Players

Players

Con Men, Hustlers, Gamblers, *and* Scam Artists

Edited by
STEPHEN HYDE *and* GENO ZANETTI

THUNDER'S MOUTH PRESS
NEW YORK

PLAYERS: *Con Men, Hustlers, Gamblers and Scam Artists*

Published by
Thunder's Mouth Press
An Imprint of Avalon Publishing Group Incorporated
161 William St., 16th Floor
New York, NY 10038

Library of Congress of Cataloging-in-Publication Data

Players : con men, hustlers, gamblers, and scam artists / edited by Stephen Hyde and Geno Zanetti.

p. cm.
ISBN 1-56025-380-0 (trade paper)
1. Gambling. 2. Gamblers. 3. Swindlers and swindling.
I. Hyde, Stephen. II. Zanetti, Geno.

HV6710 .P5 2002
795—dc21

2002018149

9 8 7 6 5 4 3 2 1

Designed by Kathleen Lake, Neuwirth and Associates, Inc.
Printed in the United States of America
Distributed by Publishers Group West

Contents

Editors' Note

PLAYERS IS A literary homage to the seedy world of gamblers, con men, and grifters, living on the edge and doing the hustle, relying on lady luck, chance, but also their wits, skill, and their sleight of hand, in a hand to hand encounter with fate. The characters we meet come from all walks of life, from aristocrat gamblers to poolroom hustlers and street level con artists but they are propelled by similar passions and highs. "The stake is money—in other words, immediate, infinite possibilities," Anatole France wrote.

If there's a mood we have tried to evoke, it is the mood of the world of Jean Pierre Melville's *Bob La Flambeur* and Jules Dassin's *Rififi*, two legendary French film noirs from the 1950s that fed off the American hard-boiled tradition of Raymond Chandler, Dashiell Hammett, Horace McCoy, Jim Thompson and Dave Goodis yet produced their own hybrid style, evoking a bohemian, underworld post-war Paris where an old school, almost artisanal code of ethics and practice is being eroded. Luc Sante characterizes this atmosphere nicely in his introduction to the new, Criterion Collection DVD edition of *Bob Le Flambeur* as an "elegiac, twilight mood," We find this mood as we encounter David Mamet in the poker room and meet Damon Runyon's Bookie Bob, Saul Bellow's immortal Yellow Kid, and learn from Herbert Asbury about the merry antics of Izzy and Moe, from David Maurer on the discreet charm of the confidence man, Ricky Jay on the story of Dice, and Walter Tevis on Fast Eddie Felson and Minnesota Fats. We have also traced the antecedents of the modern hustler to the boheme of nineteenth century Paris, to pre-revolutionary Russia and the British-ruled India of Kipling's "The Man Who Would Be King," a story that allegorizes one of the great geo-political hustles and con-tricks of all time, the British Empire's conquest of a quarter of the planet's surface.

Inevitably, as we enter the twentieth century, it is America, Gore Vidal's "Last Empire," and American writers that dominate the book. American writing has more often than not defined the atmosphere and psychology of the world of the con and the hustle, from the world of the short-con and the bookie, to the legalized forms in Las Vegas, Atlantic City and the NY and NJ State Lottery. It's a far more proletarian world, the gangsters, Hustlers and gamblers, a shadow world that resembles but is ultimately dwarfed by the fraud, theft and sleight of hand in the casino world of modern capitalism. This is one of John Molyneux's themes in an original essay, written specially for this book, about his life as a neophyte gambler in sixties London. John's closing thoughts are confirmed by much of this book: "I learned the invaluable lesson that, contrary to everything I had been taught at school, neither intelligence nor decency were linked to social status or respectability."

WE WOULD LIKE to thank Neil Ortenberg, Dan O'Connor, Ghadah Alrawi, Sam Erman, Paul Long, Dan Swift, Stefanie Ameres, Stuart Olesker, Clive Ashenden, John and Jill Molyneux, the Zanetti family, and Ana and Tony Hyde for all their help in putting this book together.

"Gambling is a hand-to-hand encounter with Fate . . . The stake is money—in other words, immediate, infinite possibilities . . . The fascination of danger is at the bottom of great passions."

—Anatole France

"Dearly beloved, never forget, when you hear anyone vaunt the progress of enlightenment, that the Devil's finest trick is to persuade you that he does not exist!"

—Charles Baudelaire

Players

1.

"Yes, but you have to wager."

—Blaise Pascal

"But for some players, luck itself is a skill . . . or an art."

—The Color of Money

The Lottery in Babylon

by Jorge Luis Borges

LIKE ALL THE men of Babylon, I have been proconsul; like all, I have been a slave. I have known omnipotence, ignominy, imprisonment. Look here—my right hand has no index finger. Look here—through this gash in my cape you can see on my stomach a crimson tattoo—it is the second letter, *Beth*. On nights when the moon is full, this symbol gives me power over men with the mark of Gimel, but it subjects me to those with the Aleph, who on nights when there is no moon owe obedience to those marked with the Gimel. In the half-light of dawn, in a cellar, standing before a black altar, I have slit the throats of sacred bulls. Once, for an entire lunar year, I was declared invisible—I would cry out and no one would heed my call, I would steal bread and not be beheaded. I have known that thing the Greeks knew not—uncertainty. In a chamber of brass, as I faced the strangler's silent scarf, hope did not abandon me; in the river of delights, panic has not failed me. Heraclides Ponticus reports, admiringly, that Pythagoras recalled having been Pyrrhus, and before that, Euphorbus, and before that, some other mortal; in order to recall similar vicissitudes, I have no need of death, nor even of imposture.

I owe that almost monstrous variety to an institution—the Lottery—which is unknown in other nations, or at work in them imperfectly or secretly. I have not delved into this institution's history. I know that sages cannot agree. About its mighty purposes I know as much as a man untutored in astrology might know about the moon. Mine is a dizzying country in which the Lottery is a major element of reality; until this day, I have thought as little about it as about the conduct of the indecipherable gods or of my heart. Now, far from Babylon and its belovèd customs, I think with some bewilderment about the Lottery, and about the blasphemous conjectures that shrouded men whisper in the half-light of dawn or evening.

My father would tell how once, long ago—centuries? years?—the lottery in Babylon was a game played by commoners. He would tell (though whether this is true or not, I cannot say) how barbers would take a man's copper coins and give back rectangles made of bone or parchment and adorned with symbols. Then, in broad daylight, a drawing would be held; those smiled upon by fate would, with no further corroboration by chance, win coins minted of silver. The procedure, as you can see, was rudimentary.

Naturally, those so-called "lotteries" were a failure. They had no moral force whatsoever; they appealed not to all a man's faculties, but only to his hopefulness. Public indifference soon meant that the merchants who had founded these venal lotteries began to lose money. Someone tried something new: including among the list of lucky numbers a few *unlucky* draws. This innovation meant that those who bought those numbered rectangles now had a twofold chance they might win a sum of money or they might be required to pay a fine—sometimes a considerable one. As one might expect, that small risk (for every thirty "good" numbers there was one ill-omened one) piqued the public's interest. Babylonians flocked to buy tickets. The man who bought none was considered a pusillanimous wretch, a man with no spirit of adventure. In time, this justified contempt found a second target: not just the man who didn't play, but also the man who lost and paid the fine. The Company (as it was now beginning to be known) had to protect the interest of the winners, who could not be paid their prizes unless the pot contained almost the entire amount of the fines. A lawsuit was filed against the losers: the judge sentenced them to pay the original fine, plus court costs, or spend a number of days in jail. In order to thwart the Company, they all chose jail. From that gauntlet thrown down by a few men sprang the Company's omnipotence—its ecclesiastical, metaphysical force.

Some time after this, the announcements of the numbers drawn began to leave out the lists of fines and simply print the days of prison assigned to each losing number. That shorthand, as it were, which went virtually unnoticed at the time, was of utmost importance: *It was the first appearance of nonpecuniary elements in the lottery.* And it met with great success—indeed, the Company was forced by its players to increase the number of unlucky draws.

As everyone knows, the people of Babylon are great admirers of logic, and even of symmetry. It was inconsistent that lucky numbers should pay off in round silver coins while unlucky ones were measured in days and nights of jail. Certain moralists argued that the possession of coins did not always bring about happiness, and that other forms of happiness were perhaps more direct.

The lower-caste neighborhoods of the city voiced a different complaint. The members of the priestly class gambled heavily, and so enjoyed all the vicissitudes of terror and hope; the poor (with understandable, or inevitable, envy) saw themselves denied access to that famously delightful, even sensual, wheel. The fair and reasonable desire that all men and women, rich and poor, be able to take part equally in the Lottery inspired indignant demonstrations—the memory of which, time has failed to dim. Some stubborn souls could not (or pretended they could not) understand that this was a *novus ordo seclorum*, a necessary stage of history. . . . A slave stole a crimson ticket; the drawing determined that that ticket entitled the bearer to have his tongue burned out. The code of law provided the same sentence for stealing a lottery ticket. Some Babylonians argued that the slave deserved the burning iron for being a thief; others, more magnanimous, that the executioner should employ the iron because thus fate had decreed. . . . There were disturbances, there were regrettable instances of bloodshed, but the masses of Babylon at last, over the opposition of the well-to-do, imposed their will; they saw their generous objectives fully achieved. First, the Company was forced to assume all public power. (The unification was necessary because of the vastness and complexity of the new operations.) Second, the Lottery was made secret, free of charge, and open to all. The mercenary sale of lots was abolished; once initiated into the mysteries of Baal, every free citizen automatically took part in the sacred drawings, which were held in the labyrinths of the god every sixty nights and determined each citizen's destiny until the next drawing. The consequences were incalculable. A lucky draw might bring about a man's elevation to the council of the magi or the imprisonment of his enemy (secret, or known by all to be so), or might allow him to find, in the peaceful dimness of his room, the woman who would begin to disturb him, or whom he had never hoped to see again; an unlucky draw: mutilation, dishonor of many kinds, death itself. Sometimes a single event—the murder of C in a tavern, B's mysterious apotheosis—would be the inspired outcome of thirty or forty drawings. Combining bets was difficult, but we must recall that the individuals of the Company were (and still are) all-powerful, and clever. In many cases, the knowledge that certain happy turns were the simple result of chance would have lessened the force of those outcomes; to forestall that problem, agents of the Company employed suggestion, or even magic. The paths they followed, the intrigues they wove, were invariably secret. To penetrate the innermost hopes and innermost fears of every man, they called upon astrologers and spies. There were certain stone lions, a sacred latrine called Qaphqa, some cracks in a dusty aqueduct—these places, it was generally believed, *gave access to the Company*, and well- or ill-wishing persons would deposit confidential reports in them. An alphabetical file held those *dossiers* of varying veracity.

Incredibly, there was talk of favoritism, of corruption. With its customary discretion, the Company did not reply directly; instead, it scrawled its brief argument in the rubble of a mask factory. This *apologia* is now numbered among the sacred Scriptures. It pointed out, doctrinally, that the Lottery is an interpolation of chance into the order of the universe, and observed that to accept errors is to strengthen chance, not contravene it. It also noted that those lions, that sacred squatting-place, though not disavowed by the Company (which reserved the right to consult them), functioned with no official guarantee.

This statement quieted the public's concerns. But it also produced other effects perhaps unforeseen by its author. It profoundly altered both the spirit and the operations of the Company. I have but little time remaining; we are told that the ship is about to sail—but I will try to explain.

However unlikely it may seem, no one, until that time, had attempted to produce a general theory of gaming. Babylonians are not a speculative people; they obey the dictates of chance, surrender their lives, their hopes, their nameless terror to it, but it never occurs to them to delve into its labyrinthine laws or the revolving spheres that manifest its workings. Nonetheless, the semiofficial statement that I mentioned inspired numerous debates of a legal and mathematical nature. From one of them, there emerged the following conjecture: If the Lottery is an intensification of chance, a periodic infusion of chaos into the cosmos, then is it not appropriate that chance intervene in *every* aspect of the drawing, not just one? Is it not ludicrous that chance should dictate a person's death while the circumstances of that death—whether private or public, whether drawn out for an hour or a century—should *not* be subject to chance? Those perfectly reasonable objections finally prompted sweeping reform; the complexities of the new system (complicated further by its having been in practice for centuries) are understood by only a handful of specialists, though I will attempt to summarize them, even if only symbolically.

Let us imagine a first drawing, which condemns an individual to death. In pursuance of that decree, another drawing is held; out of that second drawing come, say, nine possible executors. Of those nine, four might initiate a third drawing to determine the name of the executioner, two might replace the unlucky draw with a lucky one (the discovery of a treasure, say), another might decide that the death should be exacerbated (death with dishonor, that is, or with the refinement of torture), others might simply refuse to carry out the sentence. . . . That is the scheme of the Lottery, put symbolically. *In reality, the number of drawings is infinite.* No decision is final; all branch into others. The ignorant assume that infinite drawings require infinite time; actually, all that is required is that time be infinitely subdivisible, as in the famous parable of the Race with the Tortoise. That infinitude coincides remarkably well with the sinuous numbers of Chance and with the Heavenly Archetype of the Lottery beloved of Platonists. . . . Some distorted echo of our custom seems to have reached the Tiber: In his *Life of Antoninus Heliogabalus,* Ælius Lampridius tells us that the emperor wrote out on seashells the fate that he intended for his guests at dinner—some would receive ten pounds of gold; others, ten houseflies, ten dormice, ten bears. It is fair to recall that Heliogabalus was raised in Asia Minor, among the priests of his eponymous god.

There are also *impersonal* drawings, whose purpose is unclear. One drawing decrees that a sapphire from Taprobana be thrown into the waters of the Euphrates; another, that a bird be released from the top of a certain tower; another, that every hundred years a grain of sand be added to (or taken from) the countless grains of sand on a certain beach. Sometimes, the consequences are terrible.

Under the Company's beneficent influence, our customs are now steeped in chance. The purchaser of a dozen amphoræ of Damascene wine will not be surprised if one contains a talisman, or a viper; the scribe who writes out a contract never fails to include some error; I myself, in this hurried statement, have misrepresented some splendor, some atrocity—perhaps, too, some mysterious monotony. . . . Our historians, the most perspicacious on the planet, have invented a method for correcting chance; it is well known that the outcomes of this method are (in general) trustworthy—although, of course, they are never divulged without a measure of deception. Besides, there is nothing so tainted with fiction as the history of the Company. . . . A paleographic document, unearthed at a certain temple, may come from yesterday's drawing or from a drawing that took place centuries ago. No book is published without some discrepancy between each of the edition's copies. Scribes take a secret oath to omit, interpolate, alter. *Indirect* falsehood is also practiced.

The Company, with godlike modesty, shuns all publicity. Its agents, of course, are secret; the orders it constantly (perhaps continually) imparts are no different from those spread wholesale by impostors. Besides—who will boast of being a mere impostor? The drunken man who blurts out an absurd command, the sleeping man who suddenly awakes and turns and chokes to death the woman sleeping at his side—are they not, perhaps, implementing one of the Company's secret decisions? That silent functioning, like God's, inspires all manner of conjectures. One scurrilously suggests that the Company ceased to exist hundreds of years ago, and that the sacred disorder of our lives is purely hereditary, traditional; another believes that the Company is eternal, and that it shall endure until the last night, when the last god shall annihilate the earth. Yet another declares that the Company is omnipotent, but affects only small things: the cry of a bird, the shades of rust and dust, the half dreams that come at dawn. Another, whispered by masked heresiarchs, says that *the Company has never existed, and never will*. Another, no less despicable, argues that it makes no difference whether one affirms or denies the reality of the shadowy corporation, because Babylon is nothing but an infinite game of chance.

from

Poker—Bets, Bluffs and Bad Beats

by Al Alvarez

Opposite the bankholder stood some of the smart speculators and specialists in gambling who, like old criminals, were no longer afraid of the galley. They came to play three stakes and disappeared immediately after having won their livelihood.

HONORÉ DE BALZAC, *LA PEAU DE CHAGRIN*

POKER WAS ASSIMILATED into American culture so fast and so thoroughly that some historians maintain that the game is at least as old as Columbus's discovery of America and that its origins are almost as old as Western civilization itself. According to this theory, poker was derived from a Persian game called As-Nas and was brought into the country by Columbus's sailors. As-Nas, in its turn, was said to be an ancient game, dating back many hundreds of years, like chess.

Like the stories that surround most myths, this one is a mixture of truth and fiction. The true part is that As-Nas and Old Poker, as it was first played in New Orleans, were virtually the same game—a game played by four players with a twenty-card deck in which the ace was the key card. In an As-Nas deck, there were four aces, kings, ladies, soldiers, and dancing girls; in the European deck, the ladies were elevated to queens and the scandalous dancing girl became plain Jane ten. In both games, each player was dealt five cards, then each bet on them, without a draw, according to their combinations: pairs, trips, full houses (so called because they are the only combination in which all five cards are used), and four of a kind. (Straights and flushes didn't arrive until after 1837, when the game was adapted to a full 52-card deck.) The ace was the all-powerful card because there were only two hands in a twenty-card deck that could not be beaten: four aces and four kings with an ace. (The ace with the kings, of course, meant that no one else could be holding four aces.)

Those are the facts, but the antiquity of the game is fiction. There is no evidence that Columbus's sailors played poker or that As-Nas itself was played earlier than the seventeenth century, the date of its oldest surviving cards. It may not even have been a Persian game. Instead, it seems most likely that it was invented by the French diplomats, administrators, and merchants who were serving their country in Persia (Iran) around the beginning of the nineteenth century and adapted their own game of *poque* or *bouillotte* to the local As-Nas deck, then taught it to their Persian hosts.

There are two reasons for believing in this French connection, and the vital clue in both is the word "ace." First, there was no ace in the original As-Nas decks. Each deck was a work of art, elaborate, hand painted and unique; no two of them were alike, and their beauty was an indication of their owners' social status and wealth. But the most powerful card they contained, ranking higher than the king, was the lion or the sun. "As," in fact, is not even a relevant Farsi (Persian) word, as David Partlett pointed out in *A History of Card Games* (Oxford, 1990, p. 112), "but it does happen to be the French for 'Ace.'" The second clue is the key role the ace played in As-Nas and poker. "As" may not be a relevant Farsi word, but "As-Naz"—"Naz" spelled with a "z" instead of an "s"—means "my beloved ace," and that is a cry that has been echoed by countless poker players for as long as the game has been played.

In other words, As-Nas was merely the five-card Persian version of a family of related European three-card games with similar rules and similar ways of ranking the hands—pairs, three of a kind, and three of the same suit, a "flux" or "flush." All of them were gambling games in which how and when you bet played an important part. Hence the concept of bluff. At a crucial, early point in the development of the games, some smart guy must have realized that a large raise could drive out a hand that was stronger than his, but not invincible. As Shelley almost said, "If betting comes, can bluff be far behind?" "Bluff," in the early years, was an alternative name for poker. In England, the three-card variant, which is still widely played, is called "brag"; bragging or boasting is closely related to the idea of bluffing. Brag itself was developed from the Spanish and Italian primero, which may have been the game Columbus's sailors brought with them across the Atlantic. In Germany, the game was called pochspiel; *pochen* means "to knock" and when a player bet, say, ten units, he would rap the table and say, "*Ich poche zehn.*" The French adopted that phrase into their own variation, bouillotte—the bettor would announce, "*Je poque de dix*"—and eventually their game became known as poque. Since all the experts agree that American poker originated in the early years of the nineteenth century in what, until the Louisiana Purchase of 1803, had been the French colonial city of New Orleans, its most likely antecedent has to be poque. The French pronounce poque as a word with two syllables. To an English speaker with a lazy Southern drawl, that would have sounded like "pok-ah" and been transcribed as "poker."

FROM THE CASINOS of New Orleans the game spread north up the Mississippi, following the easy money on the steamboats to St. Louis, then west with the gold rush to California. The first decades of the nineteenth century were a period of great wealth in the South. The railroad had linked the cotton fields to the great river, and the thriving towns along its banks—Vicksburg, Natchez, Memphis—were crowded with professional gamblers on the lookout for rich suckers. For them, Old Poker played, As-Nas style, with a twenty-card deck, was even more profitable than a straightforward con game like three-card monte. Even the dumbest mark was unlikely to be swindled often by three-card monte, but in poker the trickery was less obvious. The cards were shuffled and cut between each deal, so it seemed like a legitimate game.

It was nothing of the kind. Old Poker, played with five cards dealt to each player, then bet and shown down without a draw to upset the distribution of the cards, was an ideal game for cardsharps, and the Mississippi steamboats were the ideal setup. They were kitted out as floating palaces and crowded with plantation owners flush with money and determined to have themselves some fun, no matter how much it cost them. It was the business of the ships' officers to make sure they got whatever they wanted, and since most of them wanted to gamble for high stakes, the officers often worked in cahoots with the cardsharps. Poker games were so much a part of the attraction of the riverboats that the various card-making companies used a common trade name: "Steamboat Playing Cards."

No wonder, then, that the first published description of the newfangled game of poker involved cheating and was located on a Mississippi steamer. It appeared in *Thirty Years Passed among the Players in England and America*, published in New York in 1844 and written by an Englishman named Joe Cowell. He himself was not a card-player, but he has earned himself a place in the history of poker as the first kibitzer. The game he described took place in December 1829, on board the steamboat *Helen M'Gregor*. Cowell was a sailor turned itinerant actor—the players in his title performed on the stage, not at the card table—and, being an actor, he wanted to milk as much drama as he could from his long boat ride from Louisville to New Orleans. Nobody, he realized, wants to read about games they don't know, but everyone is interested in bad behavior, especially when it involves sly gentlemen in tinted spectacles, with diamond stickpins in their cravats and heavy gold watch chains roped across their vests. He had hit upon what proved to be an irresistible formula. Thereafter, nineteenth-century pulp fiction is full of crooked poker games in which virtue inevitably triumphs and the cardsharp comes to a sticky end:

> It was a foggy, wretched night. Our bell was kept tolling to warn other boats to our whereabouts or to entreat direction to a landing by a fire on the shore. Suddenly a most tremendous concussion, as if all-powerful Nature had shut his hand upon us, and crushed us all to atoms, upset our cards and calculations, and a general rush was made, over chairs and tables toward the doors. The cabin was entirely cleared, or, rather, all the passengers were huddled together at the entrances, with the exception of one of the poker players: a gentleman in green spectacles, a gold guard-chain, long and thick enough to moor a dog, and a brilliant diamond breast-pin; he was, apparently, quietly shuffling and cutting the poker pack for his own amusement. In less time than I am telling it, the swarm came laughing back, in which snags, bolts blown out, and boilers burst, were most conspicuous. But all the harm the fracas caused was fright; the boat, in rounding to a woodpile, had run on to the point of an island,

and was high and dry among a never-ending supply of fuel to feed this peculiar navigation, which alone can combat the unceasing, serpentine, tempestuous current of the I-will-have-my-own-way, glorious Mississippi.

The hubbub formed a good excuse to end our game which my stupidity had made desirable long before, and I took a chair beside the poker players, who, urged by the gentleman with the diamond pin, again resumed their seats. It was his turn to deal, and when he ended, he did not lift his cards, but sat watching quietly the countenances of the others. The man on his left had bet ten dollars; a young lawyer, son to the then Mayor of Pittsburgh, who little dreamed of what his boy was about, who had hardly recovered from his shock, bet ten more; at that time, fortunately for him, he was unconscious of the real value of his hand, and consequently did not betray by his manner, as greenhorns mostly do, his certainty of winning. My chicken friend bet that ten dollars and five hundred dollars better!

"I must see that," said Green Spectacles, who now took up his hand with "I am sure to win," trembling at his fingers' ends; for you couldn't see his eyes through his glasses; he paused a moment in disappointed astonishment, and sighed, "I pass," and threw his cards upon the table. The left-hand man bet "that five hundred dollars and one thousand dollars better!"

The young lawyer, who had had time to calculate the power of his hand—four kings with an ace—it could not be beat! but still he hesitated at the impossibility, as if he thought it could—looked at the money staked and then at his hand again, and, lingeringly, put his wallet on the table and called. The left-hand man had four queens, with an ace: and Washington, the four jacks and an ace.

"Did you ever see the like on't?" said he, good-humouredly, as he pushed the money towards the lawyer, who, very agreeably astonished, pocketed his two thousand and twenty-three dollars clear!

The truth was, the cards had been *put up*, or *stocked*, as it is called, by the guard-chain-man while the party were off their guard, or, rather, on the guard of the boat in the fog, inquiring if the boiler had burst; but the excitement of the time had caused him to make a slight mistake in the distribution of the hand; and young "Six-and-eight-pence" got the one he had intended for himself. He was one of many who followed card playing for a living but not properly coming

> under the denomination of gentleman-sportsman, who alone depends on his superior skill. But in that pursuit, as in all others, even among the players, some black-sheep and black-legs will creep in, as in the present instance.

Joe Cowell's story confirmed the general belief that poker, in its original form, had a bad name. "A cheating game" is how a reformed gambler named Jonathan H. Green describes it in his book *The Exposure of the Arts and Miseries of Gambling* (New York, 1843). And even when the players were honest, Old Poker, played with a twenty-card deck by four players and without a change, was as much a gambling game as roulette.

All that began to change when poker was adapted to the full deck. Fifty-two cards meant that more than four people could play. It also meant that after the deal, even with six or seven players, there were still cards left in the deck to draw. This was a great encouragement to optimists, especially when the introduction of straights and flushes gave them something to be optimistic about. Players who wanted to stay in the action despite the cards they had been dealt could stick their money in the pot and hope to improve with the draw.

Optimism, in fact, was so endemic and poker so popular that, in 1870, a serious player from Toledo, Ohio, tried to sober up the game by introducing "jackpots" to draw poker: no one could open the betting unless he held two jacks or better. The idea was to impose discipline on the game by protecting cautious players who held fair-to-middling cards from being scared out by wild men and bullies who bet and raised with nothing, merely for the hell of it. The introduction of the fifty-two-card deck and then of jackpots were the first steps in the process that transformed poker from a gambling game into a science.

The traditionalists had no problem with playing with a full deck, but they didn't take easily to jackpots. In 1880, John Blackridge, author of *The Complete Poker Player*, missed the point of jackpots entirely when he called them "equivalent to a lottery except that all players must buy tickets." This was a paradoxical use of the word "lottery" since the whole purpose of the rule was to ensure that at least one player would have a passable hand before he threw money into the pot. Even so, the resentment about jackpots lingered on. A quarter of a century later, another traditionalist, R. F. Foster, was still complaining in his book *Practical Poker* (1904): "The jack-pot, with its accompanying small-limit game, has completely killed bluffing—that pride and joy of the old-timer. Modern poker has gradually become more of a lottery than anything else." Foster at least understood the purpose of the innovation and grudgingly accepted its inevitability. "The two great steps in the history and progress of Poker," he concluded, "have undoubtedly been the introduction of the draw to improve the hand, and the invention of the jack-pot as a cure for cautiousness. It has come to stay." Players in the Western and Eastern states agreed with him, although high-rolling Southern gentlemen considered jackpots a wimpish variation, below their dignity, and they took years to adapt to it.

Part of the genius of poker is its endless capacity for development. Jackpots are merely one of literally hundreds of variations: Cincinnati, Chicago, anaconda, Levy's game, the don's game, fiery cross, screw your neighbor, spit in the ocean, elevator, and so on. Every social game, like every ambitious restaurant, has its own speciality of the house, most of them involving wild cards. Once upon a time, in the course of a particularly unhappy evening, some disgruntled player must have said, "All I'm getting is worthless cards—deuces, treys, fours. Let's play a game where the low cards beat the big ones." And that's how low-ball, razz, misère, and hi-lo were born.

Essentially, all these games, even the craziest, are variations on two basic themes: closed or draw poker, in which all the cards are dealt facedown, and stud, in which four of the player's five or seven cards are dealt faceup. Stud was a cowboy game, named after the stud horse, and first played in the middle of the nineteenth century around Ohio, Indiana, and Illinois. It spread west with the pioneers and introduced a whole new dimension of skill into the game.

To play either form well you need to know the odds and percentages, the chances of hitting your cards, and the correct price to pay for them. You also need to read (you hope) your opponents' cards. In closed poker, where none of the cards are exposed, there are only two ways of doing that. The first is deduction: When and how much did they bet? How many cards did they draw? The second is observation: their body language, the expression in their eyes, their nervous tics. In stud the same principles apply, but the exposed cards give you extra information, which helps you calculate which cards the other players have, or don't have, in the hole.

A long time ago, for example, I was playing seven-card stud in an illegal, after-hours club near London's Piccadilly Circus. It was a seedy joint, with a steel door and a peephole, and it stank of sour frying oil. The proprietor was a menacing bull of a man, an ex-cop who had been forcibly retired from the service for tampering, in every sense, with a teenage girl witness. He had gotten to know most of the players during his time with the Metropolitan police. They were small-time crooks—burglars, pimps, con men—people who worked nights, wanted to play cards after the legal casinos closed, and preferred cash to chips; there were wads of soiled banknotes on the table, plenty more in their pockets, and no questions asked about where they got it from. There were also a few professional players in the game, as there always are when there is easy money around. One of them was a long-haired hippie, wearing a caftan and apparently high on some controlled substance; he had so many twitches and tics that none of them seemed significant. He was also afflicted with a stutter so crippling that he could scarcely string two words together. At one point during the long night, he called a large bet by someone showing what seemed, to my innocent eye, a certain straight. When the hippie turned over his two small pairs and raked in the pot, the outraged bluffer shouted, "How could you possibly call me?" The hippie opened his bleary eyes and said, "You c-c-c-couldn't huff-huff-huff had a s-s-s-s-straight." Then he reeled off every card that had fallen during the deal. And he didn't stutter once. Apart from me, everybody at the table knew him, so his stutter was obviously not a bluff. He was simply a man with a photographic memory, and whenever it clicked in his stutter vanished. He was also a true professional: he watched, he waited, he counted the cards, worked out the odds, and never contributed to a pot unless he thought he had the best of it; but when he did so he was fearless.

Seven-card stud is still widely played, but the five-card variation more or less vanished around 1980. At that time the great master of five-card stud was Bill Boyd, a courtly gentleman from Arkansas who was usually referred to, even by his friends, as Mr. Boyd. Mr. Boyd, who ran the poker room at the Golden Nugget in Las Vegas for thirty-six years, until he retired in 1982, was generally recognized to be the finest five-card stud player in America. His picture is up in Binion's Poker Hall of Fame, and even "Amarillo Slim" Preston, a man not famous for his modesty, once said, "I'd rather catch frost on my winter peaches than play stud with Bill Boyd." Mr. Boyd's skill in reading his opponents' cards and making unconventional moves was uncanny. David Spanier described one of his greatest coups in *The Little Book of Poker:*

> [Boyd] had been beaten out of $50,000 by a boastful player who made a lucky outdraw, and who then left the big game to brag about his prowess at a lower level. One night Bill followed him down and the following hand developed.
>
> Player: (x) Q-4-4-10
>
> Bill: (x) 9-3-3-Q
>
> At the opening, the queen bet $70 and Bill raised $200 on his 9. The other players passed. On the third card Mr. Show-off was quite sure he had best hand, whether Bill had paired his 9s or had an ace in the hole, and bet $500. Bill made it $1,000. His opponent merely called. (Of course he should have raised the roof, to win the pot then and there.)
>
> On the fourth card Show-off, feeling confident, bet $2,000. Bill called and raised $6,000. Naturally the man had to see. And on the last card Bill bet the pot, $18,600. The man called for what he had left, $16,100.
>
> You guessed it—Bill had a 3 in the hole. His opponent who had queens wired simply could not believe Bill would have started out on a (3) 9. The pot was worth $50,800. Bill tipped the dealer $800 and said: "That makes me evens."

Mr. Boyd won the five-card stud title at the World Series of Poker at Binion's Horseshoe every year it was played, so regularly and inevitably that in the end no one else bothered to enter the event and it was dropped from the schedule. By the time he died, in 1997, at the age of ninety-one, his mastery was so absolute that he had eliminated the opposition and the game effectively died out.

Five-card stud is still occasionally played in conservative private games but not in public card rooms. The game that has replaced it is Texas hold 'em and its four-card variant, Omaha. Hold 'em is a variation of seven-card stud in which five of the seven cards are communal. Each player is dealt two cards facedown, "in the hole." The two players to the left of the dealer are forced to bet "blind"—before they see their cards. The other players cannot check; they either call the blind bet or raise it or fold. Then three communal cards, called the "flop," are dealt faceup in the center of the table, and there is another round of betting, although this time the players may check. Then two more communal cards—known as "Fourth Street" or "the turn," and "Fifth Street" or "the river"—are dealt faceup, one at a time, with a round of betting or checking after each. The five cards in the center are common to all the players, who use them in combination with their hole cards to make the strongest possible hands.

Omaha is played the same way, except that each player is dealt four cards facedown, instead of two, and each must use two of them. Having to use two of your four hole cards makes Omaha a very different game from hold 'em and creates very different situations. In hold 'em a pair of aces in the hole is the strongest possible starting hand. In Omaha a pair of aces and a pair of kings double suited (Ah-As-Kh-Ks) is equally strong, but four running cards, such as K-Q-J-10 or 9-8-7-6, are almost as powerful, because once the flop is dealt anything can happen. Say, for example, that you have raised with your double-suited aces and kings, a player calls you with Jd-10d-7c-6c, and the flop is 9h-8s-2c. You may be ahead at the moment, but if you bet, your opponent is going to raise you, sure as sunrise, because there are twenty-four cards in the deck that will win for him—any queen, jack, ten, seven, six, or five. Four of those cards are already in his hand, but that still leaves twenty cards to help him, and he will beat you 70 percent of the time. He has one of the monster drawing hands which Omaha players call a "wraparound"—that is, he has the flop surrounded—and a wraparound is one of the most highly prized hands in the game. Omaha, in short, is more of a gambling game than hold 'em, a game in which you call more opening bets because the serious action usually begins after the flop. Hold 'em is subtler, more strategic, and more cunning, and most of the significant maneuvering takes place before the flop.

That is why Doyle Brunson, twice World Poker Champion and author of *Super/System*, the best and most sophisticated of how-to poker books, called no-limit hold 'em "the Cadillac of poker games." The possibilities and subtleties are infinite. A pair of aces in the hole may be the strongest starting hand, but after the flop everything changes: a small pair in the hole suddenly becomes three of a kind (a set); two connected or suited cards turn into a straight or a flush. The complexities are so great that Brunson devotes two hundred pages to hold 'em—three or four times the space he gives to any other form of poker. The late Johnny Moss, the Grand Old Man of Poker and three times World Champion, once said, "Hold 'em is to stud and draw what chess is to checkers." It is a game of wits and psychology and position, of bluffing, thrust and counterthrust, and it depends less on cards than on skill and character and courage.

Hold 'em has been played in Texas since the end of the nineteenth century. In the first twelve years of the World Series of Poker, four of the nine champions were Texans—Moss, Brunson, "Amarillo Slim" Preston, and the redoubtable Jack Straus—and only two of the others were not Southerners. To play hold 'em well you need the qualities that Texans most admire, the qualities associated with the frontier spirit: bravery, self-reliance, opportunism, and a willingness to take risks. The game took a long time to catch on outside the South, but in the last twenty years hold 'em and Omaha have become the most popular forms of poker, the stuff of champions, and played all over the world.

from

The Alchemy of Opposites

by Rodolfo Scarfalloto

The Criminal Always Leaves a Clue. Why?

To the habitual liar, the thing feared the most is the same thing which is wanted the most—*recognition*. Those who engage in deceptive behavior leave subtle but enticing clues. This may be done as an oversight, or it may be done intentionally as a way of being "cute" and mischievous. Either way, the underlying motivation for leaving clues is the hidden desire to get caught (recognized). Persons who hide what they do are suppressing the need to be recognized, and thus it becomes the silent ruler, manifesting itself in covert ways. We are seduced by the very thing we try to suppress. The culprits will do little things to expose themselves. The longer they remain hidden, the more blatant the clues become, for the need to be recognized "*as I am*" is a strong primal need that cannot be denied indefinitely.

The liar/criminal who absentmindedly or mischievously leaves clues, is acting out the baby's primal need to be recognized and appreciated by mother (Life).

How to Prevent Being Deceived

THE ONLY WAY that we can be deceived is if we hide the truth of our feelings. This is the same as saying that we can only be deceived if we have first deceived ourselves. If we say that *everyone* hides feelings, then we conclude that everyone, to a certain extent, is vulnerable to deception.

The rational mind receives information through words and ideas. Therefore, it can be fooled by pretty pictures and clever words. The "Heart" (feeling) cannot be fooled, because it already knows the truth, irrespective of the external scenery.

As the rational mind receives information in the form of words and pictures, the "heart" accurately recognizes their true meaning and sends this wordless knowing to the rational mind. If the rational mind receives the heartfelt truth in fullness, it experiences the unmistakable and unequivocal knowing that, "We are one," in the presence of the words and images it perceives. If the mind receives only a portion of the heartfelt truth, it may experience sadness, anger, fear or an "intuition" in the presence of the perceived words or images. If we then ignore these "partial" feelings, if we devalue them and hide them from our conscious awareness, or if we try to use them to control and exploit others, then we are primed and ready to be deceived and manipulated. Hence the proverb, "You can't cheat an honest man."

Addiction & Lying

HABITUAL LYING *IS* an addiction. If the nervous system is allowed to develop naturally, the individual finds pleasure in telling the truth. On the other hand, if the individual has learned to equate truth with punishment, the only way of experiencing safety and "normalcy" is through deception. The approach of truth produces panic and disorientation, not unlike a drug addict experiencing withdrawal.

When a drug is taken as an escape from a painful situation, the experience of euphoria (the "rush") is partially due to the experience of *no pain*. Recall that we engage in repetitive behavior because anything else is threatening or painful. If a person is in a constant state of physical and emotional pain, the deadening of that pain (by any means) is experienced as "pleasure." Deception creates the same rush of "pleasure." It is simply a sense of temporary relief, a sense of "safety" produced by the absence of painful exposure to truth. This is why addiction of any kind must be accompanied by an addiction to deception (especially self-deception).

The Revealing Language of Addiction

"Re-Covery"

THE TENDENCY OF addicts to do the program for a while and then revert to addictive behavior is reflected in the very language of "recovery." The words which are routinely used in the recovery process reveal a secret desire to hold on to the addiction by keeping it covered. Every conscious attempt to dis-cover the truth is met by an equally strong unconscious attempt to "re-cover" the truth.

Half-Way House

WHEN THE ADDICT does anything in the direction of discovering the genuine self, the addiction to deception compels them to do it just "half-way." They may be sincere in their efforts, but they find some reason to stop before the truth of self has been fully contacted. If they are institutionalized, they come out "half-way" done, and typically return in several months to repeat the process.

Even the experience of *Truth* with a capital "T" can be an addictive (half-way) experience. Many individuals have experienced the profound truth of their identity as immortal spirit. They report a sense of peace, serenity, and timeless bliss. Some individuals can even go to this place repeatedly through meditation, prayer, and other devotional practices. Yet, they do not allow themselves to sustain the feeling long enough to fully integrate it into the reality of life on Earth. So, they continue to feel alienated from everyday life, living only for the next bliss fix. Like chemically-dependent addicts, they might hide their sense of alienation behind a cloak of subtle arrogance, which says, "I am better than you because I have experienced something the Truth." This cycle is stopped when the individual makes conscious contact with Self and sustains it and nurtures it so that it is not merely a temporary high, but takes form and finds expression in the activities of earthly living.

"I Got Bored"

THE STATED (OR unstated) reason for stopping half-way on the road to truth is, "I got bored." For example, after a series of dramatic confrontations, my wife and I discovered that we were both addicted to battle and drama. Conflict was a wonderful source of entertainment for us. Upon seeing this, we decided that we wanted to stop battling. We wanted "even-ness" and steadiness in our lives. We decided to be straight with each other, and just tell the truth moment by moment without engaging in drama and battle. After a few days of this, my wife very candidly declared, "Even-ness is boring." I thought about her statement for a few seconds, and then my eyebrows shot up. I said, "Yes, even-ness is very '*boring*'; it bores into us so deeply, we can't stand it . . ." Sitting in quiet contemplation is *boring*. Staying with "the program" beyond the excitement of its newness is *boring*. The absence of stimulants and mood altering drugs (conflict, drama, chaos, blame) is *very boring*. However, if we have the endurance and tenacity to withstand being bored, we will eventually be bored to the core, at which point we are no longer capable of being bored.

The point of "boredom" is the point of change. Boredom precedes fear; the fear which says, "I am beyond my comfort zone." To be bored is to be at the crucial half-way point beyond which fear is exposed, deeper truths are discovered, and completion becomes possible.

LYING CONSCIOUSLY

THE WORDS WE use, and their funny double meanings offer clues into how we lie to ourselves unconsciously. Another surprisingly effective method of exposing unconscious lying, is to simply lie "consciously." In a situation where we are unwilling to be truthful, we simply play it out without condemning it, justifying it, or denying it. In essence, we say, "In this moment, I am lying; I am withholding my true thoughts and feelings from this person who stands before me . . ." By lying consciously (without condemnation), we begin to resurrect the natural inclination to tell the truth.

Fake It 'Til You Make It

The strategy, of "Fake it 'til you make it" is a way of lying consciously. This means that we know we are faking it; we know we are wearing a mask, and we give ourselves permission to do so without self-judgment, without justification, without making any excuses.

"Fake it 'til you make it," means that we are acting; we are "doing" a thing without actually "being" it. For example, the Tribal Shaman might put on a buffalo mask and buffalo skin and intentionally act like a buffalo, until they really do feel like a buffalo. On a more mundane level, when we act polite, we are acting out the "form" of love without necessarily feeling genuine love. However, if this is done with *total* recognition (no condemnation or justification), we are performing a powerful shamanic practice; and soon we begin to feel genuine love. That which was fake becomes real.

2.

"Even as I approach the gambling hall, as soon as I hear, two rooms away, the jingle of money poured out on the table, I almost go into convulsions."

DOSTOEVSKY, *THE GAMBLER*

"A series of lucky rolls gives me more pleasure than a man who does not gamble can have over a period of several years . . . I live a hundred lives in one."

WALLENSTEIN

Pascal's Wager

by Blaise Pascal

*Infinity nothingness. *Our soul is thrust into the body, where it finds number, time, dimension. It ponders them and calls them nature, necessity, and can believe nothing else.*

A unit added to infinity does not increase it at all, any more than a foot added to an infinite length. The finite dissolves in the presence of the infinite and becomes pure nothingness. So it is with our mind before God, with our justice before divine justice. There is not so great a disproportion between our justice and God's justice as there is between unity and infinity.

God's justice must be as vast as his mercy. But justice towards the damned is not so vast, and ought to shock less than mercy towards the elect.

We know that there is an infinite, but we do not know its nature; as we know that it is false that numbers are finite, so therefore it is true that there is an infinite number, but we do not know what it is: it is false that it is even and false that it is odd, for by adding a unit it does not change its nature; however it is a number, and all numbers are even or odd (it is true that this applies to all finite numbers).

So we can clearly understand that there is a God without knowing what he is.

Is there no substantial truth, seeing that there are so many true things which are not truth itself?

We therefore know the existence and nature of the finite, because we too are finite and have no extension.

We know the existence of the infinite, and do not know its nature, because it has extent like us, but not the same limits as us.

But we know neither the existence nor the nature of God, because he has neither extent nor limits.

BUT WE KNOW of his existence through faith. In glory we will know his nature.

Now I have already shown that we can certainly know the existence of something without knowing its nature.

Let us now speak according to natural lights.

If there is a God, he is infinitely beyond our comprehension, since, having neither parts nor limits, he bears no relation to ourselves. We are therefore incapable of knowing either what he is, or if he is. That being so, who will dare to undertake a resolution of this question? It cannot be us, who bear no relationship to him.

Who will then blame the Christians for being unable to provide a rational basis for their belief, they who profess a religion for which they cannot provide a rational basis? They declare that it is a folly, *stultitiam* (1 Cor. 1: 18) in laying it before the world: and then you complain that they do not prove it! If they did prove it, they would not be keeping their word. It is by the lack of proof that they do not lack sense. 'Yes, but although that excuses those who offer their religion as it is, and that takes away the blame from them of producing it without a rational basis, it does not excuse those who accept it.'

Let us therefore examine this point, and say: God is, or is not. But towards which side will we lean? Reason cannot decide anything. There is an infinite chaos separating us. At the far end of this infinite distance a game is being played and the coin will come down heads or tails. How will you wager? Reason cannot make you choose one way or the other, reason cannot make you defend either of the two choices.

So do not accuse those who have made a choice of being wrong, for you know nothing about it! 'No, but I will blame them not for having made this choice, but for having made any choice. For, though the one who chooses heads and the other one are equally wrong, they are both wrong. The right thing is not to wager at all.'

Yes, but you have to wager. It is not up to you, you are already committed. Which then will you choose? Let us see. Since you have to choose, let us see which interests you the least. You have two things to lose: the truth and the good, and two things to stake: your reason and will, your knowledge and beatitude; and your nature has two things to avoid: error and wretchedness. Your reason is not hurt more by choosing one rather than the other, since you do have to make the choice. That is one point disposed of. But your beatitude? Let us weigh up the gain and the loss by calling heads that God exists. Let us assess the two cases: if you win, you win everything; if you lose, you lose nothing. Wager that he exists then, without hesitating! 'This is wonderful. Yes, I must wager. But perhaps I am betting too much.' Let us see. Since there is an equal chance of gain and loss, if you won only two lives instead of one, you could still put on a bet. But if there were three lives to win, you would have to play (since you must necessarily play), and you would be unwise, once forced to play, not to chance your life to win three in a game where there is an equal chance of losing and winning. But there is an eternity of life and happiness. And that being so, even though there were an infinite number of chances of which only one were in your favour, you would still be right to wager one in order to win two, and you would be acting wrongly, since you are obliged to play, by refusing to stake one life against three in a game where out of an infinite number of chances there is one in your favour, if there were an infinitely happy infinity of life to be won. But here there is an infinitely happy infinity of life to be won, one chance of winning against a finite number of chances of losing, and what you are staking is finite. That removes all choice: wherever there is infinity and where there is no infinity of chances of losing against one of winning, there is no scope for wavering, you have to chance everything. And thus, as you are forced to gamble, you have to have discarded reason if you cling on to your life, rather than risk it for the infinite prize which is just as likely to happen as the loss of nothingness.

For it is no good saying that it is uncertain if you will win, that it is certain you are taking a risk, and that the infinite distance between the CERTAINTY of what you are risking and the UNCERTAINTY of whether you win makes the finite good of what you are certainly risking equal to the uncertainty of the infinite. It does not work like that. Every gambler takes a certain risk for an uncertain gain; nevertheless he certainly risks the finite uncertainty in order to win a finite gain, without sinning against reason. There is no infinite distance between this certainty of what is being risked and the uncertainty of what might be gained: that is untrue. There is, indeed, an infinite distance between the certainty of winning and the certainty of losing. But the uncertainty of winning is proportional to the certainty of the risk, according to the chances of winning or losing. And hence, if there are as many chances on one side as on the other, the odds are even, and then the certainty of what you risk is equal to the uncertainty of winning. It is very far from being infinitely distant from it. So our argument is infinitely strong, when the finite is at stake in a game where there are equal chances of winning and losing, and the infinite is to be won.

That is conclusive, and, if human beings are capable of understanding any truth at all, this is the one.

'I confess it, I admit it, but even so . . . Is there no way of seeing underneath the cards?' 'Yes, Scripture and the rest, etc.' 'Yes, but my hands are tied and I cannot speak a word. I am being forced to wager and I am not free, they will not let me go. And I am made in such a way that I cannot believe. So what do you want me to do?' 'That is true. But at least realize that your inability to believe, since reason urges you to do so and yet you cannot, arises from your passions. So concentrate not on convincing yourself by increasing the number of proofs of God but on diminishing your passions. You want to find faith and you do not know the way? You want to cure yourself of unbelief and you ask for the remedies? Learn from those who have been bound like you, and who now wager all they have. They are people who know the road you want to follow and have been cured of the affliction of which you want to be cured. Follow the way by which they began: by behaving just as if they believed, taking holy water, having masses said, etc. That will make you believe quite naturally, and according to your animal reactions.' 'But that is what I am afraid of.' 'Why? What do you have to lose? In order to show you that this is where it leads, it is because it diminishes the passions, which are your great stumbling-blocks, etc.

'How these words carry me away, send me into raptures,' etc. If these words please you and seem worthwhile, you should know that they are spoken by a man who knelt both before and afterwards to beg this infinite and indivisible Being, to whom he submits the whole of himself, that you should also submit yourself, for your own good and for his glory, and that strength might thereby be reconciled with this lowliness.

End of this discourse

But what harm will come to you from taking this course? You will be faithful, honest, humble, grateful, doing good, a sincere and true friend. It is, of course, true; you will not take part in corrupt pleasure, in glory, in the pleasures of high living. But will you not have others?

I tell you that you will win thereby in this life, and that at every step you take along this path, you will see so much certainty of winning and so negligible a risk, that you will realize in the end that you have wagered on something certain and infinite, for which you have paid nothing.

from

Con Men and Cutpurses

by Lucy Moore

JOHN HATFIELD *Tried and convicted of assuming a false identity, and hanged in 1803* From the police notice for Hatfield's arrest, 5 November 1802, reprinted in Knapp and Baldwin's *Newgate Calendar* and Mary Robinson's discovery of Hatfield's deception, from *The Life of Mary Robinson* (1803)

In 1792, Captain Budworth described in A Fortnight's Ramble in the Lakes *the beautiful fourteen-year-old Mary Robinson, daughter of a local innkeeper, whom he encountered on his walking tour of the Lake District. 'Her hair was thick and long, of a dark brown . . . her face was a fine oval with full eyes and lips as red as vermilion . . . She looked an angel.' The Beauty of Buttermere, as Mary came to be known, was, eight years later, just as beautiful and, according to the poet William Wordsworth, unspoiled by the attention lavished on her since the publication of Budworth's book. For the Romantics—including Thomas de Quincey and Samuel Coleridge as well as William and Dorothy Wordsworth—she came to represent Nature, Beauty and Innocence.*

It was his connection with the Beauty of Buttermere that catapulted the forty-three-year-old John Hatfield into the public eye in 1802. He had enjoyed a long career of opportunism, petty swindling and avoiding unpaid bills. Posing as Colonel Alexander Hope, brother of the Earl of Hopetoun, and an MP, Hatfield was in the Lake District trying to marry an heiress (her wedding clothes had been bought but no date was set), when he met and befriended Mary Robinson. He seems genuinely to have fallen in love with her, and at length persuaded her to elope with him to Scotland. When his deception was discovered, Hatfield ran away, deserting his bride to avoid arrest. Eventually caught and tried, his misfortune almost destroyed Mary. She bore Hatfield a son in June 1803, just before his trial, and was so anxious about her husband that her milk dried up and she could not suckle the newborn, who died of pneumonia aged only three weeks old. Hatfield protested to the end that he had never meant to harm anyone, and died proudly, calm, pale and collected, showing no signs of either levity or insensibility.

Fifty Pounds Reward

NOTORIOUS IMPOSTOR, SWINDLER AND FELON JOHN HATFIELD

Who lately married a young woman, commonly called

THE BEAUTY OF BUTTERMERE

under an assumed name.

Height about 5' 10", age about 44, full face, bright eyes, thick eyebrows, strong but light beard, good complexion with some colour, thick but not very prominent nose, smiling countenance, fine teeth, a scar on one of his cheeks near the chin, very long, thick, light hair, with a great deal of it grey, done up in a club, stout, square-shouldered, full breast and chest, rather corpulent and stout-limbed but very active, and has rather a spring in his gait, with apparently a little hitch in bringing up one leg; the two middle fingers of his left hand are stiff from an old wound and he frequently has the custom of pulling them straight with his right; has something of the Irish brogue in his speech, fluent and elegant in his language, great command of words, frequently puts his hand to his heart, very fond of compliments and generally addressing himself to persons most distinguished by rank or situation, attentive in the extreme to females, and likely to insinuate himself where there are young ladies; he was in America during the War, is fond of talking of his wounds and exploits there and on military subjects, as well as of Hatfield Hall, and his estates in Derbyshire and Chester, of the antiquity of his family, which he pretends to trace to the Plantagenets; all which are shameful falsehoods, thrown out to deceive. He makes a boast of having often been engaged in duels; he has been a great traveller also (by his own account) and talks of Egypt, Turkey, Italy, and in short has a general knowledge of subjects which, together with his engaging manner, is well calculated to impose on the credulous.

He was seven years confined in Scarborough gaol, from when he married, and removed into Devonshire, where he has basely deserted an amiable wife and a young family.

He had art enough to connect himself with some very respectable merchants in Devonshire as a partner in business, but having swindled them out of large sums of money he was made a separate bankrupt in June last, and has never surrendered to his commission, by which means he is guilty of a felony.

He cloaks his deceptions under the mask of religion, appears fond of religious conversation, and makes a point of attending divine service and popular preachers.

To consummate his villainies, he has lately, under the very respectable name of the Honourable Colonel Hope, betrayed an innocent but unfortunate young woman near the Lake of Buttermere.

He was on the 25th October last, at Ravenglass, in Cumberland, wrapped in a sailor's greatcoat and disguised, and is supposed to be now secreted in Liverpool, or some adjacent port, with a view to leave the country.

Whoever will apprehend him, and give information to MR TAUNTON, no 4, PUMP COURT, TEMPLE, so that he may be safely lodged in one of his Majesty's gaols, shall receive Fifty pounds reward.

November 5th, 1802

THE *PRETENDED* COLONEL'S second arrival at Buttermere was some time in the last ten days of August 1802. He attempted without delay, and by every artifice of looks and language, to conciliate the affections of the young woman; and in the beginning of September, if not before, he offered to make her his wife, if she would go off with him and be married in Scotland. She gave a positive refusal, assigning as her reason the short period of his acquaintance with her, which rendered it impossible that his attachment for her should have been founded on any rational esteem for her; and the utter disproportion of the match. Her natural good sense informed her, that strange events are seldom happy events.

About this time he contrived to commence an acquaintance with an Irish gentleman, a member of the late Irish Parliament, who had been resident for some months at Keswick, with his wife and part of his family. With this gentleman, and under his immediate protection, there was likewise a young lady of family and fortune, and of great personal attraction. This gentleman, in an excursion with his party to Buttermere, had, at the request of the landlord of the Queen's Head Inn, permitted his servant to convey a small package of wine to the gentleman staying at the Char public house. In a cottage, where there is only one small sitting room, persons of pleasant manners, who happen to come at the same time, as naturally form a slight acquaintance as in the cabin of a packet[-ship]. One of the means which the adventurer used to introduce himself to this respectable family was the following: — Understanding that the gentleman had been a military man, he took an army list from his pocket and pointed to his assumed name, the Honourable Alexander Augustus Hope, Lieutenant Colonel of the 14th regiment of foot. I have thought it no waste of time to mention these minute circumstances, they may possibly be useful in the detection of some other rogue. This new acquaintance daily gained strength, and he shortly paid his addresses to the daughter of the above gentleman, and obtained her consent. The wedding clothes were bought; but, previously to the wedding-day being fixed, she insisted that the pretended Colonel Hope should introduce the subject formally to her friends. He was hourly expected to do so; and the gentleman was prepared to have required, that 'Colonel Hope's enthusiasm should not seduce him into an impropriety. They were strangers to each other. He must beg that Col. Hope would write to certain noblemen and gentlemen both in England and Ireland, whose names and addresses he would furnish him with, and obtain from them every necessary information respecting himself and the young lady under his protection. As some days would elapse before the answer could be received, he proposed to employ that time in a trip to Lord Hopetoun's seat,' etc. It was this circumstance which expedited his marriage with Mary of Buttermere; and, feigning a presence for his absence, he married the *Beauty of Buttermere*.

From this time he played a double game: it seems to have been a maxim with him to leave as few *white* interspaces as possible in the *crouded map of his villanies*. His visits to Keswick became frequent, and his suit to the young lady assiduous and fervent. Still however, both at Keswick and Buttermere, he was somewhat shy of appearing in public. He was sure to be engaged in a fishing expedition on the day on which any company was expected at the public house at Buttermere; and he never attended the church at Keswick but once. The former circumstance could not excite any reasonable suspicion; it is assuredly not necessary to be an impostor, in order to avoid as carefully as possible a crowd of strange faces in a small public house: the latter circumstance appeared more extraordinary, as great and continued pretensions to religion, and to religious exercises, formed an outstanding part of his character. He himself once assigned a frivolous and foolish excuse for his continued absence from the church, but the people of Keswick, those few at least who had noticed the circumstance, candidly attributed this neglect to his being of a Scottish family and education.

A week or two after poor Mary's refusal to go off with him to Scotland, he renewed his entreaties, and gave her a written promise of marriage, which she returned to him, persevering in her former opinion, and determined at all events not to do any thing which she could not do openly, and in the face of all among whom she was born and had lived. This in a woman of her situation, must surely be considered as a great proof of virtue and uncommon good sense, if we reflect that she had no doubt of his being the man he pretended to be. Nor can there be a doubt that when the whole particulars of this unfortunate connexion are made known, her former character for modesty, virtue and good sense, will be fully established in the eyes of the world. How could she suspect him, knowing him to be received into the intimacy of persons of undoubted rank, respectability and consequent knowledge of the world? It is probable he would have desisted from this pursuit, if he could have induced the young lady beforementioned to have consented to a private marriage.

Our adventurer finding his schemes baffled to obtain this young lady and her fortune, applied himself wholly to gain possession of Mary Robinson. He made the most minute enquiries among the neighbours into every circumstance relating to her and her family, and declared his resolution to marry her publickly at her parish church by a license. Mary told him, that she was not ignorant that he had paid his addresses to Miss—, a match every way more proportionate. This he treated as a mere venial artifice to excite her jealousy, in part perhaps an effect of despair, in consequence of Mary's repeated refusal. The conclusion is already well known. The pretended Colonel Hope, in company with the clergyman, procured a license on the 1st of October, and they were publickly married in the church of Lorton, on Saturday, October the 2d. Is there on earth that prude or that bigot who can blame poor Mary? She had given her lover the best reason to esteem her, and had earned a rational love by innocent and wise conduct. Nor can it be doubted that the man had really and deeply engaged her affections. He seems to have fascinated every one, in all ranks of society; and if Mary had remained an exception, it would have detracted more from her sensibility than it would have added to her prudence.

On the day previous to his marriage, our adventurer wrote to Mr—, informing him, that he was under the necessity of being absent for ten days on a journey into Scotland, and sent him a draft for thirty pounds, drawn on Mr Crump, of Liverpool, desiring him to cash it and pay some small debts in Keswick with it, and send him over the balance, as he feared he might be short of cash on the road, this Mr—, immediately did, and sent him ten guineas in addition to the balance. On the Saturday, Wood, the landlord of the Queen's Head, returned from Lorton with the public intelligence, that Colonel Hope had married the *Beauty of Buttermere*. As it was clear, whoever he was, that he had acted unworthily and dishonourably, Mr—'s suspicions were of course awakened. He instantly remitted the draft to Mr Crump, who immediately accepted it; and at last ninety-nine in a hundred of the people at Keswick were fully persuaded that he was a true man, and no cheat. Mr M—, the friend of the young lady whom he first paid his addresses to, immediately on this, wrote to the Earl of Hopetoun. Before the answer arrived, the pretended Honourable returned with his wife to Buttermere. He went only as far as Longtown. He had bought Mary no clothes, pretending that on his arrival at the first large town they might be all procured in a few hours. A pair of gloves was the only present he made her.

At Longtown he received two letters, seemed much troubled that some friends whom he expected had not arrived there, stayed three days and then told his wife that he would again go back to Buttermere. From this time she was seized with fears and suspicions. They returned however, and their return was made known at Keswick. A Mr Harding, a Welsh judge, and a very singular man, passing through Keswick heard of this adventurer, and sent his servant over to Buttermere with a note to the supposed Colonel Hope, who observed, 'that it was a mistake, and that the note was for a brother of his'. However, he sent for four horses, and came over to Keswick, drew another draft on Mr Crump for *20l.* which the landlord at the Queen's Head had the courage to cash. Of this sum he immediately sent the ten guineas to Mr—, who came and introduced him to the judge, as his old friend Colonel Hope. Our adventurer made a blank denial that he had ever assumed the name. He had said his name was Hope, but not that he was the honourable member for Linlithgow, etc. etc. and one who had been his frequent companion, his intimate at Buttermere gave evidence to the same purpose.

On the pretender's return to Buttermere he found poor Mary in tears; she had received a letter from a gentleman at Keswick, informing her that her husband was an impostor; she gave it to him and he chid her for believing such false suggestions, threatening to call the writer to account, with whom he afterwards had an interview, and insisted on receiving satisfaction for this injury of his character. The next morning was appointed for a meeting, but the pretended Colonel took his leave before the appointed hour.

In spite however of his impudent assertions, and those of his associate, the evidence against him was decisive.—A warrant was given by Sir Frederick Vane, on the clear proof of his having forged and received several franks as the member for Linlithgow, and he was committed to the care of the constable. The constable, as may be well supposed, was little used to business of this kind. Our adventurer affected to make light of the affair, laughed and threatened by turns, and ordered a dinner at the Queen's Head at three o'clock. In the mean time he should amuse himself on the lake, which the constable unsuspiciously permitted. He went out in a boat, accompanied by his old friend the fishing tackler; and a little before three o'clock, a considerable number of the inhabitants assembled at the foot of the lake, waiting anxiously for his return, and by far the greater part disposed to lead him back in triumph. 'If he was not this great man, they were sure that he would prove to be some other great man'; but the dusk came on; neither the great man nor his guide appeared. Burkitt had led him through the Gorge of Borrowdale, up through Rosthwait and so across the Stake, the fearful Alpine Pass, which leads over Glaramara into Langdale, and left him at Langdale Chapel—a tremendous journey in the dusk! but his neck was probably predestined to a less romantic fate.

It will hardly be believed, how obstinately almost all classes at Keswick were infatuated in his favour, and how indignantly they spoke of the gentleman who had taken such prudent and prompt measures to bring the impostor to detection. The truth is, the good people of the vales had as little heard, and possessed as little notion of the existence of this sort of wickedness, as of the abominations of Tiberius[1] at Capua.—'What motive could he have to marry poor Mary? Would a sharper marry a poor girl without fortune or connexion? If he had married the Irish young lady, there would be something to say for it, etc.' It was no doubt delightful to the people of the vales, that so great a man, that a man so generous, so condescending, so affable, *so very* good, should have married one of their own class, and that to a young woman who had been so long their pride, and so much and deservedly beloved by them. Their reasonings in the impostor's favour were, to be sure, very insufficient to counteract the evidence against him; yet of themselves they were not unplausible. It is a common blunder with those who know more of the world than the inhabitants of the secluded vales among the mountains can be supposed to know, to admit of no other passion, as the motive of crimes, except the love of money or of power.

Our adventurer in his rapid flight from Keswick, left behind him his carriage, which was taken possession of by the landlord, as a pledge for his 20*l.*; and in it were found all his plate and linen, as well as a very costly dressing box, which in a few days was opened by virtue of an order from a neighbouring magistrate. It contained a very elegant pair of pistols, and complete assortment of toilet trinkets, all silver. The whole value of the box could not be less than 80*l.* There were discovered only one letter, a cash book, a list of several cities in Italy and a couple of names attached to each. From the cash book, nothing could be learned but that he had vested divers considerable sums (some stated to be on his own account) in the house of Baron Dimsdale and Co. of London; but on examining the box more narrowly, poor Mary found that it had a double bottom, and in the interspace were a number of letters addressed to him from his wife and children, under the name of Hatfield. For some days nothing else was discovered but a bill for 100*l.* drawn on a Devonshire bank, which he

[1]Tyrannical Roman Emperor (A.D 14–37), whose reign was marked by treason trials and executions.

had left behind him with Mary's father and mother; and with which they were to have paid off a mortgage on this little property, but this proved to be an old bill that had been long paid, and on his own bank.

Among the other villanous schemes of this hardened wretch, it is said that he had attempted to persuade the old people to sell their little estate, to place the money in his own hands, and to go with him into Scotland: it is not improbable that if he had not been so soon detected, he might have prevailed upon the good old people to listen to his advice, and thus would they have been completely ruined.

Gaming

by Charles Baudelaire

In faded chairs, the pale old courtesans,
Eyebrows painted, eye of fatal calm,
Smirking, and letting drop from skinny ears
Those jingling sounds of metal and of stone;

Around green cloth, the faces without lips,
Lips without colour over toothless jaws,
And fingers twisted by infernal fires,
Digging in pockets, or in panting breast;

Under the filthy ceilings, chandeliers
And lamps of oil doling out their glow
Over the brilliant poets' gloomy brows,
Who come to squander here their bloody sweat;

This is the black tableau that in my dream
I see unroll before my prescient eye.
There in an idle corner of that den
I see myself—cold, mute, and envying,

Envious of these men's tenacious lust,
The morbid gaiety of these old whores,
Trafficking gallantly before my face
In honour and in beauty, as of old!

My heart takes fright to envy this poor lot
Who rush so fervently to the abyss,
And who, drunk on their blood, prefer, in sum,
Suffering to death, and Hell to nothingness!

The Generous Gambler

Charles Baudelaire

YESTERDAY, AMIDST THE crowds on the boulevard, I felt myself brushed against by a mysterious Being whom I had always longed to know and whom I recognized immediately, although I had never seen him. He no doubt nurtured a similar desire where I was concerned for as he passed by he gave me a meaningful wink which I hastened to obey. I followed him attentively, and before long I followed him down into a dazzling underground dwelling, which glittered with a degree of luxury that none of the better Parisian abodes could come anywhere near equalling. It struck me as strange that I could so frequently have passed by this prestigious retreat without guessing the entrance to it. In that dwelling there reigned an exquisite, though heady, atmosphere, which made one forget almost instantaneously all the tiresome horrors of life; there one breathed in a sombre beatitude, like that which the lotus-eaters must have experienced when, setting foot on an enchanted island, lit by the glow of an eternal afternoon, they felt arise within them, to the soothing sounds of melodious cascades, the longing to see no more their homes, their wives, their children, and never to return again to the sea's soaring breakers.

There you could see strange faces of men and women marked by a fatal beauty which I felt I had seen already at times and in countries which I was incapable of recalling exactly and which inspired within me more a fraternal sympathy than that fear which usually arises from the sight of the unknown. Were I to try to find some way of defining the singular expression of their gaze, I would say I had never seen eyes gleaming more energetically with the horror of boredom and the undying desire to feel themselves alive.

By the time we sat down, my host and I were already old and perfect friends. We ate, and we drank exorbitantly all manner of extraordinary wines, and, what is no less extraordinary, it seemed to me, after several hours, that I was no more drunk than he was. Meanwhile, gambling, that super-human pleasure, had from time to time interrupted our frequent libations and I have to confess that I had gambled on my soul and lost it with heroic insouciance and lightness of heart. The soul is so impalpable, so often useless, and sometimes such a nuisance, that I felt no more emotion on losing it than if, on a stroll, I had mislaid my visiting card.

We spent a long time smoking a few cigars whose incomparable savour and perfume left in our hearts a sense of nostalgia for countries and joys we had not known, and, intoxicated with all these delights, I seized a brimming goblet and dared to shout, in an outburst of familiarity which did not seem to displease him: 'To your immortal health, old Cloven Hoof!'

We also chatted about the universe, its creation and its future destruction; about the great idea of the age, by which I mean progress and perfectibility, and in general of all forms of human infatuation. On that subject, His Highness poured out an unending flow of light-hearted and irrefutable jokes, and expressed himself with a smoothness of diction and a tranquil drollery that I have never found in the most celebrated human conversationalists. He explained to me the absurdity of the different philosophies which have, until now, taken hold of the human mind and even deigned to confide in me a few fundamental principles, the benefits and ownership of which it would not be fitting for me to share with anyone at all. He made no complaint whatsoever about the bad reputation he had attracted throughout the world, assured me that he himself was the person most concerned by the destruction of *superstition*, and admitted to me that as far as his own power was concerned he had been afraid on only one occasion, which was when he had heard a preacher, more subtle than his colleagues, shout out from the pulpit:

'Dearly beloved, never forget, when you hear anyone vaunt the progress of enlightenment, that the Devil's finest trick is to persuade you that he does not exist!'

The memory of that famous orator led us naturally to the subject of academies and my strange host assured me that in many cases he didn't disdain to inspire the pen, the page, and the conscience of teachers, and that he almost always attended in person, although invisible, all academic gatherings.

Encouraged by so much kindness, I asked him if he had any news of God, and if he'd seen him recently. He replied, with a carelessness tinged with a certain sadness: 'We bow to each other when we meet, like two old noblemen, in whom an innate politeness cannot completely stifle the memory of former resentment.'

It is doubtful whether His Highness has ever given so long an audience to a simple mortal and I was afraid I might be abusing his goodwill. Finally, as shivering dawn whitened the window panes, this famous person, sung by so many poets and served by so many philosophers who work for his glory unawares, said to me: 'I want you to have good memories of me, and I'd like to prove to you that I, of whom so much ill is spoken, am sometimes a *good old devil*, to use one of your everyday expressions. To make up for the irremediable loss of your soul, I'll give you the prize you would have gained if fate had been on your side, that is, the ability to soothe and defeat throughout your entire life that strange disease of Boredom which is the source of all your illnesses and all your wretched progress. Never will you form a desire without my helping you to achieve it; you will reign over your common fellow men; you will be provided with flattery and even adoration; silver, gold, diamonds, and fairy-tale palaces will come to seek you out and beg you to accept them without your having to make any effort to win them; you will change country as often as your fancy decrees; you will grow drunk on pleasure and never weary of it, in charming lands where the weather is always warm and where the women smell as sweet as flowers,—et cetera, et cetera . . . ,' he added, rising and dismissing me with a kind smile.

Had I not been afraid to humiliate myself before so great a gathering I would willingly have fallen at the feet of this generous gambler, to thank him for such unheard-of munificence. But little by little, after I'd left him, my incurable distrust returned to me; I no longer dared to believe in such prodigious good fortune and, as I went to bed, saying my prayers through a remnant of imbecilic habit, I repeated half-asleep: 'My God! Lord, my God, make the devil keep his promise to me!'

from

The Gambler

by Fyodor Dostoevsky

I CONFESS IT was disagreeable to me. Though I had made up my mind that I would play, I had not proposed to play for other people. It rather threw me out of my reckoning, and I went into the gambling saloon with very disagreeable feelings. From the first glance I disliked everything in it. I cannot endure the flunkeyishness of the newspapers of the whole world, and especially our Russian papers, in which, almost every spring, the journalists write articles upon two things: first, on the extraordinary magnificence and luxury of the gambling saloons on the Rhine, and secondly, on the heaps of gold which are said to lie on the tables. They are not paid for it; it is simply done from disinterested obsequiousness. There was no sort of magnificence in these trashy rooms, and not only were there no piles of gold lying on the table, but there was hardly any gold at all. No doubt some time, in the course of the season, some eccentric person, either an Englishman or an Asiatic of some sort, a Turk, perhaps (as it was that summer), would suddenly turn up and lose or win immense sums; all the others play for paltry guldens, and on an average there is very little money lying on the tables.

As soon as I went into the gambling saloon (for the first time in my life), I could not for some time make up my mind to play. There was a crush besides. If I had been alone, even then, I believe, I should soon have gone away and not have begun playing. I confess my heart was beating and I was not cool. I knew for certain, and had made up my mind long before, that I should not leave Roulettenburg unchanged, that some radical and fundamental change would take place in my destiny; so it must be and so it would be. Ridiculous as it may be that I should expect so much for myself from roulette, yet I consider even more ridiculous the conventional opinion accepted by all that it is stupid and absurd to expect anything from gambling. And why should gambling be worse than any other means of making money—for instance, commerce? It is true that only one out of a hundred wins, but what is that to me?

In any case I determined to look about me first and not to begin anything in earnest that evening. If anything did happen that evening it would happen by chance and be something slight, and I staked my money accordingly. Besides, I had to study the game; for, in spite of the thousand descriptions of roulette which I had read so eagerly, I understood absolutely nothing of its working, until I saw it myself.

In the first place it all struck me as so dirty, somehow, morally horrid and dirty. I am not speaking at all of the greedy, uneasy faces which by dozens, even by hundreds, crowd round the gambling tables. I see absolutely nothing dirty in the wish to win as quickly and as much as possible. I always thought very stupid the answer of that fat and prosperous moralist, who replied to some one's excuse "that he played for a very small stake," "So much the worse, it is such petty covetousness." As though covetousness were not exactly the same, whether on a big scale or a petty one. It is a matter of proportion. What is paltry to Rothschild is wealth to me, and as for profits and winnings, people, not only at roulette, but everywhere, do nothing but try to gain or squeeze something out of one another. Whether profits or gains are nasty is a different question. But I am not solving that question here. Since I was myself possessed by an intense desire of winning, I felt as I went into the hall all this covetousness, and all this covetous filth if you like, in a sense congenial and convenient. It is most charming when people do not stand on ceremony with one another, but act openly and aboveboard. And, indeed, why deceive oneself? Gambling is a most foolish and imprudent pursuit! What was particularly ugly at first sight, in all the rabble round the roulette table, was the respect they paid to that pursuit, the solemnity and even reverence with which they all crowded round the tables. That is why a sharp distinction is drawn here between the kind of game that is *mauvais genre* and the kind that is permissible to well-bred people. There are two sorts of gambling: one the gentlemanly sort: the other the plebeian, mercenary sort, the game played by all sorts of riff-raff. The distinction is sternly observed here, and how contemptible this distinction really is! A gentleman may stake, for instance, five or ten louis d'or, rarely more; he may, however, stake as much as a thousand francs if he is very rich; but only for the sake of the play, simply for amusement, that is, simply to look on at the process of winning or of losing, but must on no account display an interest in winning. If he wins, he may laugh aloud, for instance; may make a remark to one of the bystanders; he may even put down another stake, and may even double it, but solely from curiosity, for the sake of watching and calculating the chances, and not from the plebeian desire to win. In fact, he must look on all gambling, roulette, *trente et quarante*, as nothing else than a pastime got up entirely for his amusement. He must not even suspect the greed for gain and the shifty dodges on which the bank depends. It would be extremely good form, too, if he should imagine that all the other gamblers, all the rabble, trembling over a gulden, were rich men and gentlemen like himself and were playing simply for their diversion and amusement. This complete ignorance of reality and innocent view of people would be, of course, extremely aristocratic. I have seen many mammas push forward their daughters, innocent and elegant Misses of fifteen and sixteen, and, giving them some gold coins, teach them how to play. The young lady wins or loses, invariably smiles and walks away, very well satisfied. Our General went up to the table with solid dignity; a flunkey rushed to hand him a chair, but he ignored the flunkey; he, very slowly and deliberately, took out his purse, very slowly and deliberately took three hundred francs in gold from his purse, staked them on the black, and won. He did not pick up his winnings, but left them on the table. Black turned up again; he didn't pick up his winnings that time either; and when, the third time, red turned up, he lost at once twelve hundred francs. He walked away with a smile and kept up his dignity. I am positive he was raging inwardly, and if the stake had been two or three times as much he would not have kept up his dignity but would have betrayed his feelings. A Frenchman did, however, before my eyes, win and lose as much as thirty thousand francs with perfect gaiety and no sign of emotion. A real gentleman should not show excitement even if he loses his whole fortune. Money ought to be so much below his gentlemanly dignity as to be scarcely worth noticing. Of course, it would have been extremely aristocratic not to notice the sordidness of all the rabble and all the surroundings. Sometimes, however, the opposite pose is no less aristocratic—to notice—that is, to look about one, even perhaps, to stare through a lorgnette at the rabble; though always taking the rabble and the sordidness as nothing else but a diversion of a sort, as though it were a performance got up for the amusement of gentlemen. One may be jostled in that crowd, but one must look about one with complete conviction that one is oneself a spectator and that one is in no sense part of it. Though, again, to look very attentively is not quite the thing; that, again, would not be gentlemanly because, in any case, the spectacle does not deserve much, or close, attention. And, in fact, few spectacles do deserve a gentleman's close attention. And yet it seemed to me that all this was deserving of very close attention, especially for one who had come not only to observe it, but sincerely and genuinely reckoned himself as one of the rabble. As for my hidden moral convictions, there is no place for them, of course, in my present reasonings. Let that be enough for the present. I speak to relieve my conscience. But I notice one thing: that of late it has become horribly repugnant to me to test my thoughts and actions by any moral standard whatever. I was guided by something different . . .

The rabble certainly did play very sordidly. I am ready to believe, indeed, that a great deal of the most ordinary thieving goes on at the gambling table. The croupiers who sit at each end of the table look at the stakes and reckon the winnings; they have a great deal to do. They are rabble, too! For the most part they are French. However, I was watching and observing, not with the object of describing roulette. I kept a sharp look-out for my own sake, so that I might know how to behave in the future. I noticed, for instance, that nothing was more common than for some one to stretch out his hand and snatch what one had won. A dispute would begin, often an uproar, and a nice job one would have to find witnesses and to prove that it was one's stake!

At first it was all an inexplicable puzzle to me. All I could guess and distinguish was that the stakes were on the numbers, on odd and even, and on the colours. I made up my mind to risk a hundred guldens of Polina Alexandrovna's money. The thought that I was not playing for myself seemed to throw me out of my reckoning. It was an extremely unpleasant feeling, and I wanted to be rid of it as soon as possible. I kept feeling that by beginning for Polina I should break my own luck. Is it impossible to approach the gambling table without becoming infected with superstition? I began by taking out five friedrichs d'or (fifty gulden) and putting them on the even. The wheel went round and thirteen turned up—I had lost. With a sickly feeling I staked another five friedrichs d'or on red, simply in order to settle the matter and go away. Red turned up. I staked all the ten friedrichs d'or—red turned up again. I staked all the money again on the same, and again red turned up. On receiving forty friedrichs d'or I staked twenty upon the twelve middle figures, not knowing what would come of it. I was paid three times my stake. In this way from ten friedrichs d'or I had all at once eighty. I was overcome by a strange, unusual feeling which was so unbearable that I made up my mind to go away. It seemed to me that I should not have been playing at all like that if I had been playing for myself. I staked the whole eighty firedrichs d'or, however, on even. This time four turned up; another eighty friedrichs d'or was poured out to me, and, gathering up the whole heap of a hundred and sixty friedrichs d'or, I set off to find Polina Alexandrovna.

They were all walking somewhere in the park and I only succeeded in seeing her after supper. This time the Frenchman was not of the party, and the General unbosomed himself. Among other things he thought fit to observe to me that he would not wish to see me at the gambling tables. It seemed to him that it would compromise him if I were to lose too much: "But even if you were to win a very large sum I should be compromised, too," he added significantly. "Of course, I have no right to dictate your actions, but you must admit yourself . . ." At this point he broke off, as his habit was. I answered, drily, that I had very little money, and so I could not lose very conspicuously, even if I did play. Going upstairs to my room I succeeded in handing Polina her winnings, and told her that I would not play for her another time.

"Why not?" she asked, in a tremor.

"Because I want to play on my own account," I answered, looking at her with surprise; "and it hinders me."

"Then you still continue in your conviction that roulette is your only escape and salvation?" she asked ironically.

I answered very earnestly, that I did; that as for my confidence that I should win, it might be absurd; I was ready to admit it, but that I wanted to be let alone.

Polina Alexandrovna began insisting I should go halves with her in today's winnings, and was giving me eighty friedrichs d'or, suggesting that I should go on playing on those terms. I refused the half, positively and finally, and told her that I could not play for other people, not because I didn't want to, but because I should certainly lose.

"Yet I, too," she said, pondering, "stupid as it seems, am building all my hopes on roulette. And so you must go on playing, sharing with me, and—of course—you will."

At this point she walked away, without listening to further objections.

The Queen of Spades

by Alexander Pushkin

Chapter I.

There was a card party at the rooms of Naroumoff of the Horse Guards. The long winter night passed away imperceptibly, and it was five o'clock in the morning before the company sat down to supper. Those who had won, ate with a good appetite; the others sat staring absently at their empty plates. When the champagne appeared, however, the conversation became more animated, and all took a part in it.

"And how did you fare, Sourin?" asked the host.

"Oh, I lost, as usual. I must confess that I am unlucky: I play mirandole, I always keep cool, I never allow anything to put me out, and yet I always lose!"

"And you did not once allow yourself to be tempted to back the red? . . . Your firmness astonishes me."

"But what do you think of Hermann?" said one of the guests, pointing to a young Engineer: "he has never had a card in his hand in his life, he has never in his life laid a wager, and yet he sits here till five o'clock in the morning watching our play."

"Play interests me very much," said Hermann: "but I am not in the position to sacrifice the necessary in the hope of winning the superfluous."

"Hermann is a German: he is economical—that is all!" observed Tomsky. "But if there is one person that I cannot understand, it is my grandmother, the Countess Anna Fedorovna."

"How so?" inquired the guests.

"I cannot understand," continued Tomsky, "how it is that my grandmother does not punt.

"What is there remarkable about an old lady of eighty not punting?" said Naroumoff.

"Then you do not know the reason why?"

"No, really; haven't the faintest idea."

"Oh! then listen. You must know that, about sixty years ago, my grandmother went to Paris, where she created quite a sensation. People used to run after her to catch a glimpse of the 'Muscovite Venus.' Richelieu made love to her, and my grandmother maintains that he almost blew out his brains in consequence of her cruelty. At that time ladies used to play at faro. On one occasion at the Court, she lost a very considerable sum to the Duke of Orleans. On returning home, my grandmother removed the patches from her face, took off her hoops, informed my grandfather of her loss at the gaming-table, and ordered him to pay the money. My deceased grandfather, as far as I remember, was a sort of house-steward to my grandmother. He dreaded her like fire; but, on hearing of such a heavy loss, he almost went out of his mind; he calculated the various sums she had lost, and pointed out to her that in six months she had spent half a million of francs, that neither their Moscow nor Saratoff estates were in Paris, and finally refused point blank to pay the debt. My grandmother gave him a box on the ear and slept by herself as a sign of her displeasure. The next day she sent for her husband, hoping that this domestic punishment had produced an effect upon him, but she found him inflexible. For the first time in her life, she entered into reasonings and explanations with him, thinking to be able to convince him by pointing out to him that there are debts and debts, and that there is a great difference between a Prince and a coachmaker. But it was all in vain, my grandfather still remained obdurate. But the matter did not rest there. My grandmother did not know what to do. She had shortly before become acquainted with a very remarkable man. You have heard of Count St. Germain, about whom so many marvellous stories are told. You know that he represented himself as the Wandering Jew, as the discoverer of the elixir of life, of the philosopher's stone, and so forth. Some laughed at him as a charlatan;

but Casanova, in his memoirs, says that he was a spy. But be that as it may, St. Germain, in spite of the mystery surrounding him, was a very fascinating person, and was much sought after in the best circles of society. Even to this day my grandmother retains an affectionate recollection of him, and becomes quite angry if anyone speaks disrespectfully of him. My grandmother knew that St. Germain had large sums of money at his disposal. She resolved to have recourse to him, and she wrote a letter to him asking him to come to her without delay. The queer old man immediately waited upon her and found her overwhelmed with grief. She described to him in the blackest colours the barbarity of her husband, and ended by declaring that her whole hope depended upon his friendship and amiability.

"St. Germain reflected.

"'I could advance you the sum you want,' said he; 'but I know that you would not rest easy until you had paid me back, and I should not like to bring fresh troubles upon you. But there is another way of getting out of your difficulty: you can win back your money.'

"'But, my dear Count,' replied my grandmother, 'I tell you that I haven't any money left.'

"'Money is not necessary,' replied St. Germain: 'be pleased to listen to me.'

"Then he revealed to her a secret, for which each of us would give a good deal . . ."

The young officers listened with increased attention. Tomsky lit his pipe, puffed away for a moment and then continued:

"That same evening my grandmother went to Versailles to the *jeu de la reine*. The Duke of Orleans kept the bank; my grandmother excused herself in an off-handed manner for not having yet paid her debt, by inventing some little story, and then began to play against him. She chose three cards and played them one after the other: all three won *sonika,* and my grandmother recovered every farthing that she had lost."

"Mere chance!" said one of the guests.

"A tale!" observed Hermann.

"Perhaps they were marked cards!" said a third.

"I do not think so," replied Tomsky gravely.

"What!" said Naroumoff, "you have a grandmother who knows how to hit upon three lucky cards in succession, and you have never yet succeeded in getting the secret of it out of her?"

"That's the deuce of it!" replied Tomsky: "she had four sons, one of whom was my father; all four were determined gamblers, and yet not to one of them did she ever reveal her secret, although it would not have been a bad thing either for them or for me. But this is what I heard from my uncle, Count Ivan Ilitch, and he assured me, on his honour, that it was true. The late Chaplitsky—the same who died in poverty after having squandered millions—once lost, in his youth, about three hundred thousand roubles—to Zoritch, if I remember rightly. He was in despair. My grandmother, who was always very severe upon the extravagance of young men, took pity, however, upon Chaplitsky. She gave him three cards, telling him to play them one after the other, at the same time exacting from him a solemn promise that he would never play at cards again as long as he lived. Chaplitsky then went to his victorious opponent, and they began a fresh game. On the first card he staked fifty thousand roubles and won *sonika*; he doubled the stake and won again, till at last, by pursuing the same tactics, he won back more than he had lost . . .

"But it is time to go to bed: it is a quarter to six already."

And indeed it was already beginning to dawn: the young men emptied their glasses and then took leave of each other.

CHAPTER II.

THE OLD COUNTESS A——was seated in her dressing-room in front of her looking-glass. Three waiting-maids stood around her. One held a small pot of rouge, another a box of hair-pins, and the third a tall cap with bright red ribbons. The Countess had no longer the slightest pretensions to beauty, but she still preserved the habits of her youth, dressed in strict accordance with the fashion of seventy years before, and made as long and as careful a toilette as she would have done sixty years previously. Near the window, at an embroidery frame, sat a young lady, her ward.

"Good morning, grandmamma," said a young officer, entering the room. "*Bonjour, Mademoiselle Lise.* Grandmamma, I want to ask you something."

"What is it, Paul?"

"I want you to let me introduce one of my friends to you, and to allow me to bring him to the ball on Friday."

"Bring him direct to the ball and introduce him to me there. Were you at B——'s yesterday?"

"Yes; everything went off very pleasantly, and dancing was kept up until five o'clock. How charming Eletskaia was!"

"But, my dear, what is there charming about her? Isn't she like her grandmother, the Princess Daria Petrovna? By the way, she must be very old, the Princess Daria Petrovna."

"How do you mean, old?" cried Tomsky thoughtlessly; "she died seven years ago."

The young lady raised her head and made a sign to the young officer. He then remembered that the old Countess was never to be informed of the death of any of her contemporaries, and he bit his lips. But the old Countess heard the news with the greatest indifference.

"Dead!" said she; "and I did not know it. We were appointed maids of honour at the same time, and when we were presented to the Empress . . ."

And the Countess for the hundredth time related to her grandson one of her anecdotes.

"Come, Paul," said she, when she had finished her story, "help me to get up. Lizanka, where is my snuff-box?"

And the Countess with her three maids went behind a screen to finish her toilette. Tomsky was left alone with the young lady.

"Who is the gentleman you wish to introduce to the Countess?" asked Lizaveta Ivanovna in a whisper.

"Naroumoff. Do you know him?"

"No. Is he a soldier or a civilian?"

"A soldier."

"Is he in the Engineers?"

"No, in the Cavalry. What made you think that he was in the Engineers?"

The young lady smiled, but made no reply.

"Paul," cried the Countess from behind the screen, "send me some new novel, only pray don't let it be one of the present day style."

"What do you mean, grandmother?"

"That is, a novel, in which the hero strangles neither his father nor his mother, and in which there are no drowned bodies. I have a great horror of drowned persons."

"There are no such novels nowadays. Would you like a Russian one?"

"Are there any Russian novels? Send me one, my dear, pray send me one!"

"Good-bye, grandmother: I am in a hurry. . . . Good-bye, Lizaveta Ivanovna. What made you think that Naroumoff was in the Engineers?"

And Tomsky left the boudoir.

Lizaveta Ivanovna was left alone: she laid aside her work and began to look out of the window. A few moments afterwards, at a corner house on the other side of the street, a young officer appeared. A deep blush covered her cheeks; she took up her work again and bent her head down over the frame. At the same moment the Countess returned completely dressed.

"Order the carriage, Lizaveta," said she; "we will go out for a drive."

Lizaveta arose from the frame and began to arrange her work.

"What is the matter with you, my child, are you deaf?" cried the Countess. "Order the carriage to be got ready at once."

"I will do so this moment," replied the young lady, hastening into the ante-room.

A servant entered and gave the Countess some books from Prince Paul Alexandrovitch.

"Tell him that I am much obliged to him," said the Countess. "Lizaveta! Lizaveta! where are you running to?"

"I am going to dress."

"There is plenty of time, my dear. Sit down here. Open the first volume and read to me aloud."

Her companion took the book and read a few lines.

"Louder," said the Countess. "What is the matter with you, my child? Have you lost your voice? Wait—give me that footstool—a little nearer—that will do!"

Lizaveta read two more pages. The Countess yawned.

"Put the book down," said she: "what a lot of nonsense! Send it back to Prince Paul with my thanks. . . . But where is the carriage?"

"The carriage is ready," said Lizaveta, looking out into the street.

"How is it that you are not dressed?" said the Countess: "I must always wait for you. It is intolerable, my dear!"

Liza hastened to her room. She had not been there two minutes, before the Countess began to ring with all her might. The three waiting-maids came running in at one door and the valet at another.

"How is it that you cannot hear me when I ring for you?" said the Countess. "Tell Lizaveta Ivanovna that I am waiting for her."

Lizaveta returned with her hat and cloak on.

"At last you are here!" said the Countess. "But why such an elaborate toilette? Whom do you intend to captivate? What sort of weather is it? It seems rather windy."

"No, Your Ladyship, it is very calm," replied the valet.

"You never think of what you are talking about. Open the window. So it is: windy and bitterly cold. Unharness the horses. Lizaveta, we won't go out—there was no need for you to deck yourself like that."

"What a life is mine!" thought Lizaveta Ivanovna.

And, in truth, Lizaveta Ivanovna was a very unfortunate creature. "The bread of the stranger is bitter," says Dante, "and his staircase hard to climb." But who can know what the bitterness of dependence is so well as the poor companion of an old lady of quality? The Countess A—— had by no means a bad heart, but she was capricious, like a woman who had been spoilt by the world, as well as being avaricious and egotistical, like all old people who have seen their best days, and whose thoughts are with the past and not the present. She participated in all the vanities of the great world, went to balls, where she sat in a corner, painted and dressed in old-fashioned style, like a deformed but indispensable ornament of the ball-room; all the guests on entering approached her and made a profound bow, as if in accordance with a set ceremony, but after that nobody took any further notice of her. She received the whole town at her house, and observed the strictest etiquette, although she could no longer recognize the faces of people. Her numerous domestics, growing fat and old in her ante-chamber and servants' hall, did just as they liked, and vied with each other in robbing the aged Countess in the most bare-faced manner. Lizaveta Ivanovna was the martyr of the household. She made tea, and was reproached with using too much sugar; she read novels aloud to the Countess, and the faults of the author were visited upon her head; she accompanied the Countess in her walks, and was held answerable for the weather or the state of the pavement. A salary was attached to the post, but she very rarely received it, although she was expected to dress like everybody else, that is to say, like very few indeed. In society she played the most pitiable rôle. Everybody knew her, and nobody paid her any attention. At balls she danced only when a partner was wanted, and ladies would only take hold of her arm when it was necessary to lead her out of the room to attend to their dresses. She was very self-conscious, and felt her position keenly, and she looked about her with impatience for a deliverer to come to her rescue; but the young men, calculating in their giddiness, honoured her with but very little attention, although Lizaveta Ivanovna was a hundred times prettier than the bare-faced and cold-hearted marriageable girls around whom they hovered. Many a time did she quietly slink away from the glittering but wearisome drawing-room, to go and cry in her own poor little room, in which stood a screen, a chest of drawers, a looking-glass and a painted bedstead, and where a tallow candle burnt feebly in a copper candlestick.

One morning—this was about two days after the evening party described at the beginning of this story, and a week previous to the scene at which we have just assisted—Lizaveta Ivanovna was seated near the window at her embroidery frame, when, happening to look out into the street, she caught sight of a young Engineer officer, standing motionless with his eyes fixed upon her window. She lowered her head and went on again with her work. About five minutes afterwards she looked out again—the young officer was still standing in the same place. Not being in the habit of coquetting with passing officers, she did not continue to gaze out into the street, but went on sewing for a couple of hours, without raising her head. Dinner was announced. She rose up and began to put her embroidery away, but glancing casually out of the window, she perceived the officer again. This seemed to her very strange. After dinner she went to the window with a certain feeling of uneasiness, but the officer was no longer there—and she thought no more about him.

A couple of days afterwards, just as she was stepping into the carriage with the Countess, she saw him again. He was standing close behind the door, with his face half-concealed by his fur collar, but his dark eyes sparkled beneath his cap. Lizaveta felt alarmed, though she knew not why, and she trembled as she seated herself in the carriage.

On returning home, she hastened to the window—the officer was standing in his accustomed place, with his eyes fixed upon her. She drew back, a prey to curiosity and agitated by a feeling which was quite new to her.

From that time forward not a day passed without the young officer making his appearance under the window at the customary hour, and between him and her there was established a sort of mute acquaintance.

Sitting in her place at work, she used to feel his approach; and raising her head, she would look at him longer and longer each day. The young man seemed to be very grateful to her: she saw with the sharp eye of youth, how a sudden flush covered his pale cheeks each time that their glances met. After about a week she commenced to smile at him. . . .

When Tomsky asked permission of his grandmother the Countess to present one of his friends to her, the young girl's heart beat violently. But hearing that Naroumoff was not an Engineer, she regretted that by her thoughtless question, she had betrayed her secret to the volatile Tomsky.

Hermann was the son of a German who had become a naturalized Russian, and from whom he had inherited a small capital. Being firmly convinced of the necessity of preserving his independence, Hermann did not touch his private income, but lived on his pay, without allowing himself the slightest luxury. Moreover, he was reserved and ambitious, and his companions rarely had an opportunity of making merry at the expense of his extreme parsimony. He had strong passions and an ardent imagination, but his firmness of disposition preserved him from the ordinary errors of young men. Thus, though a gamester at heart, he never touched a card, for he considered his position did not allow him—as he said—"to risk the necessary in the hope of winning the superfluous," yet he would sit for nights together at the card table and follow with feverish anxiety the different turns of the game.

The story of the three cards had produced a powerful impression upon his imagination, and all night long he could think of nothing else. "If," he thought to himself the following evening, as he walked along the streets of St. Petersburg, "if the old Countess would but reveal her secret to me! if she would only tell me the names of the three winning cards. Why should I not try my fortune? I must get introduced to her and win her favour—become her lover. . . . But all that will take time, and she is eighty-seven years old: she might be dead in a week, in a couple of days even! . . . . But the story itself: can it really be true? . . . No! Economy, temperance and industry: those are my three winning cards; by means of them I shall be able to double my capital—increase it sevenfold, and procure for myself ease and independence."

Musing in this manner, he walked on until he found himself in one of the principal streets of St. Petersburg, in front of a house of antiquated architecture. The street was blocked with equipages; carriages one after the other drew up in front of the brilliantly illuminated doorway. At one moment there stepped out on to the pavement the well-shaped little foot of some young beauty, at another the heavy boot of a cavalry officer, and then the silk stockings and shoes of a member of the diplomatic world. Furs and cloaks passed in rapid succession before the gigantic porter at the entrance.

Hermann stopped. "Whose house is this?" he asked of the watchman at the corner.

"The Countess A——'s," replied the watchman.

Hermann started. The strange story of the three cards again presented itself to his imagination. He began walking up and down before the house, thinking of its owner and her strange secret. Returning late to his modest lodging, he could not go to sleep for a long time, and when at last he did doze off, he could dream of nothing but cards, green tables, piles of banknotes and heaps of ducats. He played one card after the other, winning uninterruptedly, and then he gathered up the gold and filled his pockets with the notes. When he woke up late the next morning, he sighed over the loss of his imaginary wealth, and then sallying out into the town, he found himself once more in front of the Countess's residence. Some unknown power seemed to have attracted him thither. He stopped and looked up at the windows. At one of these he saw a head with luxuriant black hair, which was bent down probably over some book or an embroidery frame. The head was raised. Hermann saw a fresh complexion and a pair of dark eyes. That moment decided his fate.

CHAPTER III.

LIZAVETA IVANOVNA HAD scarcely taken off her hat and cloak, when the Countess sent for her and again ordered her to get the carriage ready. The vehicle drew up before the door, and they prepared to take their seats. Just at the moment when two footmen were assisting the old lady to enter the carriage, Lizaveta saw her Engineer standing close beside the wheel; he grasped her hand; alarm caused her to lose her presence of mind, and the young man disappeared—but not before he had left a letter between her fingers. She concealed it in her glove, and during the whole of the drive she neither saw nor heard anything. It was the custom of the Countess, when out for an airing in her carriage, to be constantly asking such questions as: "Who was that person that met us just now? What is the name of this bridge? What is written on that signboard?" On this occasion, however, Lizaveta returned such vague and absurd answers, that the Countess became angry with her.

"What is the matter with you, my dear?" she exclaimed. "Have you taken leave of your senses, or what is it? Do you not hear me or understand what I say? . . . Heaven be thanked, I am still in my right mind and speak plainly enough!"

Lizaveta Ivanovna did not hear her. On returning home she ran to her room, and drew the letter out of her glove: it was not sealed. Lizaveta read it. The letter contained a declaration of love; it was tender, respectful, and copied word for word from a German novel. But Lizaveta did not know anything of the German language, and she was quite delighted.

For all that, the letter caused her to feel exceedingly uneasy. For the first time in her life she was entering into secret and confidential relations with a young man. His boldness alarmed her. She reproached herself for her imprudent behaviour, and knew not what to do. Should she cease to sit at the window and, by assuming an appearance of indifference towards him, put a check upon the young officer's desire for further acquaintance with her? Should she send his letter back to him, or should she answer him in a cold and decided manner? There was nobody to whom she could turn in her perplexity, for she had neither female friend nor adviser. . . . At length she resolved to reply to him.

She sat down at her little writing-table, took pen and paper, and began to think. Several times she began her letter, and then tore it up: the way she had expressed herself seemed to her either too inviting or too cold and decisive. At last she succeeded in writing a few lines with which she felt satisfied.

"I am convinced," she wrote, "that your intentions are honourable, and that you do not wish to offend me by any imprudent behaviour, but our acquaintance must not begin in such a manner. I return you your letter, and I hope that I shall never have any cause to complain of this undeserved slight."

The next day, as soon as Hermann made his appearance, Lizaveta rose from her embroidery, went into the drawing-room, opened the ventilator and threw the letter into the street, trusting that the young officer would have the perception to pick it up.

Hermann hastened forward, picked it up and then repaired to a confectioner's shop. Breaking the seal of the envelope, he found inside it his own letter and Lizaveta's reply. He had expected this, and he returned home, his mind deeply occupied with his intrigue.

Three days afterwards, a bright-eyed young girl from a milliner's establishment brought Lizaveta a letter. Lizaveta opened it with great uneasiness, fearing that it was a demand for money, when suddenly she recognized Hermann's handwriting.

"You have made a mistake, my dear," said she: "this letter is not for me."

"Oh, yes, it is for you," replied the girl, smiling very knowingly. "Have the goodness to read it."

Lizaveta glanced at the letter. Hermann requested an interview.

"It cannot be," she cried, alarmed at the audacious request, and the manner in which it was made. "This letter is certainly not for me."

And she tore it into fragments.

"If the letter was not for you, why have you torn it up?" said the girl. "I should have given it back to the person who sent it."

"Be good enough, my dear," said Lizaveta, disconcerted by this remark, "not to bring me any more letters for the future, and tell the person who sent you that he ought to be ashamed. . . ."

But Hermann was not the man to be thus put off. Every day Lizaveta received from him a letter, sent now in this way, now in that. They were no longer translated from the German. Hermann wrote them under the inspiration of passion, and spoke in his own language, and they bore full testimony to the inflexibility of his desire and the disordered condition of his uncontrollable imagination. Lizaveta no longer thought of sending them back to him: she became intoxicated with them and began to reply to them, and little by little her answers became longer and more affectionate. At last she threw out of the window to him the following letter:

"This evening there is going to be a ball at the Embassy. The Countess will be there. We shall remain until two o'clock. You have now an opportunity of seeing me alone. As soon as the Countess is gone, the servants will very probably go out, and there will be nobody left but the Swiss, but he usually goes to sleep in his lodge. Come about half-past eleven. Walk straight upstairs. If you meet anybody in the ante-room, ask if the Countess is at home. You will be told 'No,' in which case there will be nothing left for you to do but to go away again. But it is most probable that you will meet nobody. The maidservants will all be together in one room. On leaving the ante-room, turn to the left, and walk straight on until you reach the Countess's bedroom. In the bedroom, behind a screen, you will find two doors: the one on the right leads to a cabinet, which the Countess never enters; the one on the left leads to a corridor, at the end of which is a little winding staircase; this leads to my room."

Hermann trembled like a tiger, as he waited for the appointed time to arrive. At ten o'clock in the evening he was already in front of the Countess's house. The weather was terrible; the wind blew with great violence; the sleety snow fell in large flakes; the lamps emitted a feeble light, the streets were deserted; from time to time a sledge, drawn by a sorry-looking hack, passed by, on the look-out for a belated passenger. Hermann was enveloped in a thick overcoat, and felt neither wind nor snow.

At last the Countess's carriage drew up. Hermann saw two footmen carry out in their arms the bent form of the old lady, wrapped in sable fur, and immediately behind her, clad in a warm mantle, and with her head ornamented with a wreath of fresh flowers, followed Lizaveta. The door was closed. The carriage rolled away heavily through the yielding snow. The porter shut the street-door; the windows became dark.

Hermann began walking up and down near the deserted house; at length he stopped under a lamp, and glanced at his watch: it was twenty minutes past eleven. He remained standing under a lamp, his eyes fixed upon the watch, impatiently waiting for the remaining minutes to pass. At half-past eleven precisely, Hermann ascended the steps of the house, and made his way into the brightly-illuminated vestibule. The porter was not there. Hermann hastily ascended the staircase, opened the door of the ante-room and saw a footman sitting asleep in an antique chair by the side of a lamp. With a light firm step Hermann passed by him. The drawing-room and dining-room were in darkness, but a feeble reflection penetrated thither from the lamp in the ante-room.

HERMANN REACHED THE Countess's bedroom. Before a shrine, which was full of old images, a golden lamp was burning. Faded stuffed chairs and divans with soft cushions stood in melancholy symmetry around the room, the walls of which were hung with China silk. On one side of the room hung two portraits painted in Paris by Madame Lebrun. One of these represented a stout, red-faced man of about forty years of age in a bright-green uniform and with a star upon his breast; the other—a beautiful young woman, with an aquiline nose, forehead curls and a rose in her powdered hair. In the corners stood porcelain shepherds and shepherdesses, dining-room clocks from the workshop of the celebrated Leroy, bandboxes, roulettes, fans and the various playthings for the amusement of ladies that were in vogue at the end of the last century, when Montgolfier's balloons and Mesmer's magnetism were the rage. Hermann stepped behind the screen. At the back of it stood a little iron bedstead; on the right was the door which led to the cabinet; on the left—the other which led to the corridor. He opened the latter, and saw the little winding staircase which led to the room of the poor companion. . . . But he retraced his steps and entered the dark cabinet.

The time passed slowly. All was still. The clock in the drawing-room struck twelve; the strokes echoed through the room one after the other, and everything was quiet again. Hermann stood leaning against the cold stove. He was calm; his heart beat regularly, like that of a man resolved upon a dangerous but inevitable undertaking. One o'clock in the morning struck; then two; and he heard the distant noise of carriage-wheels. An involuntary agitation took possession of him. The carriage drew near and stopped. He heard the sound of the carriage-steps being let down. All was bustle within the house. The servants were running hither and thither, there was a confusion of voices, and the rooms were lit up. Three antiquated chamber-maids entered the bedroom, and they were shortly afterwards followed by the Countess who, more dead than alive, sank into a Voltaire armchair. Hermann peeped through a chink. Lizaveta Ivanovna passed close by him, and he heard her hurried steps as she hastened up the little spiral staircase. For a moment his heart was assailed by something like a pricking of conscience, but the emotion was only transitory, and his heart became petrified as before.

The Countess began to undress before her looking-glass. Her rose-bedecked cap was taken off, and then her powdered wig was removed from off her white and closely-cut hair. Hairpins fell in showers around her. Her yellow satin dress, brocaded with silver, fell down at her swollen feet.

Hermann was a witness of the repugnant mysteries of her toilette; at last the Countess was in her night-cap and dressing-gown, and in this costume, more suitable to her age, she appeared less hideous and deformed.

Like all old people in general, the Countess suffered from sleeplessness. Having undressed, she seated herself at the window in a Voltaire armchair and dismissed her maids. The candles were taken away, and once more the room was left with only one lamp burning in it. The Countess sat there looking quite yellow, mumbling with her flaccid lips and swaying to and fro. Her dull eyes expressed complete vacancy of mind, and, looking at her, one would have thought that the rocking of her body was not a voluntary action of her own, but was produced by the action of some concealed galvanic mechanism.

Suddenly the death-like face assumed an inexplicable expression. The lips ceased to tremble, the eyes became animated: before the Countess stood an unknown man.

"Do not be alarmed, for Heaven's sake, do not be alarmed!" said he in a low but distinct voice. "I have no intention of doing you any harm, I have only come to ask a favour of you."

The old woman looked at him in silence, as if she had not heard what he had said. Hermann thought that she was deaf, and, bending down towards her ear, he repeated what he had said. The aged Countess remained silent as before.

"You can insure the happiness of my life," continued Hermann, "and it will cost you nothing. I know that you can name three cards in order——"

Hermann stopped. The Countess appeared now to understand what he wanted; she seemed as if seeking for words to reply.

"It was a joke," she replied at last: "I assure you it was only a joke."

"There is no joking about the matter," replied Hermann angrily. "Remember Chaplitsky, whom you helped to win."

The Countess became visibly uneasy. Her features expressed strong emotion, but they quickly resumed their former immobility.

"Can you not name me these three winning cards?" continued Hermann.

The Countess remained silent; Hermann continued:

"For whom are you preserving your secret? For your grandsons? They are rich enough without it; they do not know the worth of money. Your cards would be of no use to a spendthrift. He who cannot preserve his paternal inheritance, will die in want, even though he had a demon at his service. I am not a man of that sort; I know the value of money. Your three cards will not be thrown away upon me. Come!" . . .

He paused and tremblingly awaited her reply. The Countess remained silent; Hermann fell upon his knees.

"If your heart has ever known the feeling of love," said he, "if you remember its rapture, if you have ever smiled at the cry of your newborn child, if any human feeling has ever entered into your breast, I entreat you by the feelings of a wife, a lover, a mother, by all that is most sacred in life, not to reject my prayer. Reveal to me your secret. Of what use is it to you? . . . May be it is connected with some terrible sin, with the loss of eternal salvation, with some bargain with the devil. . . . Reflect,—you are old; you have not long to live—I am ready to take your sins upon my soul. Only reveal to me your secret. Remember that the happiness of a man is in your hands, that not only I, but my children, and grandchildren will bless your memory and reverence you as a saint. . . ."

The old Countess answered not a word.

Hermann rose to his feet.

"You old hag!" he exclaimed, grinding his teeth, "then I will make you answer!"

With these words he drew a pistol from his pocket.

At the sight of the pistol, the Countess for the second time exhibited strong emotion. She shook her head and raised her hands as if to protect herself from the shot . . . then she fell backwards and remained motionless.

"Come, an end to this childish nonsense!" said Hermann, taking hold of her hand. "I ask you for the last time: will you tell me the names of your three cards, or will you not?"

The Countess made no reply. Hermann perceived that she was dead!

CHAPTER IV.

LIZAVETA IVANOVNA WAS sitting in her room, still in her ball dress, lost in deep thought. On returning home, she had hastily dismissed the chambermaid who very reluctantly came forward to assist her, saying that she would undress herself, and with a trembling heart had gone up to her own room, expecting to find Hermann there, but yet hoping not to find him. At the first glance she convinced herself that he was not there, and she thanked her fate for having prevented him keeping the appointment. She sat down without undressing, and began to recall to mind all the circumstances which in so short a time had carried her so far. It was not three weeks since the time when she first saw the young officer from the window—and yet she was already in correspondence with him, and he had succeeded in inducing her to grant him a nocturnal interview! She knew his name only through his having written it at the bottom of some of his letters; she had never spoken to him, had never heard his voice, and had never heard him spoken of until that evening. But, strange to say, that very evening at the ball, Tomsky, being piqued with the young Princess Pauline N——, who, contrary to her usual custom, did not flirt with him, wished to revenge himself by assuming an air of indifference: he therefore engaged Lizaveta Ivanovna and danced an endless mazurka with her. During the whole of the time he kept teasing her about her partiality for Engineer officers; he assured her that he knew far more than she imagined, and some of his jests were so happily aimed, that Lizaveta thought several times that her secret was known to him.

"From whom have you learnt all this?" she asked, smiling.

"From a friend of a person very well known to you," replied Tomsky, "from a very distinguished man."

"And who is this distinguished man?"

"His name is Hermann."

Lizaveta made no reply; but her hands and feet lost all sense of feeling.

"This Hermann," continued Tomsky, "is a man of romantic personality. He has the profile of a Napoleon, and the soul of a Mephistopheles. I believe that he has at least three crimes upon his conscience . . . How pale you have become!"

"I have a headache . . . But what did this Hermann—or whatever his name is—tell you?"

"Hermann is very much dissatisfied with his friend: he says that in his place he would act very differently . . . I even think that Hermann himself has designs upon you; at least, he listens very attentively to all that his friend has to say about you."

"And where has he seen me?"

"In church, perhaps; or on the parade—God alone knows where. It may have been in your room, while you were asleep, for there is nothing that he——"

Three ladies approaching him with the question: *"oubli ou regret?"* interrupted the conversation, which had become so tantalizingly interesting to Lizaveta.

The lady chosen by Tomsky was the Princess Pauline herself. She succeeded in effecting a reconciliation with him during the numerous turns of the dance, after which he conducted her to her chair. On returning to his place, Tomsky thought no more either of Hermann or Lizaveta. She longed to renew the interrupted conversation, but the mazurka came to an end, and shortly afterwards the old Countess took her departure.

Tomsky's words were nothing more than the customary small talk of the dance, but they sank deep into the soul of the young dreamer. The portrait, sketched by Tomsky, coincided with the picture she had formed within her own mind, and thanks to the latest romances, the ordinary countenance of her admirer became invested with attributes capable of alarming her and fascinating her imagination at the same time. She was now sitting with her bare arms crossed and with her head, still adorned with flowers, sunk upon her uncovered bosom. Suddenly the door opened and Hermann entered. She shuddered.

"Where were you?" she asked in a terrified whisper.

"In the old Countess's bedroom," replied Hermann: "I have just left her. The Countess is dead."

"My God! What do you say?"

"And I am afraid," added Hermann, "that I am the cause of her death."

Lizaveta looked at him, and Tomsky's words found an echo in her soul: "This man has at least three crimes upon his conscience!" Hermann sat down by the window near her, and related all that had happened.

Lizaveta listened to him in terror. So all those passionate letters, those ardent desires, this bold obstinate pursuit—all this was not love! Money—that was what his soul yearned for! She could not satisfy his desire and make him happy! The poor girl had been nothing but the blind tool of a robber, of the murderer of her aged benefactress! . . . She wept bitter tears of agonized repentance. Hermann gazed at her in silence: his heart, too, was a prey to violent emotion, but neither the tears of the poor girl, nor the wonderful charm of her beauty, enhanced by her grief, could produce any impression upon his hardened soul. He felt no pricking of conscience at the thought of the dead old woman. One thing only grieved him: the irreparable loss of the secret from which he had expected to obtain great wealth.

"You are a monster!" said Lizaveta at last.

"I did not wish for her death," replied Hermann: "my pistol was not loaded."

Both remained silent.

The day began to dawn. Lizaveta extinguished her candle: a pale light illumined her room. She wiped her tear-stained eyes and raised them towards Hermann: he was sitting near the window, with his arms crossed and with a fierce frown upon his forehead. In this attitude he bore a striking resemblance to the portrait of Napoleon. This resemblance struck Lizaveta even.

"How shall I get you out of the house?" said she at last. "I thought of conducting you down the secret staircase, but in that case it would be necessary to go through the Countess's bedroom, and I am afraid."

"Tell me how to find this secret staircase—I will go alone."

Lizaveta arose, took from her drawer a key, handed it to Hermann and gave him the necessary instructions. Hermann pressed her cold, powerless hand, kissed her bowed head, and left the room.

He descended the winding staircase, and once more entered the Countess's bedroom. The dead old lady sat as if petrified; her face expressed profound tranquillity. Hermann stopped before her, and gazed long and earnestly at her, as if he wished to convince himself of the terrible reality; at last he entered the cabinet, felt behind the tapestry for the door, and then began to descend the dark staircase, filled with strange emotions. "Down this very staircase," thought he, "perhaps coming from the very same room, and at this very same hour sixty years ago, there may have glided, in an embroidered coat, with his hair dressed *à l'oiseau royal* and pressing to his heart his three-cornered hat, some young gallant who has long been mouldering in the grave, but the heart of his aged mistress has only to-day ceased to beat. . . ."

At the bottom of the staircase Hermann found a door, which he opened with a key, and then traversed a corridor which conducted him into the street.

Chapter V.

Three days after the fatal night, at nine o'clock in the morning, Hermann repaired to the Convent of——, where the last honours were to be paid to the mortal remains of the old Countess. Although feeling no remorse, he could not altogether stifle the voice of conscience, which said to him: "You are the murderer of the old woman!" In spite of his entertaining very little religious belief, he was exceedingly superstitious; and believing that the dead Countess might exercise an evil influence on his life, he resolved to be present at her obsequies in order to implore her pardon.

The church was full. It was with difficulty that Hermann made his way through the crowd of people. The coffin was placed upon a rich catafalque beneath a velvet baldachin. The deceased Countess lay within it, with her hands crossed upon her breast, with a lace cap upon her head and dressed in a white satin robe. Around the catafalque stood the members of her household: the servants in black *caftans*, with armorial ribbons upon their shoulders, and candles in their hands; the relatives—children, grandchildren, and great-grandchildren—in deep mourning.

Nobody wept; tears would have been *une affectation*. The Countess was so old, that her death could have surprised nobody, and her relatives had long looked upon her as being out of the world. A famous preacher pronounced the funeral sermon. In simple and touching words he described the peaceful passing away of the righteous, who had passed long years in calm preparation for a Christian end. "The angel of death found her," said the orator, "engaged in pious meditation and waiting for the midnight bridegroom."

The service concluded amidst profound silence. The relatives went forward first to take farewell of the corpse. Then followed the numerous guests, who had come to render the last homage to her who for so many years had been a participator in their frivolous amusements. After these followed the members of the Countess's household. The last of these was an old woman of the same age as the deceased. Two young women led her forward by the hand. She had not strength enough to bow down to the ground—she merely shed a few tears and kissed the cold hand of her mistress.

Hermann now resolved to approach the coffin. He knelt down upon the cold stones and remained in that position for some minutes; at last he arose, as pale as the deceased Countess herself; he ascended the steps of the catafalque and bent over the corpse. . . . At that moment it seemed to him that the dead woman darted a mocking look at him and winked with one eye. Hermann started back, took a false step and fell to the ground. Several persons hurried forward and raised him up. At the same moment Lizaveta Ivanovna was borne fainting into the porch of the church. This episode disturbed for some minutes the solemnity of the gloomy ceremony. Among the congregation arose a deep murmur, and a tall thin chamberlain, a near relative of the deceased, whispered in the ear of an Englishman who was standing near him, that the young officer was a natural son of the Countess, to which the Englishman coldly replied: "Oh!"

During the whole of that day, Hermann was strangely excited. Repairing to an out-of-the-way restaurant to dine, he drank a great deal of wine, contrary to his usual custom, in the hope of deadening his inward agitation. But the wine only served to excite his imagination still more. On returning home, he threw himself upon his bed without undressing, and fell into a deep sleep.

When he woke up it was already night, and the moon was shining into the room. He looked at his watch: it was a quarter to three. Sleep had left him; he sat down upon his bed and thought of the funeral of the old Countess.

At that moment somebody in the street looked in at his window, and immediately passed on again. Hermann paid no attention to this incident. A few moments afterwards he heard the door of his ante-room open. Hermann thought that it was his orderly, drunk as usual, returning from some nocturnal expedition, but presently he heard footsteps that were unknown to him: somebody was walking softly over the floor in slippers. The door opened, and a woman dressed in white, entered the room. Hermann mistook her for his old nurse, and wondered what could bring her there at that hour of the night. But the white woman glided rapidly across the room and stood before him—and Hermann recognized the Countess!

"I have come to you against my wish," she said in a firm voice: "but I have been ordered to grant your request. Three, seven, ace, will win for you if played in succession, but only on these conditions: that you do not play more than one card in twenty-four hours, and that you never play again during the rest of your life. I forgive you my death, on condition that you marry my companion, Lizaveta Ivanovna."

With these words she turned round very quietly, walked with a shuffling gait towards the door and disappeared. Hermann heard the street-door open and shut, and again he saw someone look in at him through the window.

For a long time Hermann could not recover himself. He then rose up and entered the next room. His orderly was lying asleep upon the floor, and he had much difficulty in waking him. The orderly was drunk as usual, and no information could be obtained from him. The street-door was locked. Hermann returned to his room, lit his candle, and wrote down all the details of his vision.

CHAPTER VI.

TWO FIXED IDEAS can no more exist together in the moral world than two bodies can occupy one and the same place in the physical world. "Three, seven, ace" soon drove out of Hermann's mind the thought of the dead Countess. "Three, seven, ace" were perpetually running through his head and continually being repeated by his lips. If he saw a young girl, he would say: "How slender she is! quite like the three of hearts." If anybody asked: "What is the time?" he would reply: "Five minutes to seven." Every stout man that he saw reminded him of the ace. "Three, seven, ace" haunted him in his sleep, and assumed all possible shapes. The threes bloomed before him in the forms of magnificent flowers, the sevens were represented by Gothic portals, and the aces became transformed into gigantic spiders. One thought alone occupied his whole mind—to make a profitable use of the secret which he had purchased so dearly. He thought of applying for a furlough so as to travel abroad. He wanted to go to Paris and tempt fortune in some of the public gambling-houses that abounded there. Chance spared him all this trouble.

There was in Moscow a society of rich gamesters, presided over by the celebrated Chekalinsky, who had passed all his life at the card-table and had amassed millions, accepting bills of exchange for his winnings and paying his losses in ready money. His long experience secured for him the confidence of his companions, and his open house, his famous cook, and his agreeable and fascinating manners gained for him the respect of the public. He came to St. Petersburg. The young men of the capital flocked to his rooms, forgetting balls for cards, and preferring the emotions of faro to the seductions of flirting. Naroumoff conducted Hermann to Chekalinsky's residence.

They passed through a suite of magnificent rooms, filled with attentive domestics. The place was crowded. Generals and Privy Counsellors were playing at whist; young men were lolling carelessly upon the velvet-covered sofas, eating ices and smoking pipes. In the drawing-room, at the head of a long table, around which were assembled about a score of players, sat the master of the house keeping the bank. He was a man of about sixty years of age, of a very dignified appearance; his head was covered with silvery-white hair; his full, florid countenance expressed good-nature, and his eyes twinkled with a perpetual smile. Naroumoff introduced Hermann to him. Chekalinsky shook him by the hand in a friendly manner, requested him not to stand on ceremony, and then went on dealing.

The game occupied some time. On the table lay more than thirty cards. Chekalinsky paused after each throw, in order to give the players time to arrange their cards and note down their losses, listened politely to their requests, and more politely still, put straight the corners of cards that some player's hand had chanced to bend. At last the game was finished. Chekalinsky shuffled the cards and prepared to deal again.

"Will you allow me to take a card?" said Hermann, stretching out his hand from behind a stout gentleman who was punting.

Chekalinsky smiled and bowed silently, as a sign of acquiescence. Naroumoff laughingly congratulated Hermann on his abjuration of that abstention from cards which he had practised for so long a period, and wished him a lucky beginning.

"Stake!" said Hermann, writing some figures with chalk on the back of his card.

"How much?" asked the banker, contracting the muscles of his eyes; "excuse me, I cannot see quite clearly."

"Forty-seven thousand roubles," replied Hermann.

At these words every head in the room turned suddenly round, and all eyes were fixed upon Hermann.

"He has taken leave of his senses!" thought Naroumoff.

"Allow me to inform you," said Chekalinsky, with his eternal smile, "that you are playing very high; nobody here has ever staked more than two hundred and seventy-five roubles at once."

"Very well," replied Hermann; "but do you accept my card or not?"

Chekalinsky bowed in token of consent.

"I only wish to observe," said he, "that although I have the greatest confidence in my friends, I can only play against ready money. For my own part, I am quite convinced that your word is sufficient, but for the sake of the order of the game, and to facilitate the reckoning up, I must ask you to put the money on your card."

Hermann drew from his pocket a bank-note and handed it to Chekalinsky, who, after examining it in a cursory manner, placed it on Hermann's card.

He began to deal. On the right a nine turned up, and on the left a three.

"I have won!" said Hermann, showing his card.

A murmur of astonishment arose among the players. Chekalinsky frowned, but the smile quickly returned to his face.

"Do you wish me to settle with you?" he said to Hermann.

"If you please," replied the latter.

Chekalinsky drew from his pocket a number of bank-notes and paid at once. Hermann took up his money and left the table. Naroumoff could not recover from his astonishment. Hermann drank a glass of lemonade and returned home.

The next evening he again repaired to Chekalinsky's. The host was dealing. Hermann walked up to the table; the punters immediately made room for him. Chekalinsky greeted him with a gracious bow.

Hermann waited for the next deal, took a card and placed upon it his forty-seven thousand roubles, together with his winnings of the previous evening.

Chekalinsky began to deal. A knave turned up on the right, a seven on the left.

Hermann showed his seven.

There was a general exclamation. Chekalinsky was evidently ill at ease, but he counted out the ninety-four thousand roubles and handed them over to Hermann, who pocketed them in the coolest manner possible and immediately left the house.

The next evening Hermann appeared again at the table. Everyone was expecting him. The generals and Privy Counsellors left their whist in order to watch such extraordinary play. The young officers quitted their sofas, and even the servants crowded into the room. All pressed round Hermann. The other players left off punting, impatient to see how it would end. Hermann stood at the table and prepared to play alone against the pale, but still smiling Chekalinsky. Each opened a pack of cards. Chekalinsky shuffled. Hermann took a card and covered it with a pile of bank-notes. It was like a duel. Deep silence reigned around.

Chekalinsky began to deal; his hands trembled. On the right a queen turned up, and on the left an ace.

"Ace has won!" cried Hermann, showing his card.

"Your queen has lost," said Chekalinsky, politely.

Hermann started; instead of an ace, there lay before him the queen of spades! He could not believe his eyes, nor could he understand how he had made such a mistake.

At that moment it seemed to him that the queen of spades smiled ironically and winked her eye at him. He was struck by her remarkable resemblance. . . .

"The old Countess!" he exclaimed, seized with terror.

Chekalinsky gathered up his winnings. For some time, Hermann remained perfectly motionless. When at last he left the table, there was a general commotion in the room.

"Splendidly punted!" said the players. Chekalinsky shuffled the cards afresh, and the game went on as usual.

HERMANN WENT OUT of his mind, and is now confined in room Number 17 of the Oboukhoff Hospital. He never answers any questions, but he constantly mutters with unusual rapidity: "Three, seven, ace! Three, seven, queen!"

Lizaveta Ivanovna has married a very amiable young man, a son of the former steward of the old Countess. He is in the service of the State somewhere, and is in receipt of a good income. Lizaveta is also supporting a poor relative.

Tomsky has been promoted to the rank of captain, and has become the husband of the Princess Pauline.

The Man Who Would Be King

by Rudyard Kipling

THE LAW, AS quoted, lays down a fair conduct of life, and one not easy to follow. I have been fellow to a beggar again and again under circumstances which prevented either of us finding out whether the other was worthy. I have still to be broth to a Prince, though I once came near to kinship with what might have been a veritable King, and was promised the reversion of a Kingdom—army, law-courts, revenue, and policy all complete. But, today, I greatly fear that my King is dead, and if I want a crown I must go hunt it for myself.

The beginning of everything was in a railway train upon the road to Mhow from Ajmir. There had been a Deficit in the Budget, which necessitated travelling, not Second-class, which is only half as dear as First-class, but by Intermediate, which is very awful indeed. There are no cushions in the Intermediate class, and the population are either Intermediate, which is Eurasian, or native, which for a long night journey is nasty, or Loafer, which is amusing though intoxicated. Intermediates do not buy from refreshment-rooms. They carry their food in bundles and pots, and buy sweets from the native sweetmeat-sellers, and drink the road-side water. That is why in the hot weather Intermediates are taken out of the carriages dead, and in all weathers are most properly looked down upon.

My particular Intermediate happened to be empty till I reached Nasirabad, when a big black-browed gentleman in shirt-sleeves entered, and, following the custom of Intermediates, passed the time of day. He was a wanderer and a vagabond like myself, but with an educated taste for whisky. He told tales of things he had seen and done, of out-of-the-way corners of the Empire into which he had penetrated, and of adventures in which he risked his life for a few days' food.

'If India was filled with men like you and me, not knowing more than the crows where they'd get their next day's rations, it isn't seventy millions of revenue the land would be paying—it's seven hundred millions,' said he; and as I looked at his mouth and chin I was disposed to agree with him.

We talked politics—the politics of Loaferdom, that see things from the underside where the lath and plaster is not smoothed off—and we talked postal arrangements because my friend wanted to send a telegram back from the next station to Ajmir, the turning-off place from the Bombay to the Mhow line as you travel westward. My friend had no money beyond eight annas, which he wanted for dinner, and I had no money at all, owing to the hitch in the Budget before mentioned. Further, I was going into a wilderness where, though I should resume touch with the Treasury, there were no telegraph offices. I was, therefore, unable to help him in any way.

'We might threaten a Station-master, and make him send a wire on tick,' said my friend, 'but that'd mean inquiries for you and for me, and I've got my hands full these days. Did you say you are travelling back along this line within any days?'

'Within ten,' I said.

'Can't you make it eight?' said he. 'Mine is rather urgent business.'

'I can send you telegram within ten days if that will serve you,' I said.

'I couldn't trust the wire to fetch him now I think of it. It's this way. He leaves Delhi on the 23rd for Bombay. That means he'll be running through Ajmir about the night of the 23rd.'

'But I'm going into the Indian Desert,' I explained.

'Well and good,' said he. 'You'll be changing at Marwar Junction to get into Jodhpore territory—you must do that—and he'll be coming through Marwar Junction in the early morning of the 24th by the Bombay Mail. Can you be at Marwar Junction on that time? 'Twon't be inconveniencing you because I know that there's precious few pickings to be got out of these Central Indian States—even though you pretend to be correspondent of the Backwoodsman.'

'Have you ever tried that trick?' I asked.

'Again and again, but the Residents find you out, and then you get escorted to the Border before you've time to get your knife into them. But about my friend here. I must give him a word o' mouth to tell him what's come to me or else he won't know where to go. I would take it more than kind of you if you was to come out of Central India in time to catch him at Marwar Junction, and say to him: "He has gone South for the week." He'll know what that means. He's a big man with a red beard, and a great swell he is. You'll find him sleeping like a gentleman with all his luggage round him in a Second-class compartment. But don't you be afraid. Slip down the window, and say: "He has gone South for the week," and he'll tumble. It's only cutting your time of stay in those parts by two days. I ask you as a stranger—going to the West.' He said with emphasis.

'Where have you come from?' said I.

'From the East,' said he, 'and I am hoping that you will give him the message on the Square—for the sake of my Mother as well as your own.'

Englishmen are not usually softened by appeals to the memory of their mothers, but for certain reasons, which will be fully apparent, I saw fit to agree.

'It's more than a little matter,' said he, 'and that's why I asked you to do it—and now I know that I can depend on you doing it. A Second-class carriage at Marwar Junction, and a red-haired man asleep in it. You'll be sure to remember. I get out at the next station, and I must hold on there till he comes or sends me what I want.'

'I'll give the message if I catch him,' I said, 'and for the sake of your Mother as well as mine I'll give you a word of advice. Don't try to run the Central Indian States just now as the correspondent of the Backwoodsman. There's a real one knocking about here, and it might lead to trouble.'

'Thank you,' said he simply, 'and when will the swine be gone? I can't starve because he's ruining my work. I wanted to get hold of the Degumber Rajah down here about his father's widow, and give him a jump.'

'What did you do to his father's widow, then?'

'Filled her up with red pepper and slippered her to death as she hung from a beam. I found that out myself, and I'm the only man that would dare going into the State to get hush-money for it. They'll try to poison me, same as they did in Chortumna when I went on the loot there. But you'll give the man at Marwar Junction my message?'

He got out at a little roadside station, and I reflected. I had heard, more than once, of men personating correspondents of newspapers and bleeding small Native States with threats of exposure, but I had never met any of the caste before. They led a hard life, and generally die with great suddenness. The Native States have a wholesome horror of English newspapers which may throw light on their peculiar methods of government, and do their best to choke correspondents with champagne, or drive them out of their mind with four-in-hand barouches. They do not understand that nobody cares a straw for the internal administration of Native States so long as oppression and crime are kept within decent limits, and the ruler is not drugged, drunk, or diseased from one end of the year to the other. They are the dark places of the earth, full of unimaginable cruelty, touching the Railway and the Telegraph on one side, and, on the other, the days of Harun-al-Raschid. When I left the train I did business with divers Kings, and in eight days passed through many changes of life. Sometimes I wore dress-clothes and consorted with Princes and Politicals, drinking from crystal and eating from silver. Sometimes I lay out upon the ground and devoured what I could get, from a plate made of leaves, and drank the running water, and slept under the same rug as my servant. It was all in the day's work.

Then I headed for the Great Indian Desert upon the proper date, as I had promised, and the night Mail set me down at Marwar Junction, where a funny, little, happy-go-lucky, native-managed railway runs to Jodhpore. The Bombay Mail from Delhi makes a short halt at Marwar. She arrived as I got in, and I had just time to hurry to her platform and go down the carriages. There was only one Second-class on the train. I slipped the window and looked down upon a flaming red beard, half covered by a railway rug. That was my man, fast asleep, and I dug him gently in the ribs. He woke with a grunt, and I saw his face in the light of the lamps. It was a great and shining face.

'Tickets again?' said he.

'No,' said I. 'I am to tell you that he is gone South for the week. He has gone South for the week!'

The train had begun to move out. The red man rubbed his eyes. 'He has gone South for the week,' he repeated. 'Now that's just like his impidence. Did he say that I was to give you anything? 'Cause I won't.'

'He didn't,' I said, and dropped away, and watched the red lights die out in the dark. It was horribly cold because the wind was blowing off the sands. I climbed into my own train—not an Intermediate Carriage this time—and went to sleep.

If the man with the beard had given me a rupee I should have kept it as a memento of a rather curious affair. But the consciousness of having done my duty was my only reward.

Later on I reflected that two gentlemen like my friends could not do any good if they forgathered and personated correspondents of newspapers, and might, if they blackmailed one of the little rat-trap states of Central India or Southern Rajputana, get themselves into serious difficulties. I therefore took some trouble to describe them as accurately as I could remember to people who would be interested in deporting them; and succeeded, so I was later informed, in having them headed back from the Degumber borders.

Then I became respectable, and returned to an Office where there were no Kings and no incidents outside the daily manufacture of a newspaper. A newspaper office seems to attract every conceivable sort of person, to the prejudice of discipline. Zenana-mission ladies arrive, and beg that the Editor will instantly abandon all his duties to describe a Christian prize-giving in a back-slum of a perfectly inaccessible village; Colonels who have been overpassed for command sit down and sketch the outline of a series of ten, twelve, or twenty-four leading articles on Seniority versus Selection; Missionaries wish to know why they have not been permitted to escape from their regular vehicles of abuse and swear at a brother-missionary under special patronage of the editorial We; stranded theatrical companies troop up to explain that they cannot pay for their advertisements, but on their return from New Zealand or Tahiti will do so with interest; inventors of patent punkah-pulling machines, carriage couplings, and unbreakable swords and axle-trees, call with specifications in their pockets and hours at their disposal; tea-companies enter and elaborate their prospectuses with the office pens; secretaries of ball-committees clamour to have the glories of their last dance more fully described; strange ladies rustle in and say, 'I want a hundred lady's cards printed at once, please,' which is manifestly part of an Editor's duty; and every dissolute ruffian that ever tramped the Grand Trunk Road makes it his business to ask for employment as a proof-reader. And, all the time, the telephone-bell is ringing madly, and Kings are being killed on the

Continent, and Empires are saying, 'You're another,' and Mister Gladstone is calling down brimstone upon the British Dominions, and the little black copy-boys are whining, 'kaa-pi chay-ha-yeh' (copy wanted) like tired bees, and most of the paper is as blank as Modred's shield.

But that is the amusing part of the year. There are six other months when none ever comes to call, and the thermometer walks inch by inch up to the top of the glass, and the office is darkened to just above reading-light, and the press-machines are red-hot of touch, and nobody writes anything but accounts of amusements in the Hill-stations or obituary notices. Then the telephone becomes a tinkling terror, because it tells you of the sudden deaths of men and women that you knew intimately, and the prickly-heat covers you with a garment, and you sit down and write: 'A slight increase of sickness is reported from the Khuda Janta Khan District. The outbreak is purely sporadic in its nature, and, thanks to the energetic efforts of the District authorities, is now almost at an end. It is, however, with deep regret we record the death, etc.'

Then the sickness really breaks out, and the less recording and reporting the better for the peace of the subscribers. But the Empires and the Kings continue to divert themselves as selfishly as before, and the Foreman thinks that a daily paper really ought to come out once in twenty-four hours, and all the people at the Hill-stations in the middle of their amusements say: 'Good gracious! Why can't the paper be sparkling? I'm sure there's plenty going on up here.'

That is the dark half of the moon, and, as the advertisements say, 'must be experienced to be appreciated.'

It was in that season, and a remarkably evil season, that the paper began running the last issue of the week on Saturday night, which is to say Sunday morning, after the custom of a London paper. This was a great convenience, for immediately after the paper was put to bed, the dawn would lower the thermometer from 96 degrees to almost 84 degrees for half an hour, and in that chill—you have no idea how cold is 84 degrees on the grass until you begin to pray for it—a very tired man could get off to sleep ere the heat roused him.

One Saturday night it was my pleasant duty to put the paper to bed alone. A King or courtier or a courtesan or a Community was going to die or get a new Constitution, or do something that was important on the other side of the world, and the paper was to be held open till the latest possible minute in order to catch the telegram.

It was a pitchy black night, as stifling as a June night can be, and the loo, the red-hot wind from the westward, was booming among the tinder-dry trees and pretending that the rain was on its heels. Now and again a spot of almost boiling water would fall on the dust with the flop of a frog, but all our weary world knew that was only pretence. It was a shade cooler in the press-room than the office, so I sat there, while the type ticked and clicked, and the night-jars hooted at the windows, and the all but naked compositors wiped the sweat from their foreheads, and called for water. The thing that was keeping us back, whatever it was, would not come off, though the loo dropped and the last type was set, and the whole round earth stood still in the choking heat, with its finger on its lip, to wait the event. I drowsed, and wondered whether the telegraph was a blessing, and whether this dying man, or struggling people, might be aware of the inconvenience the delay was causing. There was no special reason beyond the heat and worry to make tension, but, as the clock-hands crept up to three o'clock, and the machines spun their flywheels two or three times to see that all was in order before I said the word that would set them off, I could have shrieked aloud.

Then the roar and rattle of the wheels shivered the quiet into little bits. I rose to go away, but two men in white clothes stood in front of me. The first one said: 'It's him!' The second said: 'So it is!' And they both laughed almost as loudly as the machinery roared, and mopped their foreheads. 'We seed there was a light burning across the road, and we were sleeping in that ditch there for coolness, and I said to my friend here, The office is open. Let's come along and speak to him as turned us back from the Degumber State,' said the smaller of the two. He was the man I had met in the Mhow train, and his fellow was the red-bearded man of Marwar Junction. There was no mistaking the eyebrows of the one or the beard of the other.

I was not pleased, because I wished to go to sleep, not to squabble with loafers. 'What do you want?' I asked.

'Half an hour's talk with you, cool and comfortable, in the office,' said the red-bearded man. 'We'd like some drink—the Contrack doesn't begin yet, Peachey, so you needn't look—but what we really want is advice. We don't want money. We ask you as a favour, because we found out you did us a bad turn about Degumber State.'

I led from the press-room to the stifling office with the maps on the walls, and the red-haired man rubbed his hands. 'That's something like,' said he. 'This was the proper shop to come to. Now, Sir, let me introduce to you Brother Peachey Carnehan, that's him, and Brother Daniel Dravot, that is me, and the less said about our professions the better, for we have been most things in our time. Soldier, sailor, compositor, photographer, proofreader, street-preacher, and correspondents of the Backwoodsman when we thought the paper wanted one. Carnehan is sober, and so am I. Look at us first, and see that's sure. It will save you cutting into my talk. We'll take one of your cigars apiece, and you shall see us light up.'

I watched the test. The men were absolutely sober, so I gave them each a tepid whisky and soda.

'Well and good,' said Carnehan of the eyebrows, wiping the froth from his moustache. 'Let me talk now, Dan. We have been all over India, mostly on foot. We have been boiler-fitters, engine-drivers, petty contractors, and all that, and we have decided that Indian isn't big enough for such as us.'

They certainly were too big for the office. Dravot's beard seemed to fill half the room and Carnehan's shoulders the other half, as they sat on the big table. Carnehan continued: 'The country isn't half worked out because they that governs it won't let you touch it. They spend all their blessed time in governing it, and you can't lift a spade, nor chip a rock, nor look for oil, nor anything like that, without all the Government saying, "Leave it alone, and let us govern." Therefore, such as it is, we will let it alone, and go away to some other place where a man isn't crowded and can come to his own. We are not little men, and there is nothing that we are afraid of except Drink, and we have signed a Contrack on that. Therefore, we are going away to be Kings.'

'Kings in our own right,' muttered Dravot.

'Yes, of course,' I said. 'You've been tramping in the sun, and it's a very warm night, and hadn't you better sleep over the notion? Come tomorrow.'

'Neither drunk nor sunstruck,' said Dravot. 'We have slept over the notion half a year, and require to see Books and Atlases, and we have decided that there is only one place now in the world that two strong men can Sar-a-whack. They call it Kafiristan. By my reckoning it's the top right-hand corner of Afghanistan, not more than three hundred miles from Peshawar. They have two-and-thirty heathen idols there, and we'll be the thirty-third and thirty-fourth. It's a mountainous country, and the women of those parts are very beautiful.'

'But that is provided against in the Contrack,' said Carnehan. 'Neither Woman nor Liquor, Daniel.'

'And that's all we know, except that no one has gone there, and they fight, and in any place where they fight a man who knows how to drill men can always be a King. We shall go to those parts and say to any King we find—"D'you want to vanquish your foes?" and we will show him how to drill men; for that we know better than anything else. Then we will subvert that King and seize his Throne and establish a Dy-nasty.'

'You'll be cut to pieces before you're fifty miles across the Border,' I said. 'You have to travel through Afghanistan to get to that country. It's one mass of mountains and peaks and glaciers, and no Englishman has been through it. The people are utter brutes, and even if you reached them you couldn't do anything.'

'That's more like,' said Carnehan. 'If you could think us a little more mad we would be more pleased. We have come to you to know about this country, to read a book about it, and to be shown maps. We want you to tell us that we are fools and to show us your books.' He turned to the bookcases.

'Are you at all in earnest?' I said.

'A little,' said Dravot sweetly. 'As big a map as you have got, even if it's all blank where Kafiristan is, and any books you've got. We can read, though we aren't very educated.'

I uncased the big thirty-two-miles-to-the-inch map of India, and two smaller Frontier maps, hauled down volume INF-KAN of the Encyclopaedia Britannica, and the men consulted them.

'See here!' said Dravot, his thumb on the map. 'Up to Jagdallak, Peachey and me know the road. We was there with Roberts' Army. We'll have to turn off to the right at Jagdallak through Laghmann territory. Then we get among the hills—fourteen thousand feet—fifteen thousand—it will be cold work there, but it don't look very far on the map.'

I handed him wood on the Sources of the Oxus. Carnehan was deep in the Encyclopaedia.

'They're a mixed lot,' said Dravot reflectively; 'and it won't help us to know the names of their tribes. The more tribes the more they'll fight, and the better for us. From Jagdallak to Ashang H'mm!'

'But all the information about the country is as sketchy and inaccurate as can be,' I protested. 'No one knows anything about it really. Here's the file of United Services' Institute. Read what Bellew says.'

'Blow Bellew,!' said Carnehan. 'Dan, they're a stinkin' lot of heathens, but this book here says they think they're related to us English.'

I smoked while the men poured over Raverty, Wood, the maps, and the Encyclopaedia.

'There is no use your waiting,' said Dravot politely. 'It's about four o'clock now. We'll go before six o'clock if you want to sleep, and we won't steal any of the papers. Don't you sit up. We're two harmless lunatics, and if you come tomorrow evening down to the Serai, we'll say good-bye to you.'

'You are two fools,' I answered. 'You'll be turned back at the Frontier or cut up the minute you set foot in Afghanistan. Do you want any money or a recommendation down-country? I can help you to the chance of work next week.'

'Next week we shall be hard at work ourselves, thank you,' said Dravot. 'It isn't so easy being a King as it looks. When we've got our Kingdom in going order we'll let you know, and you can come up and help us to govern it.'

"Would two lunatics make a contrack like that?" said Carnehan, with subdued pride, showing me a greasy half-sheet of notepaper on which was written the following. I copied it, then and there, as a curiosity—

This Contract between me and you persuing witnesseth in the name of God—Amen and so forth.

(One) That me and you will settle this matter together; i.e. to be Kings of Kafiristan.

(Two) That you and me will not, while this matter is being settled, look at any Liquor, nor any Woman black, white, or brown, so as to get mixed up with one or the other harmful.

(Three) That we conduct ourselves with Dignity and Discretion, and if one of us gets into trouble the other will stay by him.

Signed by you and me this day,

Peachey Taliaferro Carnehan

Daniel Dravot

Both Gentlemen at Large

'There was no need for the last article,' said Carnehan, blushing modestly; 'but it looks regular. Now you know the sort of men that loafers are—we are loafers, Dan, until we get out of India—and do you think that we would sign a Contrack like that unless we was in earnest? We have kept away from the two things that make life worth having.'

'You won't enjoy your lives much longer if you are going to try this idiotic adventure. Don't set the office on fire,' I said, 'and go away before nine o'clock.

I left them still poring over the maps and making notes on the back of the 'Contrack'. 'Be sure to come down to the Serai tomorrow,' were their parting words.

The Kumharsen Serai is the great four-square sink of humanity where the strings of camels and horses from the North load and unload. All the nationalities of Central Asia may be found there, and most of the folk of India proper. Balkh and Bokhara there meet Bengal and Bombay, and try to draw eye-teeth. You can buy ponies, turquoises, Persian pussy-cats, saddle-bags, fat-tailed sheep and musk in the Kumharsen Serai, and get many strange things for nothing. In the afternoon I went down to see whether my friends intended to keep their word or were lying there drunk.

A priest attired in fragments of ribbons and rags stalked up to me, gravely twisting a child's paper whirligig. Behind him was his servant bending undre a load of a crate of mud toys. The two were loading up two camels, and the inhabitants of the Serai watched them with shrieks of laughter.

'The priest is mad,' said a horse-dealer to me. 'He is going up to Kabul to sell toys to the Amir. He will either be raised to honor or have his head cut off. He came in here this morning and has been behaving madly ever since.'

'The witless are under the protection of God,' stammered a flat-cheeked Usbeg in broken Hindi. 'They foretell future events.'

'Would they could have foretold that my caravan would have been cut up by the Shinwaris almost within shadow of the Pass!' grunted the Eusufzai agent of a Rajputana trading-house whose goods had been diverted into the hands of other robbers just across the Border, and whose misfortunes were the laughing-stock of the basar. 'Ohé, priest, whence come you and whither do you go?'

'From Roum have I come,' shouted the priest, waving his whirligig; 'from Roum, blown by the breath of a hundred devils across the sea! O thieves, robbers, liars, the blessing of Pir Khan on pigs, dogs, and perjurers! Who will take the Protected of God to the North to sell charms that are never still to the Amir? The camels shall not gall, the sons shall not fall sick, and the wives shall remain faithful while they are away, of the men who give me place in their caravan. Who will assist me to slipper the King of the Roos with a golden slipper with a silver heel? The protection of Pir Khan be upon his labours!' He spread out the skirts of his gaberdine and pirouetted between the lines of tethered horses.

'There starts a caravan from Peshawar to Kabul in twenty days, Huzrut,' said the Eusufzai trader. 'My camels go therewith. Do thou also go and bring us good luck.'

'I will go even now!' shouted the priest. 'I will depart upon my winged camels, and be at Peshawar in a day! Ho! Hazar Mir Khan,' he yelled to his servant, 'drive out the camels, but let me first mount my own.'

He leaped on the back of his beast as it knelt, and, turning round to me, cried: 'Come thou also, Sahib, a little along the road, and I will sell thee a charm—an amulet that shall make thee King of Kafiristan.'

Then the light broke upon me, and I followed the two camels out of the Serai till we reached open road and the priest halted.

'What d'you think o' that?' said he in English. 'Carnehan can't talk their patter, so I've made him my servant. He makes a handsome servant. 'Tisn't for nothing that I've been knocking about the country for fourteen years. Didn't I do that talk neat? We'll hitch on to a caravan at Peshawar till we get to Jagdallak, and then we'll see if we can get donkeys for our camels, and strike into Kafiristan. Whirligigs for the Amir, O Lor! Put your hand under the camel-bags and tell me what you feel.'

I felt the butt of a Martini, and another and another.

'Twenty of 'em,' said Dravot placidly. 'Twenty of 'em and ammunition to correspond, under the whirligigs and the mud dolls.'

'Heaven help you if you are caught with those things!' I said. 'A Martini is worth her weight in silver among the Pathans.'

'Fifteen hundred rupees of capital—every rupee we could beg, borrow, or steal—are invested on these two camels,' said Dravot. 'We won't get caught. We're going through the Khaiber with a regular caravan. Who'd touch a poor mad priest?'

'Have you got everything you want?' I asked, overcome with astonishment.

'Not yet, but we shall soon. Give us a memento of your kindness, Brother. You did me a service, yesterday, and that time in Marwar. Half my Kingdom shall you have, as the saying is.' I slipped a small charm compass from my watch-chain and handed it up to the priest.

'Good-bye,' said Dravot, giving me hand cautiously. 'It's the last time we'll shake hands with an Englishman these many days. Shake hands with him, Carnehan,' he cried, as the second camel passed me.

Carnehan leaned down and shook hands. Then the camels passed away along the dusty road, and I was left alone to wonder. My eye could detect no failure in disguises. The scene in the Serai proved that they were complete to the native mind. There was just the chance, therefore, that Carnehan and Dravot would be able to wander through Afghanistan without detection. But, beyond, they would find death—certain and awful death.

Ten days later a native correspondent giving me the news of the day from Peshawar, wound up his letter with: 'There has been much laughter here on account of a certain mad priest who is going in his estimation to sell petty gauds and insignificant trinkets which he ascribes as great charms to H.H. the Amir of Bukhara. He passed through Peshawar and associated himself to the Second Summer caravan that goes to Kabul. The merchants are pleased because through superstition they imagine that such mad fellows bring good fortune.'

The two, then, were beyond the Border. I would have prayed for them, but, that night, a real King died in Europe, and demanded an obituary notice.

The wheel of the world swings through the same phases again and again. Summer passed and winter thereafter, and came and passed again. The daily paper continued and I with it, and upon the third summer there fell a hot night, a night-issue, and a strained waiting for something to be telegraphed from the other side of the world, exactly as had happened before. A few great men had died in the past two years, the machines worked with more clatter, and some of the trees in the office garden were a few feet taller. But that was all the difference.

I passed over to the press-room, and went through just such a scene as I have already described. The nervous tension was stronger than it had been two years before, and I felt the heat more acutely. At three o'clock I cried, 'Print off,' and turned to go when there crept to my chair what was left of a man. He was bent into a circle, his head was sunk between his shoulders, and he moved his feet one over the other like a bar. I could hardly see whether he walked or crawled—this rag-wrapped, whining cripple who addressed me by name, crying that he was come back. 'Can you give me a drink?' he whimpered. 'For the Lord's sake give me a drink!'

I went back to the office, the man following with groans of pain, and I turned on the lamp.

'Don't you know me?' he gasped, dropping into a chair, and he turned his drawn face, surmounted by a shock of grey hair, to the light.

I looked at him intently. Once before had I seen eyebrows that met over the nose in an inch-broad black band, but for the life of me I could not tell where.

'I don't know you,' I said, handing him the whisky. 'What can I do for you?'

He took a gulp of the spirit raw, and shivered in spite of the suffocating heat.

'I've come back,' he repeated; 'and I was the King of Kafiristan—me and Dravot—crowned Kings we was! In this office we settled it—you setting there and giving us the books. I am Peachey—Peachey Taliaferro Carnehan, and you've been setting here ever since—O Lord!'

I was more than a little astonished, and expressed my feelings accordingly.

'It's true,' said Carnehan, with a dry cackle, nursing his feet, which were wrapped in rags. 'True as gospel. Kings we were, with crowns upon our heads—me and Dravot—poor Dan—oh, poor, poor Dan, that would never take advice, not though I begged of him!'

'Take the whisky,' I said, 'and take your own time. Tell me all you can recollect of everything from beginning to end. You got across the Border on your camels, Dravot dressed as a mad priest and you his servant. Do you remember that?'

'I ain't mad—yet, but I shall be that way soon. Of course I remember. Keep looking at me, or maybe my words will go all to pieces. Keep looking at me in my eyes and don't say anything.'

I leaned forward and looked into his face as steadily as I could. He dropped one hand upon the table and I grasped it by the wrist. It was twisted like a bird's claw, and upon the back was a ragged red diamond-shaped scar.

'No, don't look there. Look at me,' said Carnehan. 'That comes afterwards, but for the Lord's sake don't distrack me. We left with that caravan, me and Dravot playing all sorts of antics to amuse the people we were with. Dravot used to make us laugh in the evenings when all the people was cooking their dinners—cooking their dinners, and . . . what did they do then? They lit little fires with sparks that went into Dravot's beard, and we all laughed—fit to die. Little red fires they was, going into Dravot's big red beard—so funny.' His eyes left mine and he smiled foolishly.

'You went as far as Jagdallak with that caravan,' I said at a venture, 'after you had lit those fires. To Jagdallak, where you turned off to try to get into Kafiristan.'

'No, we didn't neither. What are you talking about? We turned off before Jagdallak, because we heard the roads was good. But they wasn't good enough for our two camels—mine and Dravot's. When we left the caravan, Dravot took off all his clothes and mine too, and said we would be heathen, because the Kafirs didn't allow Mohammedans to talk to them. So we dressed betwixt and between, and such a sight as Daniel Dravot I never saw yet nor expect to see again. He burned half his beard, and slung a sheep-skin over his shoulder, and shaved his head into patters. He shaved mine, too, and made me wear outrageous things to look like a heathen. That was in a most mountaineous country, and our camels couldn't go along any more because of the mountains. They were tall and black, and coming home I saw them fight like wild goats—there are lots of goats in Kafiristan. And these mountains, they never keep still, no more than the goats. Always fighting they are, and don't let you sleep at night.'

'Take some more whisky,' I said very slowly. 'What did you and Daniel Dravot do when the camels could go no farther because of the rough roads that led into Kafiristan?'

'What did which do? There was a party called Peachey Taliaferro Carnehan that was with Dravot. Shall I tell you about him? He died out there in the cold. Slap from the bridge fell old Peachy, turning and twisting in the air like a penny whirligig that you can sell to the Amir—No; they was two for three ha'pence, those whirligigs, or I am much mistaken and woful sore . . . And then these camels were no use, and Peachey said to Dravot—"For the Lord's sake let's get out of this before our heads are chopped off," and with that they killed the camels all among the mountains, not having anything in particular to teat, but first they took off the boxes with the guns and the ammunition, till two men came along driving four mules. Dravot up and dances in front of them, singing—"Sell me four mules." Says the first man—"If you are rich enough to buy, you are rich enough to rob"; but before ever he could put his hand to his knife, Dravot breaks his neck over his knee, and the other party runs away. So Carnehan loaded the mules with the rifles that was taken off the camels, and together we starts forward into those bitter cold mountaineous parts, and never a road broader than the back of your hand.'

He paused for a moment, while I asked him if he could remember the nature of the country through which he had journeyed.

'I am telling you as straight as I can, but my head isn't as good as it might be. They drove nails through it to make me hear better how Dravot died. The country was mountaineous and the mules were most contrary, and the inhabitants was dispersed and solitary. They went up and up, and down and down, and that other party, Carnehan, was imploring of Dravot not to sing and whistle so loud, for fear of bringing down the tremenjus avalanches. But Dravot says that if a King couldn't sing it wasn't worth being King, and whacked the mules over the rump, and never took no heed for ten cold days. We came to a big level valley all among the mountains, and the mules were near dead, so we killed them, not having anything in special for them or us to eat. We sat upon the boxes, and played odd and even with the cartridges that was jolted out.

'Then ten men with bows and arrows ran down that valley, chasing twenty men with bows and arrows, and the row was tremenjus. They was fair men—fairer than you or me—with yellow hair and remarkable well built. Says Dravot, unpacking the guns—"This is the beginning of the business. We'll fight for the ten men," and with that he first two rifles at the twenty men, and drops one of them at two hundred yards from the rock where he was sitting. The other men began to run, but Carnehan and Dravot sits on the boxes picking them off at all ranges, up and down the valley. Then we goes up to the ten men that had run across the snow too, and they fires a footy little arrow at us. Dravot he shoots above their heads and they all falls down flat. Then he walks over them and kicks them, and then he lifts them up and shakes hands all round to make them friendly like. He calls them and gives them the boxes to carry, and waves his hand for all the world as though he was King already. They takes the boxes and him across the valley and up the hill into a pine wood on the top, where there was half-a-dozen big stone idols. Dravot he goes to the biggest—a fellow they call Imbra—and lays a rifle and a cartridge at his feet, rubbing his nose respectful with his own nose, patting him on the head, and saluting in front of it. He turns round to the men and nods his head, and says—"That's all right. I'm in the know too, and all these old jim-jams are my friends." Then he opens his mouth and points down it, and when the first man brings him food, he says—"No"; and when the second man brings him food, he says—"No"; but when one of the old priests and the boss of the village brings him food, he says—"Yes," very haughty, and eats it slow. That was how we came to our first village, without any trouble, just as though we had tumbled from the skies. But we tumbled from one of those damned rope-bridges, you see, and—you couldn't expect a man to laugh much after that?'

'Take some more whisky and go on,' I said. 'That was the first village you came into. How did you get to be King?'

'I wasn't King,' said Carnehan. 'Dravot he was the King, and a handsome man he looked with the gold crown on his head and all. Him and the other party stayed in that village, and every morning Dravot sat by the side of old Imbra, and the people came and worshipped. That was Dravot's order. Then a lot of men came into the valley, and Camehan and Dravot picks them off with the rifles before they knew where they was, and runs down into the valley and up again the other side and finds another village, same as the first one, and the people all falls down flat on their faces, and Dravot says—"Now what is the trouble between you two villages?" and the people points to a woman, as fair as you or me, that was carried off, and Dravot takes her back to the first village and counts up the dead—eight there was. For each dead man Dravot pours a little milk on the ground and waves his arms like a whirligig, and "That's all right," says he. Then he and Carnehan takes the big boss of each village by the arm and walks them down into the valley, and shows them how to scratch a line with a spear right down the valley, and gives each a sod of turf from both sides of the line. Then all the people comes down and shouts like the devil and all, and Dravot says—"Go and dig the land, and be fruitful and multiply," which they did, though they didn't understand. Then we asks the names of things in their lingo—bread and water and fire and idols and such, and Dravot leads the priest of each village up to the idol, and says he must sit there and judge the people, and if anything goes wrong he is to be shot.

'Next week they was all turning up the land in the village as quiet as bees and much prettier, and the priests heard all the complaints and told Dravot in dumb show what it was about. "That's just the beginning," says Dravot. "They think we're Gods." He and Carnehan picks out twenty good men and shows them how to click off a rifle, and form fours, and advance in line, and they was very pleased to do so, and clever to see the hang of it. Then he takes out his pipe and is baccy-pouch and leaves one at one village, and one at the other, and off we two goes to see what was to be done in the next valley. That was all rock, and there was a little village there, and Carnehan says—"Send 'em to the old valley to plant," and takes 'em there, and gives 'em some land that wasn't took before. They were a poor lot, and we blooded 'em with a kid before letting 'em into the new Kingdom. That was to impress the people, and then they settled down quiet, and Carnehan went back to Dravot who had got into another valley, all snow and ice and most mountaineous. There was no people there and the Army got afraid, so Dravot shoots one of them, and goes on till he finds some people in a village, and the Army explains that unless the people wants to be killed they had better not shoot their little matchlocks; for they had matchlocks. We makes friends with the priest, and I stays there alone with two of the Army, teaching the men how to drill, and a thundering big Chief comes across the snow with kettle-drums and horns twanging, because he heard there was a new God kicking about. Carnehan sights for the brown of the men half a mile across the snow and wings one of them. Then he sends a message to the Chief that, unless he wished to be killed, he must come and shake hands with me and leave his arms behind. The Chief comes alone first, and Carnehan shakes hands with him and whirls his arms about, same as Dravot used, and very much surprised that Chief was, and strokes my eyebrows. Then Carnehan goes alone to the Chief, and asks him in dumb show if he had an enemy he hated. "I have," says the Chief. So Carnehan weeds out the pick of his men, and sets the two of the Army to show them drill, and at the end of two weeks the men can manoeuvre about as well as Volunteers. So he marches with the Chief to a great big plain on the top of a mountain, and the Chief's men rushes into a village and takes it, we three Martinis firing into the brown of the enemy. So we took that village too, and I gives the Chief a rag from my coat and says, "Occupy till I come"; which was scriptural. By way of a reminder, when me and the Army was eighteen hundred yards away, I drops a bullet near him standing on the snow, and all the people falls flat on their faces. Then I sends a letter to Dravot wherever he be by land or by sea.'

At the risk of throwing the creature out of train I interrupted—'How could you write a letter up yonder?'

'The letter?—Oh!—The letter! Keep looking at me between the eyes, please. It was a string-talk letter, that we'd learned the way of it from a blind beggar in the Punjab.'

I remember that there had once come to the office a blind man with a knotted twig and a piece of string which he wound round the twig according to some cipher of his own. He could, after the lapse of days or hours, repeat the sentence which he had reeled up. He had reduced the alphabet to eleven primitive sounds, and tried to teach me the method, but I could not understand.

'I sent that letter to Dravot,' said Carnehan; 'and told him to come back because this Kingdom was growing too big for me to handle, and then I struck for the first valley, to see how the priests were working. They called the village we took along with the Chief, Bashkai, and the first village we took, Er-Heb. The priests at Er-Heb was doing all right, but they had a lot of pending cases about land to show me, and some men from another village had been firing arrows at night. I went out and looked for that village, and fired four rounds at it from a thousand yards. That used all the cartridges I cared to spend, and I waited for Dravot, who had been away two or three months, and I kept my people quiet.

'One morning I heard the devil's own noise of drums and horns, and Dan Dravot marches down the hill with his Army and a tail of hundreds of men, and, which was the most amazing, a great gold crown on his head. "My Gord, Carnehan," says Daniel, "this is a tremenjus business, and we've got the whole country as far as it's worth having. I am the son of Alexander by Queen Semiramis, and you're my younger brother and a God too! It's the biggest thing we've ever seen. I've been marching and fighting for six weeks with the Army, and every footy little village for fifty miles has come in rejoiceful; and more than that, I've got the key of the whole show, as you'll see, and I've got a crown for you! I told 'em to make two of 'em at a place called Shu, where the gold lies in the rock like suet in mutton. Gold I've seen, and turquoise I've kicked out of the cliffs, and there's garnets in the sands of the river, and here's a chunk of amber that a man brought me. Call up all he priests and, here, take your crown."

'One of the men opens a black hair bag, and I slips the crown on. It was too small and too heavy, but I wore it for the glory. Hammered gold it was—five pound weight, like a hoop of a barrel.

'"Peachey," says Dravot, "we don't want to fight no more. The Craft's the trick, so help me!" and he brings forward that same Chief that I left at Bashkai—Billy Fish we called him afterwards, because he was so like Billy Fish that drove the big tank-engine at Mach on the Bolan in the old days. "Shake hands with him," says Dravot, and I shook hands and nearly dropped, for Billy Fish gave me the Grip. I said nothing, but tried him with the Fellow Craft Grip. He answers all right, and I tried the Master's Grip, but that was a slip. "A Fellow Craft he is!" I says to Dan, "Does he know the word?—"He does," says Dan, "and all the priests know. It's a miracle! The Chiefs and the priests can work a Fellow Craft Lodge in a way that's very like ours, and they've cut the marks on the rocks, but they don't know the Third Degree, and they've come to find out. It's Gord's Truth. I've known these long years that the Afghans knew up to the Fellow Craft Degree, but this is a miracle. A God and a Grand-Master of the Craft am I, and a Lodge in the Third Degree I will open, and we'll raise the head priests and the Chiefs of the Village."

'"It's against all the law," says I, "holding a Lodge without warrant from any one; and you know we never held office in any Lodge."

'"It's a master-stroke o' policy," says Dravot. "It means running the country as easy as a four-wheeled bogie on a down grade. We can't stop to inquire now, or they'll turn against us. I've forty Chiefs at my heel, and passed and raised according to their merit they shall be. Billet these men on the villages, and see that we run up a Lodge of some kind. The temple of Imbra will do for the Lodge-room. The women must make aprons as you show them. I'll hold a levee of Chiefs tonight and Lodge tomorrow."

'I was fair run off my legs, but I wasn't such a fool as not to see what a pull this Craft business gave us. I showed the priests' families how to make aprons of the degrees, but for Dravot's apron the blue border and marks was made of turquoise lumps on white hide, not cloth. We took a great square stone in the temple for the Master's chair, and little stones for the officers' chairs, and painted the black pavement with white squares, and did what we could to make things regular.

'At the levee which was held that night on the hillside with big bonfires, Dravot gives out that him and me were Gods and sons of Alexander, and Past Grand-Masters in the Craft, and was come to make Kafiristan a country where every man should eat in peace and drink in quiet, and especially obey us. Then the Chiefs come round to shake hands, and they were so hairy and white and fair it was just shaking hands with old friends. We gave them names according as they was like men we had known in India—Billy Fish, Holly Dilworth, Pikky Kergan, that was Bazar-master when I was at Mhow, and so on, and so on.

'The most amazing miracles was at Lodge next night. One of the old priests was watching us continuous, and I felt uneasy, for I knew we'd have to fudge the Ritual, and I didn't know what the man knew. The old priest was a stranger come in from beyond the village of Bashkai. The minute Dravot puts on that Master's apron that the girls had made for him, the priest fetches a whoop and a howl, and tries to overturn the stone that Dravot was sitting on. "It's all up now," I says. "That comes of meddling with the Craft without warrant!" Dravot never winked an eye, not when ten priests took and tilted over the Grand-Master's chair—which was to say the stone of Imbra. The priests begins rubbing the bottom end of it to clear away the black dirt, and presently he shows all the other priests the Master's Mark, same as was on Dravot's apron, cut into the stone. Not even the priests of the temple of Imbra knew it was there. The old chap falls flat on his face at Dravot's feet and kisses 'em. "Luck again," says Dravot, across the Lodge to me; "they say it's the Missing Mark that no one could understand the why of. We're more than safe now." Then he bangs the butt of his gun for a gavel and says: "By virtue of the authority vested in me by my own right hand and the help of Peachey, I declare myself Grand-Master of all Freemasonry in Kafiristan in this the Mother Lodge o' the country, and King of Kafiristan equally with Peachey!" At that he puts on his crown and I puts on mine—I was doing Senior Warden—and we opens the Lodge in most ample form. It was an amazing miracle! The priests moved in Lodge through the first two degrees almost without telling, as if the memory was coming back to them. After that, Peachey and Dravot raised such as was worthy—high priests and Chiefs of far-off villages. Billy Fish was the first, and I can tell you we scared the soul out of him. It was not in any way according to Ritual, but it served our turn. We didn't raise more than ten of the biggest men, because we didn't want to make the Degree common. And they was clamouring to be raised.

'"In another six months," says Dravot, "we'll hold another Communication, and see how you are working." Then he asks them about their villages, and learns that they was fighting one against the other, and were sick and tired of it. And when they weren't doing that they was fighting with the Mohammedans. "You can fight those when they come into our country," says Dravot. "Tell off every tenth man of your tribes for a Frontier guard, and send two hundred at a time to this valley to be drilled. Nobody is going to be shot or speared any more so long as he does well, and I know that you won't cheat me, because you're white people—sons of Alexander—and not like common, black Mohammedans. You are my people, and by God," says he, running off into English at the end—"I'll make a damned fine Nation of you, or I'll die in the making!"

'I can't tell all we did for the next six months, because Dravot did a lot I couldn't see the hang of, and he learned their lingo in a way I never could. My work was to help the people plough, and now and again go out with some of the Army and see what the other villages were doing, and make 'em throw rope-bridges across the ravines which cut up the country horrid. Dravot was very kind to me, but when he walked up and down in the pine wood pulling that bloody red beard of his with both fists I knew he was thinking plans I would not advise about, and I just waited for orders.

'But Dravot never showed me disrespect before the people. They were afraid of me and the Army, but they loved Dan. He was the best of friends with the priests and the Chiefs; but anyone could come across the hills with a complaint, and Dravot would hear him out fair, and call four priests together and say what was to be done. He used to call in Billy Fish from Bashkai, and Pikky Kergan from Shu, and an old Chief we called Kafuzelum—it was like enough to his real name—and hold councils with 'em when there was any fighting to be done in small villages. That was his Council of War, and the four preists of Bashkai, Shu, Khawak, and Madora was his Privy Council. Between the lot of 'em they sent me, with forty men and twenty rifles and sixty men carrying turquoises, into the Ghorband country to buy those hand-made Martini rifles, that come out of the Amir's workshops at Kabul, from one of the Amir's Herati regiments that would have sold the very teeth out of their mouths for turquoises.

'I stayed in Ghorband a month, and gave the Governor there the pick of my baskets for hush-money, and bribed the Colonel of the regiment some more, and, between the two and the tribespeople, we got more than a hundred hand-made Martinis, a hundred good Kohat Jezails that'll throw to six hundred yards, and forty man-loads of very bad ammunition for the rifles. I came back with what I had, and distributed 'em among the men that the Chiefs sent in to me to drill. Dravot was too busy to attend to those things, but the old Army that we first made helped me, and we turned out five hundred men that could drill, and two hundred that knew how to hold arms pretty straight. Even those corkscrewed, hand-made guns was a miracle to them. Dravot talked big about powder-shops and factories, walking up and down in the pine wood when the winter was coming on.

"'I won't make a Nation," says he. "I'll make an Empire! These men aren't niggers; they're English! Look at their eyes—look at their mouths.

Look at the way they stand up. They sit on chairs in their own houses. They're the Lost Tribes, or something like it, and they've grown to be English. I'll take a census in the spring if the priests don't get frightened. There must be a fair two million of 'em in these hills. The villages are full o' little children. Two million people—two hundred and fifty thousand fighting men—and all English! They only want the rifles and a little drilling. Two hundred and fifty thousand men, ready to cut in on Russia's right flank when she tries for India! Peachey, man," he says, chewing his bard in great hunks, "we shall be Emperors—Emperors of the Earth! Rajah Brooke will be a suckling to us. I'll treat with the Viceroy on equal terms. I'll ask him to send me twelve picked English—to help us govern a bit. There's Mackray, Sergeant-pensioner at Segowli—many's the good dinner he's given me, and his wife a pair of trousers. There's Donkin, the Warder of Tounghoo Jail; there's hundreds that I could lay my hands on if I was in India. The Viceroy shall do it for me. I'll send a man through in the spring for those men, and I'll write for a dispensation from the Grand Lodge for what I've done as Grand-Master. That—and all the Sniders that'll be thrown out when the native troops in India take up the Martini. They'll be worn smooth, but they'll do for fighting in these hills. Twelve English, a hundred thousand Sniders run through the Amir's country in driblets—I'd be content with twenty thousand in one year—and we'd be an Empire. When everything was shipshape I'd hand over the crown—this crown that I'm wearing now—to Queen Victoria on my knees, and she'd say: 'Rise up, Sir Daniel Dravot.' Oh, it's big! It's big, I tell you! But there's so much to be done in every place—Bashkai, Khawak, Shu, and everywhere else."

"'What is it?" I says. "There are no more men coming in to be drilled this autumn. Look at those fat, black clouds. They're bringing the snow."

"'It isn't that," says Daniel, putting his hand very hard on my shoulder; "and I don't wish to say anything that's against you, for no other living man would have followed me and made me what I am as you have done. You're a first-class Commander-in-Chief, and the people know you, but—it's a big country, and somehow you can't help me, Peachey, in the way I want to be helped."

"'Go to your blasted priests, then!" I said, and I was sorry when I made that remark, but it did hurt me sore to find Daniel talking so superior when I'd drilled all the men, and done all he told me.

"'Don't let's quarrel, Peachey," says Daniel without cursing. "You're a King too, and the half of this Kingdom is yours; but can't you see,

Peachey, we want cleverer men than us now—three or four of 'em, that we can scatter about for our Deputies. It's a hugeous great State, and I can't always tell the right thing to do, and I haven't time for all I want to do, and here's the winter coming on and all." He put half his beard into his mouth, all red like the gold of his crown.

"'I'm sorry, Daniel," says I. "I've done all I could. I've drilled the men and shown the people how to stack their oats better; and I've brought in those tinware rifles from Ghorband—but I know what you're driving at. I take it Kings always feel oppressed that way."

"'There's another thing too," says Dravot, walking up and down. "The winter's coming and these people won't be giving much trouble, and if they do we can't move about. I want a wife."

"'For God's sake leave the women alone!" I says. "We've both got all the work we can, though I am a fool. Remember the Contrack, and keep clear o' women."

"'The Contrack only lasted till such time as we was Kings; and Kings we have been these months past," says Dravot, weighting his crown in his hand. "You go get a wife too, Peachey—a nice, strappin', plump girl that'll keep you warm in the winter. They're prettier than English girls, and we can take the pick of 'em. Boil 'em once or twice in hot water and they'll come out like chicken and ham."

"'Don't tempt me!" I says. "I will not have any dealings with a woman not till we are a dam' side more settled than we are now. I've been doing the work o' two men, and you've been doing the work o' three. Let's lie off a bit, and see if we can get some better tobacco from Afghan country and run in some good liquor; but no women."

'"Who's talking o' women?" says Dravot. "I said wife—a Queen to breed a King's son for the King. A Queen out of the strongest tribe, that'll make them your blood-brothers, and that'll lie by your side and tell you all the people thinks about you and their own affairs. That's what I mean."

'"Do you remember that Bengali woman I kept at Mogul Serai when I was a plate-layer?" says I. "A fat lot o' good she was to me. She taught me the lingo and one or two other things; but what happened? She ran away with the Station-master's servant and half my month's pay. Then she turned up at Dadur Junction in tow of a half-caste, and had the impidence to say I was her husband—all among the drivers in the running-shed too!"

'"We've done with that," says Dravot; "these women are whiter than you or me, and a Queen I will have for the winter months."

'"For the last time o' asking, Dan, do not," I says. "It'll only bring us harm. The Bible says that Kings ain't to waste their strength on women, 'specially when they've got a new raw Kingdom to work over."

'"For the last time of answering I will," said Dravot, and he went away through the pinetrees looking like a big red devil, the sun being on his crown and beard and all.

'But getting a wife was not as easy as Dan thought. He put it before the Council, and there was no answer till Billy Fish said that he'd better ask the girls. Dravot damned them all around. "What's wrong with me?" he shouts, standing by the idol Imbra. "Am I a dog or am I not enough of a man for your wenches? Haven't I put the shadow of my hand over this country? Who stopped the last Afghan raid?" It was me really, but Dravot was too angry to remember. "Who bought your guns? Who repaired the bridges? Who's the Grand-Master of the sign cut in the stone?" says he, and he thumped his hand on the block that he used to sit on in Lodge, and at Council, which opened like Lodge always. Billy Fish said nothing and no more did the others. "Keep your hair on, Dan," said I; "and ask the girls. That's how it's done at Home, and these people are quite English."

'"The marriage of the King is a matter of State," says Dan, in a white-hot rage, for he could feel, I hope, that he was going against his better mind. He walked out of the Council-room, and the others sat still, looking at the ground.

'"Billy Fish," says I to the Chief of Bashkai, "what's the difficulty here? A straight answer to a true friend."

'"You know," says Billy Fish. "How should a man tell you who knows everything? How can daughters of men marry Gods or Devils? It's not proper."

'I remembered something like that in the Bible; but if, after seeing us as long as they had, they still believed we were Gods, it wasn't for me to undeceive them.

'"A God can do anything," says I. "If the King is fond of a girl he'll not let her die."—"She'll have to," said Billy Fish. "There are all sorts of Gods and Devils in these mountains, and now and again a girl marries one of them and isn't seen any more. Besides, you two know the Mark cut in the stone. Only the Gods know that. We thought you were men till you showed the sign of the Master."

'I wished then that we had explained about the loss of the genuine secrets of a Master-Mason at the first go-off; but I said nothing. All that night there was a blowing of horns in a little dark temple half-way down the hill, and I heard a girl crying fit to die. One of the priests told us that she was being prepared to marry the King.

'"I'll have no nonsense of that kind," says Dan. "I don't want to interfere with your customs, but I'll take my own wife."—"The girl's a bit afraid," says the priest. "She thinks she's going to die, and they are a-heartening of her up down in the temple."

'"Hearten her very tender, then," says Dravot, "or I'll hearten you with the butt of a gun so you'll never want to be heartened again." He licked his lips, did Dan, and stayed up walking about more than half the night, thinking of the wife that he was going to get in the morning. I wasn't any means comfortable, for I knew that dealings with a woman in foreign parts, though you was a crowned King twenty times over, could not but be risky. I got up very early in the morning while Dravot was asleep, and I saw the priests talking together in whispers, and the Chiefs talking together too, and they looked at me out of the corners of their eyes.

'"What is up, Fish?" I say to the Bashkai man, who was wrapped up in his furs and looking splendid to behold.

'"I can't rightly say," says he, "but if you can make the King drop all this nonsense about marriage, you'll be doing him and me and yourself a great service."

'"That I do believe," says I. "But sure, you know, Billy, as well as me, having fought against and for us, that the King and me are nothing more than two of the finest men that God Almighty ever made. Nothing more, I do assure you."

'"That may be," says Billy Fish, "and yet I should be sorry if it was." He sinks his head upon his great fur cloak for a minute and thinks. "King," says he, "be you man or God or Devil, I'll stick by you today. I have twenty of my men with me, and they will follow me. We'll go to Bashkai until the storm blows over."

'A little snow had fallen in the night, and everything was white except the greasy fat clouds that blew down and down from the north. Dravot came out with his crown on his head, swinging his arms and stamping his feet, and looking more pleased than Punch.

'"For the last time, drop it, Dan," says I in a whisper, "Billy Fish here says that there will be a row."

'"A row amongst my people!" says Dravot. "Not much, Peachey, you're a fool not to get a wife too. Where's the girl?" says he with a voice as loud as the braying of a jackass. "Call up all the Chiefs and priests, and let the Emperor see if his wife suits him."

'There was no need to call anyone. They were all there leaning on their guns and spears round the clearing in the centre of the pine wood. A lot of priests went down to the little temple to bring up the girl, and the horns blew fit to wake the dead. Billy Fish saunters round and gets as close to Daniel as he could, and behind him stood his twenty men with matchlocks. Not a man of them under six feet. I was next to Dravot, and behind me was twenty men of the regular Army. Up comes the girl, and a strapping wench she was, covered with silver and turquoises, but white as death, and looking back every minute at the priests.

'"She'll do," said Dan, looking her over. "What's to be afraid of, lass? Come and kiss me." He puts his arm round her. She shuts her eyes, gives a bit of a squeak, and down goes her face in the side of Dan's flaming red beard.

'"The slut's bitten me!" says he, clapping his hand to his neck, and, sure enough, his hand was red with blood. Billy Fish and two of his matchlock-men catches hold of Dan by the shoulders and drags him into the Bashkai lot, while the priests howls in their lingo—"Neither God nor Devil but a man!" I was all taken aback, for a priest cut at me in front, and the Army behind began firing into the Bashkai men.

'"God A'mighty!" says Dan. "What is the meaning o' this?"

'"Come back! Come away!" says Billy Fish. "Ruin and Mutiny is the matter. We'll break for Bashkai if we can."

'I tried to give some sort of orders to my men—the men of the Regular Army—but it was no use, so I fired into the brown of 'em with an English Martini and drilled three beggars in a line. The valley was full of shouting, howling creatures, and every soul was shrieking, "Not a God or a Devil but only a man!" The Bashkai troops stuck to Billy Fish for all they were worth, but their matchlocks wasn't half as good as the Kabul breechloaders, and four of them dropped. Dan was bellowing like a bull, for he was very wrathy; and Billy Fish had a hard job to prevent him running out at the crowd.

'"We can't stand," says Billy Fish. "Make a run for it down the valley! The whole place is against us." The matchlock-men ran, and we went down the valley in spite of Dravot. He was swearing horribly and crying out he was King. The priests rolled great stones on us, and the regular

Army fired hard, and there wasn't more than six men, not counting Dan, Billy Fish, and Me, that came down to the bottom of the valley alive.

'Then they stopped firing and the horns in the temple blew again. "Come away—for God's sake come away!" says Billy Fish. "They'll send runners out to all the villages before ever we get to Bashkai. I can protect you there, but I can't do anything now."

'My own notion is that Dan began to go mad in his head from that hour. He stared up and down like a stuck pig. Then he was all for walking back alone and killing the priests with his bare hands; which he could have done. "An Emperor am I," says Daniel, "and next year I shall be a Knight of the Queen."

'"All right, Dan," says I, "but come along now while there's time."

'"It's your fault," says he, "for not looking after your Army better. There was mutiny in the midst, and you didn't know—you damned engine-driving, plate-laying, missionary's-pass-hunting hound!" He sat upon a rock and called me every foul name he could lay tongue to. I was too heart-sick to care, though it was all his foolishness that brought the smash.

'"I'm sorry, Dan," says I, "but there's no accounting for natives. This business is our Fifty-Seven. Maybe we'll make something out of it yet, when we've got to Bashkai."

'"Let's get to Bashkai, then," says Dan, "and, by God, when I come back here again I'll sweep the valley so there isn't a bug in a blanket left!"

'We walked all that day, and all that night Dan was stumping up and down on the snow, chewing his beard and muttering to himself.

'"There's no hope o' getting clear," said Billy Fish. "The priests will have sent runners to the villages to say that you are only men. Why didn't you stick on as Gods till things was more settled? I'm a dead man," says Billy Fish, and he throws himself down on the snow and begins to pray to his Gods.

'Next morning we was in a cruel bad country—all up and down, no level ground at all, and no food either. The six Bashkai men looked at Billy Fish hungry-way as if they wanted to ask something, but they said never a word. At noon we came to the top of a flat mountain all covered with snow, and when we climbed up into it, behold, there was an Army in position waiting in the middle!

'"The runners have been very quick," says Billy Fish, with a little bit of a laugh. "They are waiting for us."

'Three or four men began to fire from the enemy's side, and a chance shot took Daniel in the calf of the leg. That brought him to his senses. He looks across the snow at the Army, and sees the rifles that we had brought into the country.

'"We're done for," says he. "They are Englishmen, these people—and it's by blasted nonsense that has brought you to this. Get back, Billy Fish, and take your men away; you've done what you could, and now cut for it. Carnehan," says he, "shake hands with me and go along with Billy. Maybe they won't kill you. I'll go and meet 'em alone. It's me that did it. Me, the King!"

'"Go!" says I. "Go to Hell, Dan! I'm with you here. Billy Fish, you clear out, and we two will meet these folk."

'"I'm a Chief," says Billy Fish, quite quiet. "I stay with you. My men can go."

'The Bashkai fellows didn't wait for a second word, but ran off, and Dan and Me and Billy Fish walked across to where the drums were drumming and the horns were horning. It was cold—awful cold. I've got that cold in the back of my head now. There's a lump of it there.'

The punkah-coolies had gone to sleep. Two kerosene lamps were blazing in the office, and the perspiration poured down my face and splashed on the blotter as I leaned forward. Carnehan was shivering, and I feared that his mind might go. I wiped my face, took a fresh grip of the piteously mangled hands, and said: 'What happened after that?'

The momentary shift of my eyes had broken the clear current.

'What was you pleased to say?' whined Carnehan. 'They took them without any sound. Not a little whisper all along the snow, not though the King knocked down the first man that set hand on him—not though old Peachey fired his last cartridge into the brown of 'em. Not a single solitary sound did those swines make. They just closed up tight, and I tell you their furs stunk. There was a man called Billy Fish, a good friend of us all, and they cut his throat, Sir, then and there, like a pig; and the King kicks up the bloody snow and says: "We've had a dashed fine run for our money. What's coming next?" But Peachey, Peachey Taliaferro, I tell you, Sir, in confidence as betwixt two friends, he lost his head, Sir. No, he didn't neither. The King lost his head, so he did, all along o' one of those cunning rope-bridges. Kindly let me have the paper-cutter, Sir. It tilted this way.

'They marched him a mile across that snow to a rope-bridge over a ravine with a river at the bottom. You may have seen such. They prodded him behind like an ox. "Damn your eyes!" says the King. "D'you suppose I can't die like a gentleman?" He turns to Peachey—Peachey that was crying like a child. "I've brought you to this, Peachey," says he. "Brought you out of your happy life to be killed in Kafiristan, where you was late Commander-in-Chief of the Emperor's forces. Say you forgive me, Peachey."—"I do," says Peachey. "Fully and freely do I forgive you, Dan."—"Shake hands, Peachey," says he. "I'm going now." Out he goes, looking neither right nor left, and when he was plumb in the middle of those dizzy looking ropes—"Cut, you beggars," he shouts; and they cut, and old Dan fell, turning round and round and round, twenty thousand miles, for he took half an hour to fall till he struck the water, and I could see his body caught on a rock with the gold crown close beside.

'But do you know what they did to Peachey between two pine-trees? They crucified him, Sir, as Peachey's hand will show. They used wooden pegs for his hands and his feet; and he didn't die. He hung there and screamed, and they took him down next day, and said it was a miracle that he wasn't dead. They took him down—poor old Peachey that hadn't done them any harm—that hadn't done them any—'

He rocked to and fro and wept bitterly, wiping his eyes with the back of his scarred hands and moaning like a child for some ten minutes.

'They was cruel enough to feed him up in the temple, because they said he was more of a God than old Daniel that was a man. Then they turned him out on the snow, and told him to go home, and Peachey came home in about a year, begging along the roads quite safe; for Daniel Dravot he walked before and said, "Come along, Peachey. It's a big thing we're doing." The mountains they danced at night, and the mountains they tried to fall on Peachey's head, but Dan he held up his hand, and Peachey came along bent double. He never let go of Dan's hand, and he never let go of Dan's head. They gave it to him as a present in the temple, to remind him not to come again, and though the crown was pure gold, and Peachey was starving, never would Peachey sell the same. You knew Dravot, Sir! You knew Right Worshipful Brother Dravot! Look at him now!'

He fumbled in the mass of rags round his bent waist; brought out a black horsehair bag embroidered with silver thread, and shook therefrom on to my table—the dried withered head of Daniel Dravot! The morning sun that had long been paling the lamps struck the red beard and blind sunken eyes; struck, too, a heavy circlet of gold studded with raw turquoises, that Carnehan placed tenderly on the battered temples.

'You be'old now,' said Carnehan, 'the Emperor in his 'abit as he lived—the King of Kafiristan with his crown upon his head. Poor old Daniel that was a monarch once!'

I shuddered, for, in spite of defacements manifold, I recognized the head of the man of Marwar Junction. Carnehan rose to go. I attempted to stop him. He was not fit to walk abroad. 'Let me take away the whisky, and give me a little money,' he gasped. 'I was a King once. I'll go to the Deputy Commissioner and ask to be set in the Poorhouse till I get my health. No, thank you, I can't wait till you get a carriage for me. I've urgent private affairs—in the south—at Marwar.'

He shambled out of the office and departed in the direction of the Deputy Commissioner's house. That day at noon I had occasion to go down the blinding hot Mall, and I saw a crooked man crawling along the white dust of the roadside, his hat in his hand, quavering dolorously after the fashion of street-singers at Home. There was not a soul in sight, and he was out of all possible earshot of houses. And he sang through his nose, turning his head from right to left:

'The Son of Man goes forth to war,
A golden crown to gain;
His blood-red banner streams afar—
Who follows in his train?'

I waited to hear no more, but put the poor wretch into my carriage and drove him off to the nearest missionary for eventual transfer to the Asylum. He repeated the hymn twice while he was with me whom he did not in the least recognize, and I left him singing it to the missionary.

Two days later I inquired after his welfare of the Superintendent of the Asylum.

'He was admitted suffering from sunstroke. He died early yesterday morning,' said the Superintendent. 'Is it true that he was half an hour bare-headed in the sun at mid-day?'

'Yes,' said I, 'but do you happen to know if he had anything upon him by any chance when he died?'

'Not to my knowledge,' said the Superintendent.

And there the matter rests.

The End

3.

"Suckers have no business with money anyway."

CANADA BILL JONES, THREE CARD MONTE DEALER

"There's a sucker born every minute."

P. T. BARNUM

A Word about Confidence Men

by David Maurer

THE *GRIT* HAS a gentle touch. It takes its toll from the verdant sucker by means of the skilled hand or the sharp wit. In this, it differs from all other forms of crime, and especially from the *heavy-rackets*. It never employs violence to separate the mark from his money. Of all the *grifters*, the confidence man is the aristocrat.

Although the confidence man is sometimes classed with professional thieves, pickpockets, and gamblers, he is really not a thief at all because he does no actual stealing. The trusting victim literally thrusts a fat bank roll into his hands. It is a point of pride with him that he does not have to steal.

Confidence men are not "crooks" in the ordinary sense of the word. They are suave, slick, and capable. Their depredations are very much on the genteel side. Because of their high intelligence, their solid organization, the widespread connivance of the law, and the fact that the victim must virtually admit criminal intentions himself if he wishes to prosecute, society has been neither willing nor able to avenge itself effectively. Relatively few good con men are ever brought to trial; of those who are tried, few are convicted; of those who are convicted, even fewer ever serve out their full sentences. Many successful operators have never a day in prison to pay for their merry and lucrative lives spent in fleecing willing marks on the big-con games.

A confidence man prospers only because of the fundamental dishonesty of his victim. First, he inspires a firm belief in his own integrity. Second, he brings into play powerful and well-nigh irresistible forces to excite the cupidity of the mark. Then he allows the victim to make large sums of money by means of dealings which are explained to him as being dishonest—and hence a "sure thing." As the lust for large and easy profits is fanned into a hot flame, the mark puts all his scruples behind him. He closes out his bank account, liquidates his property, borrows from his friends, embezzles from his employer or his clients. In the mad frenzy of cheating someone else, he is unaware of the fact that he is the real victim, carefully selected and fatted for the kill. Thus arises the trite but none the less sage maxim: "You can't cheat an honest man."

This fine old principle rules all confidence games, big and little, from a simple three-card monte or shell game in a shady corner of a country fair grounds to the intricate *pay-off* or *rag*, played against a *big store* replete with expensive props and manned by suave experts. The three-card-monte grifter takes a few dollars from a willing farmer here and there; the big-con men take thousands or hundreds of thousands from those who have it. But the principle is always the same.

This accounts for the fact that it has been found very difficult to prosecute confidence men successfully. At the same time it explains why so little of the true nature of confidence games is known to the public, for once a victim is fleeced he often proves to be a most reluctant and untruthful witness against the men who have taken his money. By the same token, confidence men are hardly criminals in the usual sense of the word, for they prosper through a superb knowledge of human nature; they are set apart from those who employ the machine-gun, the blackjack, or the acetylene torch. Their methods differ more in degree than in kind from those employed by more legitimate forms of business.

Modern con men use at present only three *big-con* games, and only two of these are now used extensively. In addition, there are scores of *short-con* games which seem to enjoy periodic bursts of activity, followed by alternate periods of obsolescence. Some of these short-con games, when played by big-time professionals who apply the principles of the big con to them, attain very respectable status as devices to separate the mark from his money.

The three big-con games, the *wire*, the *rug*, and the *pay-off*, have in some forty years of their existence taken a staggering toll from a gullible public. No one knows just how much the total is because many touches, especially large ones, never come to light; both con men and police officials agree that roughly ninety per cent of the victims never complain to the police. Some professionals estimate that these three games alone have produced more illicit profit for the operators and for the law than *all other forms of professional crime* (excepting violations of the prohibition law) over the same period of time. However that may be, it is very certain that they have been immensely profitable.

All confidence games, big and little, have certain similar underlying principles; all of them progress through certain fundamental stages to an inevitable conclusion; while these stages or steps may vary widely in detail from type to type of game, the principles upon which they are based remain the same and are immediately recognizable. In the big-con games the steps are these:

1. Locating and investigating a well-to-do victim. (*Putting the mark up.*)
2. Gaining the victim's confidence. (*Playing the con for him.*)
3. Steering him to meet the insideman. (*Roping the mark.*)
4. Permitting the insideman to show him how he can make a large amount of money dishonestly. (*Telling him the tale.*)
5. Allowing the victim to make a substantial profit. (*Giving him the convincer.*)
6. Determining exactly how much he will invest. (*Giving him the breakdown.*)
7. Sending him home for this amount of money. (*Putting him on the send.*)
8. Playing him against a *big store* and fleecing him. (*Taking off the touch.*)
9. Getting him out of the way as quietly as possible. (*Blowing him off.*)
10. Forestalling action by the law. (*Putting in the fax.*)

The big-con games did not spring full-fledged into existence. The principles on which they operate are as old as civilization. But their immediate evolution is closely knit with the invention and development of the *big store*, a fake gambling club or broker's office, in which the victim is swindled. And within the twentieth century they have, from the criminal's point of view, reached a very high state of perfection.

from

Low Life

by Luc Sante

NEW YORK CITY represented a gamble for nearly everybody who arrived voluntarily. The odds varied somewhat: for immigrants from impoverished nations, for example, the stakes may have appeared high, but the outcome virtually had to be better than what they started with. For those coming to the city from other parts of the United States the odds were longer, because the decision involved parlaying a modest future against the big take of ambition, and chances were few. New York displayed the full range of possible outcomes, laying heaviest emphasis on big prizes and vast fortunes on the one hand and utter destitution on the other; as an advertisement for itself, it only shrank from publicizing the mediocre mid-range settlement. If life was a gamble, gambling was an essential part of life, and gambling permeated every masculine gathering in every station of the social and economic range. This was no more nor less true in a general way for New York than for any other part of America at the end of the nineteenth and the beginning of the twentieth century, a time when the main chance seemed open to all, and its capture a mysterious process that could be as much a matter of pure random luck as of the hard work so esteemed in retrospect by the winners. In New York, though, while fortunes might not be made and lost as precipitately as in the goldfields of California, fortune was a constant promise rather than a seasonal fever, and poverty was just as constant a threat. While gambling fads did not come around as frequently or as inventively as in New Orleans, there was a greater range of ways to lose one's shirt. While New York was not filled with innocent rubes for the sharper to prey upon, it was, however, filled with sophisticates who thought themselves impervious to flimflammery and who could thus throw away common sense in the name of hubris.

Gambling always existed in New York, but it took the nineteenth century to make it into a real business. Prior to that, it had been small change: euchre and whist in taverns, betting on cockfights and dogfights, and a ubiquitous feature of early America—the lottery. In the eighteenth century, this was an eminently respectable pursuit, its manifestations mostly local; many were the churches built on lottery proceeds (which in the following century would preach fervently against gambling and its ill-gotten gains). It is worth noting that the construction of both Harvard and Yale was assisted by lotteries, and that a scheme to help finance the Continental Congress in 1776 by means of a country-wide lottery was abandoned only because of the difficulty of selling tickets at that troubled time. Lotteries increased in number, size, and reach after the Revolution, but it was not until the end of the War of 1812 that crooks entered the business in substantial numbers.

Soon fraudulent lotteries were displacing the honest ones, and by 1819 the situation was such that New York State passed a measure requiring licenses, procurable for a fee of $250 a year. This proved less than effectual; two years later a provision was added to the State Constitution banning them altogether. There was, however, a loophole that permitted already extant lotteries to continue functioning, so that the state continued to possess legal lotteries until 1834. Another loophole kept the racket alive long after that; there was nothing illegal about running agencies for out-of-state lotteries, and the very crooked ones in some Southern and Western states thrived for decades afterward. Lotteries were ridiculously easy to establish, and even simpler to rig, so that they amounted to the proverbial license to mint money. For that matter, the lottery did not even have to exist; a rented office and a few printed signs and tickets would suffice. There was, after all, no shortage of customers. An 1826 handbill for the New York Consolidated Lottery, one of the post-1821 holdovers, features a cartoon of an upstate rustic who is shown saying: "How darnayshun tickled I am to see our Debbyties at Olbyna tryon to stop fokes from byen tikkets—they mite just as well hold a live eal by the tale, without having an old mitten on there hand with ashes out."

Policy, which is to say, a system of wagering on figures that most often represented combinations derived from the numbers of winning lottery tickets, existed in the eighteenth century as a form of side bet among sporting gentlemen, but not notably among the poor. Its name derived from an earlier denomination, "lottery insurance," that survived until the 1830s. Policy became so popular that in time it threatened to outdraw the lotteries themselves, which was no hardship, since they were often controlled by the same people. In 1818 it was said that a single New York City lottery office made a profit of $31,000 on policy alone in one three-day period. After the New York lotteries were finally suppressed, policy drew its figures from the New Jersey state drawing, until that, too, was banned in 1840. Then the action switched to the shady Southern lotteries, particularly the Kentucky Literature Lottery, the Kentucky State Lottery, and the Frankfort Lottery of Kentucky, taking the story up to well after the Civil War. In more recent times, policy (or numbers, as it has come to be called) has based its figures on the outcomes of horse races or stock-market totals. Bettors of policy in the nineteenth century were not confined to simple three- or four-number combinations, but could choose from a menu of complex combinations similar to horse-playing boxes and sets. Up to four numbers could be played, to appear either anywhere on the board or in fixed positions. These combinations bore names redolent of horse racing: Gig, Saddle, Horse; the Gig (three numbers anywhere) evolved into the standard numbers play, and even its magic figure—4-11-44—was handed down.

The fact that neither lotteries nor policy lent themselves to any kind of system play gave rise in the early nineteenth century to the use of dream books, and some are in print today with only minor alterations over almost two centuries. The standard dream book, then as now, is based on a classic model of dream interpretation from the tradition of soothsaying. It records a list of persons, objects, and situations that might occur in a dream—a Turk, a clock, a wedding, say—but in addition to assigning them a meaning it gives a number to be played, often followed by instructions as to whether the number should be played fixed or floating, and whether the wager should be heavy or light. Policy increased in popularity and influence with every passing decade in the nineteenth century. When the game was run by Reuben Parsons as banker and John Frink as manager, from 1840 to the 1860s, the pair controlled nearly 350 shops around Manhattan. After the Civil War, Zachariah Simmons became the boss, backed by the Tweed Ring. He ran about three-quarters of the six hundred or seven hundred operations in the city at that time and opened franchises as far west as Milwaukee and as far south as Richmond. Albert J. Adams, once a runner for Simmons, took the baton in the 1880s and ran things until 1901. He dispensed with drawings altogether, and paid out strictly on numbers that had been bet low, or not bet at all, and nevertheless saw the policy shops in the city increase to around eight hundred, with a million regular players. Reform and raids finally dampened matters, and policy began to decline around 1905, becoming defunct by 1915. Prohibition changed the city's temper once again, however, and the game was reborn in 1923, particularly in Harlem, as numbers.

On-site betting operations were for many years a feature of taverns, and their play was generally modest and did not necessarily occur on a regular basis. It was not until the late 1820s that properly constituted gambling houses began to appear in New York. The development was inevitable, as specialization and then consolidation followed a general pattern in commerce in the city at the time, when New York was becoming a full-fledged urban center. The example of Kit Burns's Sportsmen's Hall, or Rat Pit, mentioned earlier, is particularly illustrative, as it took the ancient brutal sports of alleys and farmyards and turned them into a steady proposition. The phenomenon really represented an adaptation to the new industrial era of pursuits that seem almost medieval. Even members of the merchant class did not consider it beneath them to bet on fights to the death between rats and dogs. Meanwhile, on the Bowery, men like Charley Mook, Slab Baker, Shell Burrell, and the b'hoy George Rice were opening rooms that were entirely devoted to table games, which at this time were most prominently represented by roulette, twenty-one, chuck-a-luck, and faro.

Faro, now nearly forgotten, was the gambling pursuit that seized and held the imagination of the country for more than a century. From dim origins in the middle ages, it spread gradually through Europe, first receiving wide notice in France during the *ancien régime*, probably getting its name at the same time: Pharao, or Pharaon, from the Egyptian images printed on the backs of the cards. Louis XIV banned the game in 1691, but the Duc d'Orleans revived it in 1715, and it was popularized a few years later by John Law, the legendary Scottish gambler and confidence man who lived in Paris in the eighteenth century. It made its way to North America by way of French settlers in New Orleans and Mobile around the end of the century, and in the decade after the Louisiana Purchase spread all over the United States.

It was set up on a table, behind which sat the dealer and his assistant. On the table itself was the layout, which consisted of a suit of thirteen cards, usually spades, pasted or painted on an enameled oilcloth. The cards on the layout were set out in two parallel rows, with the odd card—the seven—between and at the end of the rows to the right from the players' point of view. The row nearest the players consisted of the king, queen, jack, ten, nine, and eight; that nearest to the dealer had the ace, deuce, trey, four, five, and six. The dealer shuffled and cut and inserted the cards into a box with an open top, then he proceeded to draw them two at a time, first disposing of the top card, considered dead (as was the last card). Of each pair, the first card counted for the house, the second for the players, and they were put into two piles—the winners going on top of the dead card, unless, as happened later in unscrupulous houses, that counted for the house as well. In more decorous places, bettors waited for the draw of the dead card before placing their wagers on the remaining spaces. Each draw of the cards was called a turn, and there were twenty-five of these in a game. Bettors played single cards or combinations: king, queen, and jack made up the big figure; ace, deuce, and trey the little figure; six, seven, and eight were the pot; king, queen, ace, deuce made up the grand square; jack, three, four, ten the jack square; nine, eight, six, five the nine square. The bank paid four to one for a winner, unless two cards of the same denomination were drawn in a single turn, which was called a split and which would occur on average about three times in two games; then the house would split the bet with the players. While the dealer was drawing, his assistant would be manipulating a device called a case-keeper, a miniature of the layout in a box, which would establish what had already been drawn so that the house could keep track of what cards were left. On the last turn, additional bets were made on the order of extraction, and for many players this became the whole point of the game.

Up until the middle of the nineteenth century, faro was considered the fairest game of all time, with an advantage to the bank generally estimated at a mere one and a half to three percent. It was never permitted at Monte Carlo, possibly because of its relative unprofitability for the house if played honestly. Indeed, in a scrupulous game, the player could achieve a disadvantage only through his own efforts, and then by playing a "running limit" or "going paroli"—a term that evolved into the word "parlay"—that is to say, running up winnings, consolidating them, and then risking the whole sum on one turn, usually the last. Of course, the game never was played honestly, and the methods of rigging became more elaborate as the years went by. Dealing was the first element to be affected. In the early days the deck had been dealt from a face-down position in the dealer's left hand. In 1822 an anonymous American introduced the dealing box, made of brass, half an inch wider and a little longer than the deck, covered on top with a single thumbhole, used to push the cards out through a side slit, with a spring keeping the rest in line. The open-top model came in a few years later. Soon, however, the market was deluged with rigged boxes of all sorts, with devices that in some cases can be imagined from their names: the gaff, the tongue-tell, the sand-tell, the topsight-tell, the needle squeeze, the end squeeze, the horse box, the screw box, the lever movement, the coffee mill. All sorts of ingenious contraptions were fitted into these small instruments—springs, levers, sliding plates—to inform the dealer of the order in advance and to allow him to alter it invisibly and at will.

In addition to this, there were a variety of trimmed and marked cards and cards manufactured in such a way that any two could be made to stick together. What is remarkable is that these devices were all sold very openly, advertised in newspapers as "advantage tools," and in at least one case carried on the shelves of a specialized shop around the corner from the Bowery, so that any gambler not straight from the woods would know that the chances of his being swindled were overwhelming. (Other wares included loaded dice, crooked roulette wheels, cutters and trimmers for preparing cards, poker rings for marking cards during a game, hold-outs for concealing cards in vests, sleeves, and under the table at poker, and shiners, little mirrors that enabled the artful cheater to read the hands of his opponents.) But such is the faith of the gambler. Even with these tools, adept dealing at faro was a profession that demanded great skill, and paid accordingly. In mid-century the top practitioners, known as "mechanics" or "artists," might earn several hundred dollars a week, in addition to a cut of the profits.

Faro was popular across the country and with every class. One measure of its influence is the number of terms specific to it that have entered the language in a general way: "tabs" were sheets annotated by players to keep track of cards already dealt, hence "keeping tabs"; "losing out" meant to lose four times on the same card, and "winning out" was its opposite; "piking" was to place small bets all over the board, and a practitioner was known as a piker; to "break even" was to play a system; to "string along" was to play all odd cards or all evens; a "square deal" was one made not with round-cornered but with square-edged cards, which were harder to adulterate; a "sleeper" was a bet made on a dead card (which might be carried over to the next game); a "pigeon" was the victim of a leg—a sharper—and a "stool pigeon" was a shill; a "shoe string" involved parlaying a small bankroll into big winnings; the last card was said to be "in hock" because the first card was called "soda," after the expression "soda to hock" (hock was dry white wine). Faro generally was known as the "Tiger," from the image of a Bengal tiger, of obscure origin, that was used to indicate a house where a faro bank could be found, and to play the game was to "buck the Tiger." The tiger signs were sometimes used by players to communicate the relative honesty of the house by means of a sort of hobo alphabet that involved minute scratches in a prearranged pattern. A particularly unscrupulous house (they were all unscrupulous to some degree) was called a brace house; a very fixed game, a brace game.

Variations on faro popped up every now and again: short faro and rolling faro both enjoyed brief vogues. The legendary shyster lawyers Howe and Hummel, in their 1886 guidebook to New York vice, *In Danger*, mention something called skin faro, in which the mark was assigned the role of dealer and given a deck with a pinhole through it. The players, employees of the skin house at which the game was played, could then clean him out on the final turn; Howe and Hummel tactfully refrain from specifying how this was accomplished. The most successful variant was stuss, or Jewish faro, which completely dominated play east of the Bowery from the last decade of the nineteenth century up to World War I, although it failed to spread much outside the neighborhood. The major gangsters of the period, such as Monk Eastman, Johnny Spanish, and Kid Twist, all kept a sideline in stuss at some point. The game was a simplification of faro that literally stacked the deck in the bank's favor. After bets were made—and they could be made only on single cards—the deck was shuffled, cut, and turned over. The first card was the house's, and so were all splits. Even without the various palming, reading, and counting methods employed by dealers, the house advantage was considerably increased. All these games were moribund from around World War I; they did not fully disappear until after World War II.

The other popular game in the early Bowery hells was chuck-a-luck, also known as sweat or sweat-cloth. It was the only dice game played on the East Coast until craps came along in the early 1890s and rapidly dominated the scene. The early houses might also feature such games as loo, all-fours, seven-up, pitch, hearts, euchre, ecarté, cassino, rouge et noir, Boston, and whilst, some of them ancient, some soon to achieve respectability. Keno, which did not outlast the century except in a bowdlerized boardwalk version, was essentially the same as bingo, although cards were sold at rates that varied from a dime in the slums to a hundred dollars in the high-class joints; for the dealers it was as much of a fish-in-the-barrel as the ersatz lotteries. Monte, not to be confused with three-card monte, was played with a deck of forty or forty-four (the eights, nines, and sometimes the tens were removed). The top two and the bottom two cards of the deck were set in two layouts, top and bottom, and then players would bet on matching the face or suit of cards as they were drawn against the layout cards. Needless to say, it, too, was extremely easy to manipulate. Its heyday came in the wake of the Mexican War.

By the middle of the nineteenth century Manhattan was awash in gaming houses. The reformed gambler Jonathan H. Green, who had written exposés of the generalized cheating and rigging practices of the houses across the country and had become the general executive agent of the New York Association for the Suppression of Gambling, was commissioned by this body in 1850 to take a survey of local conditions. When he presented his findings at the Broadway Tabernacle early in 1851, he reported the existence of six thousand gambling houses in New York City, two hundred of them of the first class, and this not even counting lotteries, policy, or raffles. Although the figure sounds wildly exaggerated, it should be noted that it works out to the not unreasonable average of one house for every eighty-five inhabitants. At the time it was elsewhere estimated that 25,000 men, or one-twentieth of the city's population, depended on gambling for their livelihood.

The classes and degrees of houses were numerous. The first-class joints of the time were clustered on Park Row, Park Place, lower Broadway, and Liberty, Vesey, and Barclay Streets. Some of these were veritable mansions, where every amenity was observed. The truth was that they were skinning houses not fundamentally different from the lower orders, but to persuade the prosperous—often the newly prosperous—to separate themselves from their bankrolls, a stage set was required that would suggest that the proprietors did not need the cash, that they were sporting gentlemen who wagered for the sheer love of the pursuit. Thus, these places might feature huge mirrors in gilt frames, Old Master paintings (a much more loosely defined category at that time than now), rosewood furniture upholstered in satin and velvet, elaborate crystal chandeliers. They would serve lavish dinners to all parties as a perquisite, with costly viands laid out on silver and gold plate and esteemed vintages decanted in cut glass. Even clients who recognized the polite fiction involved might be moved to refrain from an overly close examination of the hands of the faro mechanic. Nestled among these arriviste houses were the day houses that catered to messengers and clerks, keeping regular business hours and experiencing their heaviest trade at lunchtime. Both sorts of establishments tended to be run by the same people: Jim Bartolf and Frank Stuart on Park Place, the b'hoy Handsome Sam Suydam and Harry Colton on Barclay, a certain Hillman on Liberty, Orlando Moore on Broadway. Jack Wallis, who was said to be Chinese, won his house, so legend had it, from French José and Jimmy Berry in a coin toss. For that matter, Pat Herne, established on Broadway, was so much of a gambler himself that he lost his house's take more than once, and eventually the house itself. Many houses of all grades were bankrolled by one man, the lottery king Reuben Parsons, who eventually became known as the Great American Faro Banker.

Ann and Barclay Streets at the time were a lurid gaming locus halfway between the Bowery and Wall Street, and bridging the two. Ann Street, crowned on its Broadway corner by Barnum's American Museum, was a mecca of lower-class hells, saloons, and hash houses popular with a milieu of b'hoys, firemen, thieves and footpads of all stripes, pickpockets, gangsters, and Tammany shoulder-hitters, as well as with brokerage house and express-office employees. Its particular feature were the wolf-traps, also known as snap houses, or ten percent houses, or deadfalls. These were rooms, possessing no amenities or centralized bank, that let out space to individual gamblers who got up their own games, in return for a ten percent cut. Such bazaars were totally unpredictable, since a dealer of relative honesty might set up cheek-by-jowl with the most rapacious skinner. The biggest wolf-trap of them all was the Tapi Franc, at 10

Ann, which boasted the only roulette wheel in such an establishment, as well as twenty-one, chuck-a-luck, and twenty-four-hour faro action. Here low-limit games—called snaps—set a minimum wager of $25, while the high-rolling games had bottoms of as much as $500 or $1,000. At the Tapi Franc the crowd was said to be even more lawless than the dealers; fights broke out regularly and pickpockets operated without restrictions. Only a handful of bouncers kept the peace, since cops, by common agreement assisted by graft, were nowhere to be seen. Not that the police ever did much to protect the average sucker: a story of 1849 had it that one time, when a mark complained to the authorities about his treatment in a skinning joint, these worthies told him that his motives for visiting the place were "less than honorable," and then jailed him as a material witness.

There were two main classes of professional gamblers in the mid-nineteenth century, distinguished not by income but by life-style. There were the fashionable dandies called blacklegs, who were described as pursuing an unvarying daily schedule: strolling on Broadway in the morning, driving on Fifth Avenue in the afternoon, attending the opera in the evening, and then cheating on Park Row until 5 a.m. The other class was proletarian in origin, and connected to the interlaced worlds of boxing and politics, both of which were, of course, forms of gambling themselves. Bets were made on boxing matches as on elections; politicians sponsored boxers and fixed their fights; boxers would move into either gambling or politics or both when they retired from the ring. The same names crop up again and again in chronicles of gambling, boxing, and politics of the time. In 1842, for example, Chris Lilly, who was both a member of Isaiah Rynders's clique and an employee of Jack Wallis's hell (odd for a Nativist to be working for a Chinese), was matched against one Tom McCoy in a bout at Hastings, N.Y. The fight lasted 119 rounds, over two hours and forty-three minutes, during which time McCoy was knocked down eighty-one times; the fight stopped only with McCoy's death. Lilly fled the country, but soon returned under Rynders's protection; thereafter, he went into politics, setting out for New Orleans in 1848 to spread repeat voting and other New York niceties among the local electorate.

The two unbeatable local champions were Tom Hyer and Yankee Sullivan. Both were identified with the Nativist cause (in spite of the fact that Sullivan, whose real name was James Ambrose, was Australian), and both were professional gamblers: Hyer as a roper (a tout) and shill at Frank Stuart's on Park Place, and Sullivan as proprietor of his own joint, the Sawdust House on Water Street. What was needed was a Tammany champion to uphold the honor of the Irish. That man, it turned out, was John Morrissey, known as Old Smoke, born in Ireland and brought up in Troy, N.Y. When Morrissey came to town, he worked as a freelance troublemaker, originally as a Tammany shoulder-hitter. He beat a Know-Nothing champion called Bill Poole (who subsequently was shot and killed by Morrissey associate Lew Baker) and led at least one raid on Rynders's Empire Club. Rynders was sufficiently impressed by Morrissey's prowess to offer him a job, but the vicissitudes of party political enforcement were limiting for a man of Morrissey's ambitions, and in 1851 he lit out for California. There he defeated a Western champion, George Thompson, familiarly known as Pete Crawley's Big Un, in a nineteen-minute bout, and afterward called himself Champion of America.

When he got back to New York, he found to his chagrin that this title cut no ice with the natives, so he set about becoming champion of the East. He wanted to fight Hyer, but the latter demanded a $10,000 cash bet as his condition, and Morrissey couldn't raise the sum. Instead, he settled for fighting Sullivan, and beat him in a fifty-three-round affair at Boston Four Corners, N.Y., in 1853. After that, Hyer lost his crown to Tom Heenan, known as the Benicia Boy, and then Morrissey finally claimed his title by beating Heenan—who went on to marry the storied Mazeppa, Adah Isaacs Menken—in a twenty-one-minute match at Long Point, Canada. It should be noted that in those days the fights—which were, incidentally, illegal—were fought under London Prize Ring rules: a round ended when a fighter fell, was knocked down, or was thrown; the match ended when a fighter was unable to come to scratch at the beginning of a round. The bare-knuckle fights were brutal and often lethal; one of the standard corner jobs at the time was that of bloodsucker.

After their respective defeats, Hyer seems to have faded into obscurity. Sullivan slunk off to San Francisco, where he got himself arrested by the Vigilantes and ultimately committed suicide. Morrissey, on the other hand, rose steadily in the world. He opened saloons on Broadway and on Leonard Street, and began acquiring gambling houses. Morrissey had accumulated sufficient respect and goodwill over the years that his houses were thought of as considerably more square than they actually were, a reputation that was perhaps boosted by the story of the night that

Benjamin Wood, brother of Mayor Fernando Wood, won $124,000 from Morrissey's house on Twenty-fourth Street. His other two houses, both of which had existed before he bought them and continued after he had sold them, were two of the longest-lived and most celebrated hells in the city's history. The one at 818 Broadway endured at least thirty years, and was famous for its imperviousness to raids. Under Morrissey's ownership, it was raided only twice, once in 1867 by an anti-gambling society, whose members were mollified with a bribe, and again in 1873 as a result of a political grudge, although this incident too, seems to have passed without much damage done. After Morrissey retired his interest in 1877, the house was raided with greater frequency, since later owners lacked his connections and charisma, but nothing was ever found of much consequence. This was thanks to an ingenious basement vault, not publicly revealed until the building was slated for demolition in the nineties, that permitted all the gambling apparatus and the bank to be hidden rapidly behind a false wall. Morrissey's other house, at 8 Barclay, was operated continuously as a gambling den from 1859 to 1902. The longevity of these places and their relatively untroubled existence attest to Morrissey's wits and political skills. All around, gambling houses rose and fell with alacrity. One of Morrissey's associates, a man named Bill Mike Murray, opened a large, "comprehensive" house on Eighth Street east of Broadway in the early 1870s, but a plague of raids forced him to shut it after a few years. Thereafter, he moved his operation to a smaller establishment on West Twenty-eighth, but that house was also visited by ill luck: one night a local character named Jim Murphy ran faro for a few hours and then shot himself right on the floor, effectively hexing the house and driving business away for good.

But Morrissey's continued prosperity was not to be attributed simply to luck. His energy and enterprise were formidable. His Tweed Ring connections got him elected to Congress in 1866 and reelected two years later. He then turned on Tweed and became a leader of the opposition group Young Democracy in 1870, and on that ticket was twice elected to the state senate. Meanwhile, he began to invest in the upstate resort, Saratoga, at that time a genteel and rather dull place. He began with a Club House in 1861, added the still-extant race track two years later, and then continued adding casinos and buying properties until he was in virtual control of the resort. At the height of his powers Morrissey's holdings were estimated at over a million dollars. Unfortunately, he met up with a sharper far slicker than himself, in the person of Commodore Cornelius Vanderbilt, who, for whatever reasons, counseled him to make investments of an imprudent sort, and Morrissey's estate began to dwindle. He lost $500,000 on Black Friday in 1869 alone. At the same time he spent lavishly, trying to establish himself and his wife in upstate high society, when he was perceived as a low-born gambler, and the more he spent, the more he was jeered. By the time he died of pneumonia in 1878, his fortune was down to $78,000.

The golden age of gambling in New York lasted from shortly after the Civil War until just after the turn of the century. During that time, there were untold hundreds of gambling houses of all sorts for all classes and for every specialty. A particular feature of the 1880s was the gambling resort catering, exclusively to women, offering them roulette, faro, and poker amid elegant furnishings. Such places were entirely bourgeois and were found in strictly respectable neighborhoods. The period also saw cheating and fakery achieve new heights. Three-card monte and its cousin, thimble rig, now better known as the shell game, blew in from the West and flourished; they are believed to be the only major gambling games actually invented in the United States. More elaborate schemes were developed as well; the era was the heyday of the confidence man.

The confidence game took many forms, but its underlying principle was always the same: to let the mark beat himself, using his cupidity as the motor of his doom. What was perhaps the ultimate refinement of this principle did not actually manifest itself until the beginning of the twentieth century, in the form of the game called Klondike, or Canfield: the john was sold a deck of cards for $52 which he would use to play solitaire; at the conclusion the house would pay $5 for every pip on the ace pile (in this version, kings counted as thirteen, queens as twelve, jacks as eleven). There was simply no way to so much as break even. The most famous of all sucker games, however, was the one that arrived in New York in the late 1860s: banco. This game had been known for some time in England, where it was called eight dice cloth, and it was first imported to San Francisco, where it was christened banco, or bunco; the term soon entered the language as a synonym for fraud, hence the usage "bunco squad" and H.L. Mencken's celebrated expletive, "buncombe." The game was played variously with eight dice or eight numbered cards; the layout for dice contained fourteen spaces, for cards forty-three, of which forty-two were numbered, thirteen of them additionally bearing stars, and one was blank. A throw of the dice or a draw of the cards would add up to a figure that corresponded to one of the spaces on the layout. On the card layout the unstarred numbers represented cash prizes from $2 to $5,000, while those with stars allowed the player to draw again for more money. The player would be allowed to win steadily up to a certain point and then he would be dealt a hand totaling twenty-seven, the number corresponding to a space on the board called a "conditional." This meant that, to proceed further, the player would have to put up in cash a sum equal to his total bank winnings thus far. If he did so—and he invariably did—the only way he could lose would be to hit one of the two spaces covered with metal caps, called "banco." The mark did so without fail. The pattern was unvarying: the doe was led to intoxicate himself with his own greed, winning a sum that the operators would calculate represented the limit of his ready capital, and then he would rapidly be led to unpocket himself.

The games were played in elaborate setups called banco skins; usually hotel rooms or rooms in financial-district buildings made up to look like bustling business offices. The marks were usually newcomers to the city, prosperous visiting farmers being the best targets. The skins employed a pair of touts to lure them: the feeler and the catcher. The feeler would hang around hotels, identifying wealthy rubes and tourists, and would research details of their hometowns, professions, family lives, hobbies. He would then pass this information along to the catcher, who would feign acquaintance or kinship with the mark, who could usually be induced to believe that he simply failed to recall his old army buddy or second cousin, and the camaraderie thus fired would lead to an evening on the town, complete with roistering and entertainments of varyingly risqué nature. As the hour grew late, the roper would propose one last bit of jollity, a visit to a friendly game gotten up by friends of his, and he would steer the pigeon to the banco skin. As the mark lost, the tout would be losing as well, and would accompany his loss with such a theatrical display of bad sportsmanship that the embarrassed target would temporarily be distracted from his own misfortune. The most famous catcher was Hungry Joe Lewis; his most famous catch was Oscar Wilde, on the latter's 1882 tour of the United States. Hungry Joe took the dramatist for $5,000, but was trusting enough to let him pay with a check. When Wilde figured out that he had been swindled, he simply stopped payment. Wilde refused to prosecute, however, so Hungry Joe was not finally stopped until 1888, when he was arrested for a $5,000 catch in Baltimore. Before that time, Hungry Joe was reckoned to be the greatest banco artist of them all, prodigiously successful and prolific in his swindles; his fatal flaw was that, according to Police Captain Thomas Byrnes, he was "a terrible talker," so unable to stop gabbing that he very nearly gave the operation away more than once. He ultimately wound up in the laundry business. The upper rank of the banco circuit also included Tom O'Brien and Charles P. Miller, both at various times called King of the Banco Men, and Peter Lake, aka Grand Central Pete, all of whom endured in their profession well into the 1890s. Amazingly enough, banco survives into the present day; the late 1980s saw a banco skin as elemental as any of those of the previous century setting up at various locations—hardware stores, multi-vendor bazaars—around SoHo, possibly in some of the very same buildings.

Even more elaborate than the banco setups were those skinning houses, to all outward respects ordinary gambling halls, that in the 1870s and eighties were established for the exclusive purpose of rooking one chump at a time. These would be located in the back rooms of saloons and pool halls, be rigged out with all the conventional trappings, and would employ dozens of steerers, shills, and supernumeraries. The standard premise was that employed in three-card monte: the shill won again and again as the sucker watched; the sucker would imagine that the dealer was slow-witted and vulnerable; then the sucker would play big and lose everything. The mise-en-scène was soon adapted for even more ambitious play: what came to be called the big con, the large-scale confidence game. An itinerant sharper named Ben Marks can be regarded as the father of this pursuit. A few years after the Civil War he set up a front called the Dollar Store in Cheyenne, Wyoming. The store featured display windows full of quality merchandise, all of it priced at one dollar. The johns brought in by this lure would be dissuaded from buying by a swift line of patter which would steer them instead to gambling, and then they would be fleeced in short order.

In the next few decades the principle of the Big Store was refined into its principal variations: the wire, rag, and pay-off stores. All these had several main points in common; they involved a fraudulent business location, usually a betting parlor for horse races, appropriately furnished and manned by shills, ropers, and stand-ins, and one well-heeled pigeon at a time would be brought in for the play. This involved stringing the mark along over a period of days, convincing him that he was getting in on the ground floor of an enterprise making quick money by defrauding others, getting him to pour substantial and increasing amounts of cash into the operation, with the idea that the more he put in, the more he could extract, and then, when all his liquid resources were exhausted, quickly lowering the boom and skipping town. These cons were as complex and as highly organized as any legitimate business, and they involved a network of connections oiled by graft that in a smaller city might take in the whole police department and most of the municipal administration. Although one might expect such games to flourish largely in the more pliable provincial towns, there were important stores in New York which were protected by the ever-corruptible cops and politicians. There as elsewhere the suckers were imported from the outside, and it was made certain that they were properly disoriented and vulnerable. Beginning around the turn of the century, major stores were set up by such characters as Christ Tracy, Larry the Lug, Limehouse Chappie, and 102nd Street George.

The dazzling variety of short con games in the late nineteenth century ranged from such acting exercises as the Spanish prisoner swindle (a grieving wife and children would be toured around, pleading for funds to release a prisoner of conscience from foreign confinement) to vaudeville routines like the pedigreed-dog swindle. This con would begin with a man entering a saloon, accompanied by a dog. Over a drink, he would explain to the bartender that the mutt was a prize winner, an extremely valuable specimen of some mythical breed. Then he would ask the bartender to watch the dog for half an hour while he attended to a crucial matter of business, possibly sweetening the deal by giving the bartender a small tip. While the dog owner was away, another man would come in, spot the dog, exclaim over it, and then ask the bartender if he was willing to sell. When the bartender refused, the man would pretend that the bartender was simply being canny, and he would offer greater and greater sums. Finally, just as the bartender was beginning to weaken, the man would give up and leave, adding as an afterthought that he might come back later in case the bartender had changed his mind. Soon after that, the dog's owner would return, looking distraught, announcing that he had been ruined. After accepting the bartender's sympathy, he might allow himself to think of selling the dog, and the bartender, not wanting to seem too eager, would name a smallish but still sizable figure. The dog owner would look both stricken and relieved, accept the money, and leave with tears in his eyes. The accomplice, needless to say, would never return.

The gold-brick scheme, which has given the language the term "goldbricker," was invented around the time of the Civil War by a man named Reed Waddell. He manufactured gold-plated lead bricks, stamped with the initials "U.S." after the practice of the U.S. Assayer's Office, and sold them as solid gold. His display brick contained a slug of real gold, which he would dig out to show to the scoffers. Meanwhile, an accomplice posing as an assayer would pretend to test the brick. Waddell sold the first brick he made for $4,000 and never afterward sold one for less than $3,500, and is said to have made more than $250,000 in his first few years in the business. He was a versatile con man who was also a major banco artist, and he was eventually killed by the banco king Tom O'Brien in Paris in 1895. The green goods swindle, also known as the sawdust game, arrived on the scene in 1869. Waddell dabbled in this enterprise as well, along with such legendary swindlers as Pete Conlish, George Post, and the immortal Yellow Kid Weil. The con took several forms. There was a bait-and-switch routine that involved showing suckers a bag of bills which they would be told were counterfeit; when the bait was taken and money exchanged, the saps would find themselves holding a sack of clippings or sawdust. Some operators sold a machine allegedly capable of turning out fake money; they would introduce a genuine bill, turn a crank, and two perfect copies would emerge. Still others ran the scheme as a mail fraud, buying address lists of lottery subscribers and sending them circulars that announced: "For $1200 in my goods (assorted) I charge $100," and so on, up to $10,000 counterfeit for $600. Sometimes these brochures would be illustrated with pictures of notes purported to be fakes. Buyers would either be bilked long-distance or be lured to a New York hotel room. As usual, the scheme preyed on the suckers' on lawlessness, and one of the resounding advantages of this was that they could not take their complaint to the police upon discovery of the swindle.

As the century drew to a close, the swindling and gambling establishments became larger and more intricate, and civil corruption became an art in itself. At the upper level of gambling in New York was Richard Canfield (who had nothing whatsoever to do with the afore-mentioned short-con card game named after him). His house of East Forty-fourth Street was the most refined, ambitiously decorated, exquisitely catered, and his police protection for more than two decades was the finest and most discreet. Canfield serviced the richest and most socially prominent gamblers, heirs, and tycoons. His sole rival in this field was the House with the Bronze Door, an elegant institution that lasted from 1891 to around 1917 in a town house on West Thirty-third Street remodeled in the late 1890s by Stanford White. At both this house and at Canfield's, the stories of rich men dropping enormous sums in a single evening kept topping each other, so that the phenomenon almost comes to seem like a version of potlatch, in which wealth is proven by the ability to shed it. The House was owned by a syndicate, the makeup of which was never thoroughly established, but which was known to be headed by a gambler named Frank Farrell. Farrell's partner in other enterprises was a policeman called Big Bill Devery, one of the many claimants for the distinction of most crooked cop of the era, and also known as the "meanest gambler in New York." In 1903 he and Farrell bought an American League baseball franchise they moved to town and called the New York Highlanders, which they sold in 1912 to Colonel Jacob Ruppert and Tillinghast Houston, who renamed the franchise the Yankees.

Farrell and Devery, along with Tammany boss Big Tim Sullivan, made up a syndicate that handled protection services for gambling establishments. *The New York Times*, responding in 1900 to the failure of the 1899 Mazet Committee to examine properly the state of gambling in the city, published an exposé of this syndicate that gave a breakdown of its income: 400 pool rooms at $300 per month apiece, adding up to $120,000 per year; 500 crap games at $150, $75,000 annually; 200 small gambling houses at $150 per month, $30,000; 20 large gambling houses at $1,000 per month, $20,000; 50 envelope games (pawnshop swindles) at $50 per month, $2,500; policy operations at $125,000 per annum. The whole added up to a grand total of $3,095,000 per year. The scheme was airtight, since between Sullivan's and Devery's positions, the syndicate comprised the powers of the police, the state senate, and the State Gambling Commission. The man behind this report was William Travers Jerome, who had assumed as a personal mission the abolition of gambling.

Before he could do much, however, Jerome had to wait out the administration of Tammany Mayor Robert Van Wyck (1898–1901), who let gambling houses run wide open all over town. Broadway and the Bowery were both chockablock with joints offering "high play at cards," roulette, dice, off-track betting, and wagering on prizefights, cockfights, and dogfights, while in Chinatown there were scores of places specializing in fan-tan and pi-gow. The boxing situation was completely out of control. Whereas, under some earlier reform administrations, matches had been held in an atmosphere of high secrecy and sometimes in complete silence, now the sport flourished as if it were legal. The only problem was the turf war over control of the graft, a matter contested by the Manhattan-based Farrell-Devery-Sullivan axis and the McCarren-McLaughlin syndicate in Brooklyn. On the night Van Wyck took office a match was stopped in the middle because both factions claimed the payoff. Eventually, the matter was settled, Farrell and company being awarded the state minus Brooklyn. They kept such a tight rein on the sport that even the venerable New York Athletic Club was unable to stage bouts. It was not until 1910 that the Frawley Law permitted legal ten-round matches in New York City, although it made decisions non-binding.

Reformers had their work cut out for them. Jerome was elected district attorney in November 1901, in the same election that brought reform mayoral candidate Seth Low to office. Jerome immediately began staging raids on gambling houses, ensuring the maximum publicity angle by inviting reporters to come along, and by personally wielding a hatchet to break down doors. Early in 1902, the Reverend Charles H. Parkhurst's Society for the Prevention of Crime raided the headquarters of Al Adams, the widely disliked policy king who also owned two breweries, about a hundred saloons, $2 million in real estate, and allegedly a stake in every gambling house between the Battery and 110th Street. He was arrested on evidence that linked him to eighty-two policy shops, was sentenced to twelve to eighteen months in Sing Sing, and emerged from prison a broken man. Jerome's men raided Canfield's establishment that same year, although some months after Canfield had shut the place down himself, but there were enough gambling rigs stowed in the closets to make a case. Ironically, the matter spurred Canfield to get back into business, and he kept reopening until a 1904 conviction proved conclusive. His bad luck continued: in 1907 he was forced to shut down his Saratoga Club House, and the same year lost at least half of his $13 million fortune in the stock-market panic, and he began to sell off the remainder of his property, including his collection of paintings by Whistler. When he died in 1914 of a fractured skull resulting from a fall in the Fourteenth Street subway station, his estate was assessed at $814,485.

Jerome had less luck with the resilient Honest John Kelly. Kelly was not related to the identically named and monikered Tammany politician, but acquired his sobriquet in 1888 when he refused a $10,000 bribe while serving as umpire in a pennant game between Boston and Providence. In 1890 he and the baseball star Mike Kelly opened a Tenderloin saloon that offered faro as a sideline, and in 1895 he opened a gambling house on West Forty-first Street that ran for seventeen years. This house featured a saloon on the ground floor, gambling on the second, and Kelly's domicile on the third; it was the hell of choice among boxers and their backers. Kelly was an independent, genuinely defiant of the syndicates. He steadfastly refused to pay protection, so his house was constantly raided. He acted as referee for prizefights in his spare time and was noted for calling off all bets if he sensed a fix. He did this at an important 1898 fight between Jim Corbett and Tom Sharkey, despite a warning from Big Tim Sullivan, who had a $13,000 bet riding on Sharkey. The very next day Kelly's house was raided and ransacked by the police. He promptly reopened. Many more raids followed, but it was not until 1912, when cops broke all his furniture, windows, and mirrors, and damaged the building itself, that he was compelled to announce his retirement. A month later he opened the Club Vendome on West Forty-fourth, which lasted until 1922 and grossed over a million, mostly from poker, in its last year of existence; in its last four years a uniformed cop was posted in front of the door, day and night. Kelly, despite his nickname an old-fashioned skinner, died peacefully in the Bahamas several years later.

Among the small-time gamblers downtown, chaos prevailed. Such operators as Herman "Beansy" Rosenthal, Bald Jack Rose, Bridgie Webber, and Sam Schepps were constantly feuding among themselves and with their police protectors. Rosenthal, for example, closed his house in Far Rockaway because of persistent raids instigated by a rival, then opened the Hesper Club on lower Second Avenue, which swiftly failed because of the success of Webber's nearby Sans Souci, then opened a house on West 116th Street that was soon closed by the police, then opened one on West Forty-fifth that was raided innumerable times and firebombed twice. His luck changed dramatically when he took on Lieutenant Charles H. Becker of the Gambling Squad as his partner. Becker, who extorted from prostitutes and pursued a bitter vendetta against the novelist Stephen Crane, who had exposed him in print, was called the "crookedest cop who ever stood behind a shield," which was certainly a distinction in such a crowded field. Rosenthal's security was short-lived, however. In March 1912 Rosenthal failed to contribute $500 toward the legal defense of Becker's press agent, who was charged with a killing in the course of a raid on a dice game, and the following month Becker retaliated by arranging for a raid on Rosenthal's house. When Rosenthal then threatened to spill all he knew about protection rackets to District Attorney Charles Whitman, other gamblers became alarmed and threatened Rosenthal. In June of that year the gangster Big Jack Zelig was approached in the Tombs and offered his freedom in return for disposing of Rosenthal. Zelig commissioned four of his hoods, Gyp the Blood, Lefty Louie, Dago Frank, and Whitey Lewis, to do the job. They set out to execute it in early July at the Garden Café on Seventh Avenue, but somehow suffered a collective failure of nerve. A week or two later Rosenthal published an affidavit in the *World* naming Becker as his partner at 20 percent of the cut in illegal gambling operations, and that same day was summoned to appear before the D.A. The following evening he was called away from dinner at the Hotel Metropole on West Forty-fifth by the message that a man wanted to see him outside, and Rosenthal, incredibly, complied. The minute he hit the pavement he went down in a shower of bullets fired by four men in a car. Gyp, Lefty, Dago, and Whitey were arrested almost immediately. Zelig turned state's evidence and was scheduled to testify in the trial that autumn that the execution order came from Becker, but before he could appear in court he was gunned down while boarding the Second Avenue streetcar at Thirteenth Street. Enough evidence linking Becker to the Rosenthal killing was obtained, however, and the cop and the four hoods were convicted and sentenced to the electric chair. The gunmen were executed at Sing Sing in the spring of 1913, while Becker began an appeal for clemency. Unfortunately for him, the governor whose decision it happened to be was none other than former D.A. Charles Whitman. Becker was put to death in the summer of 1915. His widow had his tombstone engraved with the words "Murdered by Governor Whitman," but later had them erased when threatened with a criminal libel suit.

The Becker case opened a can of worms that finally led to the collapse of the city's gambling establishment. By that time Sullivan was dead and Devery was in the real-estate business, and Mayor John Purroy Mitchell's reform administration was undertaking an unprecedentedly thorough sweep of gangs and vice. Gambling was reduced to a small-time clandestine activity, and it remained so for nearly a decade, until the bootlegging success of such new mobs as those of Owney Madden and Dutch Schultz inspired them to expand into such operations as policy and wire rooms. After Repeal, their successors continued these sidelines, and ran them for some thirty-five years, until legalization and state control ruined the trade in the city, or at least did so by official reckoning, since bookmaking, numbers, and many other grafts continue in spite of it all.

from

Oscar Wilde

by Richard Ellman

SOME OF WILDE'S activities in America were perilous enough. On 19 September a broker named H. K. Burris brought him to see Wall Street, until a threat of being set upon by unaesthetic employees made them retreat hurriedly through a back exit. In Moncton, New Brunswick, in mid-October Wilde came near to being arrested, and in New York, in December, he came near to being fleeced. The Moncton episode arose out of an invitation from the Young Men's Christian Association to lecture for them on a certain day. Wilde's agent proposed another day, but not having received a reply, closed with another offer. A sheriff's writ was prepared against him. Fortunately local friends went bail and brought pressure on the YMCA so that the case was dropped.

As for the New York misadventure, Wilde was approached on the street on 14 December 1882 by a young man who claimed to be the son of Anthony J. Drexel of Morgan's bank, whom he said Wilde had met. Wilde did not recall either father or son but invited the young man to lunch. 'Drexel' had just won a lottery and asked Wilde to accompany him in getting his money. The place proved to be a gambling den, and 'Drexel's' prize was the right to play a turn at house expense. He courteously announced that he would play for Wilde, won, and gave Wilde his winnings. Wilde then threw the dice for himself, and after a first success began to lose heavily. He had soon written checks for over $1,000 at which point he stopped play. 'Drexel' left with him, and said he felt Wilde had been badly treated, and promised to 'See about it.' Wilde bethought himself, rushed to his bank, and stopped payment on the checks. He then went to the 30th Street Police Station, and told the sympathetic captain that he had been 'a damned fool.' On being shown photographs of some notorious confidence men, he identified 'Drexel' as 'Hungry Joe' Sellick, one of the cleverest of his kind. The captain wanted Wilde to start proceedings, but he did not do so. Perhaps as a reward from Sellick, his uncashable checks were mailed in to the police station a few days later and then returned to Wilde. But he did not recover the cash he had lost. He wrote lugubriously to John Boyle O'Reilly, 'I have fallen into a den of thieves.'[50] The *New York Tribune* rejoiced in his plight, and took to poetry to register amusement:

And then, with the air of a guileless child,
Oh, that sweet, bright smile and those eyes aflame,
He said, 'If you'll let me, dear Mr Wilde,
I'll show you a ravishing little game.'

There's a One-Eyed Man in the Game

by Dee Brown

GAMBLING AND BARROOM drinking added to the merriment and the dramatic local color in the dance halls of the frontier. Multitudes of ongoing comedy dramas transpired within barroom walls, and may explain why dance halls (with bars and gaming tables) have been the settings for so many scenes in western novels and films.

In his study of saloons in the Old West, Richard Erdoes catalogued the many uses of that institution. It was an eatery, a hotel, a bath and comfort station, a livery stable, gambling den, bordello, barbershop, courtroom, church, social club, political center, dueling ground, post office, sports arena, undertaker's parlor, museum, trading post, grocery, and ice cream parlor.

According to a visitor to San Francisco in 1849, there were more new gambling establishments in that city "than there are catfish in the Mississippi," and he noted that they all had their own species of "bait" to lure the customers.

"In one is a very handsome Chilano girl, bejeweled like a dowager, who claps down her ounces as if they were so many brass buttons. At another . . . three comely-looking American girls tend bar, and are deep in the mystery of making rum punches, brandy smashers, and gin cocktails. In one is a band playing Hail Columbia; in another the Scotch Bagpipes are wheezing away Roy's Wife; in another is a man blowing his brains out through a key bugle; in another an Italian, who beats the bass drum, plays the cymbals, plays the Pandean pipes, rings a set of musical bells on his head, and plays on several other instruments, all at the same time; then there is the banjo and the violin, the harps, the hurdy gurdys, and the grinding organs and monkeys. Add to this sweet compound of sound the rattling and jingling of money and dice on the tables, the clinking of glasses, the roaring of some inebriate, the rumbling of carts, the knocking and banging of carpenters, and you have a very faint idea of life in California."

Another visitor to San Francisco the following year so disapproved of entertainment of this sort that he viewed the great fire of May 1850 as an act of retribution when it destroyed a considerable number of gambling and drinking establishments. "The very best part of the city was left in ashes in four or five hours," he recorded in his diary. "Truly it was a visitation of the almighty's and a just one too, the fire it is said commenced in the United States, another gambling house next to the Empire; the Greater part of the houses in the square were those of infamy in fact they could be called nothing short of houses of the Devil. I often thought this would be the end of such places, yet no person but one going in and seeing them could believe the extent to which Gambling and profanity were carried on; they also sold spirits in those places and the walls were hung with pictures of naked women in different poses, as large as life."

The recognized authority, the boss whose responsibility it was to keep the customers happy and simultaneously to maintain order, was usually the bartender, who more than likely was also the owner. As Mark Twain put it, "the cheapest and easiest way to become an influential man and be looked up to by the community at large was to stand behind a bar, wear a cluster-diamond pin, and sell whiskey."

Any good bartender arriving in a new boom town could always find plenty of help in getting a saloon started. When Joe King stopped at Salida, Colorado, in 1880, he immediately saw the need for a saloon, but could not obtain any lumber to construct one. A group of miners and mule skinners came to his aid. They hijacked a train of freight wagons loaded with lumber bound for Leadville, and removed enough boards to build a shanty. Anticipating the bartender's next requirement, they secured two barrels of whiskey in a similar manner. One of the miners donated a tin cup, and Joe King stepped behind his bar and began a brisk business.

The ethics and social responsibility of bartenders, however, were not always of the highest grade. Some enjoyed taking advantage of tenderfeet, especially naive cowboys from Texas and soldiers recently arrived from the East. Richard Ackley, who worked a bar near Fort Kearney, Nebraska, in 1858, said it was common practice to mix whiskey with large amounts of water and then sell it for a dollar a pint, or three dollars for filling a soldier's canteen. "After our whiskey began to get low," Ackley said, "I used to cut up a lot of tobacco and mix with it to give it strength, and then put in plenty of water. If they only wanted a drink we charged twenty-five cents and measured it out to them."

On the other hand, bartenders usually had a soft spot in their hearts for ministers of the gospel, although professionally they were arch-rivals, especially on Sundays. During the boom days of the 1880s in Gunnison, Colorado, Fat Jack's Place and the Red Light Dance Hall had a standing rule that their orchestras would always observe the Sabbath by playing only sacred music on Sunday evenings for the patrons to dance by.

"It was by no means an uncommon sight to see sundry couples cavorting about on the floor of a Sabbath evening," George Root recalled, "the 'ladies' bedecked and bespangled in brief and extravagantly décolleté dresses, with their sturdy companions, garbed in miner's costume of khaki, or the smart outfit of a successful gambler, or perchance the outfit of a cowboy—buckskin breeches with wide fringes running down the legs, pants tucked in boots, spurs on their high-heeled footwear, blue flannel shirt, red bandanna tied loosely about the neck with the knot at the back, a wide-brimmed hat covering their usually unkempt hair, and a brace of sixguns strapped to their hips. These were the sort of patrons who celebrated every evening, Sunday included, at which time they tripped the 'light fantastic toe' to the strains of such good old hymns as 'Jesus, Lover of My Soul' or 'The Beautiful Gates Ajar.' Other old-time sacred standbys, written to common or four-four time, also apparently served the crowd as satisfactorily while they went through the evolutions and convolutions of the old-time square dancing. No stranger could set foot in one of these dance halls without being importuned to have at least one dance or to stand treat—the 'ladies' receiving a certain percentage on every dance or treat."

In towns where the competition was fierce, operators of these centers of entertainment were among the earliest users of advertising, and they learned how to exploit everything in the public eye in order to attract customers. In Fort Scott, Kansas, which had more saloons than any other type of business, Joseph Darr (who called himself General Darr) was the leading promoter among the saloon keepers.

When the Fort Scott officials passed a law to destroy all dogs running at large after a certain date, General Darr advertised that he would serve a "Dog Lunch" to celebrate the occasion. The local newspaper, of course, carried a notice of the lunch, which consisted of highly flavored bologna sausage. "The General calls it 'Dog Lunch' and says it will be served regularly, every day at 10 A.M. All are invited."

Soon afterward Darr announced that he had acquired a splendid piano presided over by a first-class musician, and promised that a splendid violinist would soon be added. "The General also informs us," the newspaper continued, "that he has engaged the professional services of a leading prima donna of one of the eastern opera troupes, who will shortly make her *debut* in Fort Scott. These attractions together with the 'Dog Lunch,' the General thinks will 'swell the receipts enormously.'"

Although they were peripatetic by nature, seldom staying long in one town, gamblers were necessary components of the saloon and dance hall setting. When customers came for recreation, they expected gambling to be a part of the program, and they preferred to lose their money to a well-dressed gentleman instead of to a crude tin-horn lout who dressed no better than they did.

Most of the elegant gamblers who came west had learned their profession on Mississippi riverboats. They considered themselves to be aristocrats, and dressed the part. They usually wore black, with long tails on the coats, and they fancied frilled shirts and silk hats. They displayed considerably more expensive jewelry than their colleagues, the bartenders.

Gamblers by the hundreds followed the building of the railroads westward. Whenever a newly created town gave some evidence of being permanent, some of these "knights of the green table" would linger a few months in the better saloons and dance halls. Many preferred not to use their real names, adopting sobriquets. In Cheyenne, Wyoming, during the 1870s the leading gamblers were known as Poker Dan, Whiffletree Jim, Coon Can Kid, Squirrel Tooth, and Timberline. Significantly, there was one called The Preacher. Because members of both professions dressed in black, at first sight a gambler was often mistaken for a preacher until his diamond rings and stickpins came into view.

The Cheyenne gamblers arrived with the Union Pacific Railroad builders, and remained for a while when they recognized the permanence of the place. Hundreds of others, however, followed the successive Hell on Wheels towns—so called because they were "gambling hells" moved on wheeled railroad cars—that sprang up as temporary tent camps at the end of track, and then would move on to the next camp.

One such town was Benton, fifty miles west of Medicine Bow. During its heyday in 1868, Benton had twenty-three saloons and five dance halls, with an accompanying army of gamblers. In two weeks Benton became a city of three thousand people, with a mayor and aldermen, a daily newspaper, and numerous land speculators.

"The streets were eight inches deep in white dust as I entered the city of canvas tents and pole-houses," said newspaper correspondent John H. Beadle. "The suburbs appeared as banks of dirty white linen, and a new arrival with black clothes looked like nothing so much as a cockroach struggling through a flour barrel."

Beadle went on to describe "the great institution of Benton, the 'Big Tent,' sometimes with equal truth but less politeness, called the 'Gamblers' Tent.' The structure was a nice frame, a hundred feet long and forty feet wide, covered with canvas and conveniently floored for dancing to which and gambling it was entirely devoted . . .

"As we enter, we note that the right side is lined with a splendid bar, supplied with every variety of liquors and cigars, with cut glass goblets, ice-pitchers, splendid mirrors, and pictures rivaling those of our Eastern cities. At the back a space huge enough for one cotillion is left open for dancing; on a raised platform, a full band is in attendance day and night, while all the rest of the room is filled with tables devoted to monte, faro, rondo coolo, fortune-wheels, and every other species of gambling known. I acknowledge a morbid curiosity relating to everything villainous, and though I never ventured a cent but once in my life, I am never weary of watching the game, and the various fortunes of those who 'buck against the tiger.'

"During the day the 'Big Tent' is rather quiet, but at night, after a few inspiring tunes at the door by the band, the long hall is soon crowded with a motley throng of three or four thousand miners, ranchers, clerks, 'Bullwhackers,' gamblers, and 'cappers. The brass instruments are laid aside, the string-music begins, the cotillions succeed each other rapidly, each ending with a drink, while those not so employed crowd around the tables and enjoy each his favorite game. Tonight is one of unusual interest, and the tent is full, while from every table is heard the musical rattle of the dice, the hum of the wheel, or the eloquent voice of the dealer. Fair women, clothed with richness and taste, in white and airy garments, mingle with the throng, watch the games with deep interest, or laugh and chat with the players. The wife of the principal gambler—a tall, spiritual and most innocent looking woman—sits by his side, while their children, two beautiful little girls of four and six years, run about the room playing and shouting with merriment, climbing upon the knees of the gamblers and embraced in their rude arms, like flowers growing on the verge of frightful precipices . . .

"The evening wears along, many visitors begin to leave, the games languish, and a diversion is needed. The band gives a few lively touches, and a young man with a capacious chest and a great deal of 'openness' in his face, mounts the stand and sings a variety of sentimental and popular songs, ending with a regular rouser, in the chorus of which he constantly reiterates—in other words however—that he is a bovine youth with a vitreous optic 'which nobody can deny.' As he wears a revolver and bowie-knife in plain view, nobody seems inclined to deny it. A lively dance follows, the crowd is enlivened, and gambling goes on with renewed vigor."

In Virginia City, Nevada, during this period, the dance halls were slightly more refined, with a false air of permanence about them. While the Civil War was still raging in the East, the nation's foremost humorist, Artemus Ward (Charles Farrar Browne) stopped at that turbulent mining town during a lecture tour. In company with his publicist, Edward Hingston, and Mark Twain of the *Territorial Enterprise*, Ward toured Virginia City's centers of amusement.

"As we ramble through it in the evening," Hingston reported, "we find innumerable dance-houses wherein miners in their red shirts are dancing to the music of hurdy-gurdys played by itinerant maidens. At Sutcliffe's Melodeon a ball is taking place, and at the Niagara Concert Hall there are crowds assembled round the door, while from within come forth the sounds of negro minstrelsy, with the clack of bones and the twang of banjos."

The dance hall with its bar downstage was the setting for countless scenes of merriment that included spontaneous skits, one-liners, and entire situation comedies. These entertainments still survive in bastardized form in cinema and television plays about the American frontier.

For instance, during Eugene Field's days as reporter for the *Denver Tribune,* he was the leading performer in a number of extemporaneous light comedies in Perrin's Saloon. One evening when he approached the bar for a drink, the proprietor, Wesley Perrin, showed him a due bill for $31.25, and demanded that he first pay something on the arrears. Field protested that he was broke, like most newspapermen of the 1880s.

Because he admired Field, Perrin abruptly tore the bill into bits. Then he informed Field that his bill was paid. "You don't owe me a cent," Perrin said, "but don't try to run up any more bills, especially by ordering drinks for customers who would otherwise pay me in cash."

Field immediately expressed his thanks, continuing to do so while Perrin began locking up the saloon for the night. "It's time to close, Gene," Perrin said, "and time for you to get to work at the paper."

Field began strutting back and forth in front of the bar.

"Come on," Perrin called. "I could be fined for not locking up on time."

"I'm waiting for my due," Field declared.

"You've got more than your due," Perrin retorted. "What do you want now?"

"Don't you know?" Field answered. "Don't you know that it is a custom among gentlemen that when a customer's bar bill is paid, the bartender must set 'em up?"

Perrin locked the door from the inside, dimmed the lights, and set a bottle and a glass on the bar. Field took his drink leisurely, and then departed, with a cordial "good night" to the outdone Wesley Perrin.

In the back country of Colorado around this same time, there were frequent alarms of Ute Indian uprisings that ingenious men turned to their advantage, sometimes unintentionally creating comic skits in barrooms. On a cold October night a man named McCann rode up to the door of Jimmie Howard's saloon in Howardsville. He dashed breathlessly to the bar. "Git up and git out of here," McCann shouted. "The Indians have massacred everybody in Animas City and are moving on Silverton. I have got dispatches for the governor for arms and troops and am going to Antelope Springs before daylight. Jimmie! Give me a drink!"

As it turned out, the entire monologue was the invention of McCann, who had no funds but was thirsting for a drink against the chill of the autumn night.

In 1876 the population of Dodge City, Kansas, numbered twelve hundred, and for their recreation the inhabitants had a choice of nineteen saloons and dance halls. Most of these places depended, of course, upon transient trade. Into one of the saloons an unwashed buffalo hunter strode one day, taking a seat and propping his feet on the table. He demanded a glass of beer, a sandwich, and some Limburger cheese, all of which were served him promptly. After a minute or so, he shouted a complaint to the proprietor: "This cheese is no good. I can't smell it!"

The proprietor shouted back: "Damn it, take your feet down, and give the cheese a chance."

In 1877 the *Dodge City Times* printed a news item that illuminates the contemporary difference in status between dance hall girls and gambling gunmen: "Miss Frankie Bell, who wears the belt for superiority in point of muscular ability, heaped epithets upon the unoffending head of Mr. Earp to such an extent as to provoke a slap from the ex-officer, besides creating a disturbance of the quiet and dignity of the city, for which she received a night's lodging in the dog house and a reception at the police court next morning, the expense of which was about $20. Wyatt Earp was assessed the lowest limit of the law, one dollar." This news account no doubt entertained the masculine readers of Dodge City, but it was certainly not amusing to the dance hall girls.

What may have been one of the first strip teases in a frontier dance hall was reported by a Scottish poet, James Thomson, author of "The City of Dreadful Night." Thomson worked for a Colorado mining company during the 1870s, and while off duty at Central City he attended a "prostitutes' ball." According to Thomson, prizes were offered for the best dancer, and after the same girl won four times, she refused to accept the fifth award, and instead undressed down to the stockings and garters. She danced to the lively music for "five wonderful minutes," and concluded her performance with a bit of chanted doggerel: "Here's the leg that can dance, and here's the arse that can back it up!" After that she put her clothes back on and danced with the others until daylight.

And what of the ordinary women of a frontier town who might occasionally want to visit a saloon to view the action and perhaps have a drink? There was very little of that, the males having divided females into two classes, the reputable and disreputable, the good and the bad. Eventually, however, in some of the larger towns, saloon proprietors outfitted "wine rooms" into which reputable women were admitted through a side entrance. A few establishments went so far as to install roulette wheels in the wine rooms, so that women customers could gamble there, but as one woman complained, "It was a very tame affair . . . and you got only a rumble from the front, where things were really doing."

Results of the division of frontier women into "good and bad" was manifested in typical fashion at Alamosa, Colorado, when a drunk wandered out of a saloon and molested a lady on the street. Next morning his hanged body was swinging above the sidewalk with a large placard attached:

ALAMOSA PERTECKS HER WIMMEN

Like many great institutions throughout history, the saloons and dance halls gradually passed their prime and went into a decline with the ending of the nineteenth century. On January 10, 1897, the *ANACONDA* (Montana) *STANDARD* printed this observation about one of the leading drinking places in the state's capital city of Helena: "At the upper end of Main Street is a one-horse beer hall, called by courtesy a concert garden, where a pianist and violinist have performed so far without getting shot. Occasionally a woman, whose face would stop a freight train and a voice that would rasp a sawmill, comes out and assists the pianist and violinist in increasing the agony."

During the early years of the twentieth century, temperance advocates and prohibition laws began drying up entire towns. Armed with a hatchet, a muscular six-foot-tall, 175-pound woman named Carry Nation invaded saloons to intimidate bartenders and their customers. She smashed bottles, barrels, mirrors, and paintings of nude courtesans.

In 1907 a Ponca City, Oklahoma, saloon proprietor—condemned to close his bar by a local prohibition law—summed up the situation by posting this sign above his entrance door:

Hush Little Saloon
Don't You Cry
You'll Be a Drug Store
By and By.

Four Men and a Poker Game *or* Too Much Luck Is Bad Luck

by Bertolt Brecht

THEY SAT ON cane chairs in Havana and let the world go by. When it got too hot they drank iced water; in the evenings they danced the Boston at the Atlantic Hotel. All four of them had money.

The newspapers called them great men. They read it three times and chucked the paper into the sea. Or they held the paper between their hands and pierced it with their toecaps. Three of them had broken swimming records in front of ten thousand people, and the fourth had brought all ten thousand to their feet. When they had beaten the field and read the papers they boarded ship. They were headed back to New York with good money in their pockets.

To tell this story properly really calls for jazz accompaniment. It is sheer poetry from A to Z. It begins with cigar smoke and laughter and ends with a corpse.

For one of them, it was generally agreed, could coax salmon out of a sardine tin. He was what they call fortune's child. His name was Johnny Baker. Lucky Johnny. He was one of the best short-distance swimmers in either hemisphere. But the ridiculous luck he enjoyed threw a shadow over all his triumphs. For when a man can't unfold a paper napkin without finding a dollar bill, people begin to wonder whether he is good at his business, even if his name is Rockefeller. And wonder they did.

He had won in Havana just like the two others. He had won the 200 yard crawl by a length. But once again it was an open secret that his strongest opponent couldn't stand the climate and hadn't been fit. Johnny of course said they would try to pin something like that on him and go on about his 'luck' whatever happened, no matter how well he had been swimming. When he said it the other three just smiled.

This was the state of play when the story began, and it began with a little game of poker. The ship was a bore.

The sky was blue and so was the sea. The drinks were good, but they always were. The cigars smoked as well as any other cigars. In short, sky, sea, drinks and cigars were no good at all.

They thought a little game of poker might be better. It wasn't far short of the Bermudas when they began to play. They settled themselves comfortably for the game; each of them used two chairs. They agreed like gentlemen about the seating arrangements. One man's feet lay by another's ear. Thus, not far short of the Bermudas, they began to work their own downfall.

Since Johnny was feeling insulted by certain insinuations, they were only three to start with. One won, one lost, one held his own. They were playing with tin chips, each standing for five cents. Then the game got too boring for one of them and he took his feet out of the game. Johnny took his place. After that, the game wasn't boring any more. That is, Johnny began to win. If there was one thing Johnny couldn't do, it was play poker: but winning at poker was something he could do.

When Johnny bluffed, the bluff was so ridiculous that no poker player in the world would have dared go along with it. And when anybody who knew Johnny would have suspected a bluff, Johnny would innocently lay a flush on the table.

Johnny himself played stone cold for a couple of hours. The two others were het up. When the fourth man came back after watching potatoes being peeled in the galley for two hours, he observed that the tin chips were standing at a dollar.

This little increase had been the only way Johnny's partners could hope to get back some of their money. It was quite simple: they were to recoup in greenbacks what he had won in cents. Responsible family men could not have played with more caution in this situation. But it was Johnny who raked in the spondulicks.

They played six hours at a stretch. At any time during those six hours they could have left the game and lost no more to Johnny than the prize-money they had won in Havana. After those six hours of worry and effort they no longer could.

It was time for dinner. They polished off the meal in double-quick time. Instead of forks they felt straights between their fingers. They ate their steaks thinking of royal flushes. The fourth man ate much more slowly. He said he was really beginning to feel like taking a hand, since a little life seemed to have crept into their dreary diddling.

After dinner they were a foursome again. They played for eight hours. When Johnny counted their money about three in the morning they had left the Bermudas behind.

They slept rather badly for five hours and started again. By then three of them were men who, whatever happened, would be in hock for years. They had one more day ahead of them; at midnight they would arrive in New York. In the course of that day they had to make sure they were not going to be ruined for life. For among them was a lousy poker player who was sucking the marrow from their bones.

In the morning, when the appearance of several ships showed that the coast was near, they began to stake their houses. On top of everything else Johnny won a piano. Then they took two hours off at noon before squaring up to play for the shirts on their backs. At five in the afternoon they saw no choice but to go on. The man who had waited till after the Bermudas to take a hand and who was still eating calmly when the others had forgotten what their forks were for, offered to play Johnny for his girl. That is to say, if Johnny won, he would have the right to take a certain Jenny Smith to the male voice choir's Widows' Ball in Hoboken, but if he lost he would have to give back everything he had already won from the others. And Johnny took him up.

First of all he got his facts straight.

'And you won't be coming along?'

'Wouldn't dream of it.'

'And you won't hold it against me?'

'I won't hold it against you.'

'Or against her?'

'What do you mean, against her?'

'Well, the girl, you won't hold it against her?'

'Godammit no, I won't hold it against her either.'

And then Johnny won.

When you place a bet, win, pocket your winnings, raise your hat and leave, it means you have been in danger and emerged unscathed. But if you have too big a heart and give your partners another chance, then, unless you end in the poorhouse, your partners will be on your back for the rest of your life. They will eat your liver like vultures. When playing poker you have to be as hard-hearted as in any other form of expropriation.

From the moment when Johnny joined the game because another player left the table, he had let the others call the shots. They had forced him to look at several thousand cards, they had robbed him of his sleep, they had made him wolf down his meals in record time. They would really have preferred him to carry on playing and every six hours snatch the odd mouthful from a steak dangling on a string above the card-table. Johnny found it all distasteful.

When he got up from the table after playing for the girl—which so far as he was concerned had topped everything—he had in his naive way thought they had had enough. They had taken him on knowing how lucky he was, because they thought he knew as little about poker as a traindriver knows about geography. But trains have rails which know their geography: a guy goes from New York to Chicago and nowhere else. That was exactly the system with which he had won, and the only thing left was for him to return his winnings without mortally offending them. Johnny's weakness was his heart. He had too much tact.

He said straight out not to worry, it had all been in fun. They didn't answer. They sat there as they had since the previous day and watched the seagulls, which were now more plentiful.

Johnny concluded from this that, so far as they were concerned, more than 24 hours of poker was no joke.

Johnny stood by the railing and thought. Then it came to him. He suggested that they should first of all have a meal with him that evening to restore their spirits. At his expense naturally. What he had in mind was a grand function, a blow-out, a really slap-up meal. He himself would mix drinks that would loosen their tongues. In view of the circumstances no expense need be spared. He even had caviare in mind. Johnny expected big things of this meal.

They didn't say no.

They took this without exactly showing enthusiasm, but at any rate they agreed to go along with him. It was time to eat anyhow.

Johnny went off and did the ordering. He went into the kitchen and ingratiated himself with the chef. He wanted a meal dished up for himself and his friends, a banquet which would outdo anything of its kind ever produced by any first class ship's galley between Havana and New York. Johnny felt a lot better after this conversation with the chef.

During this half-hour not a single word was spoken on deck.

Johnny set the table himself downstairs. Beside his own place he put a little serving table on which he arranged the drinks. No need for him to stand up to mix. He had the chef bring his guests down. They came with a look of indifference and sat down as if it were an ordinary meal. It was all a bit flat.

Johnny had thought that they would open up during the meal. People usually unbutton when they are eating, and this meal was excellent. They tucked in but they did not seem to be enjoying it. They ate the fresh vegetables as if they were porridge, and the roast chicken as if it were cafetaria ham. They seemed to have ideas of their own about Johnny's meal. At one point one of them reached for a beautifully glazed little porcelain pot and asked 'Is this caviare?' And Johnny answered truthfully. 'Yes, the best that a leaky old tub like this has to offer.' The man nodded and emptied the pot with a spoon. Right after that another pointed out to his neighbour a little, specially packed speciality in mayonnaise. And then they smiled. Neither this nor several other aspects of their behaviour escaped their host.

But it was only over the coffee that it dawned on Johnny what a piece of impertinence it had been for him to invite them to a meal. They didn't seem to appreciate his desire to apply some of the money he had won to the common good. It seemed as if they only realised the extent of their losses once they were forced to watch their money being spent on such senseless titbits. It is more or less the same with a woman who wants to leave you. When you read her nice little parting letter, you may understand, but it is only when you see her getting into a taxi with another man that it really hits you. Johnny was quite taken aback.

It was eight in the evening. Outside you could hear the tugs hooting. It was four hours to New York.

Johnny had a vague feeling that it would be intolerable to sit in this cabin with these ruined men for four hours. But it didn't look as if he would be able simply to get up and go. Given the situation, Johnny realised that he only had one chance. He suggested playing again for the whole pot.

They put down their coffee cups, pushed the half-empty cans to one corner of the table and dealt the cards.

They played for money with the same tin chips as they had done at the beginning. It struck Johnny that the other three were unwilling to go beyond a certain stake. So they were taking the game seriously again.

At the very first hand Johnny was dealt yet another straight. Nonetheless he dropped out in the second round and threw in his hand. He had definitely learnt a thing or two.

In the second hand and in the third when the stakes were raised he bluffed and strung them along as far as he could. But then one of them calmly looked him straight in the eye and said, 'Play the game.' Whereupon he played a few hands as he had done previously, and won as before. Then he had a curious desire to play it by ear and follow his luck where he saw it. Then he saw their faces again and noticed that they scarcely looked at their cards before throwing them in, and at that he lost his nerve. He wanted to start deliberately losing, but each time he had a chance to pull a fast one he felt them watching him so closely that he drew back. And when he played badly out of sheer ignorance they played even worse, because the only thing they believed in was his luck. They took his total uncertainty for sheer malice. More and more they came to think that he was just playing cat and mouse with them.

When once again he had collected all the chips in front of him the other three all got up, and he was left sitting alone without a thought in his head, amid the cards and the cans. It was eleven o'clock, one hour out of New York.

Four men and a poker deck in a cabin between Havana and New York.

They still had a little time. Since the air in the cabin was hot and stuffy they decided to go up on deck. They thought the fresh air would help. The idea of fresh air seemed to improve their spirits. They even asked Johnny whether he wanted to go on deck with them.

Johnny didn't want to go on deck.

When the other three saw that Johnny didn't want to go on deck they began insisting.

It was then that Johnny lost his head for the first time and made the mistake of not standing up immediately. This probably gave them a prolonged glimpse of fear on his face. And this in turn made up their minds.

Five minutes later, without uttering a word, Johnny went on deck with them. The steps were wide enough for two. It just happened that one of them went up ahead of Johnny, one behind him and one at his side.

When they reached the top the night was cool and foggy. The deck was damp and slippery. Johnny was glad to be in the middle.

They passed a man at the wheel who paid no attention to them. When they had gone four paces beyond him Johnny had a distinct feeling that he had missed a chance. But by then they were heading for the stern railings.

When they reached the railings Johnny wanted to put his plan into effect and give a loud shout. But he abandoned this idea, oddly enough because of the fog; for when people have trouble seeing, they think no one can hear them.

From the railings they heaved him into the sea.

Then they sat in the cabin for a while eating what was left in the half-empty cans. They consolidated what was left of the drinks, three men and a poker deck on the way from Havana to New York, and asked one another whether Johnny Baker who was no doubt swimming behind the ship as its red navigation light disappeared into the night, was as good at swimming as he was at winning poker games.

But *nobody* can possibly swim well enough to save himself from his fellow men if he has too much luck in this world.

The Snatching of Bookie Bob

by Damon Runyon

NOW IT COMES on the spring of 1931, after a long hard winter, and times are very tough indeed, what with the stock market going all to pieces, and banks busting right and left, and the law getting very nasty about this and that, and one thing and another, and many citizens of this town are compelled to do the best they can.

There is very little scratch anywhere and along Broadway many citizens are wearing their last year's clothes and have practically nothing to bet on the races or anything else, and it is a condition that will touch anybody's heart.

So I am not surprised to hear rumours that the snatching of certain parties is going on in spots, because while snatching is by no means a high-class business, and is even considered somewhat illegal, it is something to tide over the hard times.

Furthermore, I am not surprised to hear that this snatching is being done by a character by the name of Harry the Horse, who comes from Brooklyn, and who is a character who does not care much what sort of business he is in, and who is mobbed up with other characters from Brooklyn such as Spanish John and Little Isadore, who do not care what sort of business they are in, either.

In fact, Harry the Horse and Spanish John and Little Isadore are very hard characters in every respect, and there is considerable indignation expressed around and about when they move over from Brooklyn into Manhattan and start snatching, because the citizens of Manhattan feel that if there is any snatching done in their territory, they are entitled to do it themselves.

But Harry the Horse and Spanish John and Little Isadore pay no attention whatever to local sentiment and go on the snatch on a pretty fair scale, and by and by I am hearing rumours of some very nice scores. These scores are not extra large scores, to be sure, but they are enough to keep the wolf from the door, and in fact from three different doors, and before long Harry the Horse and Spanish John and Little Isadore are around the race-tracks betting on the horses, because if there is one thing they are all very fond of, it is betting on the horses.

Now many citizens have the wrong idea entirely of the snatching business. Many citizens think that all there is to snatching is to round up the party who is to be snatched and then just snatch him, putting him away somewhere until his family or friends dig up enough scratch to pay whatever price the snatchers are asking. Very few citizens understand that the snatching business must be well organized and very systematic.

In the first place, if you are going to do any snatching, you cannot snatch just anybody. You must know who you are snatching, because naturally it is no good snatching somebody who does not have any scratch to settle with. And you cannot tell by the way a party looks or how he lives in this town if he has any scratch, because many a party who is around in automobiles, and wearing good clothes, and chucking quite a swell is nothing but the phonus bolonus and does not have any real scratch whatever.

So of course such a party is no good for snatching, and of course guys who are on the snatch cannot go around inquiring into bank accounts, or asking how much this and that party has in a safe-deposit vault, because such questions are apt to make citizens wonder why, and it is very dangerous to get citizens to wondering why about anything. So the only way guys who are on the snatch can find out about parties worth snatching is to make a connexion with some guy who can put the finger on the right party.

The finger guy must know the party he fingers has plenty of ready scratch to begin with, and he must also know that this party is such a party as is not apt to make too much disturbance about being snatched, such as telling the gendarmes. The party may be a legitimate party, such as a business guy, but he will have reasons why he does not wish it to get out that he is snatched, and the finger must know these reasons. Maybe the party is not leading the right sort of life, such as running around with blondes when he has an ever-loving wife and seven children in Mamaroneck, but does not care to have his habits known, as is apt to happen if he is snatched, especially if he is snatched when he is with a blonde.

And sometimes the party is such a party as does not care to have matches run up and down the bottom of his feet, which often happens to parties who are snatched and who do not seem to wish to settle their bill promptly, because many parties are very ticklish on the bottom of the feet, especially if the matches are lit. On the other hand, maybe the party is not a legitimate guy, such as a party who is running a crap game or a swell speakeasy, or who has some other dodge he does not care to have come out, and who also does not care about having his feet tickled.

Such a party is very good indeed for the snatching business, because he is pretty apt to settle without any argument. And after a party settles one snatching, it will be considered very unethical for anybody else to snatch him again very soon, so he is not likely to make any fuss about the matter. The finger guy gets a commission of twenty-five per cent of the settlement, and one and all are satisfied and much fresh scratch comes into circulation, which is very good for the merchants. And while the party who is snatched may know who snatches him, one thing he never knows is who puts the finger on him, this being considered a trade secret.

I am talking to Waldo Winchester, the newspaper scribe, one night and something about the snatching business comes up, and Waldo Winchester is trying to tell me that it is one of the oldest dodges in the world, only Waldo calls it kidnapping, which is a title that will be very repulsive to guys who are on the snatch nowadays. Waldo Winchester claims that hundreds of years ago guys are around snatching parties, male and female, and holding them for ransom, and furthermore Waldo Winchester says they even snatch very little children and Waldo states that it is all a very, very wicked proposition.

Well, I can see where Waldo is right about it being wicked to snatch dolls and little children, but of course no guys who are on the snatch nowadays will ever think of such a thing, because who is going to settle for a doll in these times when you can scarcely even give them away? As for little children, they are apt to be a great nuisance, because their mammas are sure to go running around hollering bloody murder about them, and furthermore little children are very dangerous, indeed, what with being apt to break out with measles and mumps and one thing and another any minute and give it to everybody in the neighbourhood.

Well, anyway, knowing that Harry the Horse and Spanish John and Little Isadore are now on the snatch, I am by no means pleased to see them coming along one Tuesday evening when I am standing at the corner of Fiftieth and Broadway, although of course I give them a very jolly hello, and say I hope and trust they are feeling nicely.

They stand there talking to me a few minutes, and I am very glad indeed that Johnny Brannigan, the strong-arm cop, does not happen along and see us, because it will give Johnny a very bad impression of me to see me in such company, even though I am not responsible for the company. But naturally I cannot haul off and walk away from this company at once, because Harry the Horse and Spanish John and Little Isadore may get the idea that I am playing the chill for them, and will feel hurt.

'Well,' I say to Harry the Horse, 'how are things going, Harry?'

'They are going no good,' Harry says. 'We do not beat a race in four days. In fact,' he says, 'we go overboard to-day. We are washed out. We owe every bookmaker at the track that will trust us, and now we are out trying to raise some scratch to pay off. A guy must pay his bookmaker no matter what.'

Well, of course this is very true, indeed, because if a guy does not pay his bookmaker it will lower his business standing quite some, as the bookmaker is sure to go around putting the blast on him, so I am pleased to hear Harry the Horse mention such honourable principles.

'By the way,' Harry says, 'do you know a guy by the name of Bookie Bob?'

Now I do not know Bookie Bob personally, but of course I know who Bookie Bob is, and so does everybody else in this town that ever goes to a race-track, because Bookie Bob is the biggest bookmaker around and about, and has plenty of scratch. Furthermore, it is the opinion of one and all that Bookie Bob will die with this scratch, because he is considered a very close guy with his scratch. In fact, Bookie Bob is considered closer than a dead heat.

He is a short fat guy with a bald head, and his head is always shaking a little from side to side, which some say is a touch of palsy, but which most citizens believe comes of Bookie Bob shaking his head 'No' to guys asking for credit in betting on the races. He has an ever-loving wife, who is a very quiet little old doll with grey hair and a very sad look in her eyes, but nobody can blame her for this when they figure that she lives with Bookie Bob for many years.

I often see Bookie Bob and his ever-loving wife eating in different joints along in the Forties, because they seem to have no home except an hotel, and many a time I hear Bookie Bob giving her a going-over about something or other, and generally it is about the price of something she orders to eat, so I judge Bookie Bob is as tough with his ever-loving wife about scratch as he is with everybody else. In fact, I hear him bawling her out one night because she has on a new hat which she says cost her six bucks, and Bookie Bob wishes to know if she is trying to ruin him with her extravagances.

But of course I am not criticizing Bookie Bob for squawking about the hat, because for all I know six bucks may be too much for a doll to pay for a hat, at that. And furthermore, maybe Bookie Bob has the right idea about keeping down his ever-loving wife's appetite, because I know many a guy in this town who is practically ruined by dolls eating too much on him.

'Well,' I say to Harry the Horse, 'if Bookie Bob is one of the bookmakers you owe, I am greatly surprised to see that you seem to have both eyes in your head, because I never before hear of Bookie Bob letting anybody owe him without giving him at least one of their eyes for security. In fact,' I say, 'Bookie Bob is such a guy as will not give you the right time if he has two watches.'

'No,' Harry the Horse says, 'we do not owe Bookie Bob. But,' he says, 'he will be owing us before long. We are going to put the snatch on Bookie Bob.'

Well, this is most disquieting news to me, not because I care if they snatch Bookie Bob or not, but because somebody may see me talking to them who will remember about it when Bookie Bob is snatched. But of course it will not be good policy for me to show Harry the Horse and Spanish John and Little Isadore that I am nervous, so I only speak as follows:

'Harry,' I say, 'every man knows his own business best, and I judge you know what you are doing. But,' I say, 'you are snatching a hard guy when you snatch Bookie Bob. A very hard guy, indeed. In fact,' I say, 'I hear the softest thing about him is his front teeth, so it may be very difficult for you to get him to settle after you snatch him.'

'No,' Harry the Horse says, 'we will have no trouble about it. Our finger gives us Bookie Bob's hole card, and it is a most surprising thing, indeed. But,' Harry the Horse says, 'you come upon many surprising things in human nature when you are on the snatch. Bookie Bob's hole card is his ever-loving wife's opinion of him.

'You see,' Harry the Horse says, 'Bookie Bob has been putting himself away with his ever-loving wife for years as a very important guy in this town, with much power and influence, although of course Bookie Bob knows very well he stands about as good as a broken leg. In fact,' Harry the Horse says, 'Bookie Bob figures that his ever-loving wife is the only one in the world who looks on him as a big guy, and he will sacrifice even his scratch, or anyway some of it, rather than let her know that guys have such little respect for him as to put the snatch on him. It is what you call psychology,' Harry the Horse says.

Well, this does not make good sense to me, and I am thinking to myself that the psychology that Harry the Horse really figures to work out nice on Bookie Bob is tickling his feet with matches, but I am not anxious to stand there arguing about it, and pretty soon I bid them all good evening, very polite, and take the wind, and I do not see Harry the Horse or Spanish John or Little Isadore again for a month.

In the meantime, I hear gossip here and there that Bookie Bob is missing for several days, and when he finally shows up again he gives it out that he is very sick during his absence, but I can put two and two together as well as anybody in this town and I figure that Bookie Bob is snatched by Harry the Horse and Spanish John and Little Isadore, and the chances are it costs him plenty.

So I am looking for Harry the Horse and Spanish John and Little Isadore to be around the race-track with plenty of scratch and betting them higher than a cat's back, but they never show up, and what is more I hear they leave Manhattan, and are back in Brooklyn working every day handling beer. Naturally this is very surprising to me, because the way things are running beer is a tough dodge just now, and there is very little profit in same, and I figure that with the scratch they must make off Bookie Bob, Harry the Horse and Spanish John and Little Isadore have a right to be taking things easy.

Now one night I am in Good Time Charley Bernstein's little speak in Forty-eighth Street, talking of this and that with Charley, when in comes

Harry the Horse, looking very weary and by no means prosperous. Naturally I gave him a large hello, and by and by we get to gabbing together and I ask him whatever becomes of the Bookie Bob matter, and Harry the Horse tells me as follows:

Yes [Harry the Horse says], we snatch Bookie Bob all right. In fact, we snatch him the very next night after we are talking to you, or on a Wednesday night. Our finger tells us Bookie Bob is going to a wake over in his old neighbourhood on Tenth Avenue, near Thirty-eighth Street, and this is where we pick him up.

He is leaving the place in his car along about midnight, and of course Bookie Bob is alone as he seldom lets anybody ride with him because of the wear and tear on his car cushions, and Little Isadore swings our flivver in front of him and makes him stop. Naturally Bookie Bob is greatly surprised when I poke my head into his car and tell him I wish the pleasure of his company for a short time, and at first he is inclined to argue the matter, saying I must make a mistake, but I put the old convincer on him by letting him peek down the snozzle of my John Roscoe.

We lock his car and throw the keys away, and then we take Bookie Bob in our car and go to a certain spot on Eighth Avenue where we have a nice little apartment all ready. When we get there I tell Bookie Bob that he can call up anybody he wishes and state that the snatch is on him and that it will require twenty-five G's, cash money, to take it off, but of course I also tell Bookie Bob that he is not to mention where he is or something may happen to him.

Well, I will say one thing for Bookie Bob, although everybody is always weighing in the sacks on him and saying he is no good—he takes it like a gentleman, and very calm and businesslike.

Furthermore, he does not seem alarmed, as many citizens are when they find themselves in such a situation. He recognizes the justice of our claim at once, saying as follows:

'I will telephone my partner, Sam Salt,' he says. 'He is the only one I can think of who is apt to have such a sum as twenty-five G's cash money. But,' he says, 'if you gentlemen will pardon the question, because this is a new experience to me, how do I know everything will be okay for me after you get the scratch?'

'Why,' I say to Bookie Bob, somewhat indignant, 'it is well known to one and all in this town that my word is my bond. There are two things I am bound to do,' I say, 'and one is to keep my word in such a situation as this, and the other is to pay anything I owe a bookmaker, no matter what, for these are obligations of honour with me.'

'Well,' Bookie Bob says, 'of course I do not know you gentlemen, and, in fact, I do not remember ever seeing any of you, although your face is somewhat familiar, but if you pay your bookmaker you are an honest guy, and one in a million. In fact,' Bookie Bob says, 'if I have all the scratch that is owing to me around this town, I will not be telephoning anybody for such a sum as twenty-five G's. I will have such a sum in my pants pocket for change.'

Now Bookie Bob calls a certain number and talks to somebody there but he does not get Sam Salt, and he seems much disappointed when he hangs up the receiver again.

'This is a very tough break for me,' he says. 'Sam Salt goes to Atlantic City an hour ago on very important business and will not be back until tomorrow evening, and they do not know where he is to stay in Atlantic City. And,' Bookie Bob says, 'I cannot think of anybody else to call up to get this scratch, especially anybody I will care to have know I am in this situation.'

'Why not call your ever-loving wife?' I say. 'Maybe she can dig up this kind of scratch.'

'Say,' Bookie Bob says, 'you do not suppose I am chump enough to give my ever-loving wife twenty-five G's, or even let her know where she can get her dukes on twenty-five G's belonging to me, do you? I give my ever-loving wife ten bucks per week for spending money,' Bookie Bob says, 'and this is enough scratch for any doll, especially when you figure I pay for her meals.'

Well, there seems to be nothing we can do except wait until Sam Salt gets back, but we let Bookie Bob call his ever-loving wife, as Bookie Bob says he does not wish to have her worrying about his absence, and tells her a big lie about having to go to Jersey City to sit up with a sick Brother Elk.

Well, it is now nearly four o'clock in the morning, so we put Bookie Bob in a room with Little Isadore to sleep, although, personally, I consider making a guy sleep with Little Isadore very cruel treatment, and Spanish John and I take turns keeping awake and watching out that Bookie Bob does not take the air on us before paying us off. To tell the truth, Little Isadore and Spanish John are somewhat disappointed that Bookie Bob agrees to settle so promptly, because they are looking forward to tickling his feet with great relish.

Now Bookie Bob turns out to be very good company when he wakes up the next morning, because he knows a lot of racetrack stories and plenty of scandal, and he keeps us much interested at breakfast. He talks along with us as if he knows us all his life, and he seems very nonchalant indeed, but the chances are he will not be so nonchalant if I tell him about Spanish John's thought.

Well, about noon Spanish John goes out of the apartment and comes back with a racing sheet, because he knows Little Isadore and I will be wishing to know what is running in different spots although we do not have anything to bet on these races, or any way of betting on them, because we are overboard with every bookmaker we know.

Now Bookie Bob is also much interested in the matter of what is running, especially at Belmont, and he is bending over the table with me and Spanish John and Little Isadore, looking at the sheet, when Spanish John speaks as follows:

'My goodness,' Spanish John says, 'a spot such as this fifth race with Questionnaire at four to five is like finding money in the street. I only wish I have a few bobs to bet on him at such a price,' Spanish John says.

'Why,' Bookie Bob says, very polite, 'if you gentlemen wish to bet on these races I will gladly book to you. It is a good way to pass away the time while we are waiting for Sam Salt, unless you will rather play pinochle?'

'But,' I say, 'we have no scratch to play the races, at least not much.'

'Well,' Bookie Bob says, 'I will take your markers, because I hear what you say about always paying your bookmaker, and you put yourself away with me as an honest guy, and these other gentlemen also impress me as honest guys.'

Now what happens but we begin betting Bookie Bob on the different races, not only at Belmont, but at all the other tracks in the country, for Little Isadore and Spanish John and I are guys who like plenty of action when we start betting on the horses. We write out markers for whatever we wish to bet and hand them to Bookie Bob, and Bookie Bob sticks these markers in an inside pocket, and along in the late afternoon it looks as if he has a tumour on his chest.

We get the race results by phone off a poolroom down-town as fast as they come off, and also the prices, and it is a lot of fun, and Little Isadore and Spanish John and Bookie Bob and I are all little pals together until all the races are over and Bookie Bob takes out the markers and starts counting himself up.

It comes out then that I owe Bookie Bob ten G's, and Spanish John owes him six G's, and Little Isadore owes him four G's, as Little Isadore beats him a couple of races out west.

Well, about this time, Bookie Bob manages to get Sam Salt on the phone, and explains to Sam that he is to go to a certain safe-deposit box and get out twenty-five G's, and then wait until midnight and hire himself a taxicab and start riding around the block between Fifty-first and Fifty-second, from Eighth to Ninth avenues, and to keep riding until somebody flags the cab and takes the scratch off him.

Naturally Sam Salt understands right away that the snatch is on Bookie Bob, and he agrees to do as he is told, but he says he cannot do it until the following night because he knows there is not twenty-five G's in the box, and he will have to get the difference at the track the next day. So there we are with another day in the apartment and Spanish John and Little Isadore and I are just as well pleased because Bookie Bob has us hooked and we naturally wish to wiggle off.

But the next day is worse than ever. In all the years I am playing the horses I never have such a tough day, and Spanish John and Little Isadore are just as bad. In fact, we are all going so bad that Bookie Bob seems to feel sorry for us and often lays us a couple of points above the track prices, but it does no good. At the end of the day, I am in a total of twenty G's, while Spanish John owes fifteen, and Little Isadore fifteen, a total of fifty G's among the three of us. But we are never any hands to hold post-mortems on bad days, so Little Isadore goes out to a delicatessen store and lugs in a lot of nice things to eat, and we have a fine dinner, and then we sit around with Bookie Bob telling stories, and even singing a few songs together until time to meet Sam Salt.

When it comes on midnight Spanish John goes out and lays for Sam, and gets a little valise off of Sam Salt. Then Spanish John comes back to the apartment and we open the valise and the twenty-five G's are there okay, and we cut this scratch three ways.

Then I tell Bookie Bob he is free to go on about his business, and good luck to him, at that, but Bookie Bob looks at me as if he is very much surprised, and hurt, and says to me like this:

'Well, gentlemen, thank you for your courtesy, but what about the scratch you owe me? What about these markers? Surely, gentlemen, you will pay your bookmaker?'

Well, of course we owe Bookie Bob these markers, all right, and of course a man must pay his bookmaker, no matter what, so I hand over my bit and Bookie Bob puts down something in a little note-book that he takes out of his kick.

Then Spanish John and Little Isadore hand over their dough, too, and Bookie Bob puts down something more in the little note-book.

'Now,' Bookie Bob says, 'I credit each of your accounts with these payments, but you gentlemen still owe me a matter of twenty-five G's over and above the twenty-five I credit you with, and I hope and trust you will make arrangements to settle this at once because,' he says, 'I do not care to extend such accommodations over any considerable period.'

'But,' I say, 'we do not have any more scratch after paying you the twenty-five G's on account.'

'Listen,' Bookie Bob says, dropping his voice down to a whisper, 'what about putting the snatch on my partner, Sam Salt, and I will wait over a couple of days with you and keep booking to you, and maybe you can pull yourselves out. But of course,' Bookie Bob whispers, 'I will be entitled to twenty-five per cent of the snatch for putting the finger on Sam for you.'

But Spanish John and Little Isadore are sick and tired of Bookie Bob and will not listen to staying in the apartment any longer, because they say he is a jinx to them and they cannot beat him in any manner, shape, or form. Furthermore, I am personally anxious to get away because something Bookie Bob says reminds me of something.

It reminds me that besides the scratch we owe him, we forget to take out six G's two-fifty for the party who puts the finger on Bookie Bob for us, and this is a very serious matter indeed, because anybody will tell you that failing to pay a finger is considered a very dirty trick. Furthermore, if it gets around that you fail to pay a finger, nobody else will ever finger for you.

So [Harry the Horse says] we quit the snatching business because there is no use continuing while this obligation is outstanding against us, and we go back to Brooklyn to earn enough scratch to pay our just debts.

We are paying off Bookie Bob's IOU a little at a time, because we do not wish to ever have anybody say we welsh on a bookmaker, and furthermore we are paying off the six G's two-fifty commission we owe our finger.

And while it is tough going, I am glad to say our honest effort is doing somebody a little good, because I see Bookie Bob's ever-loving wife the other night all dressed up in new clothes and looking very happy, indeed.

And while a guy is telling me she is looking so happy because she gets a large legacy from an uncle who dies in Switzerland, and is now independent of Bookie Bob, I only hope and trust [Harry the Horse says] that it never gets out that our finger in this case is nobody but Bookie Bob's ever-loving wife.

The Yellow Kid

by Joseph "Yellow Kid" Weil, with W. T. Brannon

Joseph "Yellow Kid" Weil, probably the most famous American confidence man of the twentieth century, reformed late in life. After his release from jail in the 1940's, Weil wrote his memoirs, detailing the methods by which he had relieved an untold number of victims of an estimated eight million dollars. Weil operated hundreds of schemes. Once he tried to go straight and took a job selling a Catholic encyclopedia. But the Weil touch crept in. Calling himself Daniel O'Connell, he told a priest in Flint, Michigan, that the Holy Father, Pius X, had expressed the wish that at least two thousand copies be placed in homes in Flint. The priest bought the first set in town. On the strength of the priest's order, Weil, in three days, sold eighty sets, on which his commission totalled $1,600. But the priest discovered the imposture and withdrew his order. Thereupon, Weil returned to his first love, selling fake or nearly worthless mining and oil stock to big businessmen, including bankers. In this portion from his autobiography, Weil makes it crystal clear why seeing is not always the best reason for believing.

MY STOCK STORY was basically the same for more than twenty years. However, each victim was different, and the situations varied. Strangely enough, the victims themselves made suggestions that helped me to improve the scheme.

For example, Bobby Sims, heir to a soap fortune in Cincinnati, called my attention to an article in *McClure's*, then one of the nation's leading monthlies. The article, titled "$100,000 A Year," was written by Edward Mott Woolley and was the success story of a mining engineer named Pope Yateman who had taken over an almost worthless mine in Chile and made it pay, though he had been compelled to pipe water for more than a hundred miles. I bought as many copies of that magazine as I could find and fetched them to Chicago. At the first opportunity I took them to Jack Jones, operator of the Dill Pickle Club.

Jones was noted principally for his operation of the Dill Pickle, and only a few knew of his real activities. These were carried on in the daytime when the club was closed. Jones had a well-equipped printing and bookbinding plant in the same building.

Jones employed linotype operators, printers, binders, and one engraver. Their specialty was first editions of famous books. The engraver, whom I knew only as Hymie, was an old-time hand-engraver who could copy anything from fifteenth century bookplates to Uncle Sam's currency. He had a secret process for giving the books the appearance of age. Jones put the volumes, with their yellowed pages, into circulation through underworld channels. For books that had cost him about a dollar to produce he received twenty-five dollars.

In his spare time at night, while Jones was busy at the Dill Pickle Club, Hymie turned his talent to engravings of United States currency. He turned out some pretty good counterfeits. He also agreed to do all my printing and engraving. He made fake letterheads, stock certificates, letters of credit, calling cards, and any other documents I needed.

Now he made a cut that showed me as the famous mining engineer, copied the rest of the article, printed the requisite pages and rebound the magazines. Even an expert would not have known the magazine wasn't exactly as it had been published. These magazines were destined to play a big part in my future activities. Who could resist the advice of the $100,000-a-year mining wizard who had taken copper from a worthless mine in Chile?

I was never so crude as to call anybody's attention to the magazine. As soon as I had picked out the victim, I sent on a couple of men with a copy of the faked magazine. These men called at the town's public library and asked for the file of *McClure's*. They removed the issue containing the Pope Yateman story and substituted the one containing my faked photograph.

Later on I started my negotiations with the victim in the role of Pope Yateman. After some preliminary talks I would mention that I had other matters to attend to and left the victim in the hands of Deacon Buckminster, who had been introduced as my secretary, Mr. Kimball.

"Did you read the article about Mr. Yateman in *McClure's*?" Buck would ask in a casual manner.

"Why, no, I don't believe I did," the victim usually replied. "Do you have a copy of it?"

"No, I don't," Buck would say. "But I'm sure you can find it in the public library if you're interested."

Naturally the victim was interested. As soon as he had read this success story and had seen my picture in a magazine on file in the library of his own town he had no doubts at all about my identity. More important, he had new respect for my business acumen. As soon as we had made certain he had read the magazine, my stooges called again at the public library and used their sleight-of-hand to remove the faked magazine and return the original. You can imagine the victim's amazement, after being swindled, to go to the library and look up that article only to find that the picture did not resemble me at all!

A variation of this scheme I used later when Franz von Papen became German ambassador to the United States. I purchased 200 copies of a Sunday issue of the Washington *Post*. They were turned over to Hymie with an article I had written, a photograph of von Papen, and photographs of Buckminster and myself. Hymie had to duplicate the first and last sheets of the main news section in order to get the article in. Prominently displayed was the picture of von Papen, flanked on one side by Buckminster and on the other by me. The article told of the two plenipotentiaries who had accompanied von Papen to America. Their mission was to purchase industrial and mining property for German capitalists and for the German government.

I always carried a copy of this paper in my bag. If I had a victim in tow, I would manage, while removing something from the handbag, to let the paper fall out. The victim would see the spread and would be properly impressed.

"May I have a copy of that?" he would ask.

"I'm sorry," I would reply, "but this is the only copy I have with me. But I shall be happy to send you a copy as soon as I get back to Washington."

The reason for this procedure was that I made it a rule never to let any documentary evidence get out of my hands. Though I displayed thousands of fake letters, documents, stock certificates, etc., to prospective victims, I was always careful to recover them. . . .

As the years passed and we gained experience in the stock swindle other props were added. These included fake letters from J. P. Morgan, Walter C. Teagle, and numerous other big figures in the financial world.

I bought a supply of postage stamps of various foreign countries. By writing letters of inquiry to hotels or firms in large cities all over the world I had a sample not only of their stationery but a specimen postmark as well. I had postmarking outfits made for all the larger cities of the world. They had loose dates that could be changed at will.

Props played a big part in my success in selling fake stocks. We usually heard of a brokerage house that was moving or going out of business and rented the quarters completely furnished. With the furnishings all in, all we had to do was hire a few girls to look busy. Generally they were students from a business college who needed typing practice so they copied names from the telephone directories.

One of the most impressive layouts I ever used was in Muncie, Indiana. I learned that the Merchants National Bank had moved to new quarters. I rented the old building, which was complete with all the necessary furnishings and fixtures for a banking venture.

For a week before I was ready to take my victim in, I had my stooges call at the new Merchants Bank. Each time they went in they secretly carried away a small quantity of deposit slips, counter checks, savings withdrawal slips, and other forms used by the bank. In that manner we acquired an ample supply to spread over our counters.

I bought as many money bags as I could find, but couldn't get enough. So I had the name of the bank stenciled on fifty salt bags. The money bags, together with large stacks of boodle and some genuine silver, were stacked in the cages of our paying and receiving "tellers."

When I brought the victim in and asked to see the president of the bank we were told we would have to wait. We waited an hour during which the place bustled with activity. People would come in to patronize the bank. Most of these were girls from the local bawdy houses, interspersed with denizens of the underworld—gamblers, thugs, touts. There was a steady stream, and the bank appeared to be thriving. Occasionally a uniformed messenger came in with a money bag. These messengers were streetcar conductors off duty. They wore their regular uniforms but left the badges off their caps. The victim never suspected a thing. Fully convinced that he was in a big active bank, he relied on the president's reference, went into the stock deal with me and ultimately lost $50,000.

I have used banks many times to convince victims of the soundness of my schemes.

Leach and Company was a large brokerage house in Youngstown, Ohio. It had a national reputation. Near by was a bank, one of the largest in Ohio. One day I went in and asked to see the president. I was shown into his private office, a spacious room with a high, paneled ceiling and expensive mahogany furnishings. I told the president I had come to Youngstown to purchase one of the steel mills. (I rather favored the Youngstown Sheet and Tube Company.) I asked his advice, and he said he thought it couldn't go wrong.

"I hope you'll remember this bank when your deal has been completed," he smiled.

"I certainly shall. By the way," I said, "do you happen to have a spare office here in the bank where I might carry on our negotiations? Any room not in use will do."

"I have an excellent place," he replied. "My own office. Any time you want to hold a conference, bring your people in here. I'll get out and you can have complete privacy."

"That is very kind of you," I said. "I'll probably take advantage of your offer within the next two or three days."

Two days later, when I had brought my victim to Youngstown, I called the bank president and asked for the use of his office at 10 A.M. He assured me that it would be available and unoccupied.

I told my victim that we were going to see Mr. Leach, the owner of Leach and Company, who was also interested in buying the stock. When we entered the big office of Leach and Company, I addressed a man in shirt sleeves who stood near one of the counters. (He was my stooge, planted there for the purpose.)

"Can you tell me where we'll find Mr. Leach?" I inquired.

"See that big bank across the street? Well, that's where he spends most of his time. He's the president of that bank."

We went across the street and entered the bank. Near the door a well-dressed man without hat or topcoat walked idly about. He was another stooge.

"Do you have a Mr. Leach here?" I asked.

"We certainly do," the stooge replied. "That's his office over there." He pointed across the room to the door marked PRESIDENT. "There's Mr. Leach now, going towards his office."

The man walking across the floor was our Jimmy Head. He was well dressed and had a dignified bearing. We hurried across the room and caught up with him just as he reached the office door.

"Mr. Leach," I said, "I'm Dr. Weed—Dr. Walter H. Weed. I've come to talk to you about some mining stock I believe you're interested in."

"Ah, yes, Dr. Weed. I've heard a great deal about you. Won't you step into my office where we can talk in private?"

He opened the door and we went in. I led the way, followed by the victim. The room was unoccupied. Jimmy Head had never before seen the inside of this office. But he sat down at the broad desk of the bank president as though he had grown up in these surroundings. We began to discuss the stock deal and remained in the office for about half an hour. Nobody bothered us. By the time we were ready to go, the victim was firmly convinced he was dealing with the biggest banker in Youngstown. Head shook hands with us and saw us to the door. He, too, left as soon as we were out of sight.

A Talk with the Yellow Kid

by Saul Bellow

"I HAVE ALWAYS affected a pearl stickpin upon my neckwear," says Yellow Kid Weil. The Kid, who is now in his eighties, is an elegant and old-fashioned gentleman; he likes round phrases and leisurely speech. One of the greatest confidence men of his day, he has publicly forsworn crime and announced his retirement. A daughter of his in Florida urges him to pass his remaining years with her, but he prefers Chicago. He will tell you that he knows of no better place, and he has lived in many places. Chicago is his city.

As we stood talking in the lobby of the Sun-Times Building not long ago, a young photographer came running up to the famous criminal, threw an arm about his narrow old shoulders, and said affectionately, "Hi' ya, Kid. Kid, how's it goin'?" At such moments his bearded old face is lit with a smile of deepest pleasure, and looks of modesty and of slyness also steal over it. Bartenders, waitresses, reporters know him. The vanishing race of old intellectuals in the neighborhood of Bughouse Square respects him. Real-estate men, lawyers, even judges and bankers will sometimes greet him. Why should he live elsewhere? He was born in Chicago, his career began there.

It was Bathhouse John Coughlin, Chicago's primitive alderman and illustrious boss, who named him the Yellow Kid. Bathhouse had started out in life as a masseur in the old Brevoort Hotel. When he attained great power he was not too proud to talk to a young fellow like Joe Weil, as the Kid was then known. Weil came often to Coughlin's saloon. An early comic strip called "Hogan's Alley and the Yellow Kid" was then appearing in the New York *Journal*, to which Coughlin subscribed. Weil followed it passionately and Bathhouse John saved the papers for him. "Why, you're the Kid himself," Coughlin said one day, and so Weil acquired the name.

The Kid is now very frail, and it becomes him. His beard very much resembles the one that the late Senator James Hamilton Lewis, a great dandy, used to wear. It is short, parted in the middle, and combed into two rounded portions, white and stiff. Underneath, the Kid's chin is visible, an old man's chin. You think you have met with a happy old quack, a small-time charlatan who likes to reminisce about the wickedness of his past, until you become aware of the thin, forceful, sharp mouth under the trembling hairs of old age. It is the mouth of a masterful man.

He must once have been very imposing. Now there is a sort of fallen nattiness about him. His shoes are beautifully shined, though not in the best of condition. His suit is made of a bold material; it has gone too often to the cleaner, but it is in excellent press. His shirt must belong to the days of his prosperity, for his neck has shrunk and the collar fits loosely. It has a green pattern of squares within squares. Tie and pocket handkerchief are of a matching green. His little face is clear and animated. Long practice in insincerity gives him an advantage; it is not always easy to know when he is being straightforward.

By his swindles he made millions of dollars, but he lost as many fortunes as he made, and he lost them always in legitimate enterprises. It is one of his favorite ironies and he often returns to it. His wife was forever urging him to go straight. He loved her, he still speaks touchingly of her, and for her sake he wanted to reform. It never worked. There was a curse on any honest business that he tried, whether it was giving pianos away as a coffee premium or leasing the Hagenbeck-Wallace circus. The voice of fate seemed to warn him to stay crooked, and he did not ignore it.

The years have not softened his heart toward the victims of his confidence schemes. Of course he was a crook, but the "marks" whom he and his associates trimmed were not honest men. "I have never cheated any honest men," he says, "only rascals. They may have been respectable but they were never any good." And this is how he sums the matter up: "They wanted something for nothing. I gave them nothing for something." He says it clearly and sternly; he is not a pitying man. To be sure, he wants to justify his crimes, but quite apart from this he believes that honest men do not exist. He presents himself as a Diogenes whose lifelong daylight quest for absolute honesty has ended in disappointment. Actually, he never expected to find it.

He is a thinker, the Kid is, and a reader. His favorite authors seem to be Nietzsche and Herbert Spencer. Spencer has always been the favorite of autodidactic Midwestern philosophers, that vanishing species. During the 1920's the Kid belonged to a Bohemian discussion group on the Near North Side called the Dill Pickle Club. Its brainy and colorful eccentrics, poets, painters, and cranks have long been dispersed by adverse winds. Once Chicago promised to become a second London, but it was not to be; bowling alleys and bars increased, bookshops did not. New York and Hollywood took away the artists. Death did the rest. Herbert Spencer also was destined for the dustbin.

But the Kid is still faithful to him; he spends his evenings at his books—so at least he says—meditating upon the laws of society, the sanctioned and the unsanctioned, power and weakness, justice and history. I do not think the Kid loves the weak, and he dislikes many of the strong, especially politicians and bankers. Against bankers he has a strong prejudice. "They are almost always shady," he says. "Their activities are usually only just within the law."

The twilight borderlands of legality attract the Kid's subtle mind. Not long ago he was picked up in the lobby of the Bismarck Hotel on suspicion. He had merely been chatting with one of the guests, he told me, but the manager was worried and phoned the confidence squad. The Kid is used to these small injustices and they do not offend him or disturb his tranquillity. In court he listened attentively to the case preceding his own, that of a bookie.

"Why should this man be fined and punished?" said the Kid when his turn came at the bar. "Why should he be punished for betting when betting is permitted within the confines of the track itself?" The judge, to hear the Kid tell it, was very uneasy. He answered that the state derived revenues from the track. "I would gladly pay revenues to the state," the Kid said, "if I could rent a building within which confidence games would be legal. Suppose the state were to license me. Then confidence men operating outside my building could be arrested and imprisoned.

Inside the door licensed operatives would be safe. It makes the same kind of sense, Your Honor." According to the Kid, the judge could make no cogent reply.

Perhaps the Kid's antagonism toward bankers rests on an undivulged belief that he would have made a more impressive banker than any of them. In his swindles, he often enough pretended to be one. . . .

At one time the Kid was actually the legitimate officer of a bank, the American State Bank on South LaSalle Street in Chicago. He and Big John Worthington, a confidence man who closely resembled J. Pierpont Morgan, together paid some seventy thousand dollars and obtained controlling interest. The Kid became a vice-president. He started a racket in phony letters of credit by which he made about three hundred thousand dollars. He was not caught. . . .

Sometimes the Kid posed as a doctor, sometimes as a mining engineer or as a financial representative of the Central Powers, a professor or a geologist. He put magazines and books into circulation from which original photographs were removed and pictures of himself inserted. All his life long he sold nonexistent property, concessions he did not own, and air-spun schemes to greedy men.

The Kid's activities landed him in jail now and then—he has served time in Atlanta and Leavenworth—but he says, and not unbelievably, that he did not have many dull days. His total gains are estimated by "the police and the daily press" at about eight millions. Most of this money he lost on his bad investments or squandered in high living. He loved wild parties, show girls, champagne suppers, European trips. He had his clothes made in Bond Street or Jermyn Street. This English wardrobe is still good; real quality doesn't go out of fashion. But almost everything else is gone.

"Before I reached the years of maturity," the Kid said, "I fell in love with a young woman of the most extraordinary pulchritude. I brought her home one night to dinner. My mother," he said with a bluster of his whiskers and looking gravely at me with the thin diffused blue of his eyes, "was renowned for her perfection in the culinary art. We had a splendid meal and later my mother said to me, 'Joseph, that is a most beautiful young woman. She is so lovely that she cannot be meant for you. She must have been meant for some millionaire.' From that moment I determined that I too would be a millionaire. And I was." The sexual incentive to be rich, the Kid told me, was always very powerful with him.

"I was of a very fragile constitution, unfit for the heavier sort of manual labor. I knew I could not toil like other men. How was I to live? My power lay in words. In words I became a commander. Moreover, I could not lead a tame life of monotony. I needed excitement, variety, danger, intellectual stimulus.

"I was a psychologist," he went on. "My domain was the human mind. A Chinese scholar with whom I once studied told me, 'People always see themselves in you.' With this understanding I entered the lives of my dupes. The man who lives by an idea enjoys great superiority over those who live by none. To make money is not an idea; that doesn't count. I mean a real idea. It was very simple. My purpose was invisible. When they looked at me they saw themselves. I only showed them their own purpose."

There are no longer such operators, says the great confidence man, perhaps jealous of his eminence. Where are they to come from? The great mass of mankind breeds obedient types. They express their protests in acts of violence, not ingeniously. Moreover, your natural or talented confidence man is attracted to politics. Why be a criminal, a fugitive, when you can get society to give you the key to the vaults where the greatest boodle lies? The United States government, according to the Kid, runs the greatest giveaway program in history.

The Kid at one time tried to form a little independent republic upon a small island made of fill, somewhere in Lake Michigan. His object was to make himself eligible under the foreign-aid program.

A public figure, something of a famous man, a dandy and a philosopher, the Kid says that he now frequently does good works. But the confidence squad still keeps an eye on him. Not so long ago he was walking down the street with a certain Monsignor, he tells me. They were discussing a fund drive in the parish. Presently the con squad drew alongside and one of the detectives said, "What you up to, Kid?"

"I'm just helping out the Monsignor here. It's on the level."

The Monsignor assured him that this was true.

The detective turned on him. "Why, you so-and-so," he said. "Aren't you ashamed to be wearin' the cloth for a swindle?"

The thought so enraged him that he took them both to headquarters.

The Kid laughed quietly and long over this morifying error; wrinkled, bearded, wry, and delighted, he looked at this moment like one of the devil's party.

"They refuse to believe I have reformed," he said. The psychology of a policeman, according to the Kid, is strict, narrow, and primitive. It denies that character is capable of change.

So much for the police, in their ancient office of criminal supervision. But what about the criminals? The Kid did not think much of criminal intelligence either. And what does the underworld think of confidence men? I asked. Gangsters and thieves greatly dislike them, he said. They never trust them and in some cases they take a peculiar and moral view of the confidence swindler. He is too mental a type for them.

"The attitude of the baser sort of criminal toward me is very interesting," he said. "They have always either shunned me or behaved with extreme coldness to me. I never will forget a discussion I once had with a second-story man about our respective relations to our victims. He thought me guilty of the highest immorality. Worst of all, in his eyes, was the fact that I openly showed myself to people in the light of the day. "Why" he said to me with an indescribable demeanor, 'you go right up to them. *They see your face*!' This seemed to him the worst of all deceits. Such is their scheme of ethics," said the Kid. "In their view you should sneak up on people and burglarize them, but to look them in the eyes, gain their confidence, that is impure."

We parted on noisy Wacker Drive, near the Clark Street Bridge. No longer listening to the Kid, I heard the voice of the city. Chicago keeps changing and amazes its old-timers. The streetcars, for instance, are different. You no longer see the hard, wicked-looking red, cumbrous, cow-like, trampling giant streetcars. The new ones are green and whir by like mayflies. glittering and making soft electrical sounds, one passed the Kid as he walked toward the Loop. Spruce and firm-footed, with his beard and wind-curled hat, he looked, beside the car, like the living figure of tradition in the city.

The Merry Antics of Izzy and Moe

by Herbert Asbury

PROHIBITION WENT INTO effect throughout the United States on January 16, 1920, and the country settled back with an air of "Well, *that's* settled." There had been a liquor problem. But a Law had been passed. Naturally, there was no longer a liquor problem. . . .

The Anti-Saloon League estimated that prohibition could be enforced for less than $5,000,000 a year, so eager were the people to enter the shining gates of the dry Utopia. Congress appropriated a little more than that amount, enough to set up an enforcement organization and to provide about 1,500 prohibition agents. These noble snoopers, paid an average of about $2,000 a year and hence immune to temptation, were supposed to keep 125,000,000 people from manufacturing or drinking anything stronger than near-beer. They didn't, but two of them made a spectacular try.

In a $14-a-month flat on Ridge Street, in New York's lower East Side, lived a bulbous little man named Isadore Einstein, whom everyone called Izzy. He had been a salesman, both inside and on the road, but was now a minor clerk at Station K of the New York Post Office. It required very shrewd management to feed, house, and clothe his family—his wife and four children and his father—on the meager salary of a postal employee. He was looking for something better, and decided that he had found it when he read in his newspaper about the government's plans to pay enforcement agents up to $2,500 a year.

But James Shevlin, Chief Enforcement Agent for the Southern District of New York, was not enthusiastic about Izzy. "I must say, Mr. Einstein," he said, "you don't look much like a detective." And that was the truth. Probably no one ever looked less like a detective than Izzy Einstein. He was forty years old, almost bald, five feet and five inches tall, and weighed 225 pounds. Most of this poundage was around his middle, so that when he walked his noble paunch, gently wobbling, moved majestically ahead like the breast of an overfed pouter pigeon.

But Izzy was accomplished. Besides English and Yiddish, he spoke German, Polish, and Hungarian fluently, and could make headway, though haltingly, in French, Italian, and Russian. He had even picked up a few words and phrases of Chinese. Moreover, Izzy had a knack of getting along with people and inspiring confidence. No one, looking at his round, jolly face and twinkling black eyes, could believe that he was a government snooper. Down on the lower East Side in New York he was the neighborhood cutup; whenever he dropped into the corner cigar stores and the coffeehouses his witticisms and high spirits never failed to draw an appreciative crowd.

"I guess Mr. Shevlin never saw a type like me," Izzy said afterward. "Maybe I fascinated him or something. Anyhow, I sold him on the idea that this prohibition business needed a new type of people that couldn't be spotted so easy."

Whatever the reason, Izzy got the job.

"But I must warn you," said Shevlin, "that hunting down liquor sellers isn't exactly a safe line of work. Some law violator might get mad and try to crack a bottle over your head."

"Bottles," said Izzy, "I can dodge."

Izzy's first assignment was to clean up a place in Brooklyn which the enforcement authorities shrewdly suspected housed a speakeasy, since drunken men had been seen staggering from the building, and the air for half a block around was redolent with the fumes of beer and whiskey. Several agents had snooped and slunk around the house; one had watched all one afternoon from a roof across the street, and another had hidden for hours in an adjoining doorway, obtaining an accurate count of the number of men who entered and left. But none had been able to get inside. Izzy knew nothing of sleuthing procedures; he simply walked up to the joint and knocked on the door. A peephole was opened, and a hoarse voice demanded to know who was there.

"Izzy Einstein," said Izzy. "I want a drink."

"Oh, yeah? Who sent you here, bud? What's your business?"

"My boss sent me," Izzy explained. "I'm a prohibition agent. I just got appointed."

The door swung open and the doorman slapped Izzy jovially on the back.

"Ho! ho!" he cried. "Come right in, bud. That's the best gag I've heard yet."

Izzy stepped into a room where half a dozen men were drinking at a small, makeshift bar.

"Hey, boss!" the doorman yelled. "Here's a prohibition agent wants a drink! You got a badge, too, bud?"

"Sure I have," said Izzy, and produced it.

"Well, I'll be damned," said the man behind the bar. "Looks just like the real thing."

He poured a slug of whiskey, and Izzy downed it. That was a mistake, for when the time came to make the pinch Izzy had no evidence. He tried to grab the bottle but the bartender ran out the back door with it.

"I learned right there," said Izzy, "that a slug of hooch in an agent's belly might feel good, but it ain't evidence."

So when he went home that night he rigged up an evidence-collector. He put a small funnel in the upper left-hand pocket of his vest, and connected it, by means of a rubber tube, with a flat bottle concealed in the lining of the garment. Thereafter, when a drink was served to him, Izzy took a small sip, then poured the remainder into the funnel while the bartender was making change. The bottle wouldn't hold much, but there was always enough for analysis and to offer in evidence. "I'd have died if it hadn't been for that little funnel and the bottle," said Izzy. "And most of the stuff I got in those places was terrible."

Izzy used his original device of giving his real name, with some variation, more than twenty times during the next five years. It was successful even after he became so well known, and so greatly feared, that his picture hung behind the bar in many speakeasies, that all might see and be warned. Occasionally Izzy would prance into a gin-mill with his badge pinned to his lapel, in plain sight, and shout jovially, "How about a drink for a hard-working prohibition agent?" Seeing the round little man trying so hard to be funny, everyone in the place would rush forward to hand him something alcoholic, and Izzy would arrest them and close the joint.

Once he went into a gin-mill where three huge portraits of himself, framed in what he described as "black, creepy crape," ornamented the back bar. He asked for a drink, and the bartender refused to serve it.

"I don't know you," he said.

"Why," said Izzy, laughing. "I'm Izzy Epstein, the famous prohibition detective."

"Get the name right, bud," growled the bartender. "The bum's name is Einstein."

"Epstein," said Izzy. "Don't I know my own name?"

"Maybe you do, but the low-life you're trying to act like is named Einstein. E-i-n-s-t-e-i-n."

"Brother," said Izzy, "I ain't never wrong about a name. It's Epstein."

"Einstein!" roared the bartender.

"Epstein!" shouted Izzy.

"You're nuts!" yelled the bartender, furiously. "I'll bet you anything you want it's Einstein!"

"Okay," said Izzy. "I'll bet you the drinks."

The bartender called his other customers, and after much argument and pointing to Izzy's pictures, they agreed that the name was Einstein. So Izzy—or rather the government—had to buy nine drinks, and the bartender served them, and shortly after went to jail.

After Izzy had been an enforcement agent for a few weeks, he began to miss his old friend Moe Smith, with whom he had spent many pleasant evenings in the East Side coffeehouses. Like Izzy, Moe was a natural comedian, and, also like Izzy, he was corpulent. He tipped the scales at about 235 pounds, but he was a couple of inches taller than Izzy and didn't look quite so roly-poly. Moe had been a cigar salesman, and manager of a small fight club at Orchard and Grand Streets, New York City, and had invested his savings in a little cigar store, where he was doing well. Izzy persuaded him to be a relative in charge of the store, and to apply for a job as enforcement agent.

As soon as Moe was sworn in as an agent, he and Izzy teamed up together, and most of the time thereafter worked as a pair. Their first assignment took them to Rockaway Beach, near New York, where they confiscated a still and arrested the operator. This man apparently took a great liking to Izzy, for after he got out of jail he made several trips to New York especially to urge Izzy to go on a fishing trip with him.

"I'll take you three miles out to sea," he said. "You'll have quite a time."

But Izzy firmly declined the invitation. "Sure he'll take me out to sea," he said, "but will he bring me back? He could leave me with the fishes."

In those early days of the noble experiment everything that happened in connection with prohibition was news, and some of New York's best reporters covered enforcement headquarters. Casting about for a way to enliven their stories and provide exercise for their imaginations, they seized upon the exploits of Izzy and Moe. The two fat and indefatigable agents supplied human-interest material by the yard; moreover, they were extraordinarily co-operative. They frequently scheduled their raids to suit the convenience of the reporters and the newspaper photographers, and soon learned that there was more room in the papers on Monday morning than on any other day of the week. One Sunday, accompanied by a swarm of eager reporters, they established a record by making seventy-one raids in a little more than twelve hours. . . .

Hundreds of stories, a great many of them truthful, were written about Izzy and Moe and their grotesque adventures, and they probably made the front pages oftener than any other personages of their time except the President and the Prince of Wales. . . .

What the newspapers enjoyed most about Izzy and Moe was their ingenuity. Once they went after a speakeasy where half a dozen dry agents had tried without success to buy a drink. The bartender positively wouldn't sell to anyone he didn't know. So on a cold winter night Izzy stood in front of the gin-mill, in his shirt sleeves, until he was red and shivering and his teeth were chattering. Then Moe half-carried him into the speakeasy, shouting excitedly:

"Give this man a drink! He's just been bitten by a frost!"

The kindhearted bartender, startled by Moe's excitement and upset by Izzy's miserable appearance, rushed forward with a bottle of whiskey. Moe promptly snatched the bottle and put him under arrest.

One of Izzy's most brilliant ideas was always to carry something on his raids, the nature of the burden depending upon the character of the neighborhood and of a particular speakeasy's clientele. When he wanted to get into a place frequented by musicians, for example, he carried a violin or a trombone, and if, as sometimes happened, he was asked to play the instrument, he could do it. He usually played "How Dry I Am." On the East Side and in the poorer sections of the Bronx, if the weather permitted, Izzy went around in his shirt sleeves carrying a pitcher of milk, the very pattern of an honest man on his way home from the grocery. Once in Brooklyn he was admitted to half a dozen gin-mills because he was lugging a big pail of dill pickles. "A fat man with pickles!" said Izzy. "Who'd ever think a fat man with pickles was an agent?"

"When Izzy operated on the beaches around New York he always carried a fishing rod or a bathing suit; he had great success one day at Sheepshead Bay with a string of fish slung over his shoulder. The doorman of the Assembly, a café in Brooklyn which catered to judges and lawyers, let him in without question because he wore a frock coat and carried a huge tome bound in sheepskin. Once inside, Izzy opened his book and adjusted a pair of horn-rimmed spectacles and, with lips moving and brow furrowed, marched with stately tread across the room and barged into the bar. Without lifting his eyes from the book, he called sonorously for "a beverage, please," and the fascinated bartender poured a slug of whiskey before he realized what he was doing. When Izzy and Moe visited Reisenweber's, a famous and expensive resort on Broadway, they carried two lovely blondes and wore "full-dress tuxedos," with rings on their fingers, sweet-smelling pomade on their hair, and huge imitation-pearl studs in their shirt fronts. The headwaiter asked them for references when they ordered liquor, and Izzy searched his pockets and pulled out the first card he found. It happened to be the card of a rabbi, with which Izzy planned to ensnare a sacramental-wine store. But the headwaiter, a man of scant perception, bowed deferentially and sold them a bottle of whiskey. "He deserved to be arrested," said Izzy, indignantly. "Imagine! A rabbi with a blonde and no beard!"

Up in Van Cortlandt Park, in New York City, near the public playing fields, was a soft-drink establishment which was suspected of being one of the retail outlets of a big rum ring. Many complaints were made to enforcement headquarters that customers had become tipsy after a few shots of the soda water sold in the place; one woman wrote that by mistake her milk shake had been filled with gin. Bad gin, too, she added. The job of getting the evidence was given to Izzy. It proved a difficult task, for the owner of the joint would sell liquor to no one he didn't know personally. So on a Saturday afternoon in November Izzy assembled a group of half a dozen dry agents, clad them in football uniforms, and smeared their arms and faces with fresh dirt. Then Izzy tucked a football under his arm, hung a helmet over his ears, and led them whooping and rah-rahing into the suspected speakeasy, where they shouted that they had just won the last game of the season and wanted to break training in a big way. The speakeasy owner, pleased at such a rush of business, sold each agent a pint of whiskey. "Have fun, boys," he said. "The same to you," said Izzy, handing him a summons.

Flushed with this striking success, which showed that at heart he was a college boy, Izzy went to Ithaca, N.Y., to investigate a complaint by officials of Cornell University that some soda fountains near the campus were not confining their sales to pop. Izzy disguised himself as an undergraduate by putting on a little cap and a pair of white linen knickers, not so little, and for several days strolled about the campus. He hummed snatches of Cornell songs which he had learned, and played safe by addressing everyone with a mustache as "Professor," and everyone with a beard as "Dean." Having located the soda fountains which sold liquor, he dashed into them one by one, establishing himself as a student by shouting, "Sizzle Boom! Sizzle Boom! Rah! Rah! Rah!" The speakeasy boys thought he was a comedian, which indeed he was, and they gladly sold him all the booze he wanted, after which he went from place to place distributing "diplomas," or summonses.

From Cornell, and without the blessing of the student body, Izzy rushed into Harlem to investigate a complaint about a grocery store. . . . Izzy disguised himself as a Negro, with his face blackened by burnt cork and a rich Southern accent rolling off his tongue. He visited the store and awaited his turn in a long line of impatient customers. He found that to buy a half-pint of whiskey (four dollars) a customer asked for a can of beans. If he wanted gin (two dollars) he asked for tomatoes. Izzy bought both beans and tomatoes and came back next day with a warrant and a truck. Besides the groceryman, he hauled away four hundred bottles of gin, some empty cans, a canning machine, three barrels of whiskey, and a barrel of pickles which contained one hundred small bottles of gin. . . .

The trail of illegal liquor led Izzy and Moe into some mighty queer places, but they followed wherever it led, and were always ready with the appropriate disguise. Dressed as a longshoreman, Izzy captured an Italian who used his cash register as a cellarette; its drawers were filled with little bottles of booze. In the guise of a mendicant, Izzy pawned an old pair of pants for two dollars in Brooklyn, and snooping about the pawnshops a bit found ten thousand dollars' worth of good liquor wrapped in clothing that had been left as pledges. He got into the Half Past Nine Club, on Eighth Avenue, as a prosperous poultry salesman, playing tipsy and carrying a sample, and found a large stock of liquor in a stuffed grizzly bear. . . .

For more than five years the whole country laughed at the antics of Izzy and Moe, with the exception of the ardent drys, who thought the boys were wonderful, and the bootleggers and speakeasy proprietors, who thought they were crazy and feared them mightily. And their fear was justified, for in their comparatively brief career Izzy and Moe confiscated 5,000,000 bottles of booze, worth $15,000,000, besides thousands of gallons in kegs and barrels and hundreds of stills and breweries. They smashed an enormous quantity of saloon fixtures and equipment, and made 4,392 arrests, of which more than 95 per cent resulted in convictions. No other two agents even approached this record. . . .

Izzy and Moe made many spectacular raids in Chicago, Detroit, and other cities ruled by the gangsters and the beer barons, but they never encountered Al Capone, Johnny Torrio, Frankie Yale, or any of the other great hoodlums who were the real beneficiaries of the Eighteenth Amendment. If they had, there is little doubt that they would have taken the triggermen in their stride, for neither Izzy nor Moe lacked courage. Izzy didn't approve of guns, and never carried one. Moe lugged a revolver around occasionally, but in five years fired it only twice. Once he shot out a lock that had resisted his efforts, and another time he shot a hole in a keg of whiskey. Izzy said later that guns were pulled on him only twice. The first time was on Dock Street, in Yonkers, N.Y., where he had spent a pleasant and profitable evening with raids on five speakeasies. To make it an even half dozen, he stepped into a sixth place that looked suspicious, bought a slug of whiskey for sixty cents, and poured it into the funnel in his vest pocket. While he was arresting the bartender, the owner of the joint came into the bar from another part of the house.

"He pulled an automatic from behind the bar," wrote Izzy. "She clicked but the trigger jammed. It was aimed right at my heart. I didn't like that. I grabbed his arm and he and I had a fierce fight all over the bar, till finally I got the pistol. I don't mind telling you I was afraid, particularly when I found the gun was loaded."

On another occasion an angry bartender shoved a revolver against

Izzy's stomach. But Izzy didn't bat an eye; he calmly shoved the gun aside.

"Put that up, son," he said, soothingly. "Murdering me won't help your family."

Fortunately, the bartender had a family, and Izzy's warning brought to his mind a vision of his fatherless children weeping at the knee of their widowed mother, who was also weeping. He stopped to think. While he was thinking, Moe knocked him cold. . . .

During the summer of 1925 the almost continual stories about Izzy and Moe in the newspapers got on the nerves of high prohibition enforcement officials in Washington, few of whom ever got mentioned in the papers at all. National headquarters announced that any agent whose name appeared in print in connection with his work would be suspended, and perhaps otherwise punished, on the ground that publicity brought discredit to the service. At the same time a high official called Izzy to Washington and spoke to him rather severely. "You get your name in the newspaper all the time, and in the headlines, too," he complained, "whereas mine is hardly ever mentioned. I must ask you to remember that you are merely a subordinate, not the whole show." For a while Izzy really tried to keep away from the reporters and out of the papers, but both he and Moe had become public personages, and it was impossible to keep the newspapermen from writing about them. When they refused to tell what they had done, the reporters invented stories about them, so a stream of angry denials and protests continued to come from Washington.

Finally, on November 13, 1925, it was announced that Izzy and Moe had turned in their gold badges and were no longer prohibition agents. Izzy's story was that he had been told he was to be transferred to Chicago. He had lived in New York since he was fifteen years old, and had no intention of ever living anywhere else, so he refused to go, and "thereby fired myself." Government officials, however, said that Izzy and Moe had been dismissed "for the good of the service." . . .

Both Izzy and Moe went into the insurance business, and did well. They dropped out of the public eye, and remained out except for an occasional Sunday feature story, and a brief flurry of publicity in 1928, when Izzy went to Europe and returned with some entertaining accounts of his adventures.

The Spanish Prisoner, the Beautiful Señorita and *You*

by Rufus Jarman

THIS MORNING — AS on any given day — a thousand or so business or professional people in this country found in their mail a mysterious letter that had arrived by air from Mexico. In twenty-three lines of typescript, it promised a chance to participate in some high adventure and romance, like Anthony Adverse or Scaramouche.

It is surprising how many good, solid Americans have secret ambitions to act like Captain Blood or Sir Lancelot, and rescue fair maidens from dark towers. Not a fortnight goes by but some good citizen, who has received one of these alluring missives from Mexico, will heed the call, load himself down with cash and go questing adventure in an unknown land — generally with ridiculous results.

The letters always promise several exciting prospects: a journey south of the border; adventure in shadowed streets, shuttered cafés and picturesque patios; intrigue revolving around an unfortunate prisoner in a fortresslike stronghold; a fortune in hidden money and the enchanting opportunity to rescue and protect a fair *señorita*, who is always beautiful and always eighteen years old.

There is only one serious weakness in this lovely dream — to wit, the whole proposition is a fake. The prisoner, the fortune and the beautiful *señorita* are all as unreal as the imaginary kingdom of Graustark or the illusive castle in Spain. In fact, the proposition is known as the Spanish-Prisoner Swindle or the Spanish Trunk Racket, or, to the Mexicans themselves, as *El Timo del Baúl*.

This ancient come-on—it has been operating now for about 368 years—is so fantastic, shallow and crude that it should be an obvious mess of malarkey to almost anybody. But, according to the United States Post Office Inspection Service, the old Spanish-Prisoner Swindle is just as effective today as it was in the time of Philip II of Spain and Sir Francis Drake. Chief Post Office Inspector Clifton C. Garner says it has been estimated that United States citizens lose annually at least $600,000—and probably much more—to the mythical prisoner languishing in romantic Mexico.

The racket appeals mostly to persons unusually gullible or tender-hearted or who are particularly bored by the lack of romance in their lives. Some of them, even while halfway recognizing it as a fraud, try to make themselves believe in it, anyway.

Not long ago, a small-town Midwestern minister brought the post-office inspectors in Omaha some Spanish-prisoner letters he had received. He suspected fraud, and the post-office men assured him that that was exactly what it was, showing him case reports of a dozen people. Through believing in letters exactly like his, they had lost their savings and some had their lives threatened by Mexican picaroons.

The minister thanked the inspectors, gathered up his swindle letters and prepared to depart. The inspectors, asked him to leave the letters with them for evidence, in case any of the swindlers were brought to trial.

"No," the preacher replied. "I think I'll take them along with me. There just might be something in it, you know."

The venerable fraud works like this: The letter writer claims to be a Mexican banker recently jailed in connection with a bankruptcy case. Before his capture he had converted all available funds into United States dollars, hidden them in the false bottom of a trunk and checked it through to a customhouse in the United States. The trunk reached its destination, but the banker, accompanied by his "dear daughter," was arrested at the border. The two suitcases he carried were impounded. In secret compartments they contained the check stub necessary to get the trunk, the trunk key, also a certified check, usually in amounts of $25,000 to $35,000, and made payable to bearer.

The police did not discover the secret compartments, so the story goes, but impounded the suitcases. The banker was sentenced to three years in prison and fined. If the fine is not paid within forty-five days of his letter's date, the suitcases will be sold at auction. And so the key to the fortune concealed in the trunk will be lost. The amount of this phantom fortune is usually $450,000 nowadays. Ten years ago it was only about $285,000, but the treasure has kept pace with inflation.

The banker prisoner claims he got the name of the American, who receives his letter, from a friend of the American, who is his fellow prisoner. He can't give his friend's name in fear of "disgracing his family," but the banker prisoner proposes that the American business or professional man—doctors are prime favorites—come to Mexico City and pay his fine and court costs—generally just under $10,000. (It used to be around $4000, but inflation has affected that too.) This payment will not release the prisoner, but it will free his two suitcases with the hidden check stub to the treasure trunk and the $35,000 certified check.

The American is expected to cash the check and keep the $35,000 for his trouble and expenses. He is to retrieve the trunk from the United States customhouse, keep one third of the treasure—about $150,000—and turn the balance over to the prisoner's "dear daughter."

She, of course, is the "beautiful eighteen-year-old *señorita*." Sometimes she is referred to as "my poor daughter," "my orphaned daughter," "my unfortunate daughter," "my darling daughter," "my beautiful daughter," or "my beautiful, eighteen-year-old daughter," but just plain "dear daughter" is the most popular term. Now and then, the prisoner will send along a picture of his "dear daughter," which is always that of a sexy-looking babe, of a type some middle-aged businessmen are said to dream about.

If a photograph is sent, it is usually in a second letter, which gives the victim his travel instructions and details of the treasure. It is dispatched only after a potential victim has risen to the bait by answering the first, shorter letter that gives only general hints. First letters are broadcast by the thousands—10,000 to 15,000 every two or three weeks, post-office inspectors estimate. The swindlers learn through them who and where the suckers are.

Usually, every mailing from Mexico turns up several suckers, from Brooklyn to Podunk. They will send self-righteous but cautious replies stating that their humanitarian instincts have been stirred. The prospect of acquiring a large fortune is usually dismissed as quite secondary. A typical reply is this one from St. Louis:

> *Dear Sir:* In regards to your letter of July 22nd, I would like to state that I will be happy to be of help in any way that I can to yourself and, in particular, to your unfortunate daughter. I will, beyond all doubt, center my energies in this direction, as long as these efforts are legitimate and within the law and are in line with the general promotion of humanitarian causes, in the same way that I have helped many others who were in need.

The victim is directed to communicate with no one except the contact man, "because of the delicacy of the matter." He is told to write air mail in care of a "brother-in-law" of a "prison guard who is friendly to the prisoner," telling his time of arrival. The brother-in-law is the contact man with the friendly guard, who will arrange for the suitcase, with its valuable secret, to be released to the American.

The sucker usually flies down. He is met at the airport by the guard's brother-in-law, who escorts him to a hotel. Gradually, a whole cast of mysterious Mexicans, like characters in a Richard Harding Davis story, begin circulating about the American. He becomes more and more mystified, confused and, at last, frightened. There is a lot of lurking about dark street corners, whispered conferences by candlelight in dark cafés and the popping in and out of sundry sinister Mexicans, who act as though they had just contrived to blow up the Texas Rangers' headquarters and kidnap Zane Grey.

The American is spirited out several times to the prison, a grim, stone-walled bastion at the edge of the city. There the friendly guard sneaks out for short conferences now and then. He confides that the plan is proving more difficult than had been anticipated, for the judge is starting to get suspicious. (Of course, he is no real guard, just a member of the gang in a uniform.)

Finally, the guard breaks the frightening news that the judge has discovered the plot and an order is being issued for the American's arrest as a conspirator in springing a prisoner. Fortunately, however, the guard has managed to break the seals on the suitcases and retrieve the claim-check stub and the certified check.

By now the American is horribly frightened. He is generally glad to shove the $10,000 he has brought into the eager hands of the guard's brother-in-law, who, in turn, slips the American a check stub, a key and the certified check. The sucker flees across the border. He learns that the certified check is no good when he tries to cash it. The customhouse reveals that there is no trunk to match the check stub. And, of course, the "beautiful *señorita*" never makes an appearance. The victim goes sadly home. He generally keeps the entire humiliating experience a dark secret, if possible.

For all its crudities, the Spanish-Prisoner Swindle is "astonishingly successful," according to the Post Office Inspection Service. It is so successful, in fact, that from time to time the service distributes circulars to all banks in the country, urging them to bring the swindle to the attention of all persons who make unusually large withdrawals. The service also has printed warnings distributed by customs officials to all travelers headed toward Mexico and the other Latin-American countries.

These warnings are only partially successful. Often the suckers on their way to the Mexico City rendezvous are so excited that they haven't time to look over papers handed them at the border. Recently, a seventy-four-year-old Chicago man on such a mission didn't take time to relax until after he had paid his cash to the swindlers and was on his way home by train. It was then that he read, for the first time, the swindle warning that had been handed him when he entered Mexico.

There was the case early this year of a West Coast doctor, himself of Spanish descent, who fell for the swindle letter, borrowed $10,000 on real-estate holdings and prepared to embark for Mexico. He told his daughter what he intended to do, but paid no attention to her notion that it sounded fishy. The daughter told her fiancé, a young man named Elmer. He had seen the Spanish-prisoner warnings, and recognized the scheme right off, but he and the daughter were then afraid to tell papa. He is an old-Spanish-grandee type, who rules his family with an iron hand. The daughter was afraid to let him know she had told her friend. So the faithful Elmer sneaked off to the post office and told the inspectors. They managed to convince the doctor that the offer was a fraud. He abandoned the trip and canceled the mortgage. But he never was told how the post-office inspectors learned about his plan, and probably won't ever know—unless he happens to read this article.

Starting two or three years ago, the swindlers have been changing their routing instructions by telling victims to come via Havana rather than directly into Mexico. This is in the hope that United States customs officials at debarkation points for Cuba, where the swindle doesn't operate, will not be so diligent in handing out swindle warnings as those along the Mexican border.

An early victim by this new route was a sixty-eight-year-old Pennsylvania physician. "In my reply to the first letter," he later informed post-office men, "I said if it was straight, honest and aboveboard, I was willing to do anything in my power to help. But if it was crooked, I wanted nothing to do with it."

Apparently deciding that everything was aboveboard, the doctor borrowed $10,000 from his bank on some securities, and flew away to Havana, as instructed. From there he wired for further directions from his Mexico City pen pal, one Luis Olvera. The latter replied, in the best secret-agent style: "Documents have arrived here. Come immediately." The doctor boarded the next plane and went.

He was given the usual comic-opera, cloak-and-dagger treatment by the cast in Mexico City. This so upset and frightened him that, as he recalled afterward, "From the looks of these men, I knew they would stop at nothing. I did not know what to do. They asked if I had the money; I said yes. They insisted I give it to them, which I did. Besides my $9600, they made me pay an eleven-dollar taxi fare."

The doctor left with all speed for Nuevo Laredo, Mexico, by air. He crossed into Laredo, Texas, by car, happy to escape the Mexican authorities or the banditti, he wasn't exactly sure which. But somehow he still believed in the scheme. He phoned his son, a student in a Midwestern medical college, to meet him in Galveston to cash the certified check. The bank people gave them a look of bored pity.

Still believing, father and son proceeded to New Orleans to get the treasure-laden trunk from the customhouse. There was no trunk either. Whereupon the son went back to college and the father returned to his practice. All he got from his adventure was a bum bank draft for $25,000, which, he told post-office inspectors, he had put away in his safe-deposit box.

The Post Office Inspection Service is convinced that it hears of only a fraction of swindle victims. They are often so embarrassed that they would rather take their losses in silence.

Occasionally, a Spanish-prisoner-letter recipient will invite some friends to share. They will go down to Mexico City as a group and all get swindled together. Not long ago, after receiving a letter, an Alabama doctor borrowed $3000 on some vacant lots, and persuaded a businessman friend to come in for $6000. The pair, accompanied by the doctor's son, then lit out for old Mexico.

As there is a certain strength in numbers, the swindlers didn't try to frighten them. Before paying over their $9850, this trio insisted on proof that the $30,000 bank draft was legitimate, and that the trunk was really being held at Laredo. They sent telegrams, they thought, to the "National City Bank" of Galveston, on which the draft was drawn, and to the Laredo customhouse.

Within a couple of hours they had replies. A telegram purporting to be from the bank stated that the draft was indeed good. Another wire, apparently sent by the customhouse, said the trunk was right there. The trio paid their cash and took off for Galveston, where they learned there was no such bank in Galveston as the National City. There was a City National Bank, of Galveston, which was of no use whatever to the three Alabamans. Of course, they found no trunk at Laredo, either.

The swindlers had merely intercepted their messages before they had reached the telegraph office. The gang had facilities to simulate telegrams, and the replies the three thought they had received were fakes.

This was possible because the Spanish-prisoner swindlers avail themselves of all modern improvements and scientific advances useful to their trade. Several years ago a United States post-office inspector managed to get into a swindle headquarters in Mexico City and found everything modern and efficient. The equipment included a dozen electric typewriters, at which the come-on letters were batted out by a whole stenographic pool.

There were Chamber of Commerce membership lists for most United States towns and cities, trade-association membership lists, city directories, Who's Who and even lists of people who had sent in cereal-box tops for toy rocket guns. Currently, the gang is believed to be an international group of some thirty smart crooks out of several Latin-American countries. They operate from Mexico City, with branch offices in Monterrey, Guadalajara, Tampico and Veracruz, and roving agents in the States to scout for prospects. Besides regular business machines, the headquarters viewed by the post-office inspector contained presses to print fake newspaper stories of the banker's arrest and fake copies of his indictment. These are usually sent in letters to victims to substantiate the prisoner's claims. Other equipment at the swindle headquarters included presses for printing the certified-check forms and for faking telegrams.

The Spanish-prisoner racket is believed to have developed as an aftermath of the Spanish Armada's defeat in 1588, when thousands of Spanish soldiers and sailors, captured in battle or driven ashore by shipwreck, were thrown into English prisons and held until ransomed. It was not long before some smart Spanish confidence men used their plight as a racket. They solicited funds from relatives, supposedly to be used for ransom, but kept the money themselves. Later on they added a yarn about hidden treasure belonging to the prisoners, which the prisoners would split with their redeemers. This was to interest persons not related to these unfortunates.

The racket kept right on after the Armada prisoners were long dead and gone. Fresh crops of sharpers wrote to wealthy persons in other lands, posing as prisoners in the dungeons of Spain—a land noted for dungeons—with vast fortunes they would divide with their benefactors. Some literary authorities, incidentally, think this racket may have inspired Dumas' Count of Monte Cristo.

As Americans became wealthy, the Spanish swindlers turned their principal attention to this country. In one two-month period in 1900, Americans turned over to postal authorities 1431 Spanish-swindle letters. In 1907, Americans are known to have lost $30,000—probably much more—to swindlers in one Spanish province alone. They usually operated near the French border, for a convenient escape. They bribed well the poorly paid postal and telegraph employees who tipped them off when dangerous-looking strangers appeared in town.

In 1922 some of the swindlers moved their bases to Latin America, principally Mexico, to be more convenient to their prey. Then the Spanish civil war in the 1930's caused all prisoner-swindle operations to move to this side, as the war had destroyed much of Spain's nostalgic glamour that had helped to make the prisoner credible. Besides, the Spanish Government became stricter.

Until about four years ago, the only known prisoner racket was the Spanish version. But, with as many characters as there are around Broadway looking for a fast buck, it was obviously only a matter of time before somebody invented an American prisoner, and set about to fleece the Latins. That distinction went to one Celedonio Sevilla, an artist of sorts who owned the Dalla Advertising Corporation, which had headquarters in the Empire State Building.

His company operated a large screen, like an outdoor-movie screen, on top of a building in Times Square. Humorous cartoon advertisements were projected upon it each evening to entertain crowds on the Great White Way. Sevilla, however, undertook to augment his advertising revenue with an American-prisoner scheme like the Spanish version, except that his potential victims were in the Spanish-speaking countries. His prisoner was a certain "Nelson Lawrence Watkins," a former millionaire, in jail for defrauding his stockholders. He had a dear daughter by the name of Kathlene, who was only fifteen years old. (The Latins like them younger.) And, of course, he had concealed a trunkful of treasure.

The come-on letters were signed by a certain "Father John Miller," supposedly a prison chaplain, acting as intermediary for the prisoner. Father Miller's letters pointed out that the lucky Latin chosen to shelter the fair Kathlene and her father's fortune would have to give proof of his social acceptability and his financial stability. The letter explained that the prisoner wished a Latin American to have this responsibility because he understood "Latins are frank, loyal and trustworthy." The letters were pounded out by the hundreds in Sevilla's Empire State office and sent to businessmen in practically all the Latin-American countries.

One of Sevilla's associates approached the priest in charge of one of New York's Catholic churches. He explained that he was a friend of Father John Miller, a resident of South America who was then touring the States. He asked permission for Father Miller's mail to be sent in care of that church. The New York priest innocently agreed. Before long, Father Miller's letters were pouring into the church at the rate of forty or fifty a day. They contained answers such as the following:

> With deep surprise I have read your pious message, sent to my humble self. I have resolved, after meditation, to offer my services in a cause so worth while as that of the unfortunate Mr. Watkins. My economic solvency and social position are such that I believe will not impede my participation.
>
> Father Miller, as mediator, I implore you to accept my help in serving Mr. Watkins. I hope you will send me the documents, etc., in order that I may have a better understanding of the task you are undertaking.

When these answers were delivered in New York, through the unsuspecting church, Father Miller wrote back, instructing the writer to come at once to New York, stop in a certain hotel on Lexington Avenue, prepare to put up a substantial cash guarantee and reap a treasure that sounded like Captain Kidd's cache.

Father Miller gave some interesting details about that—to wit:

> You must have care in taking the lining from the trunk, and separate the double walls so as not to deteriorate what is there. Among the contents are: one thousand $100 bills, eight hundred $500 bills, four thousand pounds sterling, railroad and oil shares worth many thousands of dollars. Also in the trunk are the jewels of Kathlene's mother: a pearl necklace valued at $10,000, a diamond diadem, which—that her mother may rest in peace—Kathlene must wear on her wedding day, worth $35,000. There is also the mother's wedding ring, worth $5000, a gold bracelet with the mother's name in rubies and emeralds, and some odd jewelry. There are two checkbooks on the National Bank of Argentina, with two deposits—one amounting to $16,000, the other $36,000. The little girl carries the key to the trunk on a little gold cord hanging about her neck.

In spite of all that bait, nobody got swindled in the American-prisoner racket. Sevilla had arranged with a woman who rented desk and office space in a building on West 42nd Street to accept some of Father Miller's overflow mail. She became suspicious when the person who called for it wasn't in clerical clothing, and told the post-office inspectors.

Sevilla was sentenced to seven years for mail fraud, and the new American-prisoner racket died aborning. But not before several eager businessmen from South America, with adventure in their hearts, had arrived in New York, all set to retrieve the hidden fortune and rescue the dear daughter.

And this gives us the comforting assurance that not all fools are on this side of the border.

The Grifters

by Jim Thompson

AS ROY DILLON stumbled out of the shop his face was a sickish green, and each breath he drew was an incredible agony. A hard blow in the guts can do that to a man, and Dillon had gotten a hard one. Not with a fist, which would have been bad enough, but from the butt-end of a heavy club.

Somehow, he got back to his car and managed to slide into the seat. But that was all he could manage. He moaned as the change in posture cramped his stomach muscles; then, with a strangled gasp, he leaned out the window.

Several cars passed as he spewed vomit into the street, their occupants grinning, frowning sympathetically, or averting their eyes in disgust. But Roy Dillon was too sick to notice or to care if he had. When at last his stomach was empty, he felt better, though still not well enough to drive. By then, however, a prowl car had pulled up behind him—a sheriff's car, since he was in the county rather than city of Los Angeles—and a brown-clad deputy was inviting him to step out to the walk.

Dillon shakily obeyed.

'One too many, mister?'

'What?'

'Never mind.' The cop had already noticed the absence of liquor breath. 'Let's see your driver's license.'

Dillon showed it to him, also displaying, with seeming inadvertence, an assortment of credit cards. Suspicion washed off the cop's face, giving way to concern.

'You seem pretty sick, Mr Dillon. Any idea what caused it?'

'My lunch, I guess. I know I should know better, but I had a chicken-salad sandwich—and it didn't taste quite right when I was eating it—but . . . ' He let his voice trail away, smiling a shy, rueful smile.

'Mmm-hmm!' The cop nodded grimly. 'That stuff will do it to you. Well'—a shrewd up-and-down look—'you all right now? Want us to take you to a doctor?'

'Oh, no. I'm fine.'

'We got a first-aid man over to the substation. No trouble to run you over there.'

Roy declined, pleasantly but firmly. Any prolonged contact with the cops would result in a record, and any kind of record was at best a nuisance. So far he had none; the scrapes which the grift had led him into had not led him to the cops. And he meant to keep it that way.

The deputy went back to the prowl car, and he and his partner drove off. Roy waved a smiling farewell to them and got back into his own car. Gingerly, wincing a little, he got a cigarette lit. Then, convinced that the last of the vomiting was over, he forced himself to lean back against the cushions.

He was in a suburb of Los Angeles, one of the many which resist incorporation despite their interdependence and the lack of visible boundaries. From here it was almost a thirty-mile drive back into the city, a very long thirty miles at this hour of the day. He needed to be in better shape than he was, to rest a while, before bucking the outbound tide of evening traffic. More important, he needed to reconstruct the details of his recent disaster, while they still remained fresh in his mind.

He closed his eyes for a moment. He opened them again, focussing them on the changing lights of the nearby traffic standard. And suddenly, without moving from the car—without physically moving from it—he was back inside the shop again. Sipping a limeade at the fountain, while he casually studied his surroundings.

It was little different from a thousand small shops in Los Angeles, establishments with an abbreviated soda fountain, a showcase or two of cigars, cigarettes, and candy, and overflowing racks of magazines, paperback books, and greeting cards. In the East, such shops were referred to as stationers' or candy stores. Here they were usually called confectionaries or simply fountains.

Dillon was the only customer in the place. The one other person present was the clerk, a large, lumpy-looking youth of perhaps nineteen or twenty. As Dillon finished his drink, he noted the boy's manner as he tapped ice down around the freezer containers, working with a paradoxical mixture of diligence and indifference. He knew exactly what needed to be done, his expression said, and to hell with doing a bit more than that. Nothing for show, nothing to impress anyone. The boss's son, Dillon decided, putting down his glass and sliding off the stool. He sauntered up toward the cash register, and the youth laid down the sawed-off ball bat with which he had been tamping. Then, wiping his hands on his apron, he also moved up to the register.

'Ten cents,' he said.

'And a package of those mints, too.'

'Twenty cents.'

'Twenty cents, hmm?' Roy began to fumble through his pockets, while the clerk fidgeted impatiently. 'Now, I know I've got some change here. Bound to have. I wonder where the devil . . . '

Exasperatedly, he shook his head and drew out his wallet. 'I'm sorry. Mind cashing a twenty?'

The clerk almost snatched the bill from his hand. He slapped the bill down on the cash register ledge and counted out the change from the drawer. Dillon absently picked it up, continuing his fumbling search of his pockets.

'Now, doesn't that get you? I mean, you know darned well you've got something, but—' He broke off, eyes widening with a pleased smile. 'There it is—two dimes! Just give me back my twenty, will you?'

The clerk grabbed the dimes from him, and tossed back the bill. Dillon turned casually toward the door, pausing, on the way out, for a disinterested glance at the magazine display.

Thus, for the tenth time that day, he had worked the twenties, one of the three standard gimmicks of the short con grift. The other two are the smack and the tat, usually good for bigger scores but not nearly so swift nor safe. Some marks fall for the twenties repeatedly, without ever tipping.

Dillon didn't see the clerk come around the counter. The guy was just there, all of a sudden, a pouty snarl on his face, swinging the sawed-off bat like a battering ram.

'Dirty crook,' he whinnied angrily. 'Dirty crooks keep cheatin' me and cheatin' me, an' Papa cusses me out for it!'

The butt of the bat landed in Dillon's stomach. Even the clerk was startled by its effect. 'Now, you can't blame me, mister,' he stammered. 'You were askin' for it. I—I give you change for twenty dollars, an' then you have me give the twenty back, an'—an''—his self-righteousness began to crumble. 'N-now, you k-know you did, m-mister.'

Roy could think of nothing but his agony. He turned swimming eyes on the clerk, eyes flooded with pain-filled puzzlement. The look completely demolished the youth.

'It w-was j-just a mistake, mister. Y-you made a m-mistake, an' I m-made a m-m-mistake an'—mister!' He backed away terrified. 'D-don't look at me like that!'

'You killed me,' Dillon gasped. 'You killed me, you rotten bastard!'

'Nah! P-please don't say t-that, mister!'

'I'm dying,' Dillon gasped. And, then, somehow, he had gotten out of the place.

And now, seated in his car and re-examining the incident, he could see no reason to fault himself, no flaw in his technique. It was just bad luck. He'd simply caught a goof, and goofs couldn't be figured.

He was right about that. And he'd been right about something else, although he didn't know it.

As he drove back to Los Angeles, constantly braking and speeding up in the thickening traffic, repeatedly stopping and starting—with every passing minute, he was dying.

Death might be forestalled if he took proper care of himself. Otherwise, he had no more than three days to live.

AT SEVENTEEN GOING on eighteen, Roy Dillon had left home. He took nothing with him but the clothes he wore—clothes he had bought and paid for himself. He took no money but the little in the pockets of his clothes, and that too he had earned.

He wanted nothing from Lilly. She had given him nothing when he needed it, when he was too small to get for himself, and he wasn't letting her into the game at this late date.

He had no contact with her during the first six months he was away. Then, at Christmas time, he sent her a card, and on Mother's Day he sent her another. Both were of the gooey sentimental type, dripping with sickly sweetness, but the latter was a real dilly. Hearts and flowers and fat little angels swarmed over it in an insanely hilarious montage. The engraved message was dedicated to Dear Old Mom, and it gushed tearfully of goodnight kisses and platters and pitchers of oven-fresh cookies and milk when a little boy came in from play.

You would have thought that Dear Old Mom (God bless her silvering hair) had been the proprietor of a combination dairy-bakery, serving no customer but her own little tyke (on his brand-new bike).

He was laughing so hard when he sent it that he almost botched up the address. But afterward, he had some sobering second thoughts. Perhaps the joke was on him, yes? Perhaps by gibing at her he was revealing a deep and lasting hurt, admitting that she was tougher than he. And that, naturally, wouldn't do. He'd taken everything she had to hand out, and it hadn't made a dent in him. He damned well mustn't ever let her think that it had.

So he kept in touch with her after that, at Christmas and on her birthday and so on. But he was very correct about it. He just didn't think enough of her, he told himself, to indulge in ridicule. It would take a lot better woman than Lilly Dillon to get to him.

The only way he showed his true feelings was in the presents they exchanged. For while Lilly could obviously afford far better gifts than he, he would not admit it. At least, he did not until the effort to keep up with or outdo her not only threatened his long-range objectives, but revealed itself for what it was. Another manifestation of hurt. She had hurt him—or so it looked—and childishly he was rejecting her attempts at atonement.

She might think that, anyway, and he couldn't let her. So he had written her casually that gift-giving had been over-commercialized, and that they should stick to token remembrances from then on. If she wanted to donate to charity in his name, fine. Boys' Town would be appropriate. He, of course, would make a donation in her name.

Say to some institution for Wayward Women . . .

Well, but that is getting ahead of the story, skipping over its principal element.

New York is a two-hour ride from Baltimore. At seventeen going on eighteen, Roy went there, the logical objective of a young man whose only assets were good looks and an inherent yen for the fast dollar.

Needing to earn—and to be paid—immediately, he took work selling on a flat commission. Door-to-door stuff. Magazines, photo coupons, cooking utensils, vacuum cleaners—anything that looked promising. All of it promised much and gave little.

Perhaps Miles of Michigan had made $1,380 his first month by showing Super Suitings to his friends, and perhaps O'Hara of Oklahoma earned ninety dollars a day by taking orders for the Oopsy-Doodle Baby Walker. But Roy doubted it like hell. By literally knocking himself out, he made as high as $125 in one week. But that was his very best week. The average was between seventy-five and eighty dollars, and he had to hump to get that.

Still it was better than working as a messenger, or taking some small clerical job which promised 'Good Opportunity' and 'Possibility To Advance' in lieu of an attractive wage. Promises were cheap. Suppose he went to one of those places and promised to be president some day; so how about a little advance?

The selling was no good, but he knew of nothing else. He was very irked with himself. Here he was nineteen going on twenty, and already a proven failure. What was wrong with him, anyway? What had Lilly had that he didn't have?

Then, he stumbled onto the twenties.

It was a fluke. The chump, the proprietor of a cigar store, had really pulled it on himself. Preoccupied, Roy had continued to fumble for a coin after receiving the change from the bill, and the fidgety storekeeper, delayed in waiting on other customers, had suddenly lost patience.

'For Pete's sake, mister!' he snapped. 'It's only a nickel! Just pay me the next time you're in.'

Then, he threw back the twenty, and Roy was a block away before he realized what had happened.

On the heels of the realization came another: an ambitious young man did not wait for such happy accidents. He created them. And he forthwith started to do so.

He was coldly told off at two places. At three others, it was pointed out—more or less politely—that he was not entitled to the return of his twenty. At the remaining three, he collected.

He was exuberant at his good luck. (And he had been exceptionally lucky.) He wondered if there were any gimmicks similar to the twenties, ways of picking up as much money in a few hours as a *fool* made in a week.

There were. He was introduced to them that night in a bar, whence he had gone to celebrate.

A customer sat down next to him, jostling his elbow. A little of his drink was spilled, and the man apologetically insisted on buying him a fresh one. Then he bought still another round. At this point, of course, Roy wanted to buy a round. But the man's attention had been diverted. He was peering down at the floor, then reaching down and picking up a dice cube which he laid on the bar.

'Did you drop this, pal? No? Well, look. I don't like to drink so fast, but if you want to roll me for a round—just to keep things even . . . '

They rolled. Roy won. Which naturally wouldn't do at all. They rolled again, for the price of four drinks, and this time the guy won. And, of course, that wouldn't do either. He just wouldn't allow it. Hell, they were just swapping drinks, friendly like, and he certainly wasn't going to walk out of here winner.

'We'll roll for eight drinks this time, well, call it five bucks even, and then . . . '

The *tat*, with its rapidly doubling bets, is murder on a fool. That is its vicious beauty. Unless he is carrying very heavy, the man *with-the-best-of-it* strips him on a relatively innocent number of winning rolls.

Roy's griftings were down the drain in twenty minutes.

In another ten, all of his honest money had followed it. The guy felt very bad about it; he said so himself. Roy must take back a couple bucks of his loss, and . . .

But the taste of the grift was strong in Roy's mouth, the taste and the smell. He said firmly that he would take back half of the money. The grifter—his name was Mintz—could keep the other half for his services as an instructor in swindling.

'You can begin the lessons right now,' he said. 'Start with that dice gimmick you just worked on me.'

There were some indignant protests from Mintz, some stern language from Roy. But in the end they adjourned to one of the booths, and that night and for some nights afterward they played the roles of teacher and pupil. Mintz held back nothing. On the contrary, he talked almost to the point of becoming tiresome. For here was a blessed chance to drop pretense. He could show how smart he was, as his existence normally precluded doing, and do it in absolute safety.

Mintz did not like the twenties. It took a certain indefinable something which he did not have. And he never worked it without a partner, someone to distract the chump while the play was being made. As for working with a partner, he didn't like that either. It cut the score right down the middle. It put an apple on your head, and handed the other guy a shotgun. Because grifters, it seemed, suffered an irresistible urge to beat their colleagues. There was little glory in whipping a fool—hell, fools were made to be whipped. But to take a professional, even if it cost you in the long run, ah, that was something to polish your pride.

Mintz liked the smack. It was natural, you know. Everyone matched coins.

He particularly liked the tat, whose many virtues were almost beyond enumeration. Hook a group of guys on that tat, and you had it made for the week.

The tat must always be played on a very restricted surface, a bar or a booth table. Thus, you could not actually roll the die, although of course, you appeared to. You shook your hand vigorously, holding the cube on a high point, never shaking it at all, and then you spun it out, letting it skid and topple but never turn. If the marks became suspicious, you shot out of a cup, or, more likely, a glass, since you were in a bar room. But again you did not really shake the die. You held it, as before, clicking it vigorously against the glass in a simulated rattle, and then you spun it out as before.

It took practice, sure. Everything did.

If things got too warm, the bartender would often give you a *take-out* for a good tip. Call you to the phone or say that the cops were coming or something like that. Bartenders were chronically fed up with drinkers. They'd as soon see them chumped as not, if it made them a buck, and unless the guys were their friends.

Mintz knew of many gimmicks other than the three standards. Some of them promised payoffs exceeding the normal short-con top of a thousand dollars. But these invariably required more than one man, as well as considerable time and preparation; were, in short, bordering big-con stuff. And they had one very serious disadvantage: if the fool tipped, you were caught. You hadn't made a mistake. You hadn't just been unlucky. You'd just had it.

There were two highly essential details of grifting which Mintz did not explain to his pupil. One of them defied explanation. It was an acquired trait, something each man had to do on his own and in his own way; i.e., retaining a high degree of anonymity while remaining in circulation. You couldn't disguise yourself, naturally. It was more a matter of *not* doing anything. Of avoiding any mannerisn, any expression, any tone or pattern of speech, any posture or gesture or walk— anything at all that might be remembered.

Thus, the first unexplained essential.

Presumably, Mintz didn't explain the second one because he saw no need to. It was something that Roy must certainly know.

The lessons ended.

Roy industriously went to work on the grift. He acquired a handsome wardrobe. He moved to a good hotel. Indulging himself extravagantly, he still built up a roll of more than four thousand dollars.

Months passed. Then, one day, when he was eating in an Astoria-section lunchroom, a detective came in looking for him.

Conferring with the proprietor, he described Roy to a *t*. He had no photo of him, but he did have a police artist's reconstruction, and it was an excellent likeness.

Roy could see them looking down his way, as they talked, and he thought wildly of running. Of beating it back through the kitchen, and on out the back door. Probably the only thing that kept him from running was the weakness of his legs.

And then he looked at himself in the back-counter mirror, and he breathed a shuddery sigh of relief.

The day had turned warm after he left his hotel, and he'd checked his hat, coat and tie in a subway locker. Then, only an hour or so ago, he'd got a butch-style haircut.

So he was changed, considerably. Enough anyway to keep him from being collared. But he was shaken right down to his shoe soles. He sneaked back to his hotel room, wondering if he'd ever have the guts to work again. He stayed in the hotel until dark, and then he went looking for Mintz.

Mintz was gone from the small hotel where he had lived. He'd left months ago, leaving no forwarding address. Roy started hunting for him. By sheer luck, he found him in a bar six blocks away.

The grifter was horrified when Roy told him what had happened. 'You mean you've been working here all this time? You've been working *steady*? My God! Do you know where I've been in the last six months? A dozen places! All the way to the coast and back!'

'But why? I mean, New York's a big city. Why—'

Mintz cut him off impatiently. New York *wasn't* a big city, he said. It just had a lot of people in it, and they were crammed into a relatively small area. And no, you didn't help your odds much by getting out of jampacked Manhattan and into the other boroughs. Not only did you keep bumping into the same people, people who worked in Manhattan and lived in Astoria, Jackson Heights, et cetera, but you were more conspicuous there. Easier to be spotted by the fools. 'And, kid, a blind man could spot you. Look at that haircut! Look at the fancy wristwatch, and them three-tone sports shoes! Why don't you wear a black eye-patch, too, and a mouthful of gold teeth?'

Roy reddened. He asked troubledly if every city was like this. Did you have to keep jumping from place to place, using up your capital and having to move on just about the time you got to know your way around?

'What do you want?' Mintz shrugged. 'Egg in your beer? You can usually play a fairly long stand in Los Angeles, because it ain't just one town. It's a county full of towns, dozens of 'em. And with traffic so bad and a lousy transportation system, the people don't mix around like they do in New York. *But'*—he wagged a finger severely—'but that still doesn't mean you can run wild, kid. You're a grifter, see? A thief. You've got no home and no friends, and no visible means of support. And you damned well better not ever forget it.'

'I won't,' Roy promised. 'But, Mintz . . . '

'Yeah?'

Roy smiled and shook his head, keeping his thought to himself. *Suppose I did have a home, a regular place of residence? Suppose I had hundreds of friends and acquaintances? Suppose I had a job and—*

And there was a knock on the door, and he said, 'Come in, Lilly,' and his mother came in.

from

The Hustler

by Walter Tevis

THEY HAD TO take an elevator to the eighth floor, an elevator that jerked and had brass doors and held five people. It did not seem at all right to go to a pool-room on an elevator; and he had never figured Bennington's that way. Nobody had ever told him about the elevator. When they stepped off it there was a very high, wide doorway facing them. Over this was written, in small, feeble neon letters, BENNINGTON'S BILLIARD HALL. He looked at Charlie and then they walked in.

Eddie had with him a small, cylindrical leather case. This was as big around as his forearm and about two and a half feet long. In it was an extremely well-made, inlaid, ivory-pointed, French-leather-tipped, delicately balanced pool cue. This was actually in two parts; they could be joined for use by screwing together a two-piece, machined brass joint, fastened to the maple end of each section.

The place was big, bigger, even than he had imagined. It was familiar, because the smell and the feel of a pool-room are the same everywhere; but it was also very much different. Victorian, with heavy, leather-cushioned chairs, big elaborate brass chandeliers, three high windows with heavy curtains, a sense of spaciousness, of elegance.

It was practically empty. No one plays pool late in the afternoon; few people come in at that time except to drink at the bar, make bets on the races or play the pinball machines; and Bennington's had facilities for none of these. This, too, was unique; its business was pool, nothing else.

There was a man practicing on the front table, a big man, smoking a cigar. On another table further back two tall children in blue jeans and jackets were playing nine ball. One of these had long sideburns. In the middle of the room a very big man with heavy, black-rimmed glasses—like an advertising executive—was sitting in an oak swivel chair by the cash register, reading a newspaper. He looked at them a moment after they came in and when he saw the leather case in Eddie's hand he stared for a moment at Eddie's face before going back to the paper. Beyond him, in the back of the room, a stooped black man in formless clothes was pushing a broom, limping.

They picked a table toward the back, several tables down from the nine-ball players, and began to practice. Eddie took a house cue stick from the rack, setting the leather case, unopened, against the wall.

They shot around, loosely, for about forty-five minutes. He was trying to get the feel of the table, to get used to the big four-and-a-half-by-nine-feet size—since the war practically all pool tables were four by eight—and to learn the bounce of the rails. They were a little soft and the nap on the cloth was smooth, making the balls take long angles and making stiffening English difficult. But the table was a good one, level, even, with clean pocket drops, and he liked the sense of it.

The big man with the cigar ambled down, took a chair, and watched them. Then after they had finished the game he took the cigar out of his mouth, looked at Eddie, very hard, looked at the leather case leaning against the wall, looked back at Eddie and said, thoughtfully, "You looking for action?"

Eddie smiled at him. "Maybe. You want to play?"

The big man scowled. "No. Hell, no." Then he said, "You Eddie Felson?"

Eddie grinned, "Who's he?" He took a cigarette out of his shirt pocket.

The man put the cigar back in his mouth. "What's your game? What do you shoot?"

Eddie lit the cigarette. "You name it, mister. We'll play."

The big man jerked the cigar from his mouth. "Look, friend," he said, "I'm not trying to hustle. I don't never hustle people who carry leather satchels in poolrooms." His voice was loud, commanding, and yet it sounded tired, as if he were greatly discouraged. "I ask you a civil question and you play it cute. I come up and watch and I think maybe I can help you out, and you want to be cute."

"Okay," Eddie grinned, "no hard feelings. I shoot straight pool. You know any straight pool players around this poolroom?"

"What kind of straight pool game do you like?"

Eddie looked at him a minute, noticing the way the man's eyes blinked. Then he said, "I like the expensive kind."

The man chewed on his cigar a minute. Then he leaned forward in his chair and said, "You come up here to play straight pool with Minnesota Fats?"

Eddie liked this man. He seemed very strange, as if he were going to explode. "Yes," he said.

The man stared at him, chewing the cigar. Then he said, "Don't. Go home."

"Why?"

"I'll tell you why, and you better believe it. Fats don't need your money. And there's no way you can beat him. He's the best in the country." He leaned back in the chair, blowing out smoke.

Eddie kept grinning. "I'll think about that," he said. "Where is he?"

The big man came alive, violently. "For God's sake," he said, loudly, despairingly, "You talk like a real high-class pool hustler. Who do you think you are—Humphrey Bogart? Maybe you carry a rod and wear raincoats and really hold a mean pool stick back in California or Idaho or wherever it is. I bet you already beat every nine-ball shooting farmer from here to the West Coast. Okay. I told you what I wanted about Minnesota Fats. You just go ahead and play him, friend."

Eddie laughed. Not scornfully, but with amusement—amusement at the other man and at himself. "All right," he said, laughing. "Just tell me where I find him."

The big man pulled himself up from the chair with considerable effort. "Just stay where you are," he said. "He comes in, every night, about eight o'clock." He jammed the cigar in his mouth and walked back to the front table.

"Thanks," Eddie called at him. The man didn't reply. He began practicing again, a long rail shot on the three ball.

Eddie and Charlie returned to their game. The talk with the big man could have rattled him but, somehow, it had the effect of making him feel better about the evening. He began concentrating on the game, getting his stroke down to a finer point, running little groups of balls and then missing intentionally—more from long habit than from fear of being identified. They kept shooting, and after a while the other tables began to fill up with men and smoke and the clicking of pool balls and he began to glance toward the massive front door, watching.

And then, after he had finished running a group of balls, he looked up and saw, leaning against the next table, an extremely fat man with black curly hair, watching him shoot—a man with small black eyes.

He picked up the chalk and began stroking his cue tip with it, slowly, looking at the man. It couldn't have been anyone else, not with all of that weight, not with the look of authority, not with those sharp little eyes.

He was wearing a silk sport shirt, chartreuse, open at the neck and loose on his wide, soft-looking belly. His face was like dough, like the face of the full moon on a free calendar, puffed up like an Eskimo's, little ears close to his head, the hair shiny, curly, and carefully trimmed, the complexion clear, pinkish. His hands were clasped over the great belly, above a small, jeweled belt buckle, and there were brightly jeweled rings on four of his fingers. The nails were manicured and polished.

About every ten seconds there was a sudden, convulsive motion of his head, forcing his chins down toward his left collar bone. This was a very sudden movement, and it brought an automatic grimace to that side of his mouth which seemed affected by the tic. Other than this there was no expression on his face.

The man stared back at him. Then he said, "You shoot pretty good straights." His voice had no tone whatever. It was very deep.

Eddie, somehow, did not feel like grinning. "Thanks," he said.

He turned back to the table and finished up the rack of balls. Then when the cashier, the man with the black-rimmed glasses, was racking them up, Eddie turned back to the fat man and said, smiling this time, "You play straight pool, mister?"

The man's chin jerked, abruptly, "Every once in a while," he said. "You know how it is." His voice sounded as though he were talking from the bottom of a well.

Eddie continued chalking his cue. "You're Minnesota Fats, aren't you, mister?"

The man said nothing, but his eyes seemed to flicker, as if he were amused, or trying to be amusing.

Eddie kept smiling, but he felt his fingertips quivering and put one hand in his pocket, holding the cue stick with the other. "They say Minnesota Fats is the best in the country, out where I come from," he said.

"Is that a fact?" The man's face jerked again.

"That's right," Eddie said. "Out where I come from they say Minnesota Fats shoots the eyes right off them balls."

The other man was quiet for a minute. Then he said, "You come from California, don't you?"

"That's right."

"Name of Felson, Eddie Felson?" He pronounced the words carefully, distinctly, with neither warmth nor malice in them.

"That's right too."

There seemed nothing more to say. Eddie went back to his game with Charlie. Knowing Fats was watching him, adding him up, calculating the risks of playing him, he felt nervous; but his hands were steady with the cue and the nervousness was only enough to make him feel alert, springy, to sharpen his sense of the game he was playing, his feel for the balls and for the roll of the balls and the swing of the cue. He laid it on carefully, disregarding his normal practice of making himself look weak, shooting well-controlled, neat shots, until the fifteen colored balls were gone from the table.

Then he turned around and looked at Fats. Fats seemed not to see him. His chin jerked, and then he turned to a small man who had been standing next to him, watching, and said, "He shoots straight. You think maybe he's a hustler?" Then he turned back to Eddie, his face blank but the little eyes sharp, watching. "You a gambler, Eddie?" he said. "You like to gamble money on pool games?"

Eddie looked him full in the face and, abruptly, grinned. "Fats," he said, grinning, feeling good, all the way, "let's you and me play a game of straight pool."

Fats looked at him a moment. Then he said, "Fifty dollars?"

Eddie laughed, looked at Charlie and then back again, "Hell, Fats," he said, "you shoot big-time pool. Everybody says you shoot big-time pool. Let's don't be chicken about this." He looked at the men standing by Fats. Both of them were bugged, astonished. *Probably*, he thought, *nobody's ever talked to their big tin god like this before*. He grinned. "Let's make it a hundred, Fats."

Fats stared at him, his expression unchanging. Then, suddenly, with a great moving of flesh, he smiled. "They call you Fast Eddie, don't they?" he said.

"That's right." Eddie was still grinning.

"Well, Fast Eddie. You talk my kind of talk. You flip a coin so we see who breaks."

Eddie took his leather case from where it was leaning against the wall.

Someone flipped a half dollar. Eddie lost the toss and had to break the balls. He took the standard shot—two balls out from the rack and back again, three rails on the cue ball to the end cushion—and he froze the cue ball on the rail with only a bare edge of a corner ball sticking from behind the rack, to shoot at. Then Fats walked very slowly, ponderously, up to the front of the poolroom, where there was a green metal locker. He opened this and took out a cue stick, one joined at the middle with a brass joint, like Eddie's. He picked a cube of chalk up from the front table and chalked his cue as he walked back. He did not even appear to look at the position of the balls on the table, but merely said, "Five ball. Corner pocket," and took his position behind the cue ball to shoot.

Eddie watched him closely. He stepped up to the table with short, quick little steps, stepping up to it sideways, bringing his cue up into position as he did so, so that he was holding his cue, standing sideways to the table, out across his great stomach, the left-hand bridge already formed, the right hand holding the butt delicately, much as a violinist holds his bow—gracefully but surely. And then, as if it were an integral, continuous part of his approach to the table, his bridge hand settled down on the green and almost immediately there was a smooth, level motion of the cue stick, effortless, and the cue ball sped down the table and clipped the corner of the five ball and the five ball sped across the table and into the corner pocket. The cue ball darted into the rack, spreading the balls wide.

And then Fats began moving around the table, making balls, all of his former ponderousness gone now, his motions like a ballet, the steps light, sure, and rehearsed; the bridge hand inevitably falling into the right place; the hand on the butt of the cue with its fat, jeweled fingers gently pushing the thin shaft into the cue ball. He never stopped to look at the layout of the balls, never appeared to think or to prepare himself for shooting. About every five shots he stopped long enough to stroke the tip of his cue gently with chalk; but he did not even look at the table as he did this; he merely watched what he was doing at the moment.

He made fourteen out of the fifteen balls on the table very quickly, leaving the remaining ball in excellent position for the break.

Eddie racked the balls. Fats made the break shot, shooting effortlessly but powering the cue ball into the rack so that it scattered balls all over the table. He began punching them in. He was good. He was fantastically good. He ran eighty balls before he got tied up and played Eddie safe. Eddie had seen and made bigger runs, much bigger; but he had never seen anyone shoot with the ease, the unruffled certainty, that this delicate, gross man had.

Eddie looked at Charlie, sitting now in one of the big, high chairs. Charlie's face showed nothing, but he shrugged his shoulders. Then Eddie looked the shot over carefully. It was a good safe, but he was able to return it, freezing the cue ball to the end rail, leaving nothing to be shot at. They played it back and forth, safe, leaving no openings for the other man, until Eddie made a small slip and let Fats get loose. Fats edged up to the table and started shooting. Eddie sat down. He looked around; a crowd of ten or fifteen people had already formed around the table. A neat man with pink cheeks and glasses was moving around in the crowd, making bets. Eddie wondered what on. He looked at the clock on the wall over the door. It was eight-thirty. He took a deep breath, and then let it out slowly.

He had known he would start out losing. That was natural; he was playing a great player and on his own table, in his own poolroom, and he figured to lose for a few hours. But not that badly. Fats beat him two games by one hundred and twenty-five to nothing and in the third game Eddie finally got one open shot and scored fifty on it. It was not pleasant to lose, and yet, somehow, he was not deeply dismayed, did not feel lost in the brilliance of the other man's game, did not feel nervous or confused. He spent most of each game sitting down and each time Fats won a game Eddie grinned and gave him a hundred dollars. Fats had nothing to say.

At eleven o'clock, after he had lost the sixth game, Charlie came over, looked at him, and said, "Quit."

He looked at Charlie, who seemed to be perspiring, and said, "I'll take him. Just wait."

"Don't be too sure." Charlie went back to his chair, on the other side of the table.

Then Eddie started winning. He felt it start in the middle of a game, began to feel the sense he sometimes had of being a part of the table and of the balls and of the cue stick. The stroke of his arm seemed to travel on oiled bearings; and each muscle of his body was alert, sensitive to the game and the movement of the balls, sharply aware of how every ball would roll, of how, exactly, every shot must be made. Fats beat him that game, but he had felt it coming and he won the next.

And the game after that, and the next, and then another. Then someone turned off all the lights except those over the table that they were playing on and the background of Bennington's vanished, leaving only the faces of the crowd around the table, the green of the cloth of the table, and the now sharply etched, clean, black-shadowed balls, brilliant against the green. The balls had sharp, jeweled edges; the cue ball itself was a milk-white jewel and it was a magnificent thing to watch the balls roll and to know beforehand where they were going to roll. Nothing could be so clear or so simple or so excellent to do. And there was no limit to the shots that could be made.

Fats' game did not change. It was brilliant, fantastically good, but Eddie was beating him now, playing an incredible game: a gorgeous, spellbinding game, a game that he felt he had known all of his life, that he would play when the right time came. There was no better time than this.

And then, after a game had ended, there was noise up front and Eddie turned and saw that the clock said midnight and that someone was locking the great oak door, and he looked at Fats and Fats said, "Don't worry, Fast Eddie. We're not going anyplace."

Then he pulled a ten-dollar bill out of his pocket, handed it to a thin nervous man in a black suit, who was watching the game, and said, "Preacher, I want White Horse whiskey. And ice. And a glass. And you get yourself a fix with the change; but you do that after you come back with my whiskey."

Eddie grinned, liking the feel of this, the getting ready for action. He fished out a ten himself. "J. T. S. Brown bourbon," he said to the thin man. Then he leaned his cue stick against the table, unbuttoned his cuffs, and began rolling up his shirt sleeves. Then he stretched out his arms, flexing the muscles, enjoying the good sense of their steadiness, their control, and he said, "Okay, Fats. Your break."

Eddie beat him. The pleasure was exquisite; and when the man brought the whiskey and he mixed himself a highball with water from the cooler and drank it, his whole body and brain seemed to be suffused with pleasure, with alertness and life. He looked at Fats. There was a dark line of sweat and dirt around the back of his collar. His manicured nails were dirty. His face still showed no expression. He, too, was holding a glass of whiskey and sipping it quietly.

Suddenly Eddie grinned at him. "Let's play for a thousand a game, Fats," he said.

There was a murmur in the crowd.

Fats took a sip of whiskey, rolled it around carefully in his mouth, swallowed. His sharp, black eyes were fixed on Eddie, dispassionately, searching. He seemed to see something there that reassured him. Then he glanced, for a moment, at the neat man with glasses, the man who had been taking bets. The man nodded, pursing his lips. "Okay," he said.

Eddie knew it, could feel it, that no one had ever played straight pool like this before. Fats' game, itself, was astonishing, a consistently beautiful, precise game, a deft, quick shooting game with almost no mistakes. And he won games; no power on earth could have stopped him from winning some of them, for pool is a game that gives the man sitting down no earthly way of affecting the shooting of the man he is trying to beat. But Eddie beat him, steadily, making shots that no one had ever made before, knifing balls in, playing hairline position, running rack after rack of balls without his cue ball's touching a cushion, firing ball after ball into the center, the heart of every pocket. His stroking arm was like a conscious thing, and the cue stick was a living extension of it. There were nerves in the wood of it, and he could feel the tapping of the leather tip with the nerves, could feel the balls roll; and the exquisite sound that they made as they hit the bottoms of the pockets was a sound both there, on the table, and in the very center of his own soul.

They played for a long, long time and then he noticed that the shadows of the balls on the green had become softer, had lost their edges. He looked up and saw pale light coming through the window draperies and then looked at the clock. It was seven-thirty. He looked around him, dazed. The crowd had thinned out, but some of the same men were there. Everybody seemed to need a shave. He felt his own face. Sandpaper. He looked down at himself. His shirt was filthy, covered with chalk marks, the tail out, and the front wrinkled as if he had slept in it. He looked at Fats, who looked, if anything, worse.

Charlie came over. He looked like hell, too. He blinked at Eddie. "Breakfast?"

Eddie sat down, in one of the now-empty chairs by the table. "Yeah," he said. "Sure." He fished in his pocket, pulled out a five.

"Thanks," Charlie said. "I don't need it. I been keeping the money, remember?"

Eddie grinned, weakly. "That's right. How much is it now?"

Charlie stared at him. "You don't know?"

"I forgot." He fished a crumpled cigarette from his pocket, lit it. His hands, he noticed, were trembling faintly; but he saw this as if he were looking at someone else. "What is it?" He leaned back, smoking the cigarette, looking at the balls sitting, quiet now, on the table. The cigarette had no taste to it.

"You won eleven thousand four hundred," Charlie said. "Cash. It's in my pocket."

Eddie looked back at him. "Well!" he said. And then, "Go get breakfast. I want a egg sandwich and coffee."

"Now wait a minute," Charlie said. "You're going with me. We eat breakfast at the hotel. The pool game is over."

Eddie looked at him a minute, grinning, wondering, too, why it was that Charlie couldn't see it, never had seen it. Then he leaned forward, looked at him, and said, "No it isn't, Charlie."

"Eddie . . ."

"This pool game ends when Minnesota Fats says it ends."

"You came after ten thousand. You got ten thousand."

Eddie leaned forward again. He wasn't grinning now. He wanted Charlie to see it, to get with it, to feel some of what he was feeling, some of the commitment he was making. "Charlie," he said, "I came here after Minnesota Fats. And I'm gonna get him. I'm gonna stay with him all the way."

Fats was sitting down too, resting. He stood up. His chin jerked, down into the soft flesh of his neck. "Fast Eddie," he said tonelessly, "let's play pool."

"Break the balls," Eddie said.

IN THE MIDDLE of the game the food came and Eddie ate his sandwich in bites between shots, setting it on the rail of the table while he was shooting, and washing it down with the coffee, which tasted very bitter. Fats had sent someone out and he was eating from a platter of a great many small sandwiches and link sausages. Instead of coffee he had three bottles of Dutch beer on another platter and these he drank from a pilsner glass, which he held in a fat hand, delicately. He wiped his lips gently with a napkin between bites of the sandwiches and, apparently, paid no attention whatever to the balls that Eddie was methodically pocketing in the thousand-dollar game that he, sitting in the chair and eating his gourmet's breakfast, was playing in.

Eddie won the game; but Fats won the next one, by a narrow margin. And at nine o'clock the poolroom doors were opened again and an ancient colored man limped in and began sweeping the floor and opened the windows, pulling back the draperies. Outside the sky was, absurdly, blue. The sun shone in.

Fats turned his head toward the janitor and said, his voice loud and flat, across the room, "Cut off that goddamn sunshine."

The black man shuffled back to the windows and drew the curtains. Then he went back to his broom.

They played, and Eddie kept winning. In his shoulders, now, and in his back and at the backs of his legs there was a kind of dull pain; but the pain seemed as if it were someone else's and he hardly felt it, hardly knew it was there. He merely kept shooting and the balls kept falling and the grotesque, fat man whom he was playing—the man who was the Best Straight Pool Player in the Country—kept giving large amounts of money to Charlie. Once, he noticed that, while he was shooting and the other man was sitting, Fats was talking with the man with the pink cheeks and with Gordon, the manager. The pink-cheeked man had his billfold in his hand. After that game, Fats paid Charlie with a thousand-dollar bill. The sight of the bill that he had just earned made him feel nothing. He only wished that the rack man would hurry and rack the balls.

The aching and the dullness increased gradually; but these did not affect the way his body played pool. There was a strange, exhilarating feeling that he was really somewhere else in the room, above the table—floating, possibly, with the heavy, bodiless mass of cigarette smoke that hung below the light—watching his own body, down below, driving small colored balls into holes by poking them with a long, polished stick of wood. And somewhere else in the room, perhaps everywhere in the room, was an incredibly fat man, silent, always in motion, unruffled, a man whose sharp little eyes saw not only the colored balls on the green rectangle, but saw also into all of the million corners in the room, whether or not they were illuminated by the cone of light that circumscribed the bright oblong of the pool table.

At nine o'clock in the evening Charlie told him that he had won eighteen thousand dollars.

Something happened, suddenly, in his stomach when Charlie told him this. A thin steel blade touched against a nerve in his stomach. He tried to look at Fats, but, for a moment, could not.

At ten-thirty, after winning one and then losing one, Minnesota Fats went back to the bathroom and Eddie found himself sitting down and then, in a moment, his head was in his hands and he was staring at the floor, at a little group of flat cigarette butts at his feet. And then Charlie was with him, or he heard his voice; but it seemed to be coming from a distance and when he tried to raise his head he could not. But Charlie was telling him to quit, he knew that without being able to pick out the word. And then the cigarette butts began to shift positions and to sway, in a gentle but confusing motion, and there was a humming in his ears like the humming of a cheap radio and, suddenly, he realized that he was passing out, and he shook his head, weakly at first and then violently, and when he stopped doing this he could see and hear better. But something in his mind was screaming. Something in him was quivering, frightened, cutting at his stomach from the inside, like a small knife.

Charlie was still talking but he broke him off, saying, "Give me a drink, Charlie." He did not look at Charlie, but kept his eyes on the cigarette butts, watching them closely.

"You don't need a drink."

Then he looked up at him, at the round, comic face dirty with beard and said, surprised at the softness of his own voice, "Shut up, Charlie. Give me a drink."

Charlie handed him the bottle.

He turned it up and let the whiskey spill down his throat. It gagged him but he did not feel it burn, hardly felt it in his stomach except as a mild warmness, softening the edges of the knife. Then he looked around him and found that his vision was all right, that he could see clearly the things directly in front of him, although there was a mistiness around the edges.

Fats was standing by the table, cleaning his fingernails. His hands were clean again; he had washed them; and his hair although still greasy, dirty looking, was combed. He seemed no more tired—except for the soiled shirt and a slight squinting of the eyes—than he had when Eddie had first seen him. Eddie looked away, looking back at the pool table. The balls were racked into their neat triangle. The cue ball sat at the head of the table, near the side rail, in position for the break.

Fats was at the side of his vision, in the misty part, and he appeared to be smiling placidly. "Let's play pool, Fast Eddie," he said.

Suddenly, Eddie turned to him and stared. Fats' chin jerked, toward his shoulder, his mouth twisting with the movement. Eddie watched this and it seemed, now, to have some kind of meaning; but he did not know what the meaning was.

And then he leaned back in his chair and said, the words coming almost without volition, "I'll beat you, Fats."

Fats just looked at him.

Eddie was not sure whether or not he was grinning at the fat man, at the huge, ridiculous, effeminate, jeweled ballet dancer of a pool hustler, but he felt as if something were going to make him laugh aloud at any minute. "I'll beat you, Fats," he said. "I beat you all day and I'll beat you all night."

"Let's play pool, Fast Eddie."

And then it came, the laughing. Only it was like someone else laughing, not himself, so that he heard himself as if it were from across the room. And then there were tears in his eyes, misting over his vision, fuzzing together the poolroom, the crowd of people around him, and the fat man, into a meaningless blur of colors, shaded with a dark, dominating green that seemed, now, to be actually being diffused from the surface of the table. And then the laughing stopped and he blinked at Fats.

He said it very slowly, tasting the words thickly as they came on. "I'm the best you ever seen, Fats." That was it. It was very simple. "I'm the best there is." He had known it, of course, all along, for years. But now it was so clear, so simple, that no one—not even Charlie—could mistake it. "I'm the best. Even if you beat me, I'm the best." The mistiness was clearing from his eyes again and he could see Fats standing sideways at the table, laying his hand down toward the green, not even aiming. *Even if you beat me . . .*

Somewhere in Eddie, deep in him, a weight was being lifted away. And, deeper still, there was a tiny, distant voice, a thin, anguished cry that said to him, sighing, *You don't have to win.* For hours there had been the weight, pressing on him, trying to break him, and now these words, this fine and deep and true revelation, had come and were taking the weight from him. The weight of responsibility. And the small steel knife of fear.

He looked back at the great fat man. "I'm the best," he said, "no matter who wins."

"We'll see," Fats said, and he broke the balls.

WHEN EDDIE LOOKED at the clock again it was a little past midnight. He lost two in a row. Then he won one, lost one, won another—all of them close scores. The pain in his right upper arm seemed to glow outward from the bone and his shoulder was a lump of heat with swollen blood vessels around it and the cue stick seemed to mush into the cue ball when he hit it. And the balls no longer clicked when they hit one another but seemed to hit as if they were made of balsa wood. But he still could not miss the balls; it was still ridiculous that anyone could miss them; and his eyes saw the balls in sharp, brilliant detail although there seemed to be no longer a range of sensitivity to his vision. He felt he could see in the dark or could look at, stare into, the sun—the brightest sun at full noon—and stare it out of the sky.

He did not miss; but when he played safe, now, the cue ball did not always freeze against the rail or against a cluster of balls as he wanted it to. Once, at a critical time in a game, when he had to play safe, the cue ball rolled an inch too far and left Fats an open shot and Fats ran sixty-odd balls and out. And later, during what should have been a big run, he miscalculated a simple, one-rail position roll and had to play for defense. Fats won that game too. When he did, Eddie said, "You fat son of a bitch, you make mistakes expensive."

But he kept on making them. He would still make large numbers of balls but something would go wrong and he would throw the advantage away. And Fats didn't make mistakes. Not ever. And then Charlie came over after a game, and said, "Eddie, you still got the ten thousand. But that's all. Let's quit and go home. Let's go to bed."

Eddie did not look at him. "No," he said.

"Look, Eddie," he said, his voice soft, tired, "what is it you want to do? You beat him. You beat him bad. You want to kill yourself?"

Eddie looked up at him. "What's the matter, Charlie?" he said, trying to grin at him. "You chicken?"

Charlie looked back at him for a minute before he spoke. "Yeah," he said, "maybe that's it. I'm chicken."

"Okay. Then go home. Give me the money."

"Go to hell."

Eddie held his hand out. "Give me the money, Charlie. It's mine."

Charlie just looked at him. Then he reached in his pocket and pulled out a tremendous roll of money, wrinkled bills rolled up and wrapped with a heavy rubber band.

"Here," he said. "Be a goddamn fool."

Eddie stuffed the roll in his pocket. When he stood up to play he looked down at himself. It seemed grossly funny; one pocket bulging with a whiskey bottle, the other with paper money.

It took a slight effort to pick up his cue and start playing again; but after he was started the playing did not seem to stop. He did not even seem to be aware of the times when he was sitting down and Fats was shooting, seemed always to be at the table himself, stroking with his bruised, screaming arm, watching the bright little balls roll and spin and twist their ways about the table. But, although he was hardly aware that Fats was shooting, he knew that he was losing, that Fats was winning more games than he was. And when the janitor came in to open up the poolroom and sweep the floor and they had to stop playing for a few minutes while he swept the cigarette butts from around the table, Eddie sat down to count his money. He could not count it, could not keep track of what he had counted; but he could see that the roll was much smaller than it had been when Charlie gave it to him. He looked at Fats and said, "You fat bastard. You fat lucky bastard," but Fats said nothing.

And then, after a game, Eddie counted off a thousand dollars to Fats, holding the money on the table, under the light, and when he had counted off the thousand he saw that there were only a few bills left. This did not seem right, and he had to look for a moment before he realized what it meant. Then he counted them. There was a hundred-dollar bill, two fifties, a half-dozen twenties and some tens and ones.

Something happened in his stomach. A fist had clamped on something in his stomach and was twisting it.

"All right," he said. "All right, Fats. We're not through yet. We'll play for two hundred. Two hundred dollars a game." He looked at Fats, blinking now, trying to bring his eyes to focus on the huge man across the table from him. "Two hundred dollars. That's a hustler's game of pool."

Fats was unscrewing his cue, unfastening the brass joint in its center. He looked at Eddie. "The game's over," he said.

Eddie leaned over the table, letting his hand fall on the cue ball. "You can't quit me," he said.

Fats did not even look at him. "Watch," he said.

Eddie looked around. The crowd was beginning to leave the table, men were shuffling away, breaking up into little groups, talking. Charlie was walking toward him, his hands in his pockets. The distance between them seemed very great, as though he were looking down a long hallway.

Abruptly, Eddie pushed himself away from the table, clutching the cue ball in his hand. He felt himself staggering. "Wait!" he said. Somehow, he could not see, and the sounds were all melting into one another. "Wait!" He could barely hear his own voice. Somehow, he swung his arm, his burning, swollen, throbbing right arm, and he heard the cue ball crash against the floor and then he was on the floor himself and could see nothing but a lurching motion around him, unclear patterns of light swinging around his head, and he was vomiting, on the floor and on the front of his shirt. . . .

Birds of a Feather

by David Maurer

SO MUCH SENSATIONAL material has been printed about confidence men and, generally speaking, the public entertains such romantic and even fantastic ideas regarding them, that a chapter like this would not be complete without a few modest but realistic notes regarding their personal lives.

There is nothing superhuman about confidence men, nor is there anything mysterious or occult about the methods they use. Although they sometimes perform sensational crimes, they are not the super criminals of fiction. They are neither violent, blood-thirsty, nor thieving, in the ordinary sense of that word. They are not antisocial—whatever that term really means. They hold no especial hatred or antipathy toward the individuals they fleece, nor toward society as a whole. They are not, on the one hand, the romantic and sentimental crooks of the movies, nor, on the other, the sinister, plotting, cold-blooded criminals of the crime-story magazine. They are human beings, manifesting salt-and-pepper mixtures of all the vices and virtues to which mankind is heir. If fifty of them were selected and mixed indiscriminately with a group of successful business and professional men, all the correlations and statistics of a Hooton or a Lombroso would not set them apart; and, if a census of opinions upon politics, ethics, religion, or what-not were taken from the entire group, not even a Solomon could separate the sheep from the goats on the basis of their social views. If confidence men operate outside the law, it must be remembered that they are not much further outside than many of our pillars of society who go under names less sinister. They only carry to an ultimate and very logical conclusion certain trends which are often inherent in various forms of legitimate business.

However, since all confidence men live in much the same environment, have something of the same training and background, live by a loose but nevertheless real code, are all of high intelligence, have similar attitudes toward their victims, toward the law, and one another, and run somewhat true to form in their amusements and recreations, it follows naturally that they develop certain traits in common. While these traits can hardly be said to be earmarks of the profession, and certainly they could not be used to identify a confidence man, they are, regardless of individual variations, characteristic of the group.

As we have seen, most con men have a criminal or semi-criminal background, though some, like the Yenshee Kid for instance, come from good family stock and a high middle-class background, but fall early into criminal company. Most of them have a wide variety of thieving experience before they become confidence men. They have grown up in a tradition of cheating, grifting, stealing; their habits and attitudes are fixed, sometimes from boyhood. "You are shaped by the company you keep as a youngster," said the Postal Kid. "You tangle up early with guys who cheat for a living. Then you meet other grifters through them and get hardened to their ways. You lose your dough and that hardens you up to the other side of the picture. You become hungry for dough to gamble with. Then you go out looking for a mark you can trim. You take the chances and the gamblers take the dough away from you. They are very nice to you when you are flush, but when you are chick, boy, they give you the chill. They think you might put the bite on, and gamesters don't like to associate with grifters who are chicane. So out you go for another mark. . . ."

Thus is begun a cycle which is likely to continue, with minor variations, throughout a lifetime, for most con men gamble heavily with the money for which they work so hard and take such chances to secure. In a word, most of them are suckers for some other branch of the grift. Among the old-timers, it was twisting the tiger's tail; among the present generation, it is cards, dice, roulette or stocks. It is indeed strange that men who know so much about the percentage which operates in favor of the professional gambler will risk their freedom for the highly synthetic thrill of bucking the tiger. Yet a big score is hardly cut up until all the mob are plunging heavily at their favorite game; within a few weeks, or even a few days, a $100,000 touch has gone glimmering and the con men are living on borrowed money, or are out on the tip or the smack to make expenses.

Con men are well aware of this weakness, yet few of them, it seems, are able to curb their gambling instincts and gear their lives down to the speed at which the ordinary citizen lives. Many amusing stories are told about this tendency, each con man laughing at the mote in his neighbor's eye while he ignores the beam in his own. One of these stories concerns Little Chappie Lohr and Plunk Drucker. Plunk had an insatiable lust for faro-bank and played it at every opportunity, even though he lost with distressing regularity. The two men started out on the road with a bank roll between them. Plunk promptly lost it all at faro. They borrowed from an accommodating saloon-keeper in Chicago. At Council Bluffs Plunk disappeared. Little Chappie, fearing the worst, sought him out in the den of the tiger.

"You can't do this," remonstrated Chappie. "You'll lose our bank roll again."

"Oh, no, Chappie," said Plunk, confidently, "don't worry. Back in Chicago, they were only dealing it out at $5 and $10. Here they are dealing it out at $12.50 and $25."

(For the benefit of those who do not understand faro-bank—strictly a grifter's game nowadays—the point of the story lies in the fact that Plunk felt confident that he could win just twice as fast because the cards were dealt for double the former price in Council Bluffs; in reality, of course, he was losing at more than double the rate he did in Chicago.)

Another, which is now almost legendary in the underworld, illustrates how Kid McGinley's lust for poker consumed all of his income from the grift. One time he and his partner stopped for a time in Rochester, New York, just after taking off a big touch. Every night the Kid played poker in a brace-game and lost heavily. He was rapidly going broke. His partner, who had been a professional gambler, tried to warn the Kid.

"Kid," he said, "that stud-horse poker game is Mill's lock. All those starters are subway dealers. If you play any longer, you'll be behind the six."

"What the hell can I do?" asked the Kid. "It's the only game in town."

This indulgence of the gaming instincts becomes more than relaxation; their gratification is the only motive which many con men have for grifting. With many, especially old-timers, faro-bank is an obsession. As soon as they have taken off a score and cut it up, away they go to a faro-bank to try out the systems which they hope will beat the bank in this most fascinating of all card games. They win and lose, win and lose, always losing more than they win, until they come away broke and full of reasons why their "systems" didn't work that time. The only way con men can come away substantially and consistently richer is to use the same methods the gambling house uses and beat the house from the outside. Kid S—and Jerry Daley, for instance, claim credit for inventing a crooked system (probably much older) which they called "copper on and copper off." At any rate, they perfected it to a high degree and several con men and gamblers formed a mob which traveled over the country taking scores of from $7,000 to $10,000 from each gambling house; but work as hard as they could, all the con men in the country, using the "copper on and copper off" system, could never win back all the money that the faro-dealers have taken from con men. Old-timers have lost heavily at this game, but many young grifters have never seen it played.

While no con men ever play for such high stakes as did some of the multimillionaire plungers of the Canfield era, many of them throw money over the gaming board at a rate that seems impressive to us in these degenerate days. Kid McGinley, who was infinitely more successful at making money legitimately than he was at grifting, always bet high on sporting events, especially prize fights and baseball games. It was common for him to bet as much as $2,000 per race when he was at the track. The Indiana Wonder likes horse-racing, but plunges on longshots only. The Jew Kid gambles on anything, but likes horses and craps best; there are rumors that he has a hand in fixed races. 102nd St. George concentrates on horses, while the Postal Kid, on the contrary, never liked horses but gambled away sizable fortunes on faro and craps. The High Ass Kid likes blackjack; Limehouse Chappie, Curley Carter, and the Boone Kid gamble on anything. Chappie Moran, who had himself been a bookie and should have known better, always aspired to beat the horses. So did the Honey Grove Kid. Fifth Avenue Fred is a high-rolling gambler, sometimes rolling as high as $5,000 at a pop on the crap table. Lee Reil enjoyed a little faro. The Ripley Kid loves gambling, especially bridge, but his enthusiasm exceeds his card sense and he never wins. The handsome Kid W—does likewise. Queer-pusher Nick gambles heavily. The

Square Faced Kid, himself a fine card cheater, and one of the best bridge players anywhere, is a sucker for stocks and loses his winnings in speculation. Little Bert, although an excellent bridge player, put the interests of his family first, and seldom gambled for high stakes. Wildfire John, a heavy gambler during his entire life, now in his old age lives practically in the gutter.

Naturally those confidence men who gamble heavily seldom profit much from the large sums they take from gullible marks. Others spend their cut of each score rapidly as soon as they get it, or give it to their women, who put it promptly into clothes, furs or diamonds.

In this connection, there is a tale told of E—— S——, who for years shepherded the S——s' assets, buying diamonds as fast as her husband turned over to her his end of a touch. These she carefully hoarded in a little chamois bag which fitted snugly inside her stocking above the knee. Ironically, for all her thrift, the S—— fortune came to grief in a most plebeian fashion. Several con men and their wives were crossing the southwestern desert by train; E—— retired to the ladies' room where, in the course of certain solemn rites enthroned, she let slip the little chamois bag and it skittered through to the ties beneath. She leaped for the bell cord and gave it a lusty pull. The train stopped long enough for E—— and her friends to pile out onto the blistering sands. For long hours they paraded back and forth over the right-of-way, but the winds arose and the sands shifted, and for all I know, E——'s diamonds still lie buried there.

But some eschewed gambling and bad investments, salted away their money, and became well-to-do. These would include the Narrow Gage Kid, Doc Sterling, Glouster Jack, Little Chappie Lohr, George Ryan, John Henry Strosnider, the Clinic Kid, Joe Furey (who was broken by the Norfleet case), the Black Kid of quiet demean and refined manners, Nigger Mike and the Big Alabama Kid. Christ Tracy did not gamble but gave away most of the money he made during a prosperous lifetime. The notorious Yellow Kid doesn't gamble, but indulges a vast and expensive taste for women.

Although many confidence men lose heavily to professional gamblers, a few of them are themselves first-rate gamblers with both grift sense and card sense—a rare and fortunate combination. These men are wise enough to protect their winnings from braced gambling houses, carefully hoarding them up to lose on stocks, horses, women or whatever they are suckers for. "Grifters who are gamble-wise can make a braced gambling house right away," said Tom Furey, who evaded them with enough success to leave a comfortable fortune at his death. "Why? Because when they step into a house, they look around for a short time at all the shills who are boosting. Then they'll notice from the way the sticks handle the chips that they're not interested in the play. They are professionals and handle the chips like no mark could ever handle them. They just shuffle them like cards. I think that within one hour I could pick out every shill in the gaff. But there is no gambling game invented that you can't beat either from the inside or the outside, so what the hell. . . ."

The money which a con man does not throw away over the gaming table is rapidly used up in maintaining a very high standard of living. Because he must appear at an advantage in a highly respectable world, he lives on a high and even luxurious plane. Most con men dress well, carrying with them on the road an extensive wardrobe which provides for any sort of social situation in which they may find themselves. They wear their clothes well, for most of them are well-built, substantial-looking men; this build seems to occur with remarkable frequency, though one immediately thinks of exceptions in John Singleton, short, heavy-set, portly; in the Brass Kid, short, rosy-cheeked, jolly; and in Little Bert, and the Little Alabama Kid. Probably natural selection explains the fact that most of them are well set-up and attractive physically; some of them are distinguished-looking. Their manners are excellent, their behavior during professional appearances beyond reproach.

There is at least one ill-mannered exception to this generalization who deserves a bit of space because he is widely known among con men as the prime example of everything a con man shouldn't do or be. He is the prosperous Red Lager. Ignorant and repulsive-looking, freckled to the point of blotchiness, with the nasty shade of blue eyes which often accompanies a certain cast of red hair, awkward and slew-footed, Red Lager is certainly the acme of unattractiveness among con men. He is everything and does everything which, theoretically, a good con man shouldn't. He has never heard of Dale Carnegie and is unaware of the barest rudiments of the science of "influencing" people; yet he has made a fortune on the pay-off. And he has a son, the exact replica of his father down to the duck-like walk, who, despite his addiction to drugs—one vice which the old man shunned—is today a successful confidence man.

First-class accommodations on railways and steamships are necessary if con men are to meet well-to-do people. Many of them now travel in their own chauffeured cars. Their hotels are always the best and their suites imposing. Their work takes them into swank clubs and resorts. Naturally, their personalities and their manners must not betray them. Consequently, they have cultivated the social side more than any other criminal group. They are able to fit in unobtrusively on any social level.

Although their culture is not very deep, it is surprisingly wide and versatile. They must be well informed in business and financial matters, have a glib knowledge of society gossip, and enough of an acquaintance with art, literature and music to give an illusion of culture. I have observed that many of them read widely, and that it is an almost universal habit to run through ten or a dozen newspapers daily in order to keep constantly informed on topics which may come up in conversation. Newspapers also furnish a wide variety of news vital to grifters who want to thrive in their profession and keep out of jail. A few go deeper than casual browsing among the periodicals and haunt libraries when they have time, reading books omnivorously. One con man of my acquaintance buys a great many books, reads them, and promptly gives them away.

Among those who pursue learning for its own sake, I might cite three examples. One, a man of about forty-five, has his own special interests, largely sociological, and sits in sporadically on classes in a large midwestern university. Another, a man of some sixty years of age, has never sought any formal education, but delights in literature, has read widely and indiscriminately from Shakespeare to the moderns, and has his critical views which compensate in originality for what they lack in orthodoxy. A phenomenal memory enables him to quote at will from almost anything he has read. Another has made a hobby of history, with especial emphasis on Napoleon, and has, at one time or another, acquainted himself with most of the documents in English, both here and abroad, which touch upon the career of that general.

But most confidence men read for mercenary rather than cultural reasons, seeking only information which they can use in their profession. "All grifters [con men] try to educate themselves by reading a lot," says one con man, who might well speak for the entire profession. "I read to learn something, so when I bump into Mr. Bates I can hold my own with him on most any subject. If you are posing as a banker, for instance, you must know enough about banking to get away with it. I read the financial pages and the investment journals so I won't slip up and rumble the mark. The same is true for any business I claim to be engaged in. Of course, I pick up a lot of it from just talking to people, but I have to read a lot too."

Often one encounters a creative spark in con men; if given the opportunity and the incentive, they might write quite well. Their wide experience with people, their keen powers of observation, and their fluent command of picturesque language would all stand them in good stead if they chose to record the colorful world about them. Certain of them have a genuine love of poetry and rather apologetically exhibit their own efforts at verse; I have in my files numerous manuscripts, some of which rise decidedly above the level of doggerel.

In general, however, the culture of con men is no more than a superficial veneer which, combined with attractive personalities and a ready mother-wit, gives the illusion of polish. Once a con man is thrown back on his own resources and into his own society, he relapses into the ways and the tastes of the common grifter. He has no real interests to sustain him. "A few of the boys have something they like to play around with when they have the leisure," says an old-timer, "but for most of them, I guess it is only faro, craps or just the gals. When a con man hits a new town, he can smell a faro-bank just the same as he can smell a policeman."

Almost all con men live irregular sex-lives, because they are away from their women so much of the time; much of their money is squandered in fancy brothels of one sort or another. And most con men drink when they are at leisure, some, like Roy Brooks (the Major) probably to excess. However, no competent con man drinks on the job, and drinking with the mark is always frowned upon. Certainly no con man who used alcohol continuously to excess long maintains his standing in his profession.

With the increased use of narcotics among underworld folk, it is inevitable that some con men should become addicted, though most modern big-time criminals shun narcotics like poison. Some of the old-timers took up opium around 1900 when it was considered no more dangerous than smoking cigarettes—when many citizens on the West Coast placidly puffed the pipe on their own front porches, and an opium lay-out was standard equipment for most prostitutes whose Pekes and Pomeranians often acquired a "lamp habit" from breathing the smoke while their mistresses puffed. But the Harrison Act changed all that. As opium became more difficult to buy and to take, many addicts turned to morphine and heroin. However, confidence men have always felt that there was something disgraceful about addiction, the present generation being particularly sensitive about it. Consequently, once a con man becomes addicted, he carefully conceals the fact as well as he can and only his intimate associates are aware of his misfortune. How many of the more prominent grifters are addicted it is impossible to say, but it is rumored that Kid Duff, Jack Hardaway, Charley Dixon, Pretty Willy (better known as a thief), Kid Niles, the Yenshee Kid, Claude King, Kent Marshall, Red Lager (the Younger), Jimmy the Rooter, the Sanctimonious Kid and Jackie French are, or have been, addicted. There must be many others who have successfully concealed their addiction. As one goes down the social scale among grifters, addiction becomes increasingly common.

Some con men have pleasures which are less deleterious. Many now play golf for sport, while old-timers like Wildfire John, the Honey Grove Kid, the Indiana Wonder and the High Ass Kid played it largely for business reasons. Some fancy horses and, like the Clinic Kid and Big Kentuck, maintain their own racing or saddle stables. But mostly their interests stop with gambling and girls.

On the other hand, it must not be assumed that all con men live fast, dissipated lives. Some are temperate or even ascetic. Stewart Donnelly, for instance, has a reputation among his colleagues for being exceedingly abstemious and far more decent in his living habits than many legitimate citizens. He is reputed to refuse all kinds of liquor, even beer and wine, does not use tobacco or narcotics; and, at past fifty, has the physique of a boxer. Many of his associates feel that it is to his credit that he does not gamble, that he scrupulously pays his debts, and that he has been married to the same woman for twenty years.

Confidence men, like legitimate citizens, mate once or more (usually more) during their lives. But, unlike the legitimate citizens, they seldom get divorces, probably because of the publicity which would attend such an event. If they separate, they do it quietly and without benefit of legal papers. Some con men marry into higher social levels and acquire property and status through marriage. Others associate themselves with wealthy women; Kid McGinley, who once short-changed Anita Baldwin on the circus lot and soon found himself in possession of a fortune, is a happy example of this. Some, like Cockroach Gary, scion of a wealthy family who acquired four hundred pounds, more or less, of thief in Big Cad, reverse the process. Some marry waitresses, some prostitutes. But most of them marry girls who are in one way or another connected with the grift, although few women ever work into the confidence rackets with their husbands.

Grifters differ in their opinions about the extent to which women are able to help their husbands in the business of trimming marks. "Grifters," observes one cynic, "are always marrying some squaw who is a bum and who will never make a grifter. I never knew one who married anybody who knew much, or who wanted to learn. They just never seem to meet the right sort." Another con man, an expert on the pay-off, says, "Grifters use girls and women for contacting marks around high-class resorts. If a grifter has his girl or wife with him, and if she is smart enough, why then he uses her. But few are smart enough." Another, who has himself used women as part of his roping technique, says, "Some women are smart to grifting if they have a chance to grift. A clever girl can certainly lead a mark around. She knows how to keep him on the line while he is being played, too. Sometimes she promises the mark that, after he makes all his money, they will take a little trip to Europe together. Marks like that kind of goings-on. . . ." An old-timer who remembers the genesis of big-time confidence games adds, "A long time ago I knew many women, like Ollie Roberts in St. Louis, who were roping for panel stores, and some of them were good. But most of them have passed on. Some of them should have been on the pay-off. They were natural ropers. There are plenty of women today who would make good, too, but they haven't the chance because they don't know any good grifters." The majority of con men, however, want their women safely at home while a mark is being played; then they know that a woman won't do something impulsive and ruin the play. Furthermore, some con men feel that it is beneath the dignity of their wives to work on the grift.

Other branches of the grift are peopled with women aplenty; some of the best pickpockets are women, women have been dealers in gaming houses from western frontier days on down, and have been professional gamblers since long before the Civil War. As big-time professional thieves, some of them are unsurpassed, and the small-time thieving rackets are overrun with them. They are well represented in flat-jointing and in some other branches of the short con. But the only full-fledged con woman whom I have been able to turn up, who is recognized by male colleagues everywhere as a competent professional, is Lilly the Roper, who is now over fifty and has spent her entire life on the grift. Early in life she made a reputation as a pickpocket and had her own mob. She was first married to a heavy man named Harrington. Following his death, she married a thief whom she divorced to marry her present husband, a pickpocket turned con man. "Lilly can rope a mark for the big con and trim one, too," commented one professional who has known her for many years.

The fact that there are few marriages among con folk and even fewer divorces need not imply that there is no code governing relations between the sexes. The men provide for the material needs of their women very liberally; they have good living quarters, fine clothes, servants and all the comforts that money can buy. Most of them do not discard their women when they grow old, even though there is no legal tie binding them. One con man seldom steals another's woman unless she deliberately throws herself at him, or has already left her man. However, if one does steal another's girl, the only resultant social criticism is a little good-natured ribbing directed at the loser. If he takes his loss very seriously, he may kill or try to kill his rival; usually, he takes his kidding graciously and consoles himself with another woman. And, in all justice to the women, it should be said that, in spite of the fact that they know that their husbands live free-and-easy love lives on the road, they usually remain faithful to their men. As long as they live in wedlock, they carefully observe the double standard. Probably there is no more infidelity on their parts than there is among legitimate middle-class wives. A woman who is unfaithful to her man is not regarded very highly; this is especially true when she is living or staying with friends while her husband is in prison or away. Her indiscretions are her own business, but she should not bring them into the homes of her friends. If she regards herself as still belonging to her man, she should conduct herself properly; if not, she should stay on her own, or get another man. In other words, as long as she permits her husband's friends to support her, she is obligated to maintain a respectable demeanor and behavior. And she usually does. Kid Duff's wife, for instance, held in her possession all the Kid's assets—amounting to several hundred thousand dollars—until he finished his last bit in prison, then, after his release, returned them to him and secured a divorce. She could have very easily run out on him while he was helpless, but she dealt fairly with him.

Con men get out of life little more than they can buy with money; in addition, they are beset on all sides by dangers which the legitimate citizen never has to cope with. They like to believe that their women will be the last to let them down—despite many examples to the contrary. There is sometimes a deep and somewhat pathetic attachment between the pair which may be life-long. Charley Gondorff, for instance, has always stuck to his Maude, even though wealth and wide social contacts made it possible for him to have had a choice of many clever and more handsome women. Many of the older generation have done the same thing. And Farmer Brown, king of the monte players, frequently and vociferously proclaimed in public that he was "married to the most beautiful woman who ever straddled a chamber-pot," expert testimony to the contrary notwithstanding.

The women do not always have an easy time of it, even though their wants are liberally supplied. If they are aware of their husband's occupation—and few of them are not—they live in constant fear of a "fall" with disastrous consequences. They see little of their men for weeks on end, while, at the same time, correspondence may be both difficult and dangerous. They are usually incapable of helping their men or of sharing any common interest with them. But many of them do try to do their part as well as they can. Perhaps the most pathetic case in point is that of the schoolteacher who married the illiterate Sheeny Mike. John Singleton swears that when he once visited the pair, he overheard her teaching her husband the alphabet. "I could hear Mike droning, 'Aaa, Bee, Cee,' then starting all over again, 'Aaa, Bee, Cee. . . . ' His wife said that was as far as he was ever able to get." But Singleton was having his sarcastic little joke; the teacher did make Mike literate and he became a prosperous roper.

In spite of the fact that con men live on the road almost continuously, they try to maintain more or less permanent homes, most of them in or about Chicago or New York, some of the fine ones on Long Island. The location of these homes is always carefully guarded and kept secret from all but very close friends. Grifters frequently know one another well, and even work together professionally, without revealing their addresses to one another. In fact, it is rigidly observed underworld etiquette to refrain from asking a professional where he lives; if he volunteers the information it is a mark of trust and esteem. Some con men, like Joe Furey, maintain two homes with a separate family in each; but, on the whole, con folk appear to be hardly less monogamous than legitimate middle-class society.

However, marital life on the grift is by no means always calm and unruffled, the relationship mutually faithful and felicitous. Far from it. "Storm-and-strife" is a common argot word for wife, a coinage which is probably rooted rather deeply in bitter experience. Some con men marry "sucker-broads" who trim them and run out on them; others marry "gun-molls" who are themselves "on the lam" most of the time; and not a few find themselves harboring a "rat" who only awaits an opportunity to turn stool pigeon for the police. "My boy," old John Henry Strosnider once said, "the best way to avoid the big house is not to tell your twist how clever you are. Broads have been known to put the finger on smart young apples. So cop my advice, and last longer on the outside than on the inside. . . ."

All too often the home life of the grifter, especially the small-time grifter, is like that of the famous Cheerful Charley and his girl, the Cheerful Chicken. Charley had fallen upon lean days as steerer for a mitt store in Minneapolis and had done what small-timers frequently do—"joined out the odds"—that is, he had put the Chicken on the market for all and sundry who would buy. One wintry Saturday night the Chicken came into the room, weary and stiff from pounding the pavements in her worn-out shoes. She gave Charley all her money, then showed him her toes sticking out of the wet leather.

"I have to have some new shoes, Charley," she said.

"No, by God," roared Charley, "not with my money."

Obviously, the home life of grifters does not make a desirable background against which to raise children. Yet some do raise families; and some of the children grow up without suspecting that their father is a confidence man. However, when the mother is also involved in the rackets, the offspring almost inevitably follow in their parents' footsteps, for they meet thieves at home, hear thievery discussed from their earliest recollection, and grow up in an environment which they cannot escape. There are, however, some notable exceptions like John Singleton's son—who has a legitimate profession in New York—whose name, for obvious reasons, cannot be given here.

An ironical little anecdote illustrates the relation between grifters and their children. One successful grifter had three sons, none of whom suspected his father's occupation. He determined to send them to college so that they need never know the rigors of the grift. When the first two were old enough, he bundled them off. Very shortly, and somewhat to their father's embarrassment, they were apprehended in some thievery. Said the grifter, "If they are going to be thieves, they might as well learn right." So he took them all on the road and thus ended his experiment in higher education.

4.

"The gambler is driven by essentially narcissistic and aggressive desires for omnipotence . . ."

Edmund Bergler

"The passion for gambling thus serves an autoerotic satisfaction, wherin betting is foreplay, winning is orgasm, and losing is ejaculation, defecation, and castration."

Ernst Simmel

"A man can find out a lot about himself, playing poker. Is he brave? Is he cool? Does he have any money left? I am obliged to say that I felt pretty hip and well-hung for much of the evening, in that little paradise of the private room, with its pro dealer, its full bar, its pleasant company, its complimentary poker chips—and the up coming cards, from which hope increasingly springs. By the end of the evening, I confess, I was feeling much less formidable: much less butch, and much less rich. But what an enthralling process. When can I go through it again?"

Martin Amis

from

Casino

by Nick Pileggi

"My pals thought I was the messiah."

LEFTY ROSENTHAL DID not believe in luck. He believed in the odds. In the numbers. In probability. In the math. In the fractions of data he had accumulated copying team statistics onto index cards. He believed that games were fixed and that referees and zebras could be bought. He knew some basketball players who practiced the art of missing basketball rim shots for hours every day, and he knew players who bet the middles between the odds spread and got a return of 10 percent on their money. He believed that some athletes played lazy and some of them played hurt. He believed in winning and losing streaks; he believed in point spreads and no-limit bets and card mechanics so good they could deal out cards without breaking the cellophane on the deck. In other words, where gambling was concerned, Lefty believed in everything but luck. Luck was the potential enemy. Luck was the temptress, the seductive whisperer taking you away from the data. Lefty learned early that if he was ever to master the skill and become a professional player, he had to take even the remotest possibility of chance out of the process.

* * *

Frank "Lefty" Rosenthal was born on June 12, 1929, just a few months before the stock market crash. He was raised on Chicago's West Side, an old-world, syndicate neighborhood, where bookie shops, crooked cops, corrupt aldermen, and closed mouths were a way of life.

"My dad was a produce wholesaler," Rosenthal said. "An administrative type. Good with numbers. Smart. Successful. My mother was a housewife. I grew up reading the racing form. I used to tear it apart. I knew everything there was to know about the form. I used to read it in class. I was a tall, skinny, shy kid. I was six foot one when I was a teenager and I was kind of withdrawn. I was sort of a loner, and horse racing was my challenge.

"My dad owned some horses, so I was at the track with him all the time. I lived at the track. I was a groom. A hot walker. I hung around the backstretch. I mucked out. I'd get there at four thirty in the morning. I became a part of the barn. I started hanging out there when I was thirteen and fourteen, and I was an owner's son. Everybody left me alone.

"I got some resistance at home when I started getting into sports betting. My mother knew I was gambling and she didn't like it, but I was very strong headed. I wouldn't listen to anyone. I loved going over the charts, the past performances, jockeys, post positions. I used to copy all that material onto my own eight-by-ten-inch file cards in my room late into the night.

"I cut school one day to go to the track. I went with two pals. Smart guys. We stayed for eight races and I punched out seven winners. My pals thought I was the messiah. My dad turned away when he spotted me there. He wouldn't talk to me. He was pissed that I had cut school. I didn't say anything to him when I got home. It wasn't discussed. I didn't say anything about winning, either. The next day I cut school again and went back to the track and lost it all.

"But I really learned gambling in the bleachers of Wrigley Field and Comiskey Park. There were about two hundred guys up there every game and they bet on everything. Every pitch. Every swing. Everything had a price. There were guys shouting numbers at you. It was great. It was an open-air casino. Constant action.

"If you were talented, and you had some ego, and you knew your game, you'd be tempted to take them on. You've got money in your pocket and you feel like you can take on the world. There was a guy named Stacy; he was in his fifties and he had a pocket full of cash. He'd fade anybody. 'Hey kid, they gonna score this inning or not?' Instead of passing, your pride gets in there and you make a bet and you pay the price. Stacy always got you to make a price.

"Say Chicago is winning six to two in the eighth and you want to bet they score again, or that they'll lose in the ninth. Or that they'd hit into a double play to end the inning. Or hit a home run to win the game. Or a double or a triple or a flyout. Whatever. Stacy would take the action and he'd lay the odds. He'd make a homer twenty-five to one. Bam! Just like that. A fly ball was twenty to one. An 'out' was eight to five. If you wanted the action, you made the bet and he gave you his odds.

"I didn't know it at first, but every one of those bets Stacy faded had odds backing them up. A strikeout at the end of a game was, say—I don't remember the real odds now, but say it was a hundred and sixty-six to one, not thirty to one, which was what Stacy was laying.

"A home run on a game's first pitch could be three thousand to one, not seventy-five to one. And so forth. If you were betting Stacy, you had to know those odds, or you'd be picked clean.

"After I caught on, I'd just sit and listen to him make his odds and I'd write them all down and keep a record. After a while, I started making proposition bets out there on my own. Over the years, Stacy made a little fortune in the bleachers. He cleaned up. He was terrific at getting everybody all around him to start betting. He was a great showman.

"Back then, you didn't have sports channels and magazines and newspapers and radio shows that specialized in betting sports. If you were in the Midwest you couldn't easily find out what was happening to the East and West Coast teams behind the scenes. You'd get the final score and that was about that.

"But if you're betting seriously, you've got to know a lot more than that. So I started reading everything. My father got me a shortwave radio, and I remember spending hours listening to the play-by-play of out-of-town teams I was thinking of betting. I began subscribing to different papers from all around the country. I'd go to this newsstand where they had all the out-of-town papers. That's where I met Hymie the Ace. He was a legendary professional. I don't call people legends unless they are. Hymie the Ace was a legend. He would be there at the same newsstand buying dozens of papers, just like me. He'd get into his car and start reading. I'd be there, too, except I didn't have a car. I had a bike. After a while we got to know each other. He knew what I was doing.

"Hymie was about ten or twelve years older than I was. I made it a habit to always say hello to him and to the other pros, and I was lucky that they'd all talk to me. I was still a kid, but they saw that I was serious and I had an aptitude, and they were willing to help me. They were very kind. They allowed me into their circle. I felt great.

"But I'm also getting chesty. I'm doing pretty well. I'm feeling good. There was a Northwestern-Michigan basketball game that was coming up. I had people at both schools feeding me information and I felt really strong. I liked Northwestern.

"Now I don't mean I *liked* Northwestern. That I was a fan. That I had their pennant in my room. I mean I liked them as a bet. That's all teams were to me. Bets. I'd been waiting for this game. I'd been watching it. So I bet Northwestern to beat Michigan State. It was a sellout crowd. I walked in and I saw Hymie the Ace. Hymie knows more about basketball than any man alive. We say hello. It's ten minutes to tip-off.

"I told him I played Northwestern and asked what he was doing. I was so certain about my information that I had made what I used to call a triple play—I'd bet two thousand dollars. It was as far as I could go with my bankroll. A single play for me at the time was like two hundred, a double play was five hundred, and a triple was two thousand. I'm just a kid. It's my limit. We're talking about a time when my whole bankroll was eight thousand.

"'What?' Hymie says, surprised. 'Why are you playing Northwestern? Don't you know about Johnny Green?'

"'Who?' I asked him.

"'Johnny Green. What's wrong with you?'

"Now Johnny Green was a black player who had been ineligible for the whole season. It turned out he had suddenly become eligible a couple of days before the game. I'd missed it.

"'Green's going to take every rebound in the game,' Ace said, and my heart sank.

"I ran to the phones, but there were just two booths and there were twenty-five people waiting at each booth. I'm looking to lay off some of my bets. Get rid of them. Balance some of the action. I'm still standing in line waiting for the phone when I hear the announcer and I know I'm dead. I can't get off.

"I go back and sit down. I watch Green. Just like Ace said, he controlled both backboards. At halftime I had seen enough. Michigan annihilated Northwestern. Ace had done his homework and I hadn't.

"Ace not only knew that Green was eligible, he knew what kind of a player he was, knew that he was a great rebounder, knew that that was the element that could beat Northwestern. Green went on to be an All-American and top pro player.

"I learned a hell of a lesson. I found out I wasn't as smart as I thought I was. I had depended upon people for too much. I had given them the power to make up my mind for me. I realized that if I wanted to spend my life gambling, pitting myself against the best bookmakers, there was no such thing as listening to people. If I was going to make a living doing this, I was going to have to figure it out for myself and do it all myself.

"So I started out with college basketball and football. In college games I subscribed to all the school newspapers and went through the sports pages every day. I'd call the reporters at the different schools and make up all kinds of stories to find out extra bits of information that didn't get into the papers.

"At first, I didn't tell them why I wanted the information, but pretty soon they caught on, and I picked up some sharp kids out there and I brought them along. When I won, I threw them a few bucks, and after a while I had a whole network of people who kept me informed about college games.

"As I got older I'd go to games with a tape recorder. I had spotters working for me. I'd tell some guys to just watch specific things. I'd have them watching two or three players only. I didn't care what else was happening; they had to watch who I told them to watch. I'd take their notes. Then I'd fly to the next town where the team played and I'd watch them again. I'd match lineups. The final score's never the main thing to look at if you want to make money instead of losing it. I knew if a player had hurt his ankle and was playing slower. I knew when a quarterback was sick. I knew if his girlfriend got knocked up or left him for somebody else. I knew if he was smoking dope, snorting coke. I knew about injuries that didn't get in the papers. About injuries that players kept from their coaches.

"Now, with this kind of information, it wasn't hard for me to see when the bookmakers had made an error in their odds. I didn't blame them. They were covering lots of sports and lots of games. I was concentrating on a few. I knew everything there was to know about a certain limited number of games, and I learned a very important thing—I learned that you can't bet on every game. Sometimes you can only bet one or two games out of forty or fifty. Sometimes, I learned, there wasn't a good bet on the whole weekend. If that was true, I wouldn't bet or take a serious position.

"I used to hang around a cigar store on Kinzie. George and Sam ran the place. Out front they had cigars and stuff. But in the back there was a Western Union wire, telephones, and a tote board. In those days, they had the most up-to-date information. During the baseball season, the latest list of starting pitchers would come over the wire just before game time.

"George and Sam were really big bookmakers. They had come to Chicago from Tarrytown, New York. And they had an okay from the powers that be to operate the book. It was wide open. They even had the okay from the local police captain to run poker games, which were very illegal.

"They had a bar and they'd serve drinks and food for free. The wire was always banging away. It was like a stock market ticker. The Western Union machines were hard for a bookie to get. They were meant to be sold to newspapers, but if you filed certain papers with the company and knew how to go about it, you might be able to get one. At that time I was so dumb I tried to get one for my house, and I was turned down.

"George and Sam were independent operators, but they still had to pay protection. All the card rooms and bookie rooms paid off in those days. Bookmakers took care of the cops and they took care of the outfit. And sometimes the outfit took care of the cops. In the end, everybody could wind up taking care of everybody, just as long as everybody made money.

"When I was nineteen," Rosenthal continued, "I got a job as a clerk at Bill Kaplan's sports service, Angel-Kaplan. It was great. We would be on the phones all day giving out our line to bookmakers and players. Everyone from all over the country was hooked into each other. We had special phone lines set up by retired telephone company workers. We all knew each other's voices and code names, but after a while, you get to know everybody's real name.

"I'm just a kid and still in Chicago, but now I'm hooked into the biggest office in the United States at the time—Gil Beckley's in Newport, Kentucky. Gil had the whole town of Newport locked up. The coppers. The politicians. The whole fucking town.

"Gil was Newport's main industry. He had thirty clerks working. He ran the biggest layoff operation in the country. It was where every bookmaking office in the country called to lay off bets if the action on one side was getting too heavy.

"For instance, if you're a bookmaker in Dallas, you are naturally going to get more Dallas bets than you want, because you won't have enough people betting on the other side to offset any win. So a Dallas bookmaker would call Gil Beckley's layoff operation, and Beckley's clerks would pick up enough of the Dallas bookmaker's bets to balance his book. Since Beckley is national, he can offset the Dallas bets against their opponents that week, and everything becomes even again.

"Wherever he went, Gil was the boss. In the winter he'd be in Miami. He'd invite twenty or thirty guys out to dinner. 'Let's go to Joe's Stone Crab!' 'Let's go here!' 'Let's go there!' He always had an entourage with him, and he always picked up the check.

"Naturally, I got to meet Gil Beckley only by phone. For a couple of years we're talking and he recognized that I was an up-and-coming kid. A whatever-you-want-to-call-it kid. A handicapper and a player. And my little reputation was building. But the more I talked to Beckley, the more I realized the most unbelievable thing. If you asked Gil Beckley how many men were on a baseball team, he'd have to ask someone. Literally.

"He could not tell you. That wasn't one of his things. I'm being honest. Mickey Mantle? Who? Beckley just didn't know. He didn't have a fucking clue. But then, he didn't have to know. He was a bookmaker and layoff man. He didn't bet. He just ran the biggest accounting office in the country. I was stunned.

"But I found out pretty soon it didn't matter. All a layoff man's gotta do is make sure he keeps the bets balanced and take his ten percent. You don't have to be an expert on teams or even know about the games. I was amazed, but it turned out to be true of lots of layoff men and bookies. Some of the biggest guys didn't bet. In Chicago we had Benny the Book. Benny was the biggest bookmaker in town. Benny made millions and millions as a bookmaker, and just like Gil Beckley, Benny couldn't tell you who Joe DiMaggio played for. I'm serious.

"I was betting and getting good information at the time my friend Sidney was Benny's top clerk, and he asked me, as a favor, if I would call his office if I learned something about a game, something that might affect the outcome, like that there was a fix or one of the players was injured.

"So, one day I came up with an injury that hadn't been reported, and I called my friend Sidney, but he wasn't there. Instead, I got Benny. The big boss himself. So I told Benny about the player. I remember the player. Bobby Avila. Second base for the Cleveland Indians. I said 'Avila's out.'

"I wanted to alert him so he could adjust his line and not get smashed by all the pros, who, I can assure you, would have already gotten the same information I had.

"Benny takes the information like he knows what I'm talking about, but when I finish he asks me, 'Don't they have another second baseman?' I think, 'Another Bobby Avila? Is he serious?' I couldn't believe it.

"That night I met Sidney and I asked him if he was working for a crazy person. He said Benny didn't follow the games, just the price. Benny was the biggest bookie in Chicago, not because he knew about the players and sports but because he paid on Monday. No matter what he owed you after the weekend, Benny paid on Monday. His clerk would be down there with an envelope and brand-new bills. And if you owed him, he'd always give you more time. So, whether he knew Bobby Avila or not, he had a tremendous clientele and laughed all the way to the bank."

Painter Jailed for Committing Masterpieces

In Which We Encounter The Mystery Man of Modern Art and Fall Into Another, Deeper Philosophical Abyss

by Robert Anton Wilson

"Logic!" cried the frog.
"There is no logic in this!"

— *MR. ARKADIN*

I can live without God.
I can't live without painting.

— *VINCENT AND THEO*

BUT PERHAPS WE began at the wrong point. The true nature of our plot might better begin with another, and more elaborate, Deconstruction.

In August 1968 the Spanish government imprisoned a man on the island of Ibiza for creating a long series of sketches and paintings—beautiful, intensely lyrical works that *Art Experts* had universally proclaimed as masterpieces.

The imprisonment of this Maker of Masterpieces did not represent censorship in the ordinary erotic or religious sense. Nobody even accused the artist of Political Incorrectness. He got jugged for a technical matter—namely, that he had signed the wrong name to his works . . . or several wrong names, in fact. Names like Picasso and Van Gogh and Modigliani and Matisse, for instance.

Not that anybody knew then, or knows now, what name the man *should* have signed. Generally, when the case gets recalled at all, people refer to the prisoner of Ibiza as El Myr or Elmyr de Hory, but neither of those titles have any claim to special eminence among his many aliases. In his long career, the painter had used both of those names, but he had also used Baron Elmyr von Houry, Elmyr Herzog, Louis Cassou, Baron Elmyr Hoffman, Joseph Dory, E. Raynal, Joseph Dory-Boutin and quite a few others—perhaps as many as a hundred pseudonyms, according to Francois Reichenbach, an alleged **Expert** on this case.

One trouble with Reichenbach as an **Expert**: he admits to buying and selling some of "Elmyr's" forged paintings. Another problem: he later collaborated (with Orson Welles, no less) on a film—*F For Fake*—that either exposed "Elmyr" totally or created a whole new set of myths about "Elmyr," depending on which other **Experts** you choose to believe.

(Welles himself has said—in the documentary "Orson Welles: A Life in Film," BBC-TV—that "everything in that movie was a fake." But to post-modernism, all art constitutes fake, or mask, in the Aristotelian sense of an imitation, or counterfeit of something else, and in a new non-Aristotelian sense we will explore as we advance deeper into the murk. We need to think slowly before deciding whether Welles spoke literally or metaphorically in describing *F For Fake* as itself a fake.)

Whatever the facts—if we still dare to speak of "facts" in this age of situationism and deconstructionism—we will, as a matter of typographical convenience, hereafter refer to the prisoner of Ibiza as Elmyr without dubious quotes and without any guessing about his last name—if he had a last name, like ordinary humans, and didn't arrive here by spaceship . . . "Elmyr" he preferred in his last years, and Elmyr we shall call him. And, for those who don't like to repeatedly see words they can't sound out in their heads, the Hungarian "Myr" rhymes with "deer," and "Elmyr" has the same beat approximately as "cold beer" or "my ear." Just say "cold beer, my ear, shake spear, Elmyr" and you'll have no further sounding problems as you read.

Elmyr served only two months in jail and then the Spanish further expressed displeasure with his chosen profession by expelling him from their country for one year, because he also had a reputation as a flamboyant homosexual, or in pop argot, an aging fairy godmother. But meanwhile, he had told his story to a young American writer, Cliff, who became his official biographer. According to *Fake!*, the deliberately outrageous biography concocted together by Cliff and Elmyr, this man of variable names, wobbly gender and multiple styles had committed many more masterpieces than those for which he had gotten jailed.

In fact, *Fake!* says Elmyr had painted *over a thousand* of the classics of modern art. Every time you walk through a museum and see a Picasso or a Matisse that you particularly like, you should stop and ask, "Now did Picasso or Matisse do that, or did Elmyr do it?"

Sort of changes your whole view of what critics call "the canon," doesn't it?

The canon—a term borrowed from the theologians (which should make us suspicious at once: can we borrow anything of value from a corporation widely suspected for about 200 years now of intellectual bankruptcy?)—designates those works of art and literature which have achieved the rank of Masterpieces. When does a work achieve this canonicity? When the **Experts** say it does, of course. But the Elmyr case, far more than Deconstructionist philosophy, indicates that the **Experts** do not always know shit from Shinola.

Of course, not everybody believes that Elmyr committed quite as much great art as he gleefully confesses in the biography. Many **Experts** claim *Fake!* (a title to ponder, and ponder again) engaged in shameless bragging and exaggeration, to make Elmyr seem cleverer than the facts warrant.

Unfortunately, these **Experts** had—many of them—authenticated some of the fakes that Elmyr undoubtedly did paint. As Elmyr's co-author, Cliff, says, these **Experts** do not want their cover blown—they don't want us to know how often, and how easily, they have gotten duped by Elmyr and other skilled forgers.

According to Cliff, *all* ***Experts*** *operate largely on bluff.* Some of the **Experts**, however, have counter-attacked by suggesting that this alleged "co-author," Cliff, may himself have functioned even more as a co-conspirator.

And, in fact, the same co-author, Clifford Irving to give him his full name, subsequently became even more famous, and much more infamous, for persuading a New York publisher to give him a $750,000 advance for an *authorized* biography of Howard Hughes, i.e., a biography in which Hughes himself would talk, for the record, about all the financial, political, conspiratorial and sexual scandals in his Faustian career. $750,000 had a value, in 1969, of about $5 million now, but the publishers shelled out happily. Irving had shown them a contract and various notes *in Hughes' own handwriting* . . .

You see, even though Cliff Irving had already written *Fake!*, a textbook on forgery, including charming details on forged signatures as well as counterfeit paintings, he had a boyishly sincere manner and a wickedly scintillating personality. Like all good con-men.

He and Hughes had met on a pyramid in Mexico, Irving said with a straight face. In the dead of night, of course . . . (It would make a wonderful surrealist painting, if Elmyr ever did a Dali: The ambitious young Irving and the rich old lunatic with matted hair and fingernails—*or claws*—like Bigfoot . . . signing a contract on a pyramid . . . under, I presume, a full moon . . .)

Handwriting **Experts** later testified in court, after Irving's own veracity came under suspicion. They said absolutely that Howard Hughes himself, and nobody else, had written the signature and notes produced by Irving. At this point, alas, many people began to share Irving's (and Elmyr's) low opinion of **Experts**, and soon the biography of Hughes got canceled.

Hughes himself speaking over a phone (he never did come out of seclusion . . .) denounced Irving as a fraud; but, of course, some say that the voice emanated from a Virtual Hughes—a double who had impersonated Hughes for years. The Mafia had bumped off the real Hughes, these conspiracy nuts claim, many years earlier. Had Irving faked a meeting with a man already dead and gotten "exposed" by another faker impersonating the dead man? As Swift proved to Partridge, we cannot decide matters of life and death on mere allegation.

But we will deal with that kind of conspiracy later. Right now we only confront the problem of *"the canon" itself as a kind of conspiracy*.

We simply do not know the extent to which Elmyr has entered the canon. Maybe 2 per cent of the masterpieces in modern museums emanated from his wizard's brush, as virtually everybody now admits. Maybe the figure (at least for post-impressionism, fauvism and early cubism, Elmyr's specialties) runs as high as 25 per cent, or 50 per cent . . . An *ouvre* of "more than a thousand" paintings might make up something in that percentage range of canonical 20th Century Classics. These implications appear heavily suggested in Irving's *Fake!* and even more stressed in the Welles-Reichenbach film . . .

Well, then, we must re-examine the canonicity of art as skeptically as the 18th and 19th Centuries re-examined religion. Religious canonicity survived (in the Occident) only as long as the Pope qualified as the world's leading **Expert**. When other **Experts** arose, with their own cults, religious canonicity became ambiguous and controversial. What happens when the Art **Experts** face a similar challenge?

Some Radical Feminist critics have already begun such a "Protestant heresy," and have dumped such Dead White European Males (DWEMs, in fashionable jargon) as Dante, Beethoven, Shakespeare, Michelangelo, etc. and replaced them with a new canon featuring a lot of long-forgotten ladies whose work, frankly, seems dreadfully inferior to me, and to most art critics.

For instance, Susan McClary has found Beethoven's Ninth Symphony a musical hymn to rape, which will no doubt surprise all those with less androphobic ears, who hear something quite different in it, something of cosmic grandeur . . . Says McClary, "The point of recapitulation in the first movement of the Ninth is one of the most horrifying moments in music . . . which finally explodes in the throttling, murderous rage of a rapist . . ." Sounds almost as bad as *The Texas Chain Saw Massacre,* doesn't it?

Although I write a lot of satire, I didn't make this up. You can find McClary's analysis in *Minnesota Composers' Forum Newsletter*, January 1987. She also doesn't like Western classic music in general, because of its "phallic violence" and "pelvic pounding." I insist I did not invent McClary or any of her ravings. Honest to God. Some Femigogues just happen to sound like satire when you quote them verbatim.

As for the female masterpieces set against old Ludwig, they only *appear* inferior, the Feminist revisionists say, because all of us have had our perceptions warped by the "patriarchal brainwashing" of our "phallocentric" culture. ("All of us" includes many female art critics, like Camille Paglia, who angrily claims this argument has crossed the line to an idiot caricature of Feminism)

Maybe we all need a long de-programming at a Feminist reeducation camp. Then we will realize that Hildegarde of Bingen not only outclassed Beethoven but wrote more first-rate music than Mozart, Bach and Scott Joplin together, and without any rape fantasies creeping in.

Third World revisionists have raised similar objections to the canonical centrality of DWEMs. They ask us, not too gently, do we really believe that *all* the great art of humanity came out of *one sub-continent*, created by *white males* only? Hmmm?

Do we trust these revisionists or do we trust our own sensibilities?

After Elmyr, do we dare trust *anybody?*

As a famous bard wrote,

> He stood in his socks and he wondered, he wondered
> He stood in his socks and he wondered

The post-modernists go beyond even the Feminists and the Multi—Culturalists, by casting relativistic doubts, not only on official Canons but on all alleged "eternal truths"—artistic, religious, philosophical, scientific or whatever. Worse yet, some of the **Experts** have identified me as a post-modernist. For instance, *Post-Modern Fiction: a Bio-Bibliographical Guide* by Larry McCaffrey includes me as leading post-modern novelist, "in the tradition" of Pynchon, Burroughs and Vonnegut. I have to recognize some truth in this accusation, since Pynchon, Burroughs and Vonnegut certainly lead the list of My Favorite Contemporary Writers, and have therefore undoubtedly influenced me. (James Joyce and Orson Welles, my favorite artists of this whole century, look suspiciously like premature post-modernists.). Sociologist Alfonso Montuori also includes me among the post-modernists in his *Evolutionary Competence*, although he says I have less gloom and pessimism than other post-modern novelists, a distinction that I feel glad somebody has noticed. Despite that, to the extent that post-modern means "post-dogmatic," I do shamefacedly belong with this unsavory crowd; only to the extent that post-modern has come to mean a new dogma do I part company from them.

At the end of Welles' *F For Fake*, after we have suffered prolonged doubt about how many Picassos should get reclassified as Elmyrs, one character cries passionately *"I must believe, at least, that art is real!"*—a noble thought with which I might finish this chapter . . .

But this voice of Faith and Tradition belongs to another art forger, one who allegedly faked even more of the canonical Renaissance masterpieces than Elmyr had faked of the canonical Moderns. We cannot have faith in this faker's faith . . .

A Law Degree Is Just an Illegal Technicality

by Frank W. Abagnale

A WEEK LATER I severed my connection with the hospital, my lease at Balmorhea came up for renewal and I decided to leave Atlanta. There was no compulsion for me to go; at least I felt none, but I thought it unwise to stay. The fox who keeps to one den is the easiest caught by the terriers, and I felt I had nested too long in one place. I knew I was still being hunted and I didn't want to make it easy for the hounds.

I later learned that my decision to leave Atlanta was an astute one. About the same time, in Washington, D.C., FBI Inspector Sean O'Riley was ordered to drop all his other cases and concentrate solely on nabbing me. O'Riley was a tall, dour man with the countenance of an Irish bishop and the tenacity of an Airedale, an outstanding agent dedicated to his job, but an eminently fair man in all respects.

I came to admire O'Riley, even while making every effort to thwart his task and to embarrass him professionally. If O'Riley has any personal feelings concerning me, I am certain animosity is not among such emotions. O'Riley is not a mean man.

Of course, I had no knowledge of O'Riley's existence, even at the time I vacated Atlanta. Save for the young special agent in Miami, and the Dade County officers I'd encountered there, the officers on my case were all phantoms to me.

I decided to hole up for a month or so in the capital city of another southern state. As usual, I was prompted in my choice by the fact that I knew an airline stewardess there. I was yet to find a more delightful influence on my actions than a lovely woman.

Her name was Diane and I had known her intermittently for about a year. I had never flown with her, having met her in the Atlanta airport terminal, and she knew me under the alias Robert F. Conrad, a Pan Am first officer, an allonym I used on occasion. I was forced to maintain the nom de plume with her, for we developed a close and pleasing relationship, during the course of which, initially, she had delved into my personal background, including my educational history. Most pilots have a college degree, but not all of them majored in the aeronautical sciences. I told Diane that I had taken a law degree but had never practiced, since a career as an airline pilot had loomed as not only more exciting but also much more lucrative than law. She readily accepted the premise that a man might shun the courtroom for the cockpit.

She also remembered my concocted law degree. A few days after my arrival in her city she took me to a party staged by one of her friends and there introduced me to a pleasant fellow named Jason Wilcox.

"You two ought to get along. Jason is one of our assistant state's attorneys," Diane told me. She turned to Wilcox. "And Bob here is a lawyer who never hung out his shingle. He became a pilot instead."

Wilcox was immediately interested. "Hey, where'd you go to law school?"

"Harvard," I said. If I was going to have a law degree, I thought I might as well have one from a prestigious source.

"But you never practiced?" he asked.

"No," I said. "I got my Commercial Pilot's License the same week I took my master's in law, and Pan Am offered me a job as a flight engineer. Since a pilot makes $30,000 to $40,000, and since I loved flying, I took the job. Maybe someday I'll go back to law, but right now I fly only eighty hours a month. Not many practicing lawyers have it that good."

"No, you're right there," Wilcox agreed. "Where do you fly to? Rome? Paris? All over the world, I guess."

I shook my head. "I'm not flying at the moment," I said. "I've been furloughed. The company made a personnel cutback last month and I didn't have seniority. It may be six months or a year before they call me back. Right now I'm just loafing, drawing unemployment. I like it."

Wilcox studied me with bemused eyes. "How'd you do at Harvard?" he asked. I felt he was leading up to something.

"Pretty well, I guess," I replied. "I graduated with a 3.8 average. Why?"

"Well, the attorney general is looking for lawyers for his staff," Wilcox replied. "In fact, he's really in a bind. Why don't you take the bar here and join us? I'll recommend you. The job doesn't pay an airline pilot's salary, of course, but it pays better than unemployment. And you'll get in some law practice, which sure as hell couldn't hurt you."

I almost rejected his proposal outright. But the more I thought about it, the more it intrigued me. The challenge again. I shrugged. "What would it entail for me to take the bar examination in this state?" I asked.

"Not much, really," said Wilcox. "Just take a transcript from Harvard over to the state bar examiner's office and apply to take the bar. They won't refuse you. Of course, you'd have to bone up on our civil and criminal statutes, but I've got all the books you'd need. Since you're from another state, you'll be allowed three cracks at the bar here. You shouldn't have any trouble."

A transcript from Harvard. That might prove difficult, I mused, since the university and I were strangers. But then I'd never had any pilot's training, either. And I had a valid-appearing FAA pilot's license in my pocket stating I was qualified to fly passenger jets, didn't I? My bumblebee instincts began buzzing.

I wrote to the registrar of the Harvard Law School and asked for a fall schedule and a law school catalogue, and within a few days the requested material was deposited in my mailbox. The catalogue listed all the courses necessary for a doctor of law from Harvard, and it also boasted some lovely logos and letterheads. But I still didn't have the foggiest notion of what a college transcript looked like.

Diane was an Ohio University graduate, who had majored in business administration. I casually engaged her in a conversation revolving around her student years.

She had been heavily involved in campus activities, it developed, something of a playgirl in college. "You must not have done much studying," I said jestingly.

"Oh, yes, I did," she maintained. "I had a 3.8 average. In fact, I was on the dean's list my senior year. You can have fun and still make good grades, you know."

"Aw, come on! I don't believe you had that kind of average. I'd have to see your transcript to believe that," I protested.

She grinned. "Well, smart-ass, I just happen to have one," she said, and returned from her bedroom a few minutes later with the document.

The transcript consisted of four legal-sized sheets of lined paper and was, in fact, a certified photocopy of her four years of college work, attested to and notarized by the registrar. The first page was headed by the name of the university in large, bold letters, beneath which appeared the state seal of Ohio. Then came her name, the year she had graduated, the degree she had received and the college (College of Business Administration) awarding the degree. The remainder of the pages was filled, line by line, with the courses she had taken, the dates, the hours of credit she had accumulated and her grades. A grade average was given at the end of each year and a final entry noted her over-all average, 3.8. In the bottom right-hand corner of the last page was the Ohio University seal, with a notary's seal superimposed and bearing the signature of the school registrar.

I committed the structure of the transcript to memory, absorbing it as a sponge absorbs water, before handing it back. "Okay, you're not only sexy, you're also brainy," I said in mock apology.

I went shopping the next day at a graphic arts supply house, a stationery store and an office-supply firm, picking up some legal-sized bond paper, some layout material, some press-on letters in several different type faces, some artist's pens and pencils, an X-Acto knife, some glue and a right-angle ruler, some gold seals and a notary's press.

I started by simply cutting out the Harvard Law School logo and pasting it at the top of a piece of bond paper. I then affixed the school seal, also filched from the catalogue, beneath the school heading. Next I filled in my name, year of graduation, degree and then, using the right angle and a fine artist's pen, I carefully lined several pages of the legal-sized bond. Afterward, using block press-on letters, I carefully entered every course required for a law degree from Harvard, my electives and my fictitious grades. Since Wilcox might see the transcript, I gave myself a three-year over-all grade average of 3.8.

The finished, pasted-up product looked like leavings from a layout artist's desk, but when I ran the pages through a do-it-yourself copying machine, it came out beautifully. It had all the appearances of something coughed out by a duplicating computer. I finished the six-page counterfeit by attaching a gold seal to the bottom of the last page and impressing over it, in a deliberately blurred manner, the notary stamp, which I filled in by hand, using a heavy pen, and signing with a flourish the name of the Harvard Law School registrar, noting below the forgery that the registrar was also a notary.

Whether or not it resembled an actual Harvard transcript, I didn't know. The acid test would come when I presented the phony document to the state bar examiner's office. Wilcox had been practicing law for fifteen years, and had been an assistant state's attorney for nine years. He also had a wide acquaintance among the state's lawyers. He said I was the first Harvard graduate he'd ever met.

I spent three weeks poring over the volumes in Wilcox's office library, finding law a much easier, if somewhat duller, subject than I had assumed, and then with bated breath presented myself at the state bar examiner's office. A law student acting as a clerk in the office leafed through my fake transcript, nodded approvingly, made a copy of the phony instrument and handed my original counterfeit back to me, along with an application to take the bar examination. While I was filling out the form, he thumbed through a calendar and called someone on the telephone.

"You can take the exam next Wednesday, if you think you're ready," he stated, and then grinned encouragingly. "It should be no hill at all for a Harvard stepper."

His colloquialism might have been true in regard to an actual Ivy League law graduate. For me it was a mountain, eight hours of surmises, I hopes, maybes, confident conjecture and semi-educated guesses.

I flunked.

To my astonishment, however, the notification that I had failed was attached to the test I had taken, which reflected the answers I had correctly given and the questions I had missed. Someone in the SBE's office obviously liked me.

I went back to Wilcox's office and camped in his library, concentrating on the sections of the test I had missed. Whenever possible Wilcox himself tutored me. After six weeks I felt I was ready to attempt the test a second time.

I blew it again. But again my test papers were returned to me, showing where I had succeeded and where I had failed. I was gaining. In fact, I was delighted at the number of legal questions I had answered correctly and I was determined to pass the examination on my final try.

I took the third examination seven weeks later and passed! Within two weeks I received a handsome certificate attesting to the fact that I had been admitted to the state bar and was licensed to practice law. I cracked up. I hadn't even finished high school and had yet to step on a college campus, but I was a certified lawyer! However, I regarded my actual lack of academic qualifications merely a technicality, and in my four months of legal cramming I'd learned the law is full of technicalities. Technicalities are what screw up justice.

Wilcox fulfilled his promise. He arranged a job interview for me with the state attorney general, who, on Wilcox's recommendation, hired me as an assistant. My salary was $12,800 annually.

I was assigned to the corporate law division, one of the AG's civil departments. The division's attorneys handled all the small claims made against the state, trespass-to-try-title suits, land-condemnation cases and various other real estate actions.

That is, most of them did. The senior assistant to whom I was assigned as an aide was Phillip Rigby, the haughty scion of an old and established local family. Rigby considered himself a southern aristocrat and I impinged on two of his strongest prejudices. I was a Yankee, but even worse, I was a Catholic Yankee! He relegated me to the role of "gopher"—go for coffee, go for this book or that book, go for anything he could think of for me to fetch. I was the highest-paid errand boy in the state. Rigby was a rednecked coprolite. Mine was an opinion shared by many of the other younger assistants, most of whom were natives themselves but surprisingly liberal in their views.

I was popular with the young bachelors in the division. I still had over $20,000 in my boodle and I spent it freely on the friends I made on the AG's staff, treating them to dinners in fine restaurants, riverboat outings and evenings in posh night clubs.

I deliberately gave the impression that I was from a wealthy New York family without making any such direct claim. I lived in a swank apartment overlooking a lake, drove a leased Jaguar and accumulated a wardrobe worthy of a British duke. I wore a different suit to work each day of the week, partly because it pleased me but mostly because my extensive wardrobe seemed to irritate Rigby. He had three suits to my knowledge, one of which I was sure was a hand-me-down from his Confederate colonel grandfather. Rigby was also penurious.

If my grooming was resented by Rigby, it was approved by others. One day in court, during a short delay in the case at hand, the judge leaned forward on his bench and addressed me:

"Mr. Conrad, you may not contribute much in the way of legal expertise to the proceedings before this court, but you certainly add style, sir. You are the best-dressed gopher in Dixie, Counselor, and the court commends you." It was a genuine tribute and I was pleased, but Rigby nearly had an apoplectic seizure.

Actually, I was satisfied with my errand-boy role. I had no real desire to actually try a case. There was too much danger that my basic lack of knowledge of the law would be exposed. And the work Rigby and I did was dull and uninteresting the majority of the time, a boresome task that I was content to let him handle. Occasionally he did throw me a bone, allowing me to present some minor land issue or make the opening argument in a given case, and I did enjoy those incidents and on the whole handled them without detriment to the law profession, I thought. Rigby was a highly competent lawyer, and I learned a lot sitting behind him, much more than I had gleaned from the lawbooks or the examinations.

Basically, my position was a haven, a lair not likely to be discovered by the hounds. When you're looking for a criminal, you don't often think to look for him on the attorney general's staff of prosecutors, especially if you're seeking a teen-age high school dropout.

Several weeks after I joined the AG's staff, Diane was transferred to Dallas. I was only momentarily saddened at losing her. I was soon dating Gloria, the daughter of a high state official. Gloria was a lively, personable, vibrant girl, and if our relationship had a fault, it was that she was not exactly a bosom companion. But I was learning that a woman can also be delightful with her clothes on.

Gloria was a member of a staunch Methodist family and I often squired her to her church, with the understanding that I was not a candidate for conversion. It was a gesture of interdenominational respect on my part that was appreciated by her parents, and actually I enjoyed it. In fact, I formed a close friendship with the young pastor of the church and he persuaded me to become involved in the church's youth programs. I participated actively in building several children's playgrounds in blighted areas of the city and served on several committees governing other urban youth projects. It was an odd pastime for a con man, but I had no real sense of hypocrisy. For the first time in my life I was giving unselfishly of myself, with no thought of any return, and it made me feel good.

A sinner toiling in the vineyards of the Church, however, no matter how worthy his labors, shouldn't put in too much overtime. I accepted one too many committee appointments and the grapes began to sour.

There was a real Harvard graduate on this particular panel. Not just a Harvard graduate, but a Harvard *Law* graduate, and he was delighted to meet me. He was practically delirious with joy. I have since learned something about Harvard men. They're like badgers. They like to stick together in their own barrows. A lone badger is going to find another badger. A Harvard man in a strange area is going to find another Harvard man. And they're going to talk about Harvard.

This one pounced on me immediately, with all the enthusiasm of Stanley encountering Livingstone in darkest Africa. When had I graduated? Who had my instructors been? Who were the girls I knew? To what club had I belonged? What pubs had I frequented? Who had my friends been?

I successfully fended him off that first night, with either inane answers or by ignoring him and concentrating on the committee business at hand. But thereafter he sought me out at every opportunity. He'd call me to have lunch. He'd drop by my office when he chanced to be in the area. He called me to invite me to parties or outings, to play golf or to take in some cultural event. And always he managed to steer the conversation around to Harvard. What buildings had I had classes in? Didn't I know Professor So-and-So? Had I been acquainted with any of the old families of Cambridge? Harvard men around other Harvard men seem to be rather limited in their conversational topics.

I couldn't avoid him, and of course I couldn't answer many of his questions. His suspicions aroused, he began to build a *res gestae* case against me as a bogus Harvard man if not a phony lawyer. It became *res judicata* for me when I learned he was making numerous inquiries into my background on several fronts, seriously questioning my honesty and integrity.

Like the proverbial Arab, I folded my tent and silently stole away. Not, however, without drawing a final paycheck. I did say good-bye to Gloria, although she wasn't aware it was a final farewell. I merely told her I'd had a death in the family and had to return to New York for a couple of weeks.

I turned in my leased Jaguar and purchased a bright orange Barracuda. It wasn't the most inconspicuous set of wheels for a wanted fugitive to drive, but I liked it and I wanted it, so I bought it. I justified the action by telling myself that since the car, if not the driver, was cool, it would probably prove a wise investment. Largely it was an astute move, for in the past I had simply rented cars and then abandoned them at airports when I was through with them, and O'Riley, unknown to me, was making good use of this practice to compile a pattern of my movements.

I had posed as a doctor for nearly a year. I had played the role of lawyer for nine months. While I was hardly leading a straight life during those twenty months, I hadn't passed any bad checks or done anything else to attract the attention of the authorities. Provided Rigby or the AG himself didn't press the issue of my sudden departure from my post as assistant attorney general, I felt justified in assuming I was not the object of any pressing manhunt. And I wasn't save for O'Riley's dogged efforts, and despite his persistence he was as yet following a cold trail.

I attempted to keep it that way, since I was still in no bind for funds. My flight from my "Harvard colleague's" inquisition turned into something of a vacation. I meandered around the western states for several weeks, touring Colorado, New Mexico, Arizona, Wyoming, Nevada, Idaho and Montana, dallying wherever the scenery intrigued me. Since the scenery usually included some very lovely and susceptible women, I stayed perpetually intrigued.

Although the image of myself as a criminal gradually blurred and dimmed, I entertained no thoughts of rehabilitation. In fact, looking to the future, I stopped long enough in a large Rocky Mountain metropolis to equip myself with dual identities as a fictitious airline pilot.

Using the same procedures that had enabled me to assume the alias of Frank Williams, a first officer for Pan Am, I created Frank Adams, an alleged co-pilot for Trans World Airways, complete with uniform, sham ID and counterfeit FAA pilot's license. I also assembled a set of duplicitous credentials that would allow me, in my posture as Frank Williams, to be a pilot for either Pan Am or TWA.

Shortly afterward I was in Utah, a state notable for not only its spectacular geography and Mormon history but also for its proliferation of college campuses. Having purloined a couple of college degrees, I thought it only fair that I at least acquaint myself with a university campus and so I visited several Utah colleges, strolling around the grounds and taking in the academic sights, especially the coeds. There were so many lovely girls on one campus that I was tempted to enroll as a student.

Instead I became a teacher.

While I was lolling around my motel room one afternoon, reading the local newspaper, my attention was drawn to an expected shortage of summer instructors at one university. The news item quoted the faculty dean, one Dr. Amos Grimes, as being most concerned about finding summer replacements for the school's two sociology professors. "It appears we will have to look out of state for qualified people willing to teach for only three months," said Dr. Grimes in the story.

A vision of myself ensconced in a classroom with a dozen or so nubile beauties took hold of my imagination, and I couldn't resist. I rang up Dr. Grimes.

"Dr. Grimes, Frank Adams here," I said briskly. "I have a Ph.D. in sociology from Columbia University in New York. I'm visiting here, Doctor, and I see by the newspaper that you're looking for sociology instructors."

"Yes, we're definitely interested in finding some people," Dr. Grimes replied cautiously. "Of course, you understand it would be only a temporary position, just for the summer. I assume you do have some teaching experience?"

"Oh, yes," I said airily. "But it's been several years. Let me explain my position, Dr. Grimes. I am a pilot for Trans World Airways, and just recently I was furloughed for six months for medical purposes, an inflammation of the inner ear that bars me at the moment from flying status. I've been looking around for something to do in the interim, and when I saw the story it occurred to me that it might be pleasant to get back into a classroom again.

"I was a professor of sociology at City College of New York for two years before I joined TWA."

"Well, it certainly sounds like you're a likely candidate for one of our positions, Dr. Adams," said Dr. Grimes, now enthusiastic. "Why don't you come by my office tomorrow morning and we'll talk about it."

"I'd be delighted to do that, Dr. Grimes," I replied. "Since I'm a complete stranger in Utah, could you tell me what documents I will need to apply for a faculty position with your college?"

"Oh, just a transcript from Columbia will do, really," said Dr. Grimes. "Of course, if you can obtain a couple of letters of recommendation from CCNY, it would be desirable."

"No problem," I said. "I'll have to send for both my transcript and the letters of recommendation, of course. I came here unprepared on either score, since I didn't even contemplate a temporary teaching position until I saw the story."

"I understand, Dr. Adams," replied Dr. Grimes. "I'll see you in the morning."

I wrote Columbia University that afternoon, requesting a complete catalogue and any pertinent brochures on the school. I also dashed off a letter to the registrar of CCNY, stating I was a Utah graduate student seeking a teaching position in New York, preferably in sociology. I arranged to rent a box at the local post office before mailing off the missives.

My meeting with Dean Grimes was a very pleasant one. He seemed immediately impressed with me, and we spent most of the time, including a leisurely luncheon interlude in the faculty club, discussing my "career" as a pilot. Dr. Grimes, like many men with sedentary jobs, had a romantic view of airline pilots and was eager to have his exciting perspective validated. I had more than enough anecdotes to satisfy his vicarious appetite.

"I have no doubt at all that we can use you this summer, Dr. Adams," he said on my departure. "I'm personally looking forward to your being here on campus."

The materials I had requested from Columbia and CCNY arrived within the week, and I drove to Salt Lake City to purchase the supplies necessary for my current counterfeiting venture. My finished "transcript" was a beauty, giving me a 3.7 grade average and listing my doctoral thesis as a dissertation on "The Sociological Impact of Aviation on the Rural Populations of North America." As I had anticipated, the reply from the registrar of CCNY was on official college stationery. I clipped off the letterhead and, using clear white plastic tape and high-quality bond paper, created a fine facsimile of the college's stationery. I trimmed it to regulation typewriter-paper size and then sat down and wrote myself two letters of recommendation, one from the registrar and one from the head of the sociology department.

I was cautious with both letters. They merely noted that I had been a sociology instructor at CCNY during the years 1961–62, that the faculty rating committee had given me very satisfactory marks and that I had resigned voluntarily to enter the field of commercial aviation as a pilot. I then took the letters to a Salt Lake City job printer and had him run off a dozen copies of each, telling him I was applying at several universities for a teaching position and thus needed extra copies on fine-grade bond. Apparently mine was not an unusual request, for he did the job perfunctorily.

Dr. Grimes barely glanced at the documents when I presented them to him. He introduced me to Dr. Wilbur Vanderhoff, assistant head of the sociology department, who also gave the instruments only a cursory examination before sending them on to faculty personnel for filing. I was hired within the hour to teach two six-week semesters during the summer at a salary of $1,600 per semester. I was assigned to teach a ninety-minute freshman course in the morning, three days a week, and a ninety-minute sophomore course in the afternoon, twice weekly. Dr. Vanderhoff provided me with the two textbooks to be used in the classes, as well as student attendance ledgers. "Any other supplies you might need, you can probably find in the bookstore. They have standard requisition forms on hand," said Dr. Vanderhoff. He grinned. "I'm glad to see you're young and strong. Our summer sociology classes are usually large ones, and you'll earn your salary."

I had three weeks before the first summer semester started. On the pretense of refreshing myself, I audited several of Dr. Vanderhoff's classes, just to get an idea of how a college course was conducted. At night I studied the two textbooks, which I found both interesting and informative.

Vanderhoff was right. Both my classes were large ones. There were seventy-eight students in my freshman class and sixty-three students in my sophomore course, the majority in both instances being female students.

That summer was one of the most enjoyable of my life. I thoroughly enjoyed my role as a teacher. So did my students, I'm certain. My courses were taught by the book, as required, and I had no difficulty there. I just read one chapter ahead of the students and selected what portions of the text I wanted to emphasize. But almost daily I deviated from the textbook in both classes, lecturing on crime, the problems of young adults from broken homes and the effects on society as a whole. My departures from textbook contents—which were largely drawn from my own experiences, unknown to the students—always sparked lively discussions and debates.

Weekends I relaxed by immersing myself in one or the other of Utah's scenic wonderlands, usually accompanied by an equally wondrous companion.

The summer was gone as swiftly as the desert spring, and I knew real regret when it ended. Dr. Vanderhoff and Dr. Grimes were delighted with my work. "Keep in touch with us, Frank," said Dr. Grimes. "If ever we have a permanent opening for a sociology professor, we'd like a chance to lure you down from the skies," said Dr. Grimes.

At least fifty of my students sought me out to tell me how much they had enjoyed my classes and to wish me good-bye and good luck.

I was reluctant to leave that Utah Utopia, but I could find no valid reason for staying. If I lingered, my past was certain to catch up, and I did not want these people's image of me to be tarnished.

I headed west to California. There was a storm building in the Sierras when I crossed the mountains, but it was nothing compared to the whirlwind of crime I was soon to create myself.

from

Fear and Loathing in Las Vegas

by Hunter S. Thompson

SATURDAY MIDNIGHT . . . MEMORIES of this night are extremely hazy. All I have, for guide-pegs, is a pocketful of keno cards and cocktail napkins, all covered with scribbled notes. Here is one: "Get the Ford man, demand a Bronco for race-observation purposes . . . photos? . . . Lacerda/call . . . why not a helicopter? . . . Get on the phone, *lean* on the fuckers . . . heavy yelling."

Another says: "Sign on Paradise Boulevard—'Stopless and Topless' . . . bush-league sex compared to L.A.; *pasties* here—total naked public humping in L.A. . . . Las Vegas is a society of armed masturbators/gambling is the kicker here/sex is extra/weird trip for high rollers . . . housewhores for winners, hand jobs for the bad luck crowd."

A LONG TIME ago when I lived in Big Sur down the road from Lionel Olay I had a friend who liked to go to Reno for the crap-shooting. He owned a sporting-goods store in Carmel. And one month he drove his Mercedes highway-cruiser to Reno on three consecutive weekends—winning heavily each time. After three trips he was something like $15,000 ahead, so he decided to skip the fourth weekend and take some friends to dinner at Nepenthe. "Always quit winners," he explained. "And besides, it's a long drive."

On Monday morning he got a phone call from Reno—from the general manager of the casino he'd been working out on. "We missed you this weekend," said the GM. "The pit-men were bored."

"Shucks," said my friend.

So the next weekend he flew up to Reno in a private plane, with a friend and two girls—all "special guests" of the GM. Nothing too good for high rollers. . . .

And on Monday morning the same plane—the casino's plane—flew him back to the Monterey airport. The pilot lent him a dime to call a friend for a ride to Carmel. He was $30,000 in debt, and two months later he was looking down the barrel of one of the world's heaviest collection agencies.

So he sold his store, but that didn't make the nut. They could wait for the rest, he said—but then he got stomped, which convinced him that maybe he'd be better off borrowing enough money to pay the whole wad.

Mainline gambling is a very heavy business—and Las Vegas makes Reno seem like your friendly neighborhood grocery store. For a loser, Vegas is the meanest town on earth. Until about a year ago, there was a giant billboard on the outskirts of Las Vegas, saying:

DON'T GAMBLE WITH MARIJUANA!
IN NEVADA: POSSESSION—20 YEARS
SALE—LIFE!

So I was not entirely at ease drifting around the casinos on this Saturday night with a car full of marijuana and head full of acid. We had several narrow escapes: at one point I tried to drive the Great Red Shark into the laundry room of the Landmark Hotel—but the door was too narrow, and the people inside seemed dangerously excited.

WE DROVE OVER to the Desert Inn, to catch the Debbie Reynolds/Harry James show. "I don't know about you," I told my attorney, "but in my line of business it's important to be Hep."

"Mine too," he said. "But as your attorney I advise you to drive over to the Tropicana and pick up on Guy Lombardo. He's in the Blue Room with his Royal Canadians."

"Why?" I asked.

"Why *what?*"

"Why should I pay out my hard-earned dollars to watch a fucking corpse?"

"Look," he said. "Why are we out here? To entertain ourselves, or to *do the job?*"

"The job, of course," I replied. We were driving around in circles, weaving through the parking lot of a place I thought was the Dunes, but it turned out to be the Thunderbird . . . or maybe it was the Hacienda . . .

My attorney was scanning *The Vegas Visitor,* looking for hints of action. "How about " 'Nickel Nick's Slot Arcade?' " he said. " 'Hot Slots,' that sounds heavy . . . Twenty-nine cent hotdogs . . ."

Suddenly people were screaming at us. We were in trouble. Two thugs wearing red-gold military overcoats were looming over the hood: "What the hell are you doing?" one screamed. "You can't park *here!*"

"Why not?" I said. It seemed like a reasonable place to park, plenty of space. I'd been looking for a parking spot for what seemed like a very long time. Too long. I was about ready to abandon the car and call a taxi . . . but then, yes, we found this *space.*

Which turned out to be the sidewalk in front of the main entrance to the Desert Inn. I had run over so many curbs by this time, that I hadn't even noticed this last one. But now we found ourselves in a position that was hard to explain . . . blocking the entrance, thugs yelling at us, bad confusion. . . .

My attorney was out of the car in a flash, waving a five-dollar bill. "We want this car parked! I'm an old friend of Debbie's. I used to *romp* with her."

For a moment I thought he had blown it . . . then one of the doormen reached out for the bill, saying: "OK, OK. I'll take care of it, sir." And he tore off a parking stub.

"Holy shit!" I said, as we hurried through the lobby. "They almost had us there. That was quick thinking."

"What do you expect?" he said. "I'm your *attorney* . . . and you owe me five bucks. I want it now."

I shrugged and gave him a bill. This garish, deep-orlon carpeted-lobby of the Desert Inn seemed an inappropriate place to be haggling about nickel/dime bribes for the parking lot attendant. This was Bob Hope's turf. Frank Sinatra's. Spiro Agnew's. The lobby fairly reeked of high-grade formica and plastic palm trees—it was clearly a high-class refuge for Big Spenders.

We approached the grand ballroom full of confidence, but they refused to let us in. We were too late, said a man in a wine-colored tuxedo; the house was already full—no seats left, at *any* price.

"Fuck seats," said my attorney. "We're old friends of Debbie's. We drove all the way from L.A. for this show, and we're goddamn well going in."

The tux-man began jabbering about "fire regulations," but my attorney refused to listen. Finally, after a lot of bad noise, he let us in for nothing—provided we would stand quietly in back and not smoke.

We promised, but the moment we got inside we lost control. The tension had been too great. Debbie Reynolds was yukking across the stage in a silver Afro wig . . . to the tune of "Sergeant Pepper," from the golden trumpet of Harry James.

"Jesus creeping shit!" said my attorney. "We've wandered into a time capsule!"

Heavy hands grabbed our shoulders. I jammed the hash pipe back into my pocket just in time. We were dragged across the lobby and held against the front door by goons until our car was fetched up. "OK, get lost," said the wine-tax-man. "We're giving you a break. If Debbie has friends like you guys, she's in worse trouble than I thought."

"We'll see about this!" my attorney shouted as we drove away. "You paranoid scum!"

I drove around to the Circus-Circus Casino and parked near the back door. "This is the place," I said. "They'll never fuck with us here."

"Where's the ether?" said my attorney. "This mescaline isn't working."

I gave him the key to the trunk while I lit up the hash pipe. He came back with the ether-bottle, un-capped it, then poured some into a kleenex and mashed it under his nose, breathing heavily. I soaked another kleenex and fouled my own nose. The smell was overwhelming, even with the top down. Soon we were staggering up the stairs towards the entrance, laughing stupidly and dragging each other along, like drunks.

This is the main advantage of ether: it makes you behave like the village drunkard in some early Irish novel . . . total loss of all basic motor skills: blurred vision, no balance, numb tongue—severance of all connection between the body and the brain. Which is interesting, because the brain continues to function more or less normally . . . you can actually *watch* yourself behaving in this terrible way, but you can't control it.

You approach the turnstiles leading into the Circus-Circus and you know that when you get there, you have to give the man two dollars or he won't let you inside . . . but when you get there, everything goes wrong: you misjudge the distance to the turnstile and slam against it, bounce off and grab hold of an old woman to keep from falling, some angry Rotarian shoves you and you think: What's happening here? What's going on? Then you hear yourself mumbling: "Dogs fucked the Pope, no fault of mine. Watch out! . . . Why money? My name is Brinks; I was born . . . born? Get sheep over side . . . women and children to armored car . . . orders from Captain Zeep."

Ah, devil ether—a total body drug. The mind recoils in horror, unable to communicate with the spinal column. The hands flap crazily, unable to get money out of the pocket . . . garbled laughter and hissing from the mouth . . . always smiling.

Ether is the perfect drug for Las Vegas. In this town they love a drunk. Fresh meat. So they put us through the turnstiles and turned us loose inside.

THE CIRCUS-CIRCUS is what the whole hep world would be doing on Saturday night if the Nazis had won the war. This is the Sixth Reich. The ground floor is full of gambling tables, like all the other casinos . . . but the place is about four stories high, in the style of a circus tent, and all manner of strange County-Fair/Polish Carnival madness is going on up in this space. Right above the gambling tables the Forty Flying Carazito Brothers are doing a high-wire trapeze act, along with four muzzled Wolverines and the Six Nymphet Sisters from San Diego . . . so you're down on the main floor playing blackjack, and the stakes are getting high when suddenly you chance to look up, and there, right smack above your head is a half-naked fourteen-year-old girl being chased through the air by a snarling wolverine, which is suddenly locked in a death battle with two silver-painted Polacks who come swinging down from opposite balconies and meet in mid-air on the wolverine's neck . . . both Polacks seize the animal as they fall straight down towards the crap tables—but they bounce off the net; they separate and spring back up towards the roof in three different directions, and just as they're about to fall again they are grabbed out of the air by three Korean Kittens and trapezed off to one of the balconies.

This madness goes on and on, but nobody seems to notice. The gambling action runs twenty-four hours a day on the main floor, and the circus never ends. Meanwhile, on all the upstairs balconies, the customers are being hustled by every conceivable kind of bizarre shuck. All kinds of funhouse-type booths. Shoot the pasties off the nipples of a ten-foot bull-dyke and win a cotton-candy goat. Stand in front of this fantastic machine, my friend, and for just 99¢ your likeness will appear, two hundred feet tall, on a screen above downtown Las Vegas. Ninety-nine cents more for a voice message. "Say whatever you want, fella. They'll hear you, don't worry about that. Remember you'll be two hundred feet tall."

Jesus Christ. I could see myself lying in bed in the Mint Hotel, half-asleep and staring idly out the window, when suddenly a vicious nazi drunkard appears two hundred feet tall in the midnight sky, screaming gibberish at the world: "*Woodstock Über Alles!*"

We will close the drapes tonight. A thing like that could send a drug person careening around the room like a ping-pong ball. Hallucinations are bad enough. But after a while you learn to cope with things like seeing your dead grandmother crawling up your leg with a knife in her teeth. Most acid fanciers can handle this sort of thing.

But *nobody* can handle that other trip—the possibility that any freak with $1.98 can walk into the Circus-Circus and suddenly appear in the sky over downtown Las Vegas twelve times the size of God, howling anything that comes into his head. No, this is not a good town for psychedelic drugs. Reality itself is too twisted.

GOOD MESCALINE COMES on slow. The first hour is all waiting, then about halfway through the second hour you start cursing the creep who burned you, because nothing is happening . . . and then ZANG! Fiendish intensity, strange glow and vibrations . . . a very heavy gig in a place like the Circus-Circus.

"I hate to say this," said my attorney as we sat down at the Merry-Go-Round Bar on the second balcony, "but this place is getting *to* me. I think I'm getting the Fear."

"Nonsense," I said. "We came out here to find the American Dream, and now that we're right in the vortex you want to quit." I grabbed his bicep and squeezed. "You must *realize*," I said, "that we've found the main nerve."

"I know," he said. "That's what gives me the Fear."

The ether was wearing off, the acid was long gone, but the mescaline was running strong. We were sitting at a small round gold formica table, moving in orbit around the bartender.

"Look over there," I said. "Two women fucking a polar bear."

"Please," he said. "Don't *tell* me those things. Not now." He signaled the waitress for two more Wild Turkeys. "This is my last drink," he said. "How much money can you lend me?"

"Not much," I said. "Why?"

"I have to go," he said.

"Go?"

"Yes. Leave the country. Tonight."

"Calm down," I said. "You'll be straight in a few hours."

"No," he said. "This is serious."

"George Metesky was serious," I said. "And you see what they did to him."

"Don't fuck around!" he shouted. "One more hour in this town and I'll kill somebody!"

I could see he was on the edge. That fearful intensity that comes at the peak of a mescaline seizure. "OK," I said. "I'll lend you some money. Let's go outside and see how much we have left."

"Can we make it?" he said.

"Well . . . that depends on how many people we fuck with between here and the door. You want to leave quietly?"

"I want to leave *fast*," he said.

"OK. Let's pay this bill and get up very slowly. We're both out of our heads. This is going to be a long walk." I shouted at the waitress for a bill. She came over, looking bored, and my attorney stood up.

"Do they *pay* you to screw that bear?" he asked her.

"What?"

"He's just kidding," I said, stepping between them. "Come on, Doc—let's go downstairs and gamble." I got him as far as the edge of the bar, the rim of the merry-go-round, but he refused to get off until it stopped turning.

"It won't stop," I said. "It's not *ever* going to stop." I stepped off and turned around to wait for him, but he wouldn't move . . . and before I could reach out and pull him off, he was carried away. "Don't move," I shouted. "You'll come around!" His eyes were staring blindly ahead, squinting with fear and confusion. But he didn't move a muscle until he'd made the whole circle.

I waited until he was almost in front of me, then I reached out to grab him—but he jumped back and went around the circle again. This made me very nervous. I felt on the verge of a freakout. The bartender seemed to be watching us.

Carson City, I thought. Twenty years.

I STEPPED ON the merry-go-round and hurried around the bar, approaching my attorney on his blind side—and when we came to the right spot I pushed him off. He staggered into the aisle and uttered a hellish scream as he lost his balance and went down, thrashing into the crowd . . . rolling like a log, then up again in a flash, fists clenched, looking for somebody to hit.

I approached him with my hands in the air, trying to smile. "You fell," I said. "Let's go."

By this time people *were* watching us. But the fool wouldn't move, and I knew what would happen if I grabbed him. "OK," I said. "You stay here and go to jail. I'm leaving." I started walking fast towards the stairs, ignoring him.

This moved him.

"Did you see that?" he said as he caught up with me. "Some sonofabitch kicked me in the back!"

"Probably the bartender," I said. "He wanted to stomp you for what you said to the waitress."

"Good *god!* Let's get out of here. Where's the elevator?"

"Don't go *near* that elevator," I said. "That's just what they *want* us to do . . . trap us in a steel box and take us down to the basement." I looked over my shoulder, but nobody was following.

"Don't run," I said. "They'd like an excuse to shoot us." He nodded, seeming to understand. We walked fast along the big indoor midway—shooting galleries, tattoo parlors, money-changers and cotton-candy booths—then out through a bank of glass doors and across the grass downhill to a parking lot where the Red Shark waited.

"You drive," he said. "I think there's something wrong with me."

Pool Halls

by David Mamet

THE NOVEL *THE Hustler* is set in a Chicago poolroom called 'Benningtons,' pool-shooting capital of the world.

The actual name of the Chicago poolroom was Bensinger's. The Bensinger family owned Brunswick Corporation. Brunswick held, and perhaps still holds, the copyright on the word 'pool,' which is a trademark name for pocket billiards, and I used to play pocket billiards at Bensinger's in Chicago.

The pool hall I played at was not quite the one immortalized in the novel. A postwar cleanup of Chicago's Downtown Area eradicated much of the demimonde living there, and the passing of the railroads took care of the rest.

When I was a habitué, Bensinger's had moved from Randolph Street up to the North Side, and its sign said that it was called Clark and Diversey Billiards, but the clientele, of course, still called it Bensinger's.

The pool hall opened, if memory serves, at eleven o'clock in the morning. And that was a wonderful time to arrive, especially in the summer, when Chicago was hot. You'd come out of the glare and the concrete-trapped heat, down a long flight of stairs, and there you were in this dark cavern.

In the cavern were forty pool tables, six three-cushion-billiard tables, snooker tables, a separate exhibition room, a bar, and a short-order kitchen. So there you are. It's eleven o'clock of a hot morning, you walk through the louvered doors and are greeted by Bob Siegel, who either did or did not own the place. Bob had been a postman, and remembered everybody's name that he had ever met. So if you'd been there every day since the Downtown Days, or if you'd been in once ten years ago, when you came by he greeted you by name, and he'd say 'regular table?' and you'd say 'yes,' and he'd hand you the tray with the balls on it, and you'd say 'I'm going on sixteen,' or whatever table you were particularly enamored of in that period, and he'd nod, and you'd start off to your table.

Then—here comes the best part—you would say—over your shoulder—'would you send *John* over with a cup of *coffee*, please?' and Bob would say 'sure thing.' So you walk back to table sixteen or table seventeen far in the back of the hall. Everything is brown, the light is brown, the tables are brown, the oak benches are brown, the air is brown but it's cool. And you arrange your book, or your hat, or your newspaper on the bench next to your table, and you turn on the light over the table, and you spill the balls out of the tray and onto the table with a jerk of the wrists; when you do it right, they hardly bounce at all, and they don't hurt the surface. Then you kind of fling the tray under the table and you sit down on the bench.

Now the thing is if you're going to have a cigarette before your coffee comes, and, of course, you are, and so you light your Camel, or your Lucky, maybe the pack's crumpled, and maybe it's the last cigarette from last night. You light it and you're in the Perfect Place.

People are supposed to gamble here, people are supposed to drink here, people are supposed to spend their days here in pursuit of skill, cunning, comradeship, and money. No one is supposed to be pompous here, or intrusive, or boring; no one will be held unaccountable for the bets they make, or the way that they comport themselves. But if they choose, they can choose to be left alone.

Well, there I am getting high on my first cigarette, or however it felt, getting cool down in the basement. There's the click of a couple of guys shooting pool back near the entrance. John brings my cup of coffee, and I say 'thank you.' He asks me if I want breakfast, and I tell him 'thank you, yes, a little later . . . '

Several years later, and in the last years of Mayor Daley's life, there was a pool hall called The Golden Eight Ball, down off Rush Street on Walton, and it had Muzak, and orange-yellow felt on the tables, and it was decorated. You could find businessmen there, and young couples on a fun date, and it lasted for a couple of years, and then it was gone.

Just as Bensinger's was gone. In the mid-seventies, the neighborhood got a tad too upscale, and all us warbabies needed somewhere to live, and so there went the neighborhood.

On Clark and Diversey where once an American could shoot pool for an hour in the summer and then dash across the street to the Parkway Cinema and catch a double feature at the before-twelve price of seventy-five cents (program changed thrice-weekly, hard to believe, but it's true), now there were candle stores, and restaurants with cunning names, and the beautiful 3,500-seat Century Movie Palace gutted to house a shopping mall.

Bensinger's moved again, down the street and up a flight of stairs over a record store. There were ten tables and Bob Siegel kept apologizing that they hadn't got the carpet in, so one had to stand on concrete all day long.

Bob, of course, never got the carpet in before the place got closed, a year or so later, and then there was nowhere to go.

Similarly in New York, on Eighth Avenue amid the girlie peep shows, you could walk down two flights into McGirr's Pool Hall and there the same setup, minus the bar and grill; and people were selling dope and people were selling stolen merchandise and booking horses over the telephone and shooting a little pool into the bargain, and, around 1980, they closed that one down, too; they opened on Seventy-ninth and Broadway in New York, which currently is a Rug Warehouse. My question is where are the pool halls? And the answer is they're gone.

There is one on the main street in Gloucester, Massachusetts, and I went in there one day and tipped the guy five dollars to disconnect the video games for one hour so I could shoot pool in peace. After the hour was up, he was pressured from the teenagers and he wouldn't renew my deal, so I packed up and left.

There used to be a pool hall in the airport in Detroit, which I thought was the most civilized accoutrement I could imagine for an airport, and very advanced. It may still be there. And there was a pool hall downstate Illinois where they took a lot of money from me while I was waiting for a train to get me out of downstate Illinois one time.

But, basically, I think we have to say they're gone.

The point was not to play pool. One can do that, to a certain extent, in the Family Billiard Centers one sees stuck now and then in the Concrete Suburbs. And dads go there to have some sort of fun with their progeny. But the point of the pool hall was not fun. The point of the pool hall was the intersection of two American Loves: the Game of Skill and the Short Con.

The denizens of the pool hall came in to practice their skill, and the transients were those upon which the skill was practiced.

So you had to be near a transient neighborhood; you had to be in a neighborhood in transition; you had to be near the railroad.

Well, I guess that America is gone. We no longer revere skill, and the short con of the pool hustle and the Murphy Man and the Fuller Brush Man. The short con, which flourished in a life lived on the street and among strangers, has been supplanted by the Big Con of a life with no excitement in it at all.

You see the clunky old elephant-legged pool tables from those old pool halls for sale from time to time, refinished, lovely leather pockets, beautiful new felt; and you might have a fantasy of taking them and housing them someplace, and that's what happened to the Country-at-Large: we turned America into a Den. Where could you be more wonderfully alone than in those old pool halls? You could sit there all day and no one would bother you except the occasional guy come over to say 'shoot a game of eight-ball. Split the time?' and you'd say 'no,' thank God, and you could stay all day.

You could sit there and drink your coffee and go find the good House cue where you hid it up behind the ventilator (where you'd have to sort through the *other* House sticks that everyone *else* hid up behind the ventilator) and you'd shoot a little pool.

If you got hungry, you could raise your head and John would come over and you'd order breakfast and a *Daily News*, and maybe another pack of Camels.

Later you could amble to the bar, where they would have the Cubs (who played three blocks away) on the TV, and have a beer. Bob would call over 'time off, Dave?' and you'd say 'yeah, time off.'

One night in the Exhibition Room, Sr. Juan Navarro, billed as Billiards Champion of the World, ran any number of straight-rail billiards, shot left-handed, made a billiard shooting *from one table to the next*. One night at the joint on Seventy-ninth Street me and a friend got lured from a nine-ball game where we had beat the local hustler, and he got us into the backroom and involved in a crap game where he cleaned us out with Shapes. One night I beat a guy in eight-ball at a bar, and he paid up and later followed me out into the night, until I turned around and looked at him, and I could see that he was just confused.

The best times were the days—the late mornings and the afternoons away from the world in a pool hall. 'Let everything else revolve,' you would think, 'I've gone fishin'. I am nowhere to be found. I am nowhere. No one can find me here.'

Things I Have Learned Playing Poker on the Hill

by David Mamet

IN TWENTY YEARS of playing poker, I have seen very few poor losers.

Poker is a game of skill and chance. Playing poker is also a masculine ritual, and, most times, losers feel either sufficiently chagrined or sufficiently reflective to retire, if not with grace, at least with alacrity.

I have seen many poor winners. Most are eventually brought back to reality. The game itself will reveal to them that they are the victim of an essential error: they have attributed their success to divine intervention.

The poor winner is celebrating either God's good sense in sending him down lucky cards, or God's wisdom in making him, the lucky winner, technically superior to the others at the table. In the first case, the cards will eventually begin to even out and the player will lose; in the second case, both the Deity and the players will tire of being patronized. The Deity will respond how he may, but the players will either drop out of the game or improve. In either case the poor winner will lose, and pride, once again, will go before a fall.

Speaking of luck: is there such a thing as luck? Yes. There is such a thing as luck. There is such a thing as a *run of luck*. This is an instructive insight I have gained from poker—that all things have a rhythm, even the most seemingly inanimate of statistics.

Any mathematician will tell you that the cards at the poker table are distributed randomly, that we remember the remarkable and forget the mundane, and that 'luck' is an illusion.

Any poker player knows—to the contrary—that there are phenomenal runs of luck which defy any mathematical explanation—there are periods in which one cannot catch a hand, and periods in which one cannot *not* catch a hand, and that there *is* such a thing as absolute premonition of cards: the rock-bottom *surety* of what will happen next. These things happen in contravention of scientific wisdom and common sense. The poker player learns that sometimes both science and common sense are wrong; that the bumblebee *can* fly; that, perhaps, one should never trust an expert; that there are more things in heaven and earth than are dreamt of by those with an academic bent.

It is comforting to know that luck exists, that there is a time to push your luck and a time to gracefully retire, that all roads have a turning.

What do you do when you are pushing your luck beyond its limits? You must behave like a good philosopher and ask what axiom you must infer that you are acting under. Having determined that, you ask if this axiom, in the long run, will leave you a winner. (You are drawing to a flush. You have a 1-in-4½ chance. The pot is offering you money odds of 5 to 1. It seems a close thing, but if you did it all day, you must receive a 10 percent return.)

If the axiom which you are acting under is not designed to make you money, you may find that your real objective at the game is something else: you may be trying to prove yourself beloved of God.

You then must ask yourself if—financially and emotionally—you can afford the potential rejection. For the first will certainly and the second will most probably ensue.

Poker is boring. If you sit down at the table to experience excitement, you will consciously and subconsciously do those things to make the game exciting; you will take long-odds chances and you will create emergencies. They will lose you money. If your aim, on the other hand, is to win money, you will watch the game and wait for the good cards, and play the odds-on chance, and, in the long run, you must be a winner. And when you do *not* win, you can still go home without mumbling, for, as Woodrow Wilson said: 'I would rather lose in a cause which will eventually prevail than triumph in a cause doomed to failure.' (I'll bet that most of you didn't even know he was a poker player.)

Playing poker you must treat each hand, as Epictetus says, as a visit to the Olympic Games, each hand offering you the chance to excel in your particular event—betting, checking, managing your money, observing the players, and, most often, waiting.

The poker players I admire most are indeed like that wise old owl who sat on the oak and who kept his mouth shut and his eyes on the action.

As for observation, Confucius said man cannot hide himself—look what he smiles at, look what he frowns at. The inability to hide is especially true of men under pressure, which is to say, gamblers. This is another reason for stoic and correct play.

When you are proud of having made the correct decision (that is, the decision which, in the long run, *must* eventually make you a winner), you are inclined to look forward to the results of that decision with some degree of impassivity. When you are so resolved, you become less fearful and more calm. You are less interested in yourself and more naturally interested in the other players: now *they* begin to reveal themselves. Is their nervousness feigned? Is their hand made already? Are they bluffing? These elections are impossible to make when you are afraid, but become easier the more content you are with your own actions. And, yes, sometimes you lose, but differences of opinion make both horse races and religious intolerance, and if you don't like to take a sporting chance, you don't have to play poker.

Poker will also reveal to the frank observer something else of import—it will teach him about his own nature.

Many bad players will not improve because they cannot bear self-knowledge. Finally, they cannot bear the notion that everything they do is done for a reason. The bad player will not deign to determine what he thinks by watching what he does. To do so might, and frequently would, reveal a need to be abused (in calling what must be a superior hand); a need to be loved (in staying for 'that one magic card'); a need to have Daddy relent (in trying to bluff out the obvious best hand); et cetera.

It is painful to observe this sort of thing about oneself. Many times we'd rather suffer on than fix it. It's not easy to face that, rather than playing cards in spite of our losses, we are playing cards because of them.

But poker is a game played among folks made equal by their money. Each player uses it to buy his time at the table, and, while there, is entitled to whatever kind and length of enjoyment that money will buy.

The pain of losing is diverting. So is the thrill of winning. Winning, however, is lonelier, as those you've taken money from are not likely to commiserate with you. Winning takes some getting used to.

Many of us, and most of us from time to time, try to escape a blunt fact which may not tally with our self-image. When we are depressed, we recreate the world around us to rationalize our mood. We are then likely to overlook or misinterpret happy circumstances. At the poker table, this can be expensive, for opportunity may knock, but it seldom nags. Which brings us to a crass thought many genteel players cannot grasp; poker is about money.

The ability of a poker player is judged solely by the difference between his stack when he sat down and his stack when he got up. The point is not to win the most hands, the point is not even to win in the most games. The point is to *win the most money*. This probably means playing less hands than the guy who has just come for the action; it means not giving your fellow players a break because you value their feelings; it means not giving some back at the end of the night because you feel embarrassed by winning; it means taking those steps and creating those habits of thought and action which, in the long run, must prevail.

The long run for me—to date—has been a period of twenty years.

One day in college I promoted myself from the dormitory game to the *big* poker game Up on the Hill in town.

After graduation I would, occasionally, come back to the area to visit. I told myself my visits were to renew friendships, to use the library, to see the leaves. But I was really coming back to play in the Hill game.

Last September one of the players pointed out that five of us at the table that night had been doing this for two decades.

As a group, we have all improved. Some of us have improved drastically. As the facts, the statistics, the tactics are known to all, and as we are men of equal intelligence, that improvement can be due to only one thing: to character, which, as I *finally* begin to improve a bit myself, I see that the game of poker is all about.

from

Cut Numbers

by Nick Tosches

HE PULLED A Partagas cigar from his breast pocket, removed it from its copper-colored metal tube, and carefully snipped its rounded end with his teeth. "Newark made New York look like a Methodist tank town." He struck a match, held it to the cigar, then puffed. "Ah, well, like your uncle used to say, as goes Newark, so goes the world."

"How is he?"

"Rock of Gibraltar." Ernie smiled. "We walked down to the bar the other day. He had his few. Every year, same thing. He starts in talkin' 'bout those barrels of bock beer the bars used to get in the springtime; then it's 'What do you say we go down for a cold one?' He's still got that bottle of brandy up there. A shot in the morning, maybe one at night." Ernie tapped an ash onto the sidewalk. "Yesterday I went with him to get his hair cut." Ernie laughed a little. "You ever see that barber he goes to over there on New Street? I think he's older than your uncle. Holds the damn scissors with two hands." Then Ernie blew smoke, and he seemed to think awhile, and the smile faded from his face. He looked into the younger man's eyes. "There is somethin', Lou," he said. "You ever known your uncle to use a telephone?"

"Are you kiddin', Ernie. Forget about it." Louie shook his head. "When I was a kid, my old man told me that when he was a kid, when they were all livin' together—my great-grandfather and great-grandmother, my grandfather and grandmother, all the brothers—in the house in Jersey City, my grandmother wanted a telephone. My grandfather wouldn't allow it to be listed in his name. It had to be listed in hers. And they never went near that phone, either Uncle John or my grandfather. If it rang and there was no one home but them, they just let it ring. They wouldn't even look at it except to curse it.

"I remember one time, Uncle John came home with my grandfather after visiting Mayor Gangemi or one of those guys. I asked him what the mayor's house was like, and all he said was, 'He had two phones.' It was like he'd caught the guy wearin' women's underwear or somethin'."

Ernie was silent for a moment, and he looked away before he spoke again. "Well, I'll tell you something. A few weeks ago, he had a couple of the guys from Local 827 come by and put in a phone. You believe that? And he keeps lookin' at it, like he's waitin' for it to ring."

Louie looked at Ernie and uttered a low sound of dismay, which Ernie could not hear.

"And there's somethin' else," Ernie said. "He sent off to the Justice Department in New York for a copy of his citizenship papers. Then he had me take him to the camera shop over there on Park Place to get his picture taken." He tapped more ashes onto the pavement; then he looked quizzically at Louie. "It was for a passport," he said. "He upped and got himself a damn passport."

The two men looked at each other; then Louie patted Ernie on the shoulder. "Let me go up and see him," he said. "I'll catch you later."

He unlocked the front door with a key from his pocket, and he entered.

He had known the inside of this building since he was a child. He had climbed the stairs to his uncle's rooms countless times with his father, and with other uncles; then countless times alone. As a boy, passing from the minatory din of downtown Newark into the sudden quietude of this vestibule, he always had felt as if he were entering a sanctuary, so remarkable was the contrast between the tumult on the one side of the great steeled oak door, the silence on the other. It was as if that door shut out more than the troublesome streets. It was as if it shut out the world and time itself.

Louie glanced at the little painting in the pine-molding frame that hung at the foot of the stairs: a view of foreboding trees beyond a gloomy lake. Over the years, Louie had seen the little painting slowly darken with age till, now, it seemed not a picture of trees and water at all, but only of foreboding and gloom. He laid his hand on the dark-varnished banister, and he ascended the creaking stairs to the second floor, every creak seeming, now as forever past, to summon forth from the stillness of this sanctuary shades of the dead, and to stir within himself some vague undying thing that felt, at times, like power.

The creaking ceased. He rapped lightly on the door, and he heard the old man's shuffling steps, as slow and regular as a sleeping heart.

"Hello, stranger," the old man said.

Louie followed his uncle to the easy chairs by the window. As he moved, the old man maneuvered his suspenders onto his shoulders. Slowing his pace so as to keep behind him, Louie glanced around. The window was closed, as usual, just as, Louie knew, the windows in the kitchen and the bedroom were open, as usual. The lace curtains transmuted the streaming sunshine into soft, delicate rays, which purled like churchlight on the room's familiar furnishings and pale blue walls. Like all but one of the old man's walls, these were bare. Only above the head of his bed was there any graven image of anything or anyone: a heavy bronze crucifix, adorned year-round with the woven palm leaf that Louie brought him during the last week of every Lent. The old man's cane was propped against the mahogany end table between the two easy chairs. His tweed cap was on the table. A magnifying glass lay on a folded copy of the day's *Star-Ledger*. There were White Owl cigars in cellophane wrappers, and a box of De Nobilis, but the big crystal ashtray was clean. And, yes, there was that thing, the last thing that Louie would ever have expected to see atop this table: a shining black telephone.

They sat. The old man adjusted his hearing aid, then offered Louie a cigar, as he always did. Louie declined, as he always did, and lighted a cigarette.

"New haircut," the old man said happily, gesturing toward his head.

"Yeah. Ernie told me." Louie smiled, looking at the thick silver hair that had defied all aging for the last twenty years, then at the face below it, the face of his kindred blood.

"New slippers," the old man said, pointing to his feet. Louie looked down at the fancy slippers of soft brown leather, and he grinned, so incongruous were they with the old man's shabby gabardine trousers and plaid flannel shirt. "Every time I see you," the old man smiled, "you ask me what's new. I figured I'd beat you to the punch today." And they both laughed without making a sound, beholding each other in the church-light.

"Somethin' else new, too," Louie said slyly. He tilted his head toward that black plastic improbability.

Uncle John neither spoke nor smiled then. His face relaxed into the vague, inscrutable frown of age, but Louie saw the flicker of censure behind the old man's spectacles. Then the laconic frown turned upward into the semblance of a grin.

"Phone sex," the old man said solemnly. "They got that now. You call up and you pay and the woman talks to you. They had all about it on 'Donahue' the other day. Imagine payin' a woman to talk? That's like payin' a bird to fly." He took his glasses off and rubbed them with his handkerchief. "Imagine payin' *anybody* to talk," he said quietly. Then he looked sternly into Louie's eyes. "So, how have you been, kid?"

"Good," Louie said, indecisively.

Uncle John nodded, grimacing in approval. "Next time I see you, you'll bring the palm." It was neither a question nor a statement, really, but more of an oblique musing on the passing cadences of time. "Then, the week after that, baseball." He gestured toward the dead television set across the room. "Maybe I'll go with the Mets again this year. What do you think?"

"They got a shot."

The old man nodded very slowly, and he looked blankly through the delicate rays. He sat in this manner, breathing softly, peering abstractedly, as if he were alone, not only in this room but in this world as well. When, at last, he slowly nodded once again, it seemed that he was signaling his assent to some impalpable sovereignty beyond the slivered light, or merely acknowledging those shards of himself that through the years had been lost to the rayless drift. Then he turned to Louie as if to say: I'm still here, and you're here with me. They grinned softly at the absurdity of fate that had cast them together, two stubborn links from a shattered chain.

"You ever think of settling down and having kids?" the old man asked.

"Once in a while. How about you?" Louie watched the old man soundlessly laugh. "Why?"

"Because otherwise it ends with you. You're the last card in the boot. Granted, that doesn't mean much. Like just about everybody else in this world, we were only flies on history's back. Still, you get old, you think about these things. *L'ultimo di casa Brunellesches,*" he said and grinned. "That's what you are. Unless you have a son."

"I think of it," Louie said, and he turned his hand nonchalantly.

"That's what I did. I thought about it. I'm still thinkin' about it," he laughed quietly. "That's one thing my brother Virgilio, your grandfather, did right. He got married young. Seemed like he shaved for the first time one day, got hitched the next. That's the way to do it, jump right in there before you know the score. Once you get used to going it alone, it's hard to give up the elbow room."

Louie breathed agreement through his nose. The old man fell still. Louie waited awhile and then asked: "Do you know a guy named Joe Brusher?"

The old man looked at him, and there was no smile. "Yeah," he said. "Do you?"

"No. But somebody asked me to ask you whatever happened to Joe Brusher."

The old man nodded sternly, as if there were something to accept in Louie's words. He closed his hand into a fist, and he beheld it, remembering the strength that once had lain therein. He unclenched it slowly before his eyes; then he lowered his hand calmly to the arm of his chair, braced himself, and slowly stood. He reached into his pocket and removed a dollar. He sat down and placed the bill on the end table, closer to Louie than to himself. "What is it, Louie?" he asked.

"It's a dollar bill," Louie said warily.

"Right. It's a piece of paper called a dollar. When I was a kid, a dollar bill represented a one-dollar gold piece. It was like that until the Depression. Then Roosevelt outlawed gold, and a dollar bill represented a silver dollar. It was called a Silver Certificate, and it said 'one silver dollar payable to the bearer on demand.' You remember those. Eventually, twenty years ago, they put an end to that, and a dollar note stopped representing anything: payable to the bearer on demand *un' gazz'*. But, yeah, for the sake of convenience, we'll call it a dollar bill.

"Now turn it over. See where it says 'In God We Trust'? That's something they added in the late fifties, when they were getting ready to renege on the 'payable to the bearer' bit. Look to the left there. What's that pyramid with the eye on it?"

Louie looked at it, that strange symbol that he had looked at, without seeing, every day of his grown life; and he said he did not know.

"It's the reverse of the Seal of the United States, and the back of the dollar is the only place you'll ever see it. It's Mason horseshit. The people that started this country—Benjamin Franklin, Thomas Jefferson, Paul Revere—they were all Masons. And it was Masons who made that seal and passed it through Congress in the seventeen hundreds. Think about that sometime, Louie.

"But look at the words over the eye. What does it say there?"

Louie slowly pronounced the Latin words.

"That's no Mason mumbo-jumbo," the old man said. "They're about two thousand years old, those words. They were written by Virgil during the days of the first Roman emperor, Augustus. Augustus ran the first lottery in history."

The dollar-bill routine, Louie mused, was a new one. But now the old man had returned to familiar ground. He was on his Roman kick, Louie told himself; next stop, Albania. By now, Louie had ceased to wonder what all this had to do with the question that had brought it on. That question itself, along with the name of Joe Brusher, had faded from Louie's mind, swept away by the strange slow tide of his uncle's words.

"What Augustus started two thousand years ago was still going strong in Italy when I was born. They called it the Giuoco del Lotto. I've told you all about the Giuoco, Louie, and about the *albanese*, Il Santo, I worked for. We took bets all over the Lower East Side, everything from a penny to a dollar. Everybody, no matter how poor, had something to bet. They figured they couldn't go wrong for a penny or a nickel or a dime. We must've handled more change in a week than the Federal Reserve Bank on Liberty Street.

"But, see, the thing was, those people who figured they couldn't go wrong for a penny or a nickel or a dime, they were going wrong. If they were lucky—and they all believed in luck more than they believed in anything; luck is the religion of failure—they stood to be paid off at a million to one. They thought that was great. But the real odds they were up against were almost forty-four million to one. It was a sucker's bet.

"I watched those people, day in and day out, and I took their money and I gave it to the Devil and the Devil gave me my pence. By the time I was twenty, I saw those people the way a whore sees a drunken sailor. Of course, I didn't think I was a whore. See, they've got bad names for women who sell flesh, but they don't have any for men who sell dreams."

Uncle John stopped for a minute, thinking back, almost receding into the shadows of those days. Then he turned to Louie. "I had hair just like you then," he said.

"Then all that shit happened. You know, Louie, they say you can't fight City Hall. And they're right. It's solid granite and marble." He looked through the lace; then his eyes rested on the rainbow in the prism of the crystal ashtray. "I think you know about that, Louie. I never told you, but I'm sure your father or somebody else did."

He did not look at Louie when he said this; he did not want him to feel as if he had to say anything. And Louie did not say anything, but he recalled a drunken argument he had overheard as a boy; recalled the bellowing voices of his father and Uncle John in the cellar, the slam of a fist on the table, then the constrained fury of his father's words: "What can you do about it? Kill them like you did those two fuckin' donkeys? Get locked up for another five years?" Louie remembered his mother, distraught, trying to call him away from the cellar stairs. It was the dead of summer.

"See, Louie, by 1930, the Giuoco was becoming a thing of the past. Uptown, Harlem had been running its own racket for years. At first, they had what they called Treasury tickets. In the early twenties, Treasury tickets gave way to what they called the clearing-house numbers. Everybody just called them 'the numbers.' You picked three digits. If they matched the last two figures in the millions of the exchange's total and the last figure in the millions of the balances announced that day by the New York Clearing House down on Nassau and Cedar, you got paid off at five hundred to one.

"These numbers became the biggest thing in New York. They spread everywhere, like fire, till there wasn't a city in the country without the numbers. It got so out of hand that the U.S. attorney—Roper was his name—strong-armed the newspapers into not printing the clearing-house figures in the financial pages. That was in the fall of '29, right around the time of the Crash. Soon after that, the New York Clearing House itself agreed to stop disclosing its figures. That's when the Harlem bosses switched to the Cincinnati Clearing House figures. There was no stopping the numbers.

"Il Santo had known about the Harlem numbers for a long time. He'd done a lot of business up there, in the Italian part of East Harlem, and that's where a lot of his *bubbonia*, his dope, went. But he laughed at the numbers. *La Borsa negra*, he called them: the nigger stock exchange. Then it was too late, and he was too old to care.

"All he wanted was to go back to Italy and die in the little town where he was born. He still had people there. He used to talk about how when a man died there, the women laid him out and washed his body down with their tears and their hair, the old *albanese* way. So, that's what he wanted, to take his money and go like a lord to that town and sit in the sun and die in the shade and have those broads cry on his corpse. But it didn't happen that way.

"The few guys that were his partners were never what you'd call equal partners. He shared the Giuoco money, in his way, but the *bubbonia* money was always his alone. He wouldn't even tolerate talk of that money. And when he made up his mind to go back to the other side, he gave the Giuoco to his partners, but he said nothing about the heroin. Those men knew that the Giuoco was dying. And they knew that the heroin business was worth a fortune. They knew that as soon as Prohibition was over—and the writing was on the wall, it was only a matter of time—there'd be a mad scramble for the *bubbonia*. But Il Santo had someone, or something, other than them in mind for his operation. So they decided that the only way to take control was *la vuoda*. And that was the end of Il Santo: five in the head sitting at his kitchen table on the third day of September, 1930."

The old man paused and blew his nose into his plaid handkerchief. He asked Louie to bring him a glass of cold mineral water from the bottle in the refrigerator, and to get himself one, too. Louie did so, and the old man drank.

"Best drink in the world," he said. Then he breathed gravely and continued on.

"They threw the Giuoco to us like a bone. Me and three others. We were just punk kids, but we knew enough to bury that bone in Harlem.

"Downstairs at the corner of Mott and Hester, right where that shit joint, that Vincent's Clam Bar, came to be, there was an old *capozzell'* joint. They sold Coke bottles of wine for a dime, bowls of *capozzell'* for a buck. That's where I told the others how we could break the numbers without getting our shirts dirty.

"That was a little before Thanksgiving 1930. The next week, we took a train to Cincinnati and checked into a hotel. The Cincinnati Clearing House was on the fourth floor of the First National Bank Building at Fourth and Walnut. We went there and found the guy whose job it was to write the figures on the slate for the press each morning. His salary was something like fifty dollars a week. We offered him two grand to round off three digits to zeros. He didn't hesitate, not for a minute. We set the date for December eleventh. It was as easy as that.

"Two of us stayed there, in Cincinnati, and two of us came back to New York. There was a man named Castiglia who went by the name of Costello. We knew him through Il Santo. He was in the process of putting Tammany Hall into his back pocket. When you looked over this guy's shoulder, you didn't see six guineas from Thompson Street, you saw City Hall. So, we went to see him. I talked to him in Italian. He agreed to back us. He would put up the money for the clearing-house clerk, and he would put our bets, along with his own, straight into Harlem through his people—people that Miro and the other Harlem bosses wouldn't dare fool with.

"By three o'clock that Wednesday afternoon—December tenth—Harlem was holding more than five thousand dollars' worth of action on zero-zero-zero. There was a pawnshop up there called Blue White Diamonds, where you could lay a grand on a number and get paid off half a million in cash if you hit. At the end of that afternoon, Castiglia walked in there and laid down ten hundred-dollar bills. 'I had a dream,' he told the shine.

"The next day, there it was, over the wires and in the papers: zero-zero-zero. Harlem went crazy. Castiglia and his people got what money there was from the numbers banks, then they went to Blue White Diamonds for the rest. Miro and the other bosses were busted. One of them blew out his own brains, another left town. And Castiglia and his friends became the partners of those who remained. I figured I was one of those friends."

The old man lifted his glass in his left hand to drink, and Louie's eyes caught the familiar, august gleam of the big diamond ring that his uncle never removed. As a boy, when his family was poor, Louie had learned the meaning of *malocchio* by watching the eyes of his aunts as they gazed upon that stone.

"Castiglia gave me twenty grand. He told me there would be more. In the meantime, he wanted me to come up with a new numbers system, one that couldn't be rigged as easily as the clearing-house numbers.

"I gave it some thought and figured the last three digits of the New York Stock Exchange summary would be a good gimmick. And, for a while, it was. But after a few months, the board of directors of the exchange wised up and started substituting ciphers for the last three digits. It was almost as if, with the Depression and all, the exchange was worried about becoming a subsidiary of the numbers.

"That's when I came up with what came to be called the New York numbers. You took the payoff prices of the first three races at the track each afternoon and added them up. Say those eighteen prices totaled $91.50. Then you added on the payoff prices of the next two races. Say the new total was $192.00. Then you added on the payoff prices of the sixth and seventh races. Say you ended up with $415.20. You took the last digit before each of the three decimal points and put them together. Here it would be one-two-five. That was your number for the day."

Louie had grown up with people playing the numbers all around him, and he had been told by his grandfather that there would be no numbers, as people knew them, had it not been for Uncle John. He had believed this as a boy. Unaware that the numbers were illegal—even his first-grade teacher and the cop on the corner played them—he was sure that, when he was able to read books without pictures, he would find Uncle John's name written as bold in history as the names of Columbus and Einstein. But then, in adolescence, he had ceased believing it, and it became just another of the lies that died with his grandfather. After that, he had believed it and disbelieved it, until his father, not long before he died, denied the truth of it in a way that left no doubt in Louie's mind that it was true. Yet, until this moment, Uncle John himself had never broached the subject. Like most of what lay between them, it had been unspoken.

"It was a beautiful system," the old man reflected. "Later, they added the Brooklyn numbers. You just looked at the bottom of the racing charts in the paper each day and whatever the last three digits of the track handle were, that was the Brooklyn number. With two numbers, the New York and the Brooklyn, drawing action every day, and with both paying off at five hundred on a dollar, against real odds of nine hundred ninety-nine to one, the racket was bringing in millions a week. Then they added the single action, sending runners out in the afternoon to take bets on the New York number one digit at a time, as it came out. They paid off seven to one, with real odds of nine to one; fifty-nine to one on what they called a bleeder, two digits bet at once.

"People were crazy for numbers. It was a disease. And, like every disease, it was a goldmine. But they don't give out copyrights in the rackets, and they don't pay royalties. That twenty grand I got didn't last too long. I bought myself a Packard coupe—a convertible. I bought this ring. I had a lady friend; I bought her a sable coat, and one day when I was drunk I paid off the mortgage on her mother's house in Brooklyn. A dime here, a grand there. Like they say, a fool and his money.

"So I went to see Castiglia. Was I not his friend? Of course I was. I reminded him of his promise, that there would be more money coming to me. I talked in Italian to him, and he answered me in Italian. '*E meglio il cuor felice che la borsa piena,*' he said. 'Better a happy heart than a full purse.' "

The old man drew breath.

"I thought awhile, then I drank awhile. Then I got some blood on my shirt, and that was that. The government took those five years from me. That was all right. I tacked them on to this end."

He pointed to the floor of the here and now.

"At that time, Louie, Sing Sing was a very bad place. I did nothing but sit in the dark for months. I smoked cigars and I spat and I thought the worst things a man can think. Then, one morning—it was this time of year; you could smell spring in the breeze from the river—I woke up and I was strong. I had caught that breeze.

"The way Sing Sing was set up at the time, the library was on the first level, in the open area where you came down to go into the yard. So, I walked in there that morning. The librarian was a faggot, a little guy from down South somewhere. They called him Betty Boop. He kept a box of old Kotex pads in his cell. 'Come by for a sniff,' he'd say. 'It's almost like bein' with a broad.' Eventually, he cut his own throat. They sewed it up, and he ripped it open again with his bare hands.

"Anyway, I walked in there, and I looked around. It wasn't much of a library. But, then again, Sing Sing was never known for its readers.

"I knew what I wanted, but not exactly. See, that breeze I had caught, Louie, was the first suspicion of truth. And the truth was that I was blind. All those years, from the time I went to work for Il Santo to when those big doors shut behind me, I'd looked down on the suckers who were my bread and butter. I'd looked down on them without seeing that my road ran parallel to theirs, and that it led to the same place. The difference between their end and mine was only the difference between a coffin made of pine and a coffin made of bronze. After all was said and done, I was just a fancier make of sucker than them. While I stuck it to them, somebody was sticking it to me. I knew all about the odds they were blind to, but I was blind to the odds that governed my own fate. I had fallen for the oldest sucker's game in the world: faith. I'd trusted somebody named Frankie Scarpa. And while I was talking Italian to Castiglia, Frankie Scarpa was talking English. Frankie Scarpa and Castiglia's friend Dutchie got the numbers, and I got *un' gazz'*. Then one day, Dutchie trusted, too. A guard showed me a *Mirror* with Dutchie's picture in it. He was lying in a pool of his own blood, just a few blocks from where we are now. And the day came when Castiglia trusted, too.

"See, it hadn't really sunk in yet that whenever a man talks about trust and honor, there's a good chance that if you look over your shoulder, you'll see a brass cock aimed right at your asshole. It's just like that dollar bill: They put "In God We Trust' on it one day, the next day it's worthless. I was blind to all that. I had figured out how to rig the numbers, but I didn't see that I was being rigged. I wasn't alone. That's what that place, Sing Sing, was full of, blind men.

"Anyway, Louie," he said, with force in his voice, "I was in Sing Sing five years, and I learned some things. I taught myself to read Latin, and I learned *potestas*—power, Louie—from men who knew it. From them, in their tongue. And I learned that those two words, *annuit coeptis*, on the back of that dollar bill, were from a prayer for *potestas*. I learned that that's what that dollar was.

"What I really learned, Louie, was that the ways of the world are ancient. Il Santo, Castiglia, all of them: they had done nothing that hadn't been done two thousand years before. The same holds for everybody. Any man who thinks he has a new idea is only a fool who hasn't been around. Like the Jews said, 'The thing that has been, it is that which shall be; and that which is done is that which shall be done; and there is no new thing under the sun.' Understanding the truth of that can give a man the greatest edge in the world."

The old man looked into Louie's eyes, and he did not look away from them until his own failing sight had ascertained that there was light in them.

"I got out of that place in 1936, and I went my own way. I got involved in politics, if you want to call it that, with Frank Hague there in Jersey City, around the time of the '37 election. Eventually, I settled here. I did all right. I stayed my own man. I never started trouble, and I never ran from it. It's more than half a century since I caught that breeze, and you know, Louie, it just got stronger and sweeter with time.

"I watched what happened to the numbers. As I said, Dutchie got his.

There's a big gray stone in the Gate of Heaven Cemetery with his name on it. In '39, Jimmy Hines, the Tammany Hall boss who was Castiglia's real partner in the numbers, got sent away by Dewey, who was another cocksucker. Things were shaken up for a while, and the numbers ended up in a lot of new hands. My old pal Frankie Scarpa got knocked down a few pegs. And they all just got greedier.

"That was their downfall. They came up with that cut-numbers shit figuring they'd increase their take by a good ten percent. Now certain numbers, they said—anything with a one in the middle; seven sixty-nine, which most of the dreambooks gave as the number of death; those three zeros—paid off at only four hundred on a dollar. But say a guy has been playing one seventeen for ten years. Now the runner comes to him and says that his number's cut and it won't pay five hundred on one anymore. I don't care how stupid that guy is, he's going to think. And that's why when the State decided to take over the numbers, all it had to do was pay off at five hundred on one across the board, no cut numbers. The man that advised the State to do it that way was a smart man." He grinned slyly. "Whoever he was."

Louie drank the last of his water, peering at the old man through the bottom of his raised glass.

"More than a few times in the forties and fifties, even since then, I was asked by certain men to come back into the numbers. They knew about those three zeros I told you about. But I turned them down. I knew the day was coming when the State would move in. And in your lifetime, Louie, you'll see the day when the State takes over the numbers completely. In Jersey, they've nearly done it already, and last year, in New York, the State took in close to half a billion in numbers action." He looked to Louie. "Fifteen percent of that went to what they call 'administration.'"

It seemed to Louie that his uncle savored the syllables of that last, droll word. Perhaps he was only slowing to the long pause that followed. Louie saw that there was actual weariness now in the old man's face.

"There are people, Louie, who believe I've held a grudge against the numbers since that touch of *la fede* sixty years ago." He slowly, sternly shook his head. "They don't know about that breeze, Louie. And they don't know me." He looked again at his nephew.

"And so now here we sit, Louie. We've never talked, you and me, of trusting each other, or love or honor or any of that *mut*." Louie had not heard the sound of that Albanian obscenity for years. "I'm an old man who's done all right, an old man who's spent most of what he made, but who caught a breeze and got to breathe it for longer than most men.

"And now you come and you say to me that somebody says to ask me whatever happened to Joe Brusher."

The old man nodded firmly, as he had done when Louie had first said those words and the sun washed brightly through the lace.

"And I know that the somebody you're speaking of is the man you pay your union dues to. I know he is one of the men who came up with that cut-numbers shit, and I know that he is one of those who believe that I have a grudge. He's a man as bad as Il Santo, but he lacks in the brains and in the balls. His name is Frankie Scarpa, and they call him Il Capraio.

"And Joe Brusher is a man who was born with the eyes of a corpse, and who kills men.

"It's not really a question, Louie, that your friend"—and he did savor that word—"is asking me. He knows as well as I do where Joe Brusher is. No, it's not a question. It's a threat. It means nothing to me. I'm not brave, but I don't scare, either. What means something to me is that he is low enough to send my own flesh and blood as an errand boy against me. I hope you think about that, Louie.

"Now get me a pen and paper from the kitchen."

Louie brought him what he wanted. The old man thanked him, then put the paper on the table and brought his left hand steadily down upon it. Lowering his face to within inches of it, he carefully wrote Joe Brusher's name, and below the name an address on Fairmount Avenue in Jersey City. Then he folded it and handed it to Louie.

"There," he said, his tired face smiling with a last glimmer of strength. "There's his answer."

They sat in silence while the room slowly darkened. Louie watched the old man peer into the drift, and, as he watched, he knew that what he saw was all that remained for him of a past that he alternately cherished and despised. The room grew darker still, and Louie rose to switch on the lamp. Light flooded the room, and the old man raised his head.

"So, what do you say, pal, we'll go with the Mets again?"

"Yeah," Louie said. "We'll go with the Mets."

They talked awhile more, about batting averages and artificial turf, beer and the weather. Louie offered to bring him *abbacchio*, a fresh-killed baby lamb, when he brought the palm next week. The old man wanted him to take a fifty-dollar bill for the lamb, but Louie would not have it.

"Keep it," he said. "Maybe there's something on the back you missed."

When they said good-bye, the old man reached up with one arm, and Louie bent to hug him.

The reflection of the lamplight on the windowpane was bright against the falling gloom of dusk. The old man looked out and watched Louie walk away through the long springtime shadows.

The old man turned. Glancing at a piece of paper from his pocket, he lifted the gleaming black receiver from its cradle, then dialed.

"Yeah," Joe Brusher said.

"The kid bought it," the old man said.

from

London Fields

by Martin Amis

KEITH TALENT WAS a bad guy. Keith Talent was a very bad guy. You might even say that he was the worst guy. But not *the* worst, not the very worst ever. There *were* worse guys. Where? There in the hot light of CostCheck for example, with car keys, beige singlet, and a six-pack of Peculiar Brews, the scuffle at the door, the foul threat and the elbow in the black neck of the wailing lady, then the car with its rust and its waiting blonde, and off to do the next thing, whatever, whatever necessary. The mouths on these worst guys—the eyes on them. Within those eyes a tiny unsmiling universe. No. Keith wasn't *that* bad. He had saving graces. He didn't hate people for ready-made reasons. He was at least *multiracial* in outlook—thoughtlessly, helplessly so. Intimate encounters with strange-hued women had sweetened him somewhat. His saving graces all had names. What with the Fetnabs and Fatimas he had known, the Nketchis and Iqbalas, the Michikos and Boguslawas, the Ramsarwatees and Rajashwaris—Keith was, in this sense, a man of the world. These were the chinks in his coal-black armour: God bless them all.

Although he liked nearly everything else about himself, Keith hated his redeeming features. In his view they constituted his only major shortcoming—his one tragic flaw. When the moment arrived, in the office by the loading bay at the plant off the M4 near Bristol, with his great face crammed into the prickling nylon, and the proud woman shaking her trembling head at him, and Chick Purchase and Dean Pleat both screaming *Do it. Do it* (he still remembered their meshed mouths writhing), Keith had definitely failed to realize his full potential. He had proved incapable of clubbing the Asian woman to her knees, and of going on clubbing until the man in the uniform opened the safe. Why had he failed? Why, Keith, why? In truth he had felt far from well: half the night up some lane in a car full of the feet-heat of burping criminals; no breakfast, no bowel movement; and now, to top it all off, everywhere he looked he saw green grass, fresh trees, rolling hills. Chick Purchase, furthermore, had already crippled the second guard, and Dean Pleat soon vaulted back over the counter and self-righteously laid into the woman with his rifle butt. So Keith's qualms had changed nothing—except his career prospects in armed robbery. (It's tough at the top, and it's tough at the bottom, too; Keith's name was muck thereafter.) If he could have done it, he would have done it, joyfully. He just didn't have . . . he just didn't have the talent.

After that Keith turned his back on armed robbery once and for all. He took up racketeering. In London, broadly speaking, racketeering meant fighting about drugs; in the part of West London that Keith called home, racketeering meant fighting about drugs with black people—and black people are better at fighting than white people, because, among other reasons, they *all* do it (there aren't any civilians). Racketeering works through escalation, and escalation dominance: success goes to the men who can manage the exponential jump, to the men who can regularly *astonish* with their violence. It took Keith several crunchy beatings, and the first signs of a liking for hospital food, before he concluded that he wasn't cut out for racketeering. During one of his convalescences, when he spent a lot of time in the street cafés of Golborne Road, Keith grew preoccupied by a certain enigma. The enigma was this. How come you often saw black guys with white girls (always blondes, always, presumably for maximum contrast-gain), and never saw white guys with black girls? Did the black guys beat up the white guys who went out with black girls? No, or not much; you had to be discreet, though, and in his experience lasting relationships were seldom formed. Then how was it done? It came to him in a flash of inspiration. The black guys beat up the black *girls* who went out with white guys! Of course. So much simpler. He pondered the wisdom of this and drew a lesson from it, a lesson which, in his heart, he had long understood. If you're going to be violent, stick to women. Stick to the weak. Keith gave up racketeering. He turned over a new leaf. Having renounced violent crime, Keith prospered, and rose steadily towards the very crest of his new profession: non-violent crime.

Keith worked as a *cheat*. There he stands on the street corner, with three or four colleagues, with three or four fellow *cheats*; they laugh and cough (they're always coughing) and flap their arms for warmth; they look like terrible birds . . . On good days he rose early and put in long hours, going out into the world, into society, with the intention of cheating it. Keith cheated people with his limousine service at airports and train stations; he cheated people with his fake scents and colognes at the pavement stalls of Oxford Street and Bishopsgate (his two main lines were Scandal and Outrage); he cheated people with non-pornographic pornography in the back rooms of short-lease stores; and he cheated people on the street everywhere with the upturned cardboard box or milk crate and the three warped playing cards: Find the Lady! Here, often, and occasionally elsewhere, the boundaries between violent crime and its non-violent little brother were hard to descry. Keith earned three times as much as the Prime Minister and never had any money, losing heavily every day at Mecca, the turf accountants on the Portobello Road. He never won. Sometimes he would ponder this, on alternate Thursday lunchtimes, in sheepskin overcoat, his head bent over the racing page, as he queued for his unemployment benefit, and then drove to the turf accountants on the Portobello Road. So Keith's life might have elapsed over the years. He never had what it took to be a murderer, not on his own. He needed his murderee. The foreigners, the checked and dog-toothed Americans, the leering lens-faced Japanese, standing stiff over the cardboard box or the milk crate—they never found the lady. But *Keith* did. Keith found her.

Of course, he already had a lady, little Kath, who had recently presented him with a child. By and large Keith had welcomed the pregnancy: it was, he liked to joke, quite a handy new way of putting his wife in hospital. He had decided that the baby, when it came, would be called Keith—Keith Jr. Kath, remarkably, had other ideas. Yet Keith was inflexible, wavering only once, when he briefly entertained the idea of calling the baby Clive, after his dog, a large, elderly and unpredictable Alsatian. He changed his mind once more; Keith it was to be, then . . . Swaddled in blue, the baby came home, with mother. Keith personally helped them from the ambulance. As Kath started on the dishes, Keith sat by the stolen fire and frowned at the new arrival. There was something wrong with the baby, something seriously wrong. The trouble with the baby was that it was a girl. Keith looked deep into himself, and rallied. 'Keithette,' Kath heard him murmur, as her knees settled on the cold lino. 'Keithene. Keitha. Keithinia.'

'No, Keith,' she said.

'Keithnab,' said Keith, with an air of slow discovery. 'Nkeithi.'

'No, Keith.'

' . . . Why's it so fucking yellow?'

After a few days, whenever Kath cautiously addressed the baby as 'Kim', Keith no longer swore at his wife or slammed her up against the wall with any conviction. 'Kim', after all, was the name of one of Keith's heroes, one of Keith's gods. And Keith was cheating hard that week, cheating on everyone, it seemed, and especially his wife. So Kim Talent it was—Kim Talent, little Kim.

THE MAN HAD ambition. It was his dream to go all the way; he wasn't just messing. Keith had no intention, or no desire, to be a *cheat* for the rest of his life. Even he found the work demoralizing. And mere cheating would never get him the things he wanted, the goods and services he wanted, not while a series of decisive wins at the turf accountants continued to elude him. He sensed that Keith Talent had been put here for something a little bit special. To be fair, it must be said that murder was not in his mind, not yet, except perhaps in some ghostly *potentia* that precedes all thought and action . . . Character is destiny. Keith had often been told, by various magistrates, girlfriends and probation officers, that he had a 'poor character', and he had always fondly owned up to the fact. But did that mean he had a poor destiny? . . . Waking early, perhaps, as Kath clumsily dragged herself from the bed to attend to little Kim, or wedged in one of the traffic jams that routinely enchained his day, Keith would mentally pursue an alternative vision, one of wealth, fame and a kind of spangled superlegitimacy—the chrome spokes of a possible future in World Darts.

A casual darter or arrowman all his life, right back to the bald board on the kitchen door, Keith had recently got serious. He'd always thrown for his pub, of course, and followed the sport: you could almost hear angels singing when, on those special nights (three or four times a week), Keith laid out the cigarettes on the arm of the couch and prepared to watch darts on television. But now he had designs on the other side of the screen. To his own elaborately concealed astonishment, Keith found himself in the Last Sixteen of the Sparrow Masters, an annual interpub competition which he had nonchalantly entered some months ago, on the advice of various friends and admirers. At the end of that road there basked the contingency of a televised final, a £5,000 cheque, and a play-off, also televised, with his hero and darting model, the world number one, Kim Twemlow. After that, well, after that, the rest was television.

And television was all about everything he did not have and was full of all the people he did not know and could never be. Television was the great shopfront, lightly electrified, up against which Keith crushed his nose. And now among the squirming motes, the impossible prizes, he saw a doorway, or an arrow, or a beckoning hand (with a dart in it), and everything said—Darts. Pro-Darts. World Darts. He's down there in his garage, putting in the hours, his eyes still stinging from the ineffable, the heart-breaking beauty of a brand-new dartboard, stolen that very day.

MAGNIFICENT ANACHRONISM. THE lights and mores of the modern criminal Keith held in disdain. He had no time for the gym, the fancy restaurant, the buxom bestseller, the foreign holiday. He had never taken any exercise (unless you counted burgling, running away, and getting beaten up); he had never knowingly drunk a glass of wine (or only when he was well past caring); he had never read a book (we here exclude *Darts: Master the Discipline*); and he had never been out of London. Except once. When he went to America . . .

He journeyed there with a friend, also a young *cheat*, also a dartsman, also called Keith: Keith Double. The plane was overbooked and the two Keiths were seated twenty rows apart. They stilled their terror with murderous drinking, courtesy of stewardess and duty-free bag, and by shouting out, every ten seconds or so, 'Cheers, Keith!' We can imagine the amusement of their fellow passengers, who logged over a thousand of these shouts during the seven-hour flight. After disembarking at New York, Keith Talent was admitted to the public hospital in Long Island City. Three days later, when he began to stagger out to the stairwell for his smokes, he encountered Keith Double. 'Cheers, Keith!' The mandatory health insurance turned out to cover alcohol poisoning, so everyone was happy, and became even happier when the two Keiths recovered in time to make their return flight. Keith Double was in advertising now, and had frequently returned to America. Keith hadn't; he was still cheating on the streets of London.

And the world, and history, could not be reordered in a way that would make sense to him. Some distance up the beach in Plymouth, Massachusetts, there once lay a large boulder, reputedly the first chunk of America to be touched by the Pilgrims' feet. Identified in the eighteenth century, this opening sample of US real estate had to be moved closer to the shore, in order to satisfy expectations of how history ought to happen. To satisfy Keith, to get anywhere with Keith, you'd need to fix the entire planet—great sceneshiftings, colossal rearrangements at the back of his mind. And then the tabloid face would have to crease and pucker.

Keith didn't look like a murderer. He looked like a murderer's dog. (No disrespect to Keith's dog Clive, who had signed on well before the fact, and whom Keith didn't in the least resemble anyway.) Keith looked like a murderer's dog, eager familiar of ripper or bodysnatcher or gravestalker. His eyes held a strange radiance—for a moment it reminded you of health, health hidden or sleeping or otherwise mysteriously absent. Though frequently bloodshot, the eyes seemed to pierce. In fact the light sprang off them. And it wasn't at all pleasant or encouraging, this one-way splendour. His eyes were television. The face itself was leonine, puffy with hungers, and as dry as soft fur. Keith's crowning glory, his hair, was thick and full-bodied; but it always had the look of being recently washed, imperfectly rinsed, and then, still slick with cheap shampoo, slow-dried in a huddled pub—the thermals of the booze, the sallowing fagsmoke. Those eyes, and their urban severity . . . Like the desolating gaiety of a fundless paediatric hospital (Welcome to the Peter Pan Ward), or like a criminal's cream Rolls-Royce, parked at dusk between a tube station and a flower stall, the eyes of Keith Talent shone with tremendous accommodations made to money. And murder? The eyes—was there enough blood in them for *that*? Not now, not yet. He had the talent, somewhere, but he would need the murderee to bring it out. Soon, he would find the lady.

Or she would find him.

from

Love Is a Racket

by John Ridley

"Tiiin," HE WHINED. He whined it again. "Tiiin." Some kind of accent obscured most of his English. A voice like a cat caught under a truck tire hid the rest of it. An Oriental guy, the market owner was, but not Korean.

Don't mess with Koreans.

Koreans got no love of black people. Out here a while back, a Korean shop owner shot a little black girl in the head for stealing a thing of orange juice. Judge gave the shop owner probation. Might as well have thrown in a foot massage with it. What's Korean for "open season on niggers"?

Once more with the whine: "I give you tiiin, you give me five and five single, riiight?"

He was following along. He was asking questions, slowing the whole trick down. From the street I thought he'd be an easy mark. Look at him: greasy hair, sweat-sheened face, Hawaiian-print shirt—washed dull—worn over a dirty T-shirt and pale gray pants. Sandals and black socks.

Sandals and black socks!

He wore stuff the Salvation Army wouldn't take, and here he was screwing up my grift.

Truth: People aren't always as dumb as they dress.

"You give me fiiive, and I give your tiiin back."

"Uh, yeah." I smiled. This was going nowhere.

The electric eye at the door buzzed as it opened. Someone else coming in. Someone else watching. Someone else rushing me along so they could get served, busting my groove. This I didn't need.

I didn't know how much I didn't need it.

"Let's go, Jeffty."

I went tight; my muscles stitched together. The voice plenty familiar.

"Dumas wants to see you." Ty. One of Dumas's boys. His best boy. The same one who took my usable fingers from ten down to eight.

"Give me a minute," I said. Cool, as if being cool was going to buy me anything.

"No minute. No nothing." Ty was cool, too; it's just his went further. His cool talked tougher. "Dumas wants to see you."

"Just let me—"

"Tiiin, tiiin." The Oriental worked his whine in.

"Yeah, I—" I started.

"Give me a tiiin."

I was fazed from the second Ty walked in. The last time Dumas went looking for me I got bones broken. I knew him wanting to see me now, there wasn't likely any flowers and thank-yous involved.

I handed a ten to the Oriental without even thinking about it. I was trying to work out other things, like if maybe I'd be alive at the end of the day.

Ty said again: "Come on, Dumas—"

"You said. He wants to see me." I turned and looked Ty straight in the eyes. Straight *up* into his eyes. Ty was big and beefy in a 100 percent muscle kind of way. I think he was born big, and I'm pretty sure he was one of those guys who didn't need a gym to keep looking that way. Some things came natural to Ty. His size, his ability to look good—despite his size—in a suit and tie, and, foremost, his ability to fuck you up.

I tried to give him a stare that was hard and cold and tough the way guys in movies looked hard and cold and tough. Imitating movie actors was the only way I knew how as I wasn't naturally hard or cold, and certainly not tough.

Ty smiled heavy, like this was the most amusing thing he'd seen all morning.

I walked out of the store.

Ty fell in behind me.

As I left, it came to me that I never took any money back from the Oriental.

Fuck.

In the midst of all my nervous jangling over how Dumas was going to respond to me not having his money—again—while I was trying to take the Oriental, the Oriental took me.

FOUNTAIN TO HIGHLAND. South toward Century. Inglewood, we were going to.

Ty had a Benz. S-class. Snowflake white, like all Dumas boys rolled in. I sat in back, like I was getting chauffeur-drove to my own execution. I tried the little doohickey that worked the window and got nothing.

"Nice day out," I said, like I was saying it to no one in particular. "Sure would be nice if I could breathe some of it."

Ty looked up at me in the rearview mirror. Nothing in his eyes. No anger. No pity. No nothing. He just looked up at me like he was looking at a sack of food he was carrying home from the grocer. He reached over to the armrest and the window next to me sank. Not far. Not far enough for me to jump out, as if jumping out of a moving car into traffic is ever a good idea. I just sat there and sucked up lungful after lungful of that thick chocolaty LA air.

As we rode south into the shitty—even shittier—parts of LA, we passed some ghetto houses, which was a peculiar thing to Los Angeles: houses in the ghetto. Our poor had houses, and our bums had tans.

Outside one of the houses, kids played with a shipping box they had gotten hold of. A big box for a dishwasher or refrigerator or something.

And now what was it? A castle, a fort, a spaceship? Something out of nothing. The kids—they smiled; they laughed. They didn't have a thought about anything beyond that box. Not the people on the street, not the traffic, not the big white Benzes that took guys where they didn't want to go. They just played. Fuck Disneyland. Who needs that when you've got a box? That's the way it is when you're a kid: Nothing is ever just nothing, and everything is fresh with possibilities.

I don't know why I thought about that, about those kids as they played. I just did. And I thought about how I used to be like them—young and full of chances.

Used to be.

Maybe.

Before I even knew I was saying anything, I was saying: "Why do you do this?" Ty didn't know if I was talking to him. I didn't know *why* I was talking to him, but I was, so I said it again. "Why do you do this?"

Ty laughed a little, then came back with: "'Cause you owe, Jeffty. You owe big."

"I don't mean that. I don't mean why you taking me to Dumas. Why do you work for him? Why do you do this for a living?"

More laughing. "What should I be doing, Jeffty? Huh? Selling shoes, maybe? Maybe patio furniture? Or how about used cars? Same kind of business, sort of; milking people, I guess. You tell me: What should I be doing?"

"You're not like them."

"Who? I'm not like—"

"Dumas. His whole crew."

"I'm not Haitian. That what you mean?"

"I mean you're not a goon. They're goons—big, dumb, and slow. You're not any of that. Big, sure, but you've got a brain. You've got . . ." I caught Ty looking at me in the rearview; staring at me full of suspicion.

"What are you trying to do? Make nice so I'll go soft on you?"

"I'm just saying. You're different from them. So, why do you do it?"

Ty thought about it. He gave it more thought than most would a question I had no business asking. When he got done thinking, he said: "Compton."

"Whereabouts?"

"Alvaro. Near Central."

I knew that area. Knew enough to stay away from it.

"'Round there a brother just spends his days marking time. When you're a kid, you dodge bullets on the playground, and the dope dealers who line up for business outside the schoolyard. Get to be ten, eleven, twelve you got to start choosing sides: which gang you gonna run with. And soon as you're in one, you start watching the older kids, the soldiers, get killed." Ty made a sound, part huff and part laugh. "Older kids. Some thirteen, some almost fifteen. Yeah, but 'round there that's about as old as you get. I decided I wanted to get a little older."

"So you got with Dumas."

"Got with Dumas. Got paid well. Got an education. Took the money I made running for him and hooked up some extension courses at Cal State, Long Beach. Most of those niggas where I come from couldn't point to Long Beach if you opened a map right to it. Now look at me: I know shit. I speak right. I read. And I'm not just talking about titty magazines. You want to know who I'm not like, Jeffty? I'm not like those shines back where I grew up."

"And all that learning's kept you humble, too."

"It's kept me alive. I'm twenty-four, Jeffty. In my part of the world that's goddamn ancient. Dumas isn't a banger. He's a bookie, pure and simple. Bookies don't deal with hard-asses; no dope, no gangs—"

"What kind of people do they deal with?"

"People like you."

"And what kind is that?"

Without a thought: "Losers. Look at you, Jeffty. How old are you?"

"Thirty-five." I lied, short by two years.

Ty's head shook. "Thirty-five," he repeated, like he knew what he repeated wasn't quite true. "Thirty-five and you're nothing but a scared little con with busted fingers."

"Thanks to you."

"Sorry about that."

It was the second time Ty had apologized to me for breaking my fingers. And, as with the first time, I felt he sincerely meant it. All that sincerity wouldn't keep him from snapping them again, or any other part of me, if Dumas told him to.

Ty went on. "You've got to admit, Jeffty, you're a little pathetic. More than that. I whistle, and you come crawling into the car like a lost dog gone days without food."

"Go on," I said like I didn't care. But it's hard not to care when a guy is poking you with a knife.

"Fifteen thousand. How long did it take you to get that deep?"

"Year and a half. Not including how the interest built up, about that."

"I could understand that all at once: A bad run, and you drop that in no time. But to let it eat away at you for a year and a half. To see it coming and not put on the brakes . . ." He laughed again. He was getting his money's worth on this ride. "Hell, Jeffty, even a horse isn't so dumb it won't swat the flies biting it. You're not even as smart as a big dumb animal."

I couldn't argue with that, so I didn't. "Yeah. I'm stupid."

"You are. You're the kind of brother who gives the rest of us a bad name."

"Sure. If it wasn't for me you'd be a bookie's flunky people could look up to. A real pillar of society; a strong-arm thug and a credit to his race." It was my turn to laugh, so I let loose. "Yeah, I'm stupid, but I'm smart enough to know it. You're not even that."

I thought my words clever. I guess they were. But from there on in things got very unamusing.

"Shut up, Jeffty. Do yourself a favor and shut up, or—"

"Or what? You'll beat me? You'll kill me? Take a number and wait your turn."

Big talk I tossed him. Why shouldn't I? I was feeling tough. I was feeling unstoppable. I had no fear, because in my heart I knew I was going to die. When a man knows he's going to die there isn't anything he can't do.

We made the rest of the ride in silence. Ty rolled up my window to mess with me. It wasn't much, but it was enough to get me hot and bothered. It was enough to give me a sweat so that my clothes were nothing but wet rags.

Inglewood. We pulled up to the Hollywood Park Casino. I knew it well enough. My antes alone must have built the carport. At least that.

A little Mexican in a red vest hopped in the car and valet-parked it. Ty clutched at my elbow, an unwilling date being forced to the prom, and walked me from the casino to Hollywood Park.

Hollywood Park was neither. It wasn't in Hollywood and it wasn't a park. It was a horse track, but *park* sounded nicer than *track*, same as "I spent my afternoon at the park" sounds nicer than "I lost this week's pay in the third at the track."

Big and beige and freckled with palm trees, it was just about out of place with the hard, hot asphalt reality all around it. The park was like an oasis come up out of the urban desert. Drink our cool water, it said. Relax awhile out of the sun. Play your money and dream a little dream. We're the sport of kings.

Ty guided me toward the Turf Club turnstile. Fifteen bucks just to get in. It was supposed to make the Turf Club more exclusive; keep the dregs out. I'd been up there before, and it wasn't fifteen bucks' worth of a better way to lose money than betting at trackside, but I guess for some people a ten and a five is a small price to pay to feel superior.

Ty watched as I worked some crumpled bills out of my pocket and fed them to the ticket girl. Dumas wants to see me, Dumas wants to kill me, and I've got to pay fifteen bucks out of my own pocket for the pleasure. Ty got more laughs out of this. I was making his day.

We walked in, me and Ty, his hand still on my elbow, past a cheap little man in a cheap little tux. It was the park's attempt at a touch of class. Except that it was white-hot out. The cheap little man in the cheap little tux was soaking in his own sweat. He stamped our hands with one of those inks that only show up under fluorescent light. More of the exclusivity the fifteen bucks bought you.

We worked our way up the track: the grandstands, the clubhouse. Middle of the day, middle of the week. The joint was packed. Grubby little people who looked like they thought the sole function of the U.S. government was to write checks and hand out cheese bumped up against Yuppies who'd most likely told their bosses they were just going to the mail room to run off some copies. Pretty much anyone who had two bucks to rub together had a passport to the glamorous world of horse racing and daydreaming.

Check it out over there: a fat one-legged guy in a wheelchair working a crooked arm up to the window to lay a bet. Sad. That big stain spreading over his trousers where he'd just pissed himself couldn't even make it sadder. Sport of kings.

Sure.

Sport of stupid bastards who don't know that losers are always losers, and there ain't a trifecta in the world that'll change that.

The stamp on my hand glowed under the fluorescent lamp just like it was supposed to for the guy at the Turf Club door to see, if he had been looking, which he wasn't. The park's little con ran out of steam right there. This guy, the guy at the door, might work for them, but he's not buying into their show. Everything about him—the way he slouched against the door frame, the way his head lolled as if he was in the middle of a death-defying act of sleeping upright—everything said: Go on. Go on in. Upstairs, downstairs; I don't care where you lose your money. It's all five and a quarter an hour to me.

The stands of the Turf Club were less than half-full. Ty escorted me in just as a race started. The crowd, what crowd there was, let go with yelps for their horses as if with the shrill of their voices they could push the animals down the backstretch. Such a real thrill, such a genuine excitement for horses that weren't there.

It was off-season at the park. No racing. No horses. Just a flock of pink flamingos that soaked in the pond at center track, and a pair of water trucks that circled the turf wetting it down. Other than that, nothing. The races were being run at Santa Anita, or up at Golden Gate. Every single person at the track had paid their money and laid their bets to watch races run miles away on closed-circuit TV.

Dumas sat at a table, his usual table, eating his usual meal and drinking his usual cool drink. He was surrounded by his usual boys; hangers-on who yes-manned him to death and ate his shit for the money he paid. But he paid good, and the right amount of cash helped choke down even the unpalatable taste of feces. Most of his boys were interchangeable. Just scum that was dipped off the top of a Haitian cesspool, had made its way Stateside, and would make more dough working for their man than I could dream of in a week of fantasizing.

Dumas was too busy watching the race to pay me much mind. At least he was too busy acting like he was watching the race to pay any attention to me. Let me stand there soaking up the sun, waiting; that was Dumas's style, and Dumas was all style. Skin that was dark and rich and clean of defect. Get a load of the way he drapes it in a white silk shirt and white pants. Ninety-five, a hundred out, hot so you break a sweat just coming up with a deep thought, and not a drop of perspiration on him. Cool. Always cool. That was his style, too.

Hair cut nice and tight, clean shaven. Dumas even flashed a manicure. You can be that way when you don't have to lift a finger. Not to work, not to live, not to count your gambling money . . . not to get a man dead, which was also his style.

And his voice; his accent: French, or French-Haitian if that mattered, but French-sounding. Soft. Soft so you'd think he was a fag if you didn't know. Sweet. Sweet so that he could make anything he was talking about sound pleasant—beatings, torture, breaking limbs, which were all things he talked of often. His voice had a way of making them seem . . . not so bad.

Miles away, in Santa Anita, the horses rounded the far turn and thundered down the straightaway. Most of them, horses that ran like all they thought about was the day when they'd finally get to be put to stud, were out of the money. Most, but not two. It was more than close for a bit as the pair of beasts charged full out. Ever see a cartoon of a horse when it's racing hard and they draw steam puffing from its nostrils? Look real close at these two and tell me what you see. I didn't have dollar one down, and I could feel myself getting a hard-on for this race.

Maybe it was in my head—had to be, since they were running in Santa Anita—but I could hear the jockeys going to the whip. The jockeys flogged, and the horses worked it. Two dumb animals that didn't know any more than getting beaten every couple of days. They didn't know why; they didn't know what for. It's just get hit and run, get hit and run. And if you're a good boy when it's all over we'll set you in a field and let you fuck your brains out. But first: Get hit and run.

I could relate. Except for the getting to fuck your brains out part, I could relate.

One of the horses crossed the line first.

If Dumas won or lost, you couldn't tell. One of the horses crossed the line first, and Dumas didn't move, or flinch, or yelp, or tear his tickets, or give them to one of his boys to collect. One of the horses took a beating, blew steam out its nose, crossed the line first, and Dumas played it like it didn't matter. It didn't. If his horse won, then he made a little more of what he's already got a lot of. If his horse lost, then it lost for a whole lot of other saps who'd taken bets with him and would now owe. Inside and outside, coming and going: When you can't lose no matter what you try, that's when you can play all things cool.

After a while, Dumas got around to noticing me. "Jeffty," he cooed, French and island mixed winsome. "Why is it I have not seen you around, I suppose? Why is it I have not seen you when I know, and you know, you are in my debt?"

"I haven't got what I owe."

"And why do you suppose that is?"

"Can't earn much with these." I held up my invalid fingers to him.

Dumas curled a perfectly healthy finger toward himself. "Let us have a look."

I stepped to him. I held out my hand, my fingers. He took them in his. I got nervous, him holding what he had broken, but his touch was gentle like he cared for my hurting. Just like he cared.

The caring that I felt was in his voice as well. "Not so bad. Healed up rather nicely. Rather."

He looked my fingers over, slow and careful and full of concern. So very much like he cared. Dumas looked up at me. He smiled.

And smiled.

And smiled.

His fingers twisted a bit. Just a small little bit they twisted, and twisted my broken fingers with them.

A piece of metal that had been stoking on a fire for days got jabbed into my hand. It got jabbed all the way up to my shoulder, then curved around back down to my knees. My eyes shot back in my head, and I enjoyed a quick out-of-body experience as my mind tried to run as far and as fast as it could away from the pain. It couldn't beat it.

A sweet voice sang at me: "Where is my money?"

When I got back to my body it had been painted over with a nice sheen of sweat. A stream of spittle ran over my lip and dripped from my chin. Dumas's boys, all of them, were helping themselves to a good laugh. It was just one of those days when I couldn't help but entertain people.

Dumas: "I don't like having to do that. Maybe a little, but not really. Still, at times it has to be done, do you know?"

I gave a casual response. "Whatever." I was doing too much sweating and shaking for anyone to buy my faux disassociation with pain.

"So, then, where is my money?"

"Don't have it. If I did," wiping drool from my mouth, "I would have paid it, and I wouldn't be standing here letting you work me over." I was getting a little too sharp for my own good, but the smoldering in my hand and the just-now-fading snickers made me that way.

Dumas stared off a bit like something out on the track, like maybe those two water trucks just driving around and around were more interesting than what I was about. He stared off a bit, then he laughed. His boys, who had barely finished with their previous bout of hysteria, started up again. They laughed 'cause Dumas was laughing, and Dumas was laughing at me.

Between the laughs Dumas said: "I could kill you."

Goddamn his voice was sweet.

"I could kill you right here, right now, and no one in this place—no one anywhere—would have a care, do you know? I could kill you, and you talk as if you wouldn't die; you talk as if you were a man." He laughed again. His boys laughed some more, too. "And that is exactly why I do not kill you: You amuse me. You are like a little clown, do you know? That's what you are: a little circus clown."

A sip of his fag drink, a leg raised and crossed the other.

Continuing with his dissertation on the state of me: "Certainly I'll break a finger here and there. You don't pay, I must do something. But you are too funny to kill, and it is so difficult to find a good clown in this day."

Dumas smiled Times Square–bright. An "I'm better than you" smile. An "I'm better than you, and you're nothing but an ant and you know it" smile. So much for one smile.

He should have twisted my fingers again. Dumas should have hacked them right off with that dull, dirty knife sitting on his table. It would have hurt less than his grin did.

"It's a funny thing, no?" Dumas asked. "You have nothing, Jeffty. You are dirt-poor and becoming poorer by the moment."

If that was funny, I couldn't see how.

He went on: "Here I am, an immigrant to your country. People here, Americans, they hate immigrants. A nation full of them, and they all hate the next who come. But I work hard, I've made a . . . well, let us say a fortune. Yes, let us call it that. I pay taxes. Do you pay taxes, Jeffty? Of course you do not. You don't even possess enough money to bury yourself well. That is the problem with this country. It is you lazy natural-borns who are spoiling it for the rest of us."

On the TV, in San Francisco, at Golden Gate, they walked the horses toward the starting gate.

Dumas glanced at the screen. Through his many-meaninged smile: "Make a little wager, care to?"

My head shook. I held up my freshly reswollen fingers. "That's how I worked these in the first place."

"How deep are we now?"

We?

I shrugged. I knew how much I owed. I knew, and I knew he knew, and to hell with him if I was going to let him get a hard-on listening to me choke out the number.

Dumas to Ty: "How much?"

"Fifteen and change." Ty was there with the number same as a dog bringing slippers to its master, but quicker. "Fifteen and change up-to-date on interest."

Dumas rolled the number around in his mouth for a bit. "Now you have an opportunity to win it off."

"I got no taw."

"Double or nothing. What matters owing thirty when you haven't even got fifteen?"

Dumas flipped a finger. Another one of his lapdogs grabbed up a *Racing Form* from the table and jabbed it at me. Nobody said a word, but we all spoke the same language. Dumas wants me to play, I play, and nobody's trying to hear otherwise.

I took the form, fumbled the pages, and came up with the fifth from Golden Gate. The page was worked up, the margins bloated with notations, numbers, stats. . . . It was like Dumas was trying to figure cold fusion.

The sweet voice: "I prefer Weatherly, number three. I like her works. She's ready to stretch out on the grass."

Number eight was named Terri's Song. I knew a Terri for a day once. She didn't fuck me over. Just like that: "I'll take eight." I tossed the form back down on the table for punctuation.

More smiles all around. Big stupid grins. Grab 'em up, boys. They're on the house.

Dumas threw in a few shakes of the head. A few "Isn't this dumb fuck pathetic?" shakes. He spread his hands to his minions as if to say: You see how pathetic, don't you? You see that?

Their ignorant smiles responded: Yeah, we see, boss. We see.

After Dumas had enough head shaking and grinning he got around to: "You would bet against the chalk? Eighteen to one, your long shot."

"Like you said, what's it matter owing thirty when you don't have fifteen? I win and you're off me, and that's all I'm thinking about."

On the monitors, up at Golden Gate, they finished herding the horses into the starting gate. Number eight gave the boys a little trouble about it—rearing, fighting, acting up, as if to emphasize to anyone who was even thinking about betting her, Don't.

She got settled, finally, after giving everyone around Dumas one more thing to laugh at. The bell rang, and a guy with a bad English accent said: "And they're off," just like a guy with a bad English accent says at every horse race everywhere.

Dumas's horse was smooth in second; looked like water running over a fall. There were some other horses behind it. And then there was mine, number eight, in the back, making sure the rest of the pack wasn't being followed.

"What's the fun part of gambling?" Dumas asked to no one in particular.

I didn't figure he was talking to me, so I let it go.

He asked again. "What's the fun part of gambling?"

Now I knew he was talking to me but just didn't want to waste the energy looking in my direction.

"Winning," I said.

"Winning," he repeated. "But if you won all the time it wouldn't be a gamble." His face scrunched up as if to show all the thought he was giving this incredibly complex issue. "No, I don't believe so. I think what is enjoyable is that even though you know the odds are against you, you know you will lose, there is one brief moment when the dice is rolled, or the ball drops, or"—he raised a finger at the monitor—"when the horses crash from the gate; a brief moment, a rush of excitement, when you believe there is a chance you might actually win, do you know?"

Hebrew he might as well have been talking for what I got from it all. "So?" I said.

Dumas worked up the most bored voice he could find. "So, it is the expectation of winning in the face of losing, not the winning itself, that makes gambling exciting. What pleasure is there if you know you're going to win?" As if to punctuate all that, as if to explain it to me, Dumas's horse slid easy into first.

Condensation gathered on Dumas's glass. A droplet formed and ran down the side. It swallowed up other droplets, got bigger, ran faster, and swallowed up more droplets, on and on like that all the way down the glass, and when it was done there was nothing left behind it.

Out on the track, the water trucks didn't do much gaining on each other.

Something happened.

I wasn't looking at the monitor when it did, so I wasn't sure what, or why, or how, but in the instant I was watching the droplet devour all other droplets on Dumas's glass and the water trucks chase each other, Terri's Song, number eight, my horse, had swung to the outside of the pack.

The thing about horse racing is you can load up on all the homework you want. You can read the forms, watch a horse do her works, dig up the history of the jockey like you were going to vote for him, not bet on him. . . . But the one thing no one's ever been able to do, the one thing that would make racing a sure bet every time: You can't ask a horse if it feels like running. Sometimes it does, sometimes it doesn't.

This morning, number eight felt like saying a big "Fuck you" to the world. Fuck the odds; fuck the works; fuck the dirt or the weeds. This morning, Terri's Song felt like running the hell out of herself.

Even going wide on the turn she gobbled up the other horses two at a time. Dumas got all uncomfortable in his chair like he was sitting on hot tacks. It wasn't so much that he minded losing money; it was that he minded losing at all. He minded more losing to me and losing to me in front of his boys. That cocktail was a bit strong for him. He didn't have much time to get a taste for it. This was no neck-and-neck race, no photo finish. Terri's Song just blew up the stretch and across the line like she had someplace to be.

I didn't smile. I'm pretty sure a smile would have gotten me a bullet in the face. I took my horse kicking the shit out of Dumas's very matter-of-factly while fireworks went off in my gut.

The results got posted down on the totalisator at center track. All around us people were talking, or laughing, or tearing up their race tickets in disgust. But we—me and Dumas and Dumas's boys—were in a long tunnel of silence that seemed to go on and on. Who knew what to say? Not Dumas, and sure as hell not his flunkies. Finally, quiet as he could, but still loud as thunder, a word worked its way out of Dumas.

"Well . . ."

Yeah. Well. As in: Well, how's it feel to get your ass kicked, you stupid Haitian bastard? That's the thought that came to me, all full of myself as I bit at my lip to keep from grinning. Inside my head I was having my own little private party.

I thought again, How's it feel to be the bitch for a change, Dumas? You picked the wrong brother to mess with. Today you did. I made that horse win; you're goddamn right I did, you black whore. With force of will shooting straight out of my head I made that nag run. I'm only going to let you push me so much, Dumas. I'm only gonna let you and your girlfriends get so many laughs out of me. After that? After that, I'm gonna stick it to you where it hurts. All your fine clothes and fancy talk, and you're still just a loser like everybody else. Ain't ya, Dumas? Ain't ya?

That's what I thought. "How about that" is all I said. I started to inch my way back up the stairs. As casual as I could make it sound: "I guess I'll just . . . you know . . . go."

Something happened.

Maybe I half saw it, or maybe I sensed it, or maybe in my heart I was just waiting for it to happen, but my head jerked hard around and locked on the tote board. The results that had been posted were flashing. The guy with the bad English accent came on the PA and told me what I already knew.

"There's been a steward's inquiry into the fifth race," he said with heated needles that boiled the inside of my brain box. One of Dumas's boys stepped in front of me—a big tree in the road cutting off my path. I wasn't going nowhere.

Still in that long, quiet tunnel. Nobody said anything, and nobody had to. Something had happened in the fifth. Something like . . . I don't know, but the kind of something where the officials have to sit around and talk about it. Something where a horse could get itself disqualified. Real quick I thought about the instant number eight pulled to the outside. She didn't bump another rider. She didn't cut another horse off . . . did she? No, I was sure she hadn't . . . almost sure.

The board kept flashing. The results there one second, gone the next. My victory there, and gone. My freedom there, and gone. The longer the board flashed, the worse things were. Whatever happened on the track wasn't some little matter—some runner-up jockey making a complaint just to be a pain in the ass. This was a genuine situation. A horse was coming off the board.

Dumas finally drove us out of that quiet tunnel. "I remember a story," he started, detached from his own words. Didn't matter what was going on up at Golden Gate; Dumas sounded like he could have been getting ready for a nap: "When I was a child, maybe no older, I heard it. The story of a boy whose father was a killer. Two men, I think, he murdered."

It was a clean break to the outside—that's what my mind was on. Some other horse—the inquiry had to be about some other horse.

"And his father, the boy's grandfather, had also killed. How many, I do not know. It's not important, but he was a killer, do you know? People thought this child, too, might grow up to take blood as his father and father before him had done, so the boy was removed from his parents. Taken away to another city, another family. Taken away where he might grow up to be . . . normal, I suppose, but at least not a killer."

I heard Dumas, his voice a warm buzz in the back of my head, but that's all it was to me. I stared at the board as it flashed. There, and gone. There, and gone.

"The little boy became a man, married, raised children. He had no notion of his true father, his grandfather, or the blood that ran through him. One day, he was in a mishap. His car. A . . . what? Fender bender? Nothing really. But he got into an argument with the other driver. The argument became heated, not more so than one would expect after an auto mishap. Not so much that a man could not walk away from it. But not this man; not this child of his father, and his father's father. This man took up a tire iron and beat the skull of the other driver until his brain oozed like pink jelly from the pulped stump that now hung from his neck."

Even as I watched the board, this last bit snagged me. So awful it was, so pleasant Dumas made it sound.

"Go where you like, do as you please, pretend whatever you wish, but we are all who we were born to be. Some lovers. Some killers. Some winners. And some . . ."

The board stopped flashing. My horse, number eight, Terri's Song, was gone.

The bad-accented guy came back to explain things. I caught the words that mattered: *Illegal. Disqualified. Bets void.* The guy talked on. The world seemed to slip under my feet having turned into a viscid fluid.

As the ground melted away, Dumas said: "Thirty thousand dollars. Oh, what in the hell. Twenty-five. You make me laugh, do you know?"

from

Son of a Grifter

by Kent Walker

I'D NEVER HEARD the word *grifter* till my family was arrested. Then I heard and read it everywhere. The New York tabloids loved the detective-novel feel of the word, and it kept appearing in boldface attached to Mom's and Kenny's names.

I grew to hate the term. It was useful shorthand, but inadequate. I didn't think that *grifter* or *con artist* quite captured the tangle of my mother's psyche or the confused motives of my little brother. Part of Mom was detached and calculated, dead to feeling the way con artists were supposed to be when they separated people from their money. But her desperation and emotional volatility and need for chaos weren't the hallmarks of a seasoned, professional crook. If she were such a great grifter, she wouldn't have been broke and scrambling for money in her early sixties. She wouldn't have blown her big score, Ken Kimes.

Because the word *grifter* had been burned into my brain, I began to notice it everywhere, even after the initial press furor about my family had died down. When Kenny and Mom were in jail awaiting trial, I came across a film called *The Grifters*. I was in a video rental place and the title jumped out at me. When I read the back of the box, I realized the movie was about a mother-and-son team of con artists. I decided I had to rent it.

The Grifters turned out to be an entertaining, hard-boiled crime flick set in 1930s Los Angeles. It starred Anjelica Huston and John Cusack, and I quickly got caught up in the convoluted plot and stopped taking notes about the parallels between my family and theirs.

At the climax of the movie, though, I got a jolt of too much reality. Mother and son are arguing, and the mom accidentally jabs a broken glass into her offspring's jugular. He bleeds to death in front of her. She's as shocked as the viewer and starts to cry, and then the con half of her brain takes over. Her grief evaporates, and she makes the best of the situation. She picks up a bag of money and walks out the door.

In that scene I saw what my mother had done to my little brother. She'd sacrificed him, and I knew she felt no guilt about it. I saw her as a grifter for an instant. I saw her the way the rest of the world does, now that she's famous.

It had been almost a year since the Macaroni Grill incident when I got that phone call from my friend Carl in July 1998 and saw my mother on page four of the Vegas paper. During the year before the Silverman disappearance, I'd seen Mom and Kenny very little. I was trying to stay true to my no-contact vow, but I accepted the occasional phone call, and a few days after Easter of 1998 I relented and let Mom see her grandkids.

Our encounter reminded me of court-ordered visitations after a divorce. Mom and Kenny met me and my three children, ages two to thirteen, for dinner at a local restaurant called the Lone Star. Throughout the meal, I cut off my mother's and brother's attempts at conversation. I told them to talk to the kids, not to me. But my mother still managed to make me laugh.

The place served free peanuts and encouraged customers to throw the shells on the floor. Five-year-old Carson loved flinging them around, so Mom handed him basket after basket, until the floor was no longer visible.

Our college-girl waitress sighed and pouted as the mound around the table grew deeper. When she couldn't take it anymore, she complained, as politely as she could. "You guys are making a bit of a mess, aren't you?"

Mom attacked. With mock sweetness, she said, "I know—why don't you get a broom and sweep the shells up?" She paused. "And then, when you're done, you can ride the broom right on out of here!"

When Mom and Kenny did call me, it was liable to be from anywhere. I was accustomed to Mom's travels, but they tended to be from one fixed point to another in her known world—Hawaii to Vegas to Santa Barbara to the Bahamas and back. Now she was popping up in places like Louisiana and Utah and Cuba and Bahrain. Something was up, and I had my suspicions that soon enough I'd get a call from jail on a fraud beef, shoplifting again, grand larceny, even arson. That was crime Sante style, which now meant Kenny style too. I waited for the phone to ring.

What finally happened was unexpected. Despite the Jeff David plot in 1981 and the drunken confession about Elmer Holmgren in 1992, I hadn't considered murder a possibility. When the news came, however, I was like Anjelica Huston in *The Grifters*. Soon after the initial shock had faded, I was assembling the facts in my mind with a certain detachment. The pieces of the puzzle fit.

I knew before I finished reading the first newspaper article that Mom and Kenny weren't innocent bystanders. It was murder, and it was over the top, but it sounded just like them. I knew they were guilty right away because I knew them so well.

I didn't know what they'd done, however, other than what I read in the paper. I could fill in some of the blanks, and I could guess the motivation for their activities. They'd been rich, and now, by Mom's standards, they were poor. She had a desperate need for cash.

For a year after their arrest I lived in fear that Mom would somehow find a way to implicate me in her crimes or otherwise draw me into the vortex. She wanted my attention and my help, and that would be her way of getting it. A horrified fascination, a concern for my wife and my children, as well as worries about Mom and Kenny, drove me to suck up every factoid I could find about the Silverman case.

MOM HAD MET and schmoozed a Prudential-Bache executive, either at an investment seminar in Florida or at an antiaging conference in Vegas. She wanted him to give her the names of high-end rental apartments in exclusive neighborhoods in Manhattan. The exec didn't refer her to a real estate agent or a homeowner but to a butcher. Paul Vaccari, owner of an Italian meat store at 633 Ninth Avenue called Piccinini Brothers, had told the man about an interesting, outgoing old lady who'd been his customer for years. The woman, whose name was Irene Silverman, rented out apartments in a multimillion-dollar mansion on the Upper East Side. She was eighty-two and her house was on 65th Street between Fifth and Madison Avenues, steps from Central Park. She accepted tenants for short-term or long-term stays, and she lived in the most elegant zip code in the richest city in the world. Mom pounced.

In April, posing as a secretary named Eva, Mom called Irene Silverman, probably via cell phone from the mobile home or the town house in Florida, and inquired about renting a flat. Eva's boss, Manny Guerin, aka little brother Kenny, would arrive in June and take up residence in Apartment 1B.

So here again, as in Bel Air, was the worldly, maybe eccentric woman with the big house in the fabulous neighborhood, the right address in her town, who for money or company rented out rooms for a high price. Kenny arrived, cash in hand, deploying the scent of money and entitlement.

But Mom and Kenny's act worked best on people who'd never been around money before. For Kay Frigiano and our other Vegas friends, Mom was a window into a world of possibility. Without her, they never would have gone to Mexico or Hawaii or eaten every night at expensive restaurants. They'd overlook the fake rock on her finger and the bullshit in her patter because the airline tickets and the meals were real.

Mom acted Jackie Susann, Jackie Collins rich. I'd already seen how people who were more comfortable with their wealth behaved, and I'd seen how they reacted to Mom. With some education and polish, you'd be skeptical about the things Mom did. She drove everybody away eventually, even her only life-long friend, Ruth Tanis. The more sophisticated they were, the faster they ran.

There had always been plenty of people who sensed right off that there might be something nasty underneath Mom's domineering eccentricity. Vegas had probably been the right playpen for her, since there were lots of people there prone to vulgar displays of wealth, people who behaved as if they'd found their money in a bag on the street. Because of the slots and the blackjack tables, many mooks there were rich for a week or two at a time. Vegas was the apogee of Okie-wins-lotto, or street kid hits the jackpot, either of which could be applied to my mother and stepfather.

Transposed to the more sophisticated venue of Bel Air, Mom's gaudy front had failed. Mom and Kenny's landlady had a private eye on their backs within weeks. Four months later, on the Upper East Side of Manhattan, her poorly schooled protégé fared even worse. Kenny skulked around the Silverman mansion acting strange, arousing suspicion, and he and Mom got found out just as quickly. Their victim saw them coming.

WHENEVER I READ about Irene Silverman, the woman my mother killed, I feel compelled to make an observation that some people might find in bad taste. Irene and Sante had a lot in common besides humble beginnings. I don't think they would ever have been friends, but Irene's story and Mom's are similar.

Irene was born the same year as Ken, 1916. My mom claimed to be the daughter of an Indian immigrant and a prostitute and to have been abandoned on the streets of Los Angeles before my grandparents adopted her and took her north to Carson City at the age of thirteen. Irene Silverman claimed to have been born above a New Orleans whorehouse and to have spent her childhood living next to a second one. Her parents were a Greek immigrant seamstress and a gambler named Zambelli, who'd grown up in an orphanage. George Zambelli left the family when Irene Zambelli was sixteen, and she moved north with her mother to New York.

Her mother, also named Irene, sewed for a living, while little Irene, five feet tall and less than a hundred pounds, caught on as one of the thirty-six dancers with the Radio City Music Hall Ballet Corps. She danced hard for low wages, but she and her mom were getting by in the Depression.

I don't know what passed between mother and daughter, or whether the two Irenes ever had the kind of discussions I had with my mother in Palm Springs in the sixties, but it sounds as if in later years Irene was frank about her affection for money and status. She and Mom both had a habit of flashing hundred-dollar bills. When I was a boy, Sante—at that time

Santee—was open with me about her designs on a rich man. She ran through a string of real estate types, moving mostly up the economic scale, until she landed Ken Kimes in the early seventies. She was pushing forty by the time she found her Papa.

At age twenty-five, in 1941, Irene Zambelli married a millionaire who'd been hanging around the Radio City stage door trying to meet her. Like Ken Kimes, Sam Silverman was a divorced father of two who would serve in the army during World War II. Like Ken, he made his millions in the real estate business. Ken was a motel builder; Sam was a mortgage broker. Sam affected a false Ivy League pedigree and had left a legal career in Florida under a cloud—he was shading the details of his past, à la Mom.

Sam and Irene were like an Upper East Side version of my mother and stepfather. Both pairs were considered odd couples, composed of an extrovert and an introvert, an eccentric, vivacious female with attention-getting clothes and dyed hair, and a rich, natty, proper, very reserved but devoted male. Neither new wife got along with the two kids from her husband's first marriage. My mother the bigot used to kid Ken that his hooked nose looked Jewish, and Ken, equally bigoted, would bristle. Sam Silverman was a Jew who could pass for a WASP.

Perhaps their paths crossed on Oahu in the late seventies. The Silvermans had a condo on Waikiki, and Ken and Sante had the Portlock house, and both of them were associates of the Ho family, well-known Hawaiian real estate developers. We hit Hawaii in 1975, five years before Sam Silverman passed away in 1980.

After their spouses died, the Widow Silverman and the Widow Kimes took the same approach to replacing the lost income. Mom rented rooms (and gouged tenants), filling her house with Shade Tree types. Irene and Sam Silverman had rented apartments in their five-story 65th Street town house for many years before Sam's death. In 1985, with Big Irene and Sam gone, Irene Silverman chopped the apartments in half, creating ten rentable units, and began to focus on short-term tenants.

Silverman decorated every unit in her own idiosyncratic style. My mother's taste in clothes has inspired some mirth among observers since she became a public figure, but Irene shared her belief that turbans were classy headgear. You could argue that Mom and Irene had similarly nouveau riche sensibilities. Exotic flowers filled Irene's town house, especially white ones, the color my mother first wore for Ken and continued wearing after he was gone. Irene had a huge painting of herself from her ballerina days hanging on the main floor of the house. She'd edited it slightly to make the hips smaller—she was planning to get plastic surgery before she disappeared. Her pink ballet slippers had been set up in a kind of shrine.

For all their superficial similarities, however, Irene lacked the glitch in her soul that has made Mom's life a catastrophe. Maybe it was her long, close relationship with her mother, who was there with her only child when she nearly died of typhus at fourteen, who moved in when she married Silverman and never left, but Irene sounds like a healthy, settled, benevolent version of Sante. She sounds like Sante with the kinks ironed out, and with a bigger score.

Irene lived at 20 East 65th Street, a Parisian-looking limestone town house built in 1880, from 1957 until her death. The ballroom, swathed in oak, marble, and gilt, was a replica of the Petit Trianon at Versailles. Besides the condo in Hawaii, she had two homes in and near the real Paris. She tried to compensate for dropping out of high school by taking courses at Columbia and inviting professors to dinner. She had a wide circle of long-term friends. Irene Silverman had a real marriage ceremony and benefited from a real will when her husband died. He didn't hide money from her. He left her $3.2 million and the house with the junipers out front. It was valued at more than $7 million by the time Irene disappeared.

She was a domineering presence in her household, intrusive in the lives of her tenants, but in a motherly, busybody kind of way. Her employees were devoted, including her version of Mom's Latina maids. Most of her tenants liked her too. She didn't lock them in the house, and they weren't down-and-outers from the shabby dream capital of the West, like Mom's zombie renters. They tended to be fabulous, the minor boldface names of the entertainment world. Jennifer Grey, Chaka Khan, Daniel Day-Lewis, society bandleader Peter Duchin, the Jordanian royal family. They were the kind of contacts my mother might have wanted, and could have had, were she not so helplessly destructive.

When Kenny and Mom entered her life, Irene Silverman was eighty-two and getting ready to die. Mom's response to fading health and advancing age was selfish. She pursued "longevity," hoping to put off the inevitable and scam a few more people in the process. Irene plowed her money into a non-profit foundation that would honor her mother, something called the Coby Foundation, dedicated to the decorative art of embroidery and the women who labor at it.

But she shared something with my mother that was her undoing. She liked money, even if it was all going into the Coby coffers. She'd sleep in the basement on a cot sometimes so that she could rent out her own apartment in the town house.

Normally Irene had a woman at Feathered Nest realty check out her prospective tenants. The applicants were supposed to supply references, and Feathered Nest vetted them.

In June, a thin-lipped, well-dressed young man with a big nose that looked as if it had been broken rang her doorbell. He was the Manny Guerin whose secretary had been calling Irene's office, and he didn't want to deal with the real estate agent. He offered to pay a month's rent up front, six thousand dollars. He pulled out a roll of hundreds and started to count them. He was willing to pay in cash, on the spot. Irene decided to forgo the reference check and let the young man move into 1B. She gave him a key.

Everybody, no matter how smart or sophisticated they are, has a weakness. My mother is correct in assuming that for most people, it's money.

I WOULD HAVE been a better protégé for Mom than Kenny. I can manipulate people—if not with Sante's ardor and finesse, then often enough. I can keep a low profile. I can make detached, rational decisions. And I can tell, usually, where my (or Mom's) fantasies end and the outside world begins.

For those very reasons, though, I chose not to be my mother's soldier. In the short run, I had a weakness for money and I could be seduced by the scent of an easy score. But in the long run, as hard as she pulled, and as often as I wavered, I declined the offer. I knew better, because of that moral core of unknown origin, a certain worldliness, and simple fear.

Kenny had some of the right skills. He could be charming. He dressed well. He could lie with confidence, which is job one for a confidence man. Kenny's problem was that he really didn't know how he came across. He could embarrass you in a room full of people, like the time I went to the steakhouse with him and Mom and he abused the wait staff.

Part of that was the uncomplicated smugness of youth. Jet-setting around the islands in his expensive suits, cigar clamped between his teeth and money in the bank, he felt sophisticated. The cigars and the web-page design were part of his self-conscious trendiness; he'd been a follower of fashion since his alternative rock days as a preteen.

But most of the problem was that Kenny was too much my mother's son, and too much the spawn of Ken Kimes. Nothing had tempered his mood swings, his hyperactive demand for instant gratification. He jittered and chattered and flashed his big-toothed grin to grab attention. If he saw a camera, he'd jump in front of it, mugging.

He was over the top by nature and nurture. Sometimes, to be a good con artist, one really needs to be invisible. Quite often, in fact. Kenny, like his mother, couldn't manage it.

From his first days at 20 East 65th, Manny Guerin attracted too much attention. He put his hands over his face and ducked his head when he came through the black iron front doors and walked down the marble hall to 1B. He didn't want to be seen on Irene Silverman's security camera. The moves made him as conspicuous as the grimacing gargoyle that hung over the mansions's front door.

Kenny stood at the peephole of 1B and stared out at passersby, and they could see the shadow of his feet in the crack under the door. He added a dead bolt to his bedroom door. He wouldn't let the maids clean his room. He brought in Mom and Jose Alvarez, "sneaking" them past the security camera with the duck-and-cover move. Everyone was aware that he was keeping this older woman in his room, because sometimes it was the woman's voice that shooed away the maids.

Kenny's behavior put the whole house on alert. Silverman realized within days that she'd made a mistake. The strange new tenant wouldn't sign his rental agreement form, but instead asked if he could look at the penthouse and offered to pay thirty thousand dollars in cash for a month's stay. He was snooping around other floors of the mansion and asking the staff alarming questions, like "What's Irene Silverman's Social Security number?"

"He smells like jail," griped Silverman. She told friends and employees that there was something amiss with her new tenant and that she was thinking of calling an attorney to get him out. Like Mom, she wrote things down. She sketched Kenny, with his big and unmistakable Roman nose, barely altered by his failed plastic surgery, and she took notes on his activities. When she confronted him about the rental agreement, and he blathered about having given it to a lawyer to review and then to one of Silverman's employees, she cut him off. "That's a lie," she said. His ears turned red. When she saw him at the peephole of his door, the eighty-two-year-old would flip him the bird.

Irene Silverman had made Kenny as a con artist. She knew he wanted something from her, but I doubt she guessed the scale on which her unwelcome boarder was working. Silverman was irate and ready to evict Kenny because he'd dismantled an antique chest in his room, worth thousands, but Mom and Kenny planned to take over the entire mansion, worth millions. One of her employees warned Irene to leave the house and protect herself from the weird guy with the blazing blue-green eyes in 1B. She retorted, "This is my house. I'll stay in my house, and *he'll* have to leave."

My mother had written out a step-by-step procedure for stealing the home of someone old, wealthy, and vulnerable. She and Kenny had a list of names when they arrived in Manhattan. Their first prospect, an old woman many blocks north whose name they seem to have procured in the Bahamas, refused to accept Kenny as a tenant.

Silverman was their second try. Once Kenny was inside, he and Mom got busy. To get the house, they needed Silverman's Social Security number and signature on a whole series of documents, culminating with a fake deed.

Kenny tapped Irene's phones and kept a diary of her behavior ("Thursday night, stayed up. Went upstairs to sleep. *By Herself*"). Mom was Mrs. Outside in the scheme. When she wasn't bunking at 1B, she lived in the nearby high-end hotels like the Plaza Athénée, at three hundred dollars and up a night, piling many of the charges on the credit card of the old man from Florida. She had shoved her son out front, the way she used to urge me through windows in Newport Beach. She might have figured that she was too hot because of her rap sheet and the Utah Lincoln, she might have been training Kenny, or she could have been hanging back because her highest good was always and forever self-preservation. Better Kenny than Sante if the cops came.

When Kenny failed to weasel Silverman's Social Security number out of the maids, Mom called Irene Silverman directly. Pretending to be the promotions director for a casino, Mom told Irene that she'd won a free trip to Vegas, complete with a complimentary stack of chips. All she had to do was cough up that magic nine-digit number.

Mom had misjudged her mark. Mom's idea of glamour was low-brow—big cars, big jewels, big steaks, and Frank Sinatra. Ken Kimes would have jumped at the free trip to Vegas. Irene Silverman preferred Paris, ballet, and the opera. Mom had a house next to a golf course; Irene's Paris house abutted a theater, and she boasted about how she could hear the actors through her wall. She didn't fall for Mom's Vegas scam, or for three other calls offering her island cruises.

Lacking a real Social Security number, Mom and Kenny generated a fake one. By the end of June they had a number and all the documents they needed. Mom had a tax form, a power of attorney, a rental agreement, a transfer form, and she'd obtained a copy of the deed—she'd had to buy it, since Carolene Davis couldn't get her a freebie. She forged Irene Silverman's name on all the papers, tracing over the lone shaky signature that Kenny had cadged out of the landlady, on his rental receipt. Mom was ready to spend real money to complete the deal. She had her offshore banks send her checks for seventy-five hundred dollars, the amount that would be owed in taxes upon sale.

With the papers ready, Mom and Kenny had to find a notary who'd stamp them without witnessing Silverman's signature. On July 1 at 11:20 P.M., having renamed himself Mr. Win, Kenny arranged to meet a part-time notary named Don Aoki at the bar of the Plaza Athénée. He escorted Aoki to the Silverman mansion a few yards away, and into apartment 1B.

Aoki saw a scene from *Little Red Riding Hood*. In the dim bedroom of the apartment lay an elderly woman in a nightgown, red wig, and hat. Mr. Win told Aoki that this feeble old Grandma, with the covers pulled up to her chin and the paperwork beside her, was Irene Silverman. It was, of course, Sante Kimes in disguise.

The Manhattanites were proving more difficult than the suckers in Vegas. It was New York nature to mistrust an easy smile and be suspicious of a slick story. Despite the fact that Kenny had offered to pay him several hundred dollars, far above his normal fee, Aoki refused to notarize Grandma Silverman's documents. He declined because they were already signed. He asked the old lady, who wouldn't get out of bed, to autograph a separate piece of paper so he could make a comparison. She demurred, and then staged an argument with Mr. Win so that Aoki wouldn't have time to ask why. Aoki took a cab home.

The next day, July 2, another notary, a woman named Noel Sweeney, did what Aoki wouldn't. Mom and Kenny had succeeded. They had a signed, sealed, and delivered deed to the property. For $396,000, Irene Silverman had transferred her $7.5 million home to the Atlantis Group Ltd., a corporation based on the Caribbean island of Antigua. The nominal president of the Atlantis Group was one of Mom's Shade Tree drifters, Manuel Guerrero (not Manny Guerin). Back in Nevada, Guerrero had no clue that he was a corporate president.

Everything was in order for the final phase of the operation. It's the part I have the hardest time accepting, though I don't deny that it happened, and it was almost certainly premeditated. Before July 5, 2000, Mom and Kenny between them had apparently killed at least three people. In each case, Mom could invoke the Kimes family logic and paint the victim as an enemy—a traitor or a threat who had to be eliminated. Holmgren, Kazdin, and the Caribbean banker all could have put Mom in prison with a phone call. Mom framed their murders, in her mind and to her youngest son, as self-defense. That's the way she's wired.

Killing Irene Silverman, however, was a crime of a different order. Making her disappear seems to have been implicit from the minute Kenny rang her doorbell. I wonder whether even Sante Kimes could convince herself that Irene Silverman deserved to die.

I've told myself sometimes that Mom meant to bully the woman into signing papers and something went wrong, or she was going to dope her up and keep her hidden until she could take out a whopping mortgage on the mansion and flee with the cash. Too bad the evidence says otherwise.

Mom had called one of her Vegas minions several times before July 5 to offer him a new job. She told Stan Patterson, a pizza deliveryman/jack-of-all-trades who lived in a trailer park, that he should fly to New York to manage a fancy East Side apartment house. He was supposed to fire Silverman's employees and then start restaffing. Mom contacted a homeless shelter in Queens and asked a man there to be the building's new superintendent.

She was trying to re-create her Geronimo house on a grandiose, delusional scale. She would hire homeless people, as always, and mistreat and abuse them, and she would milk her rich tenants for cash. It was the luxury boardinghouse of which she'd long dreamed. She told Patterson that there'd be a crazy old ballerina living there, dancing through the halls with no panties, but in reality the plan required, sooner or later, the absence of Irene Silverman.

Locals flee New York City on July Fourth weekend. They go to the beach or the country, and the richer precincts of town are especially empty of people. Mom and Kenny had learned that Irene was going to slap Kenny with an eviction order on Monday, July 6.

At noon on July 5, Silverman dialed a pal to chat. She scribbled out a note about her suspicious tenant, Manny Guerin. He'd skulked up to the door of her first-floor suite and asked her if she had the latest issue of the *Wall Street Journal* or *Barron's*. She'd brushed him off and written down the details. Neither paper publishes on the weekend.

Irene was last seen alive sitting in her suite with the door open around the time of that phone call. At one-thirty, a friend called Irene's apartment and got no answer. Around that time, Manny Guerin, who'd refused maid service for three weeks, twice badgered a maid named Marta to clean up his room, offering the enticement of a major tip. She said no. She then watched on the security camera as a furtive man in a white shirt left the building by the basement entrance. Marta assumed he was Manny, the weirdo in 1B, because all the other tenants were gone for the weekend.

Several hours later, a person named Lucy called Marta and told her that if any officials or tax people came to the door over the next few days, she should say nothing. Lucy also asked Marta to take Irene's bulldog, Georgie, home with her when she left for the day. The requests alarmed Marta, and the voice sounded too deep and masculine to belong to anyone named Lucy. Rattled, Marta rushed from the basement to her boss's ground-floor apartment. Irene Silverman was gone.

Between noon and seven, Mom and Kenny disposed of Irene Silverman so completely that not one drop of blood has ever been found. According to the police, they zapped her with a 50,000-volt stun gun, strangled her with a clothesline or smothered her with a pillow, then shoved her into a duffel bag and made her go poof. Dogs sniffing the house, the sidewalk, and every inch of the Lincoln came up empty. Cops dug up the swamps of New Jersey and chased down countless tips in vain. Cell phone records, restaurant receipts, and a parking garage ticket prove that Mom never left the island of Manhattan; if Kenny had, it wasn't for more than a few hours. As far as anyone could tell, Silverman's tiny body, less than five feet tall and 115 pounds, might have been consigned to a Dumpster across the street. This time, however, no homeless person stumbled across it.

Mom and Kenny, on the other hand, were all too noticeable. Marta had contacted a friend of Irene's, the same buddy to whom Irene had been kvetching about her bizarre tenant. The friend called the rental agent, the rental agent buzzed the 19th Precinct, and all parties converged on the mansion in a rush. It wasn't hard to sell the cops on the idea that Silverman wasn't out for a walk. The victim herself had made a police sketch of the suspect, with little arrows pointing out his distinguishing features.

Irene Silverman was the wrong victim. Old and rich didn't mean addled and vulnerable. This wasn't some lonely, isolated dowager in a transient town like Vegas. Her friends and employees noticed her missing within three hours. If they hadn't, the tenants would have. Mom had homeless drifters for tenants on Geronimo Way; that July, *Nanny* producer Peter Jacobson was staying at Mrs. Silverman's. Mom had picked a building full of the kind of people who call the police, their lawyers, and maybe the media too when something goes wrong.

Still, I wonder if Mom and Kenny might have slipped away from New York and onto an interstate to elsewhere, with zip to show for the Silverman scam but *free*, were it not for Mom's repeated calls to her gofer Stan Patterson. When Kazdin's body turned up in a trash bin, a joint task force of the LAPD and the FBI had started searching for Sante and Kenny. They'd connected my mother and brother to the Utah Lincoln and the fake credit card from Florida, and they'd busted Patterson for buying guns in Nevada. Rather than facing charges of procuring firearms under false pretenses for Mom the convicted felon, Patterson agreed to turn snitch. The cops urged him to accept the invite to New York from the woman he knew as Ellen.

Sante bought Patterson a ticket on the America West red-eye from Vegas to JFK. Cops met him at the gate. He was so scared of being caught in the crossfire between the law and my family, or of being executed by

Mom and Kenny for snitching, that he wore a bulletproof vest under his shirt in the dead of summer. The police made him take it off, and slapped a black baseball cap on his head. Stan was the bait in a sting.

That afternoon, Mom and Stan went barhopping in midtown while the cops watched. Mom downed several of her late husband's favorite drinks, Seven-and-Sevens, at the bar of the New York Hilton on 53rd Street and Sixth Avenue, and then wine at a restaurant a block away called Ciao Europa.

Stan sat next to her, listening to her ramble, sweating under his cap. He and his invisible escort of cops had waited six hours in the Hilton lobby for Sante, and when she finally arrived it had been without Kenny. The sting dragged on from the afternoon into early evening, and still Kenny hadn't materialized.

Mom and Patterson wandered out into one of Manhattan's ubiquitous street fairs. Vendors clogged the sidewalks of Sixth Avenue, and traffic was rerouted. It was the only crowd to be found in Manhattan on a quiet summer Sunday. Mom carried a big vinyl purse, the same kind that had swung from her arm since Palm Springs, thirty years before. Had I been there, I would have expected to see some of the cheap junk from the sidewalk tables disappear into the bag.

Mom liked shopping. She'd chosen the fair so she could browse, and because the throng provided cover for her reunion with Kenny. He didn't appear till almost seven P.M., and he hung back several yards from Mom and Stan when he did, so he could make sure he wasn't being followed.

My brother and mother hugged. Stan pulled off his baseball cap. Kenny pissed his pants when the police grabbed and cuffed the three of them. My mother and little brother were in custody.

It was only Kenny's second or third arrest, but Mom had stopped counting. She didn't panic. From the second a cop's hand touched her, Mom was spinning. "That's not my purse," she said, without blinking, of the mammoth bag attached to her side.

In the bag that didn't belong to her, Mom was carrying $10,580, as well as checks, payroll stubs, five bank books, and seven different passports. She'd stolen Silverman's passport and pasted her own picture over her victim's face. Kenny had Silverman's American Express charge plates and her fake Social Security card.

At FBI headquarters Kenny and Mom blustered and stalled, denying everything. They thought, and the cops didn't contradict them, that the bust might be about nothing more than the Utah car, and they had an explanation for that. They'd written the bad check in good faith.

They also benefited from police brainlock on a massive scale, the sort of unmissable but missed connections that makes you wonder how anybody gets arrested except people who turn themselves in. Mom and Kenny had bags and pockets full of the name Irene Silverman. They were practically wearing T-shirts with their victim's picture on the front. The police had been hunting them because they killed a man to hide a real estate fraud. Stan Patterson had told the feds that Sante wanted him in New York so he could manage a building she was taking over. Yet, incredibly, neither the NYPD nor the FBI, supposedly the finest police agencies in the land, bothered to add one plus one. Nobody tried to make a single call to find out who this Irene Silverman lady might be and whether she was upset that her passport was missing. They seemed to buy Mom's excuse that the Silverman documents belonged to a friend. At some point, Mom or Kenny or both of them must have realized—they don't know. They don't know!

Using a ticket stub from Kenny's pocket, the task force traced the Lincoln to a garage on 44th Street in midtown Manhattan. Inside, on the floor of the front seat, they could see a discarded cardboard stun-gun container. The backseat was obscured by a mound of plastic bags, topped by a quilt. The spare tire and the jack had been dumped in the backseat, leaving the trunk empty. The FBI moved the car to its downtown headquarters without searching the bags, not making the link between the vacant trunk and Irene Silverman, still not aware of who they had in custody.

The next evening, unbeknownst to the Kazdin task force, the lead cop investigating the disappearance of Irene Silverman scheduled a press conference for 8 P.M. Deputy Inspector Joseph Reznick appealed to the public for information. All the city's TV news outlets broadcast the department's sketch of the mysterious Manny Guerin.

A member of the Kazdin task force—an NYPD officer, not a fed—happened to be watching TV that night. He heard the name Irene Silverman and glimpsed the sketch. At six A.M. Tuesday morning, he phoned a detective working the Silverman case and told him "Manny Guerin" was already in custody. Mom and Kenny's luck had run out.

Now the New York cops scoured the Lincoln. They understood why the jack was in the backseat and the trunk was empty. They sifted through the contents of the garbage bags in the backseat. Besides clothes, they cataloged pepper spray, a tape recorder, the semiautomatic Glock handgun Patterson had purchased in Vegas, unused hypos, handcuffs, license plates from Nevada, Florida, and Georgia, a container of the date-rape drug Rohypnol, and thirteen notebooks in which Mom outlined every step of the Silverman caper. In apartment 1B, police collected garbage bags and duct tape. They found Kenny's fingerprint on a piece of tape.

I don't see Mom killing Irene Silverman, though she's capable of it. Instead, I'm sure she delegated the task to Kenny. The tranquilizer, the stun gun, the pistol—by whatever means Silverman was dispatched, she wound up with duct tape on her mouth, wrapped in garbage bags, shoved into a duffel bag, and carted into the beyond atop a shower curtain in the trunk of the Lincoln.

You're reading this, and you're disgusted by my family. I can't argue with you, because so am I. But my anger and revulsion are complicated by shame. I'm ashamed of my mother, and I feel guilty about my little brother. In the retelling he seems as monstrous as Mom, an eager, precocious young murderer. I have to stop myself from wallowing in if-onlys. Chief among them, if only I'd done more to save him from Mom.

I'm also struck by different things than you might be when I hear about Mom and Kenny's deeds. Details affect me. For example, the ancient container of the date-rape drug makes me think of the time Mom doped my wife. It was probably from the same jar. The pepper spray, like the brass knuckles and knife from Kenny's pocket, and his scribbled plans to order how-to books on money laundering and homemade silencers, reminds me of the scary stuff I used to find in his room. He'd made the leap from *The Anarchist Cookbook* to murder. And the name that Mom gave the police, and the manner in which she did it, makes me sad. "Want to know my real name?" Mom had asked the cops, as if sharing a secret. "It's Sandra Louise Walker." That was her name when she was married to my dad, back in Palm Springs in the sixties. We'd come full circle.

After the cops made the connection between Manny and Kenny, my mother and brother became larger than life. They became tabloid headlines, the kind with the ink so heavy it stains your fingers black. While I scanned those stories in the *New York Post* and elsewhere, I was thinking something very different from what you might have been thinking. Number one, I thanked God they'd been nailed for the New York murder before the task force had a chance to extradite them to Los Angeles. In California, they would have faced the death penalty. Number two, based on everything that had transpired in the first thirty-six years of my life, as of July 8, 2000, I thought Mom and Kenny had a better than even chance of somehow, some way, getting away with murder.

The Chelsea Rip

by David McCumber

"The present in New York is so powerful that the past is lost."
JOHN JAY CHAPMAN, 1909

October 10—We took lodging in an inexpensive (for Manhattan) little hotel, the San Carlos, that was still a third more than the Palmer House cost us. In a sense, the high daily nut fed our purpose, made us sharper, conveyed a sense of urgency to our planned hustle in a city that had seen every hustle. If you can make it there, you can make it anywhere, except of course in Toronto, where Napoleon wears goggles and does not miss a shot.

ONE THING WAS certain: we couldn't just walk into a poolroom and give weight to the best players in New York. We'd get eaten alive. This situation called for some old-fashioned trickery and deceit—a billiards tradition, of course, and particularly necessary here, where everyone we met would be holding back some speed to make a game with us. If the pool players' golden rule was applicable anywhere, it was here: Do Unto Others, Before They Run the Table, Kick You in the Nuts, and Take Your Bankroll.

This required planning, and so we went to an all-night deli called Stars on Lexington Avenue for dinner and a strategy session. Compared to the San Francisco restaurant of the same name, Stars was, well, chopped liver. But the Train Rule was still in effect: Anything—food, drink, shelter—seemed luxurious after getting off the damn thing.

The plan we came up with over bagels, scrambled eggs, and coffee required the nerve of Jimmy Doolittle, or at least Willie Sutton. We proposed to go into an establishment called Chelsea Billiards, described recently as "the last bastion of the pool hustler in America," albeit by a cutesy *L.A. Times* travel writer who didn't know that there are probably twice as many card-carrying pool hustlers at Hard Times Billiards in Bellflower, California, well within his own circulation area. We would be patient, spend several days in there, showing some cash and some gamble, and clock the place well enough to find a weaker player to whom we would lay down a spread, then get the game we wanted and snap off the entire poolroom. As plans went, it was hardly original, but it was better than nothing.

It was midnight—a good-enough time to start. We put on coats and ties—we wanted to look like appleheads—and cabbed over to Chelsea. The room was on West Twenty-first Street, a vaguely ominous area of clubs and dark storefronts with seedy loiterers loitering seedily outside. Chelsea was one of the prototypical yuppie billiard places, but at this hour on a Thursday night the place didn't seem to be attracting too many MBAs—or anybody else. The place had maybe six tables going out of the thirty or so visible when we walked in. There were another twenty or so tables downstairs; not one soul was playing there.

We ordered coffee from the house man (a mistake, it was awful coffee), who was playing a desultory game of nine-ball with a racehorse-thin kid in a Duke Blue Devils T-shirt. Something was off with the kid; his movements were jerky, his eyes huge and black. He was either high or crazy or both, but he displayed a nice stroke.

A money game started on one of the back tables, just as we came back upstairs from checking out the basement. A young Latino in a baseball cap had matched up with an older Asian guy. They put a couple of hundred on the lamp and started playing nine-ball. The younger guy had a pretty nice stroke. He seemed like a shortstop; he wasn't getting out every time, but of course he could have been stalling. He definitely shot better than the guy he was playing, who was acting like a psycho, talking to himself, talking to the balls, already taking the heat in the first couple of racks.

We hadn't been watching for ten minutes when a sketchy-looking character, maybe fifty, with slicked-back black hair, missing several teeth, dressed in a ragged leather jacket and torn Levis', came up and asked us to play.

"No, thanks."

"Me, neither, I just want to watch for a while." He turned away wordlessly.

The Asian guy gagged the eight, leaving it and the nine both hanging, and slammed his cue down viciously. As he racked the balls, the kid in the Duke shirt came up and stood in front of us. "Want to play me some nine-ball for fifty bucks?" He needed to work on his approach. When we both refused, he stared at us for maybe thirty seconds, pupils as big as quarters, then turned on his heel and glided out the front door.

"The kid's a crackhead, but he can play real good. You're smart not to mess with him." The speaker was another pretty hard case—a fortyish hippie type who featured a worn brown-leather snapbrim cap, long brown hair, jeans, sneakers, and a bad limp. "You guys wanna play *me* some, maybe some eight-ball or nine-ball?"

We demurred once again, and the guy nodded pleasantly, looked at Tony a little more closely than I would have liked, and limped over to the other side of the room, where he curled up on two chairs and went to sleep. Tony whispered in my ear, "My God, that's Waterdog."

"Who?"

"Waterdog. Fuck, I haven't seen him in damn near twenty years. He came through San Mateo when I was eighteen or nineteen, and then he was beatin' everybody in the world. Jeez, he looks horrible, I heard he's had some tough times."

We watched the nine-ball game for an hour or so. The first guy who had approached us was sitting across the table with two or three other men, and they were paying close attention to the action, as though they might have a piece. But they were also clocking us from time to time. Just as we were ready to leave, Waterdog woke up and wandered back over. "You guys want to do something, before it's too late?" "You must be a pretty good player, man, coming up and asking strangers to play. Or we must look real easy." Waterdog just smiled, and we walked out.

In the back of a cab, on the way back to the hotel, Tony told me about Waterdog. "His name's Edwards, I think, but they call him Waterdog because he's from Watertown, New York. He used to be one of the very best road players. The night he came into Town and Country, I had just beaten some stiff out of two hundred, and he and Billy Teeter came into the room. I knew Billy a little, but I'd never seen Waterdog. He asked me if I wanted to play and I was feeling pretty good after winning, so I said, "Rack 'em." I think he ran seven racks. He sure took that two hundred off me in a hurry. Then he went into Cochran's and beat everybody in there." Tony shook his head at the memory. "I heard he got fucked up on smack. It's too bad, he's a real nice guy. I don't think he recognized me. But we need to be careful, stay out of his way as much as possible. We don't want him to knock our game."

October 12—We came back the next night, at about 1 A.M. This time twenty-first street was jammed with cabs, and Chelsea's tables were full of sharply dressed young people, couples, groups of friends, all rolling the balls around and having a great time. It was good to see the club doing a decent trade, but none of these players was relevant to our purpose. We watched for a while, until some of the clubsters thinned out, and then we got a table and began the floor show.

WE PLAYED RAGGED nine-ball, grabassing around, ties at half-mast, trading hundred-dollar bills back and forth loudly and carelessly, the loser throwing the bills on the cloth after each rack. The effect was somewhat like casting a grasshopper into a streamful of hungry trout.

Within the first five minutes, a fat man waddled up to the table and said, "Can I get in?" He looked like Peter Lorre's ugly cousin, maybe fifty-five years old, five-six and rotund, with stringy black hair smeared in streaks across his scalp like bacon grease on a cheap plastic bowl.

"No, thanks, private game, we can't beat anybody but ourselves," I said, and he snorted and went over and sat down with a couple of other scraggly types, including the guy with the missing teeth from last night. We played for another half an hour, then sat down. "Fuck, I don't know, all these guys look like busted-out mooches," Tony said quietly. "Maybe this won't work."

"Don't worry, there's money here, I can smell it," I whispered back. "Let's just keep playing it out."

The tall, thin crackhead hit on us again, and Tony said, "I was watching you play, you're way too good for me."

Then the fat guy wheeled around and said, "Cut the shit, you must want to gamble or you wouldn't be in here. How about I play one-handed, you play both hands?"

"You must be a hell of a player, man, comin with that shit."

"Oh, yeah, the hell with you. I wouldn't really play that way, I just wanted to see what you'd say."

I liked it; they were getting impatient, aggressive.

Waterdog was in action across the room, I noticed, playing some kid, giving him a huge spot—what's called the "Orange Crush," meaning the five ball and the breaks. They were playing for all of ten bucks a game, and Waterdog was getting out consistently.

Missing Teeth came up and introduced himself: His name was Eddie. He wore the same skaggy leather jacket and knock-off Converse All-Stars and had a cigarette in the corner of his mouth, and he wasted no time hitting on us again. "Come on, you guys, you were just playing for some cash, why don't you try me some nine, twenty bucks a game."

We blew him off—"No thanks, Fast Eddie"—and kept watching Waterdog. He was running out, running out, running out, gimping around the table but looking solid once the bridge hand was down. I said to Tony, "This kid's going to pull up, he's getting murdered," and right then the victim shook his head and unscrewed his cue.

Waterdog came over and handed Eddie four tens and the cue he was using. Eddie didn't look too happy with the split, but he didn't argue overmuch. Then came more entertainment: On the front table, a match for a hundred dollars a set between two psychos—a thin, bespectacled sharp dresser in pleated suit pants and tie, versus a guy who looked like a tripwire Vietnam vet: Sinéad O'Connor haircut, camouflage T-shirt, eyes like glowing charcoal.

Both of them were nuts. Suit Pants grimaced with every shot, muttering loudly when he missed. Sinéad was even more violent, using massive body English, lunging viciously into the shot, twisting the cue high over the table to urge a ball down the rail. He stepped up and fired very fast each time, as if he were playing polo or hockey instead of pool. They seemed pretty well matched, in skill level and invective. Sweating their match was tense, like watching McEnroe play Nastase, waiting for one of them to blow.

At about 2 A.M. a young Latino kid, tall, maybe eighteen or nineteen, came over and said, "Hey, you guys, let's play some for fun, maybe twenty a set."

Tony said, "Oh, man, I don't know, we're business guys, just out on the town, I've had a couple drinks . . . but I don't know, I sort of want to play." He looked at me questioningly. "No way, buddy," I said. "You'd be giving the money away."

"I don't know," Tony said. "We do like to gamble but we don't play good like these guys in here."

"Come on," the kid said. "Hustler's move, businessmen my ass, let's play. I'm just learning, I work construction over in Jersey during the day. I tell you what, I'll give you the wild eight."

He was a likable kid, much less obnoxious than the other sleazeballs. Tony said to me, "Come on, bud, what do you say, what's the worst that could happen? Let's give the kid forty or fifty bucks, what the hell."

"Not with my money, but go ahead, knock yourself out."

The house man put us on a pretty tight table in the back, the one Waterdog had just been using. When Tony pulled out his cue, the kid said, "Southwest, holy shit, I'm a dead man, you telling me this guy ain't a player? *Shit.*"

Meanwhile he went over and got the same cheap Meucci that Waterdog had been using. Some hustler's den. This was a one-cue poolroom. Several of the railbirds came over to look at Tony's cue. "I got a deal on it, I know a guy works for them," Tony said. "Doesn't mean shit, it can't make me play any better." The Southwest *was* a bit of a knock. It was fifteen hundred bucks' worth of cue, minimum, and people did tend to notice. On the other hand, it fit our profile as well-heeled suckers.

Tony and the kid started playing, and it was ludicrous. They were both stalling so bad nobody made more than one ball for the first five minutes. Tony managed to lose the first two games, but the kid left the next nine ball right in the hole, as if he were daring Tony to miss again. It went back and forth like that, with Tony overcutting shots, undercutting, scratching, misplaying position. I was grateful that this was not our usual pattern. I hated to watch this. To me, it was a defilement, like holding Secretariat up in the stretch. As with any fine art, Tony's game was a mix of technical knowledge, expertise, and inspiration, and this adulteration was small and ugly, no good for the soul.

The young player didn't show much more speed than Tony did, but he went three games up. Both Eddie and Peter Lorre came over then, asking to bet five a game on the side. Finally I decided it would hurt our credibility if I didn't bet with them, so I did. The kid left Tony another hanging nine, but Tony managed to give away the next rack. His opponent started to let it out a bit, and he would have run the next rack, except he scratched on the nine.

Peter Lorre asked to up the bet to ten, and I agreed. Tony lost the next rack and I threatened to quit him. "Shit, my guy's drunk, he can't beat this kid, he can't beat anybody the way he's playing tonight." Meanwhile I kept a running line of abuse going with Tony. "Jesus, how could you miss that? Don't you know I'm betting on you? Shit, that's probably it, you dogging bastard, you'd rather lose just to watch me pay off, wouldn't you?" Then, as Tony lined up one shot, I sharked him brutally, saying in midstroke, "Can you handle this one? It's a hanger."

He acted really hot with me. "Hey, asshole, you're costing both of us money. Can't you shut up while I'm playing?"

"Man, it wouldn't make any difference if you were playing in a fuckin' cemetery, you'd still dog those shots. Don't blame it on me."

The kid won the first set and I quit the side action and got on Tony to leave. "Come on, he kicked your ass, it's late, let's get out of here, you'll never beat him."

"Shit, what's twenty bucks? I like the game. I'm going to play him one more."

The kid, who introduced himself after the first set as Robert Saez, kept on Tony's ass about stalling. Once when Tony made four balls in a row, he said, "Hey, look out, you're showing too much." As if he agreed, Tony gagged the next ball and Saez rolled his eyes.

The entire rail was on me to bet on the side. Peter Lorre said nastily, "Come on, no balls, why don't you back your man?"

"Go fuck yourself."

As Tony continued to lose, Saez's confidence obviously grew, and I could sense doubt in the room. We were laying it down so perfectly according to the book that they were confused. They naturally assumed Tony was a road player on the stall, but he was playing worse, not better. Maybe he *was* just a drunken salesman.

Tony dropped the second twenty and said to me, "All right, all right, you were right, fuck you, let's get out of here and get some sleep."

We refused two or three other offers to play and headed for the door. The railbirds were solicitous. "Tough luck, guys. Come on back tomorrow, you'll probably do better."

We walked out and somehow caught the same cabbie of the night before, a wonderful gravel-voiced character named Willie Owens, a black man of maybe fifty-five or sixty. "You all win?" he asked, eyeing our cue cases. "No, we got tortured," Tony said, like an actor staying in character offstage between scenes. "We're not very good. I can beat this guy"—he gestured to me with a thumb—"but I play anybody else and I lose."

"They's some slicks around that poolroom," Willie Owens said. "You know, hustlers. They be layin down and losin on purpose like, get you playin, you know, and nex when the cabbage come out it all be over in two seconds, they shootin out the lights."

"Yeah," Tony said. "I've heard that's done."

"Hey, I used to shoot before I got so old. I don't see good now, but yeah, I used to shoot all up and down Broadway, playin those Puerto Ricans. Yeah, those boys could play."

"Do they still play high up in Harlem?"

"Shoot, yeah, they's still big games up there, some big halls. They's a good one up 145th and Broadway, but they be a lot of hustlers in there. You can look at they hands and tell they never do a hard day's work in they life. They hustlin pool, pimpin, shootin dice, sellin drugs, they gettin they fingernails taken care of just like a woman, they wearin five-hundred-dollar suits, playin pool for five hundred a game."

"Hey, that sounds like what I like," Tony said.

"You must be pretty good you like to play high like that."

"Shit, no, man, I lose, I just like to gamble."

Owens laughed, softly—heh heh heh—and lit a big cigar as he wheeled the cab around a corner against a red light. "They gamble witchou up there."

"Can you get in and out?"

"What you mean?"

"If you're a pair of honkies like us?" I added.

This time Willie Owens laughed out loud. "Oh yes, no problem," he said. "They like honkies like you up there, want to play pool for big money."

In the hotel, Tony said, "If we end up getting the action we want, watch, it's going to be with that kid. He's on the lemon, big time. He kind of reminds me of me, when I was his age. Except I was better."

"Okay, Mr. Modesty," I said. "When are you going to start firing?"

"Do you know what we're going to do tomorrow?"

"Take the whole joint off?"

"Nope. You've got to learn some patience," he said. "Patience." He laughed. "We're going to do this thing right. I'm going to pick out the worst mooch in the place and lose to him."

October 13—Tony needed practice. It was hard, playing on the lemon all night, purposely missing balls, trying to disguise your stroke. It can put a good player off his game for real, so that when he tries to come off the stall, he finds he can't. We didn't want that to happen, so in the afternoon we sought out a place to practice.

WE FIGURED WE'D be relatively safe across town on the west side. We went to a place called Amsterdam Billiards, a beautiful, modern club part-owned by comedian David Brenner, who is a pool fanatic. Amsterdam is a thoroughgoing player's room, designed beautifully to allow some natural light in during the day without interfering with the table lighting. The equipment was perfect and all around us were serious players. Tony pointed out Tony Robles, one of the best players in New York, practicing on one of the front tables.

We decided to play a game of straight pool. It is one of the most elegant and uncompromising games played on a pool table, and although it's rare anymore to find a good money game playing straight pool, Tony loves it for practice.

The rules are relatively simple. The player pockets balls until he misses; one ball is left on the table and the remaining fourteen are reracked, without the ball at the top of the rack, with the object being to make the remaining ball and break up the rack with the cue ball, in order to be able to continue making balls. A world-class player can run a hundred or more balls without missing. Tony and I made a competitive game called "Fifty No Count": He had to make fifty balls without missing in order to count any points. On the other hand, any ball I made counted, so if I made two balls, I added two points to my score; if Tony made forty-nine balls and missed the fiftieth, he got no points. Today, we were playing to a hundred, for twenty-five dollars.

Straight pool can be a very painful game. In nine-ball or straight pool, when one player is on a long run, the other player, left to watch from his perch on the sidelines, is said to be "in the electric chair," as in, "I tortured him, ran five straight racks. I really put him in the electric chair." It is an apt idiom. I did not play well that day; the longest run I could put together was ten balls. Tony was making shots with his usual easy grace, and I was spending a lot of time sitting down. It is a horrible feeling, watching your opponent firing in shots and being powerless to stop him. One feels rather like the legendary Texas A&M twelfth man, the football player who was moved to run onto the field from the sidelines to tackle the opposing ballcarrier.

My only consolation in the early going was that Tony wasn't actually scoring. He ran thirty, thirty-eight, forty, but couldn't quite break the fifty mark. So, in spite of being thrashed, my huge handicap had enabled me to take the lead, thirty-six-0, when I overcut a ball down the rail and left the table wide open.

As Tony started making balls, there was a palpably different feeling. From my perch in the electric chair I could see that he was getting absolutely perfect position on each shot. After he cleared all but one ball, I racked the other fourteen, and he broke them, effortlessly and precisely, the cue ball exploding the rack as he made the open ball. This time, fifty was not a problem; he passed that point early in the fourth rack. Now, every ball he made on this run would count. And he didn't look like stopping.

I was squirming for a while, but after a time I could not help but be entranced. Witnessing talent on this level is a rare privilege. When straight pool is being played correctly, a rhythm develops, not too fast, not too slow, the cue ball rarely traveling more than two or three feet from shot to shot. Tony was carving up rack after rack with surgical precision, clearing lanes to the pockets whenever he could, breaking the clusters of balls apart, but not so hard that they scattered down the table, moving from shot to shot like a drill sergeant scrutinizing soldier after soldier, lined up awaiting his attention.

Everything was perfect; the table, the cloth, the balls, everything. I could tell that Tony could *feel* the way the balls were rolling, feel how much spin the cloth would take, how the ball would cut, how the rails took a bank shot, how far he could "cheat" the pocket to make the ball and maximize position on the next shot. For the first time on this trip, Tony was *there*, in that wondrous mental realm of awareness and acuity that pool players call "dead stroke," "dead punch," "having the cue ball on a string," "in a trance." It is Bill Bradley's "sense of where you are." It is a cliché in team sports like basketball and baseball to describe players as being "in the zone" or playing "in another league," when you know that twenty-foot jump shot is going in *before* you shoot it, or the baseball is going out of the park as soon as you begin to swing, but it does happen. It is not limited to sport; it happens in ballet, lovemaking, riding cutting horses, arguing before a jury, in almost every field of endeavor. There is that attainable but ephemeral "zone," born of confidence, competence, concentration, and the positive focusing of emotion and spirit, that produces spectacular results. It is the essence of success, the Holy Grail of sports psychologists. In some measure, it is what we all seek in our lives. Dead stroke.

As I watched the balls roll in their hypnotic, deadly patterns, I remembered the only other time in my life I had such an extended stay in the electric chair. I was eighteen, and I was in the Stag Tavern for the biggest evening of my young life. The legendary Cowboy Jimmy Moore was giving a trickshot exhibition—and then he was going to play a game of straight pool. Against me. When I got to the Stag he was already there, a big square kindly grandfatherly man with short-cropped white hair and steel-rimmed glasses in front of eyes that managed to smile even though his mouth was otherwise occupied, sucking on a wet cigar butt.

He broke. I tried a safety and botched it, and he ran thirty balls. I stepped back to the table and ran nine balls before missing an easy shot in the side and then he ran one hundred twenty balls and out.

I found out that night, with all of my friends watching, what the electric chair felt like. I remember gripping my Willie Hoppe so tightly my knuckles felt as though they would pop, willing him to miss and at the same time not wanting him to.

I asked him later that night, "Mr. Moore, do you play much snooker?"

He chuckled softly in his throat. "Boy, I was the United States champion." We went to the snooker table and he sat me down in my chair for another fifteen minutes while he danced the cue ball in and out of the rack of red balls until they had all disappeared. Now, twenty-two years later, it was all happening again.

Finally, ending the ninth rack, Tony missed position by a hair and got too close to the break ball, leaving himself an unmakeable shot. After his attempt bounced off the rail, it was over: One hundred twenty-six balls. Tony's career-high run. And, of course, it had to come against me. My tab with him had grown to $150. Wonderful. We were starved for action, and he was beating my brains out. Still, it was great to see him play like this. Over the next two days, he would run 114 and 93 in his next two practice innings.

Before we left Amsterdam Billiards, I noticed a board with names and *pictures* showing who had run more than a hundred balls in tournament competition at the club. Some of New York's well-known young players were there, including Tony Robles and a couple of other players Tony had heard of: Frankie Hernandez and the luxuriantly named Ginky Sansucci. I kidded Tony; his run would place him in the top five at the club.

"No pictures, no pictures," he said.

October 15—At 2 A.M. we walked into Chelsea, as we had the past few nights. The upstairs was practically deserted, but as I walked downstairs to clock the basement I ran into Robert Saez on the stairs. "I'm playing a Canadian downstairs," he said. "He's a good player. He beat me last week."

THE CANADIAN TURNED out to be Paul Potier, like John Bear a converted snooker player who spends a lot of time stateside playing nine ball. Tony was sweating; Potier knew him, and he had the potential to knock our game instantly after several days of careful preparation.

Potier was giving Robert Saez a huge spot: the wild six, meaning that the six ball got the money any time for Robert, on the break or any other way, and also the last two, meaning the ball in front of the nine, whatever it was, cashed a ticket for Robert.

They were playing on a corner table downstairs, and the biggest rail we had seen yet was sitting in judgment. All the characters from the past couple of days were there, and then some: Waterdog, Peter Lorre, Eddie, Suit Pants, Sinéad, the Asian guy, a big, silent black man in a little porkpie hat, and several other familiar faces. It was a ghostly scene; the only light on the floor came from the bulbs over that table, and the faint glow of a Coke machine clear across the room. Occasionally, a match would flare and a face would be illuminated for a second, then fade back into darkness.

These railbirds' lives were much the same, I thought, lit for a few isolated seconds by action, however it came. It was as strong as anything Waterdog ever put in his arm, and it was fueled by the memory of past triumph. Addiction is nothing more than a good memory, after all, in this case the memory of the score. They took their pleasure vicariously, to be sure; they'd tell you they loved the game, and they'd love to be the one playing for the money, but of course most of them couldn't compete at this level; to step up and play Paul Potier for the money, you'd better be able to *play*. Gambling was their way of being players, participants in the struggle.

I looked at the sweaters' faces, and I realized that I was looking at myself. I loved this action, the competing, the *risking*—as much as they did. That was a sobering thought; these boys had been doing this for a while, and the lines and scars and booze noses and red eyes and pot bellies and bad teeth and the cheapness of shiny pants and dull shoes told a story about how the life had treated them.

This kid, Saez, was certainly the darling of the room; the stakehorses evidently liked his scrambling safety game. He was carrying the wallets of the homies on his back. Watching this match, two things were immediately evident: One, Robert Saez was showing a lot more speed tonight, and two, the table was brutally tight. It may have been the toughest pool table we'd run across so far, but tough in a way that rewards great play: excellent condition, tiny pockets, very fast cloth. The pace of the game, therefore, was very deliberate.

Saez was not a great player, but he was inordinately careful. He played some stylish, ball-spinning safeties, giving me the feeling he'd rather play safe than run out. Sometimes he'd get burned—missing the hook or leaving a makeable kick. But not often. Potier displayed formidable all-around skills. He had a lot of offensive firepower and a fine understanding of safety play—both part of his snooker legacy. The first race to nine took nearly two hours, but Saez eventually won, 9–7.

Potier rallied to start the second set, making some spectacular shots and beating Saez at the safety game. But the game was ultimately a loser for him. He probably could have given that much weight fairly comfortably if it were not for the table. It was so tight that he couldn't run out consistently when Saez missed, and that changed the game, making it much easier for Saez to get to the six ball. Saez won the second set 9–7, too, and Potier pulled up, four hundred down. He was too experienced to continue in a low-percentage game, and he maintained his equanimity perfectly in defeat.

"Tough table," he said philosophically as Saez was congratulated by his backers. He saw Tony and gave him a slow, almost imperceptible wink, as if to say, I won't knock your game, clean these fuckers out.

"Just learning, eh?" I said to Saez. He shrugged and grinned. "He gave me a big spot."

"Save that, man," Tony said to him. "You tortured the guy. I got off light last night."

"Nah, we'll play again," the kid said. "You were hanging back last night, I know it."

During the match, Tony had been woofing back and forth with Eddie the Mooch, and they finally made a game. Eddie agreed to give Tony the breaks for fifteen bucks a game. Tony tossed five straight, while I bitched and whined. Finally I told him, "Pull up or I'm leaving without you," and so he did, but not before Eddie offered him the eight.

When Saez slipped up next to us on the way out and said, "Look, if you want to play for some real money, I can get a stakehorse tomorrow night and we'll see who was stalling," we figured we had it laid down right for sure.

October 17—We watched Game Two of the World Series in our hotel room. Toronto's Ed Sprague was the unlikely hero, homering off Jeff

Reardon with Dave Winfield on base to win the game 5–4. I was actually pleased for the Jays, although I didn't like being reminded of Le Spot.

BOTH OF US were keyed up during the baseball game. Tony prowled the room in his sweats, washing each of his cue's four shafts with a damp washrag, meticulously, slowly, like a warrior sharpening his lance for battle, his thoughts turning inward. This was the most interesting, delicate—and dangerous—spot we'd been in so far. It had taken far more finesse to get to this point than we had needed to get in action in Seattle or Toronto, and even though there might not be quite so much money at stake it would be incredibly satisfying to make it pay off. Particularly after Toronto. But it was no sure thing. We didn't know what kind of weight we would end up getting, or if we'd even seen Saez's true speed yet. From all I'd seen Tony could give him the seven and beat him, but you never knew.

We walked in about 11 P.M. On this Sunday evening, the clubs were all closed and Chelsea Billiards was empty again, pared back to the hard core. Eddie hit us up at the door. This guy probably hadn't made a seventy-five-dollar score in years, and by God he wanted to do it again. Sorry. He was lucky to have been the beneficiary of our advertising, but enough was enough. On this night, we had come for the money.

"Shit, I'm sick of getting beat up for nickels and dimes," Tony said loudly. "If I'm going to go off I might as well spend some money. Otherwise we might as well go to Atlantic City and play some blackjack."

We sat down in the back of the room, with the rest of the rail, and in a few minutes Robert Saez came up to us. "If you guys want to play a little higher, I can get my guy here tonight."

"What kind of weight do I get?" Tony asked.

"I'll give you the seven for two hundred a game."

"Seven and the breaks."

"No way."

"Okay, I'll take the seven, but let's freeze up some money, post a grand, play five ahead."

"Just a minute."

Saez went over and whispered to a couple of people. We waited, and waited. Maybe we'd overplayed our hand. Finally Saez came back and counted out five hundreds. He said, "We got to wait for one more guy for the rest, we called him."

"Shit," Tony said. "New York Fucking City and these mooches can't raise a thousand bucks."

"Chill, man, it'll happen," Saez said. "Gimme ten minutes."

"You're nuts, we ought to get out of here right now," I said to Tony. "They'll never raise the cash."

"Fuck you. I'll put up a hundred of it," Peter Lorre said to me.

"We'll wait for whoever's coming, but let's just take this man's hundred on the side," I said.

"Fine with me," said Tony.

"Anybody else want any?" I asked. "My guy hasn't been drinking tonight, I warn you, and he's ready to kick ass, we're sick of losing." I figured it wouldn't hurt to come out firing. And the rail was ready.

"I'll take fifty."

"Give me another C?"

"How about twenty a game, straight?"

"Two hundred on the set?"

I went all around the sweaters covering side action, putting the money in little stacks all along one rail of the table next to the one we were going to use, with our cue cases on top of it. Then, sure enough, a short, dark, familiar-looking guy came in and walked up to Saez. He looked at Tony, then nodded and pulled out a bankroll. Saez walked over to us with five more hundreds. "Let's play some pool," he said.

This was it. We had Tony in action getting the seven against someone to whom he could give the seven pretty easily. Tony could probably beat Potier straight up and Potier gave the kid the six and the last two. Of course, Potier got beat, too, and the memory of Toronto was fresh enough in my mind that I wasn't exactly sanguine.

The match started well enough. Saez hooked Tony on the four, but Tony went to the long rail and kicked the ball in, then ran out the rest. As he started to break the second rack, I got the scare of my life. Waterdog.

He sidled up to me and whispered, "You all from California? I played out there some."

"Is that right?" I whispered back, not looking at him, keeping focused on the game. *What the shit is this,* I wondered.

"Yeah, I saw a lot of good players out there, Ronnie Allen, Cole Dickson, boy, that guy Cole could play, he made some shots I never seen."

Oh fuck. "Yeah, Cole can shoot the eyes out when he's right," I whispered, still staring at the table.

"How about Tony Annigoni, you ever run into him out there?" Waterdog whispered.

"Yeah, I run onto that doggin motherfucker," I whispered back. "Waterdog, step over here for a minute." We walked a couple of tables away.

"I'll make this quick," he whispered. "I can't talk to you for long. These guys will know something's up. So you know who I am, too, huh?" He smiled at me.

"Of course I do. Look—"

"Don't worry, I'm not here to knock your game. I like these guys but I knew Tony twenty years ago and I owe him one. I hope you get em, just slide me a gapper, that's all I ask."

"You've got it. I'll treat you right." I was relieved; he wasn't threatening to pull the plug on us, he just wanted a gapper—a taste of the action—and I was happy to do that.

"I thought that was Tony. He's changed his bridge a little bit, but he still sets up solid like he used to. He's older, but hell, we're all older. I can't believe he's getting the seven from this kid, it's robbery," Waterdog whispered and limped away. I walked back to the table, and watched Tony make a nice combination on a nine ball to go two up. Saez shook his head and racked.

Tony came over to me. "What's up with Waterdog?" he whispered.

"He made you."

"Fuck, we're done, man, we may not get out of here."

"Don't worry, it's cool, I'm gonna gap him," I whispered in his ear. "He wants you to take these guys off."

Tony just shook his head. "Fuckin amazin," he said, and made two balls on the break.

"Sweet Jesus!" the black guy with the porkpie hat swore in a low groan. He had fifty on the set with me, and he wasn't liking what he was seeing. "Where the fuck did this guy come from?"

"He says he's a businessman," whined Peter Lorre with a sidelong glare at me.

"He *doin* some fuckin business," Porkpie Hat growled. "That's one businessman with some motherfuckin *stroke*. Shit. He get his motherfuckin thumbs broken, comin with that shit in here."

It took Tony only nine games to get to five ahead and the money. He was trying not to show too much, but he wasn't taking any chances with the cash, either.

"You got to give me a chance to get my money back, man, you came off the stall big time," Saez said, rolling the balls around the table. He wasn't happy but he wasn't that angry, either. He understood the game. So did the railbirds, now, though, and they were very pissed off. "Okay, give me the eight and I'll try you like that," Tony said.

"No." Saez shook his head, hard. "Even." He looked over at his backers, who were gathered in a downcast little knot at the end of the next table. They nodded vigorously. "Don't give him shit, man, make him step up and play you even," one of them said.

"Shit, you should probably give me weight," Saez said. He bent down and fired in a couple of banks.

"Play him even, Tony, let's see if these guys want to gamble some more." I turned to the rail.

"Fuck you," Peter Lorre said.

"Come on, man, he lost five straight to Eddie last night, he might shoot straight up in the air in this set."

"He lost to Eddie, he did it on purpose," Porkpie Hat rumbled. "I don't want no more of it." I was only able to get a hundred out of the rail for the second set, but that wasn't too surprising. These guys weren't here to get beat, and they knew they'd been scammed the first time.

It took a little longer, about an hour and a half, to knock down the second set. Tony had to play very well to beat Saez, who was playing even better than he had against Potier. "You guys fucked up," Robert Saez said cheerfully when it was over. "You showed too much speed."

He was right, in a way, but we were handicapped by our circumstances. Saez and his backers didn't have huge money. If we could have hung around there for two or three weeks and waited, somebody with some real money might have stepped up to play, and we could have made ten thousand or more.

But so what? It was an interesting intellectual exercise. We probably wouldn't do it again; most of the time, these days, good players are too well known, and the risks of hustling are too great. It's easier to simply match up with another good player, perhaps even one who doesn't have a high regard for your game, such as Billy Cress, and take the money. But when Saez's stakehorse, the small, dark guy who had looked so familiar, said, "I'll play you some, man, straight up for two hundred a game, same way," Tony passed.

"No thanks, Ginky," he said. "You're too fast for me. I saw your picture on the wall at Amsterdam, run a hundred twenty fuckin balls, and I don't need to play you."

It was a pity to pass up another high-stakes game. We were fairly confident the room still had Tony's game underrated by a ball, maybe two, but matching up with Ginky would be no picnic. We didn't know exactly how strong he was, but Tony had heard enough to know it would be a tough game. We had worked hard for almost a week for this payday, and there was no reason to risk losing it all in a game that tough.

Anyway, we got the money that night, what there was of it. Twenty-seven hundred and change. I gapped Waterdog a hundred and he was thrilled. He told Tony he was on a methadone program, and doing pretty well. "My biggest problem is this gout," he said, pointing to his leg. "It's a bitch."

"Hey, we heard there's some action up in Harlem," I said to him. "You ever play up there?"

Waterdog snorted. "Are you fuckin crazy, man? They'll cut off your nuts before they'll let you out of there with any of their money. Those rooms up there make this place look like the Waldorf. Speaking of that, I'd get out of here pretty quick if I was you." We took his advice.

October 20—On Tuesdays, we had heard, there was a tournament in Jersey—week in, week out, probably the toughest weekly tournament in the country. Why not? we probably weren't going to make any more money in Chelsea, or anywhere else in the city for that matter. Tony and I had slept most of the day on Monday. Now, we were ready to move.

WE PAID THE tab at the San Carlos out of our winnings, and I called around to find a decent car to rent. Alamo had a special deal on Cadillac

Sevilles—unlimited miles, two hundred bucks a week flat. I had to take a shuttle out to Newark Airport to pick it up, but it seemed like a good idea. And it beat the hell out of Amtrak.

The great thing, though, was that the car was brand new, just delivered that morning: white with a red interior, ugly as a scratch on the break but extremely comfortable for the road. The stakehorse special. When I wheeled it out of the lot into the damp gray decay of an October morning in Newark and gunned it up onto the Parkway, headed back into the city, it had three and seven-tenths miles on it.

West End Billiards in Elizabeth, N.J., is a pool player's shrine. Some of the game's true greats play there often: Steve Mizerak, Allen Hopkins, Pat Fleming, "Neptune Joey" Fratte, the Philadelphia players including Jimmy and Petey Fusco, women's tour star Loree Jon Jones, and all the New York City players.

The Tuesday night tournament at West End is known all over the East Coast for a consistently strong field, approaching the level of competition at a pro tour stop. It's a good place to play, and a good place to clock other good players, and maybe to make a game. We showed up at 5 P.M., two and a half hours before tournament time, to sign Tony up. "We have one spot left," the guy said, and so I paid him twenty dollars and Tony was in. We got a table for some practice.

Tony proposed a game of nine-ball. What he suggested seemed like a huge spot: I got the three out, but he got the breaks. That meant that if I legally made the three or any ball after the three—any of the four through nine—I would win the rack; he could only win by legally making the nine.

Sounds ridiculous, doesn't it? After all, I could play a little. But first of all, he was breaking, and maybe 40 percent of the time he would make a ball and run the table, winning without my getting a shot. So in order to come out ahead, I had to win *almost every one* of the remaining 60 percent of the games. And that, I found out, was next to impossible. Sometimes he broke, made nothing, but hooked me. Other times he broke and made a ball but didn't leave himself a shot, so he simply hooked me and waited for a ball in hand, or at worst a better-looking shot than he had just passed up. And of course if I missed a ball or misplayed a safety at any time after the break, chances were maybe 75–25 in favor of him getting out. Basically, it came down to this: For me to win at this game, he had to miss, which he was not in the habit of doing, and I then *could not miss a shot*. That's pressure. Also, it was hard for me to get in stroke playing this game, because I never got a chance to make more than one or two balls in a rack.

The game did afford me the opportunity to consider the psychological aspects of losing. I thought about Dino, how he seemed almost to like losing. I thought about Billy Cress. I thought about our experience in Toronto. And I learned firsthand how it felt, and I will be happy to share that with you now: It felt like being hit in the nuts with a hot steam iron. At the same time, though, I thought it was a valuable thing, knowing how to lose, because it seemed to me that only in that frame of reference could the sweetness of winning be fully appreciated.

I was certainly ready for a little sweetness. By tournament time my tab with Tony was up to $450.

"What kind of an asshole would rob his own stakehorse like this?"

"We've already been through all that. If you don't like the game don't gamble with me anymore."

"I'm stuck like a pig, and you advise me to quit."

"Hey, there's stuck and then there's stuck. It could get a lot worse."

"You're a real beauty, you know that? I should have left you in Toronto to play Insect Man for the rest of your life."

"Oh, now we're coming with the real low shots."

"Talk about low shots, let's talk about my four-fifty."

"Yeah, let's. Let's go over exactly how you lost all of it."

"Go over this."

He laughed. I actually considered our little gambling series an entertaining diversion. Mind you, I wanted to win. And I knew I'd get my opening, sooner or later. The truth was, I was learning a lot about gambling. And about pool. Each day that I woke up, took my bankroll from under my pillow and padded into the bathroom past the snoring machine in the other bed to brush my teeth, I was slipping deeper and deeper into this milieu, as exotic and unforgiving as a tropical rain-forest. As I gained understanding, I appreciated my player and the way he handled himself under pressure. This boy had a few moves. Each new challenge we faced helped me understand him a little more. Horrible contretemps between road partners are legendary in pool, but we were actually becoming more comfortable with each other as we went. The interdependence we felt on the road was profound. It certainly lessened the strain of walking into hostile places. The Chelsea success was a measure of our growing ability to work together.

Not that we verbalized any of this. Despite his salesman's ability to articulate, Tony wasn't much for long, serious discussion. He was much more comfortable with the needling, bantering exchange that we had fallen into, and it worked for me as well. We used it to prop each other up when we were discouraged, and to punctuate the highs as well.

After my latest thrashing, we went upstairs to the tournament room. It was beautifully equipped, with a tournament board, six tight, well-lit black Gold Crowns in perfect shape, spectator seating on one side, and a couple of card tables in the back. It was not in any way fancy, though; it had a blue-collar Jersey feel about it, with painted paneling, a few beer signs, and about a hundred men and maybe half a dozen women sitting around waiting for something to happen.

It turned out that Hopkins and Mizerak and Fleming and a few others were at a tournament in Memphis, but the field was plenty strong nevertheless: Neptune Joey, Tony Robles, Frankie Hernandez, and quite a few others. It was single-elimination, race to five, with five hundred for the winner, half that much for second.

Tony drew a local player I'd never heard of in the first round, but when the announcer called his match, Tony wasn't around. He had five minutes to avoid a forfeit. Panicked, I rushed downstairs with Waterdog, who had materialized at the tournament along with a few other rail types from Chelsea. We scoured the poolroom and then, in desperation, dashed outside. Waterdog finally spotted Tony in a restaurant across the street, calmly buying a cup of soup, and I ran in to get him.

"Are you nuts? You've got two minutes."

"That's okay, I've already won enough off you to make my daily nut."

He made it, barely, and more important, won his match. Now he had to play Frankie Hernandez, a top New York player with an attitude to match. A big, muscular twenty-five-year-old known for his loud mouth, he was fresh from a couple of big tournament upsets, and was regarded as one of the best players on the East Coast right now. Tony, unimpressed, drilled him, 5–0.

"I'll play you for money any time, asshole," Hernandez told Tony. "I'll kick your ass." We were going to Philly the next day, and not planning to return to New York, so Tony said, "Let's play tonight. But I know how good you are, I've heard of you. I got lucky here. You've got to give me a ball."

"Fuck you, you just beat me five to nothing. Get a fuckin heart transplant and come back and play me."

"Get a cash transplant and we'll play tonight," Tony said. "But I'm not playing you any two-hundred sets. Let's play some for five hundred a game."

Hernandez left, sneering.

Next, Tony had to play Tony Robles, whose quiet courtesy provided a striking contrast to Hernandez. Tony won that match, too, 5–1, and Robles simply shook his hand, smiled, and walked out.

Porkpie Hat, the guy who had grumbled about losing the fifty dollars to me at Chelsea, was sitting in front of me for that match. When it was over, he turned around to me and shook his head in disgust. "Businessman," he snorted. Tony won two more matches to end up in the finals.

Now all the tables save one in the center were idle, and all the lights in the place were turned off except for the single table's overhead lights. Tony's opponent was a local player named Don Henderson, an enormous fellow with a beefy face and a white work shirt, straining over a huge belly. Despite his size, Henderson played delicately and stylishly, controlling the cue ball beautifully. As I watched him warm up for the final, I couldn't help but admire him. He was not a "name" player. According to the patch on the shoulder of his shirt, he was a municipal bus driver, but he had beaten five good players, including Neptune Joey, to get to this point.

It was the match of the night. He and Tony were an odd pair of combatants; he must have outweighed Tony by 150 pounds. Both men played beautiful position and defense, both made tough shots when the game was on the line, and both made very few errors.

Tony won the first rack to take the lead, but Henderson ran three straight to take a 3–1 lead. Tony then ran three racks right back to take a 4–3 lead in the race to five. He made nothing on the ensuing break, and Henderson played a fine hook shot, curling the cue ball into a corner hard behind two balls. Tony was unable to hit the one, and his opponent calmly took cue ball in hand and ran two racks and out.

Tony collected $250, but it seemed like a Pyrrhic victory. There would be no more easy gambling money to be had around here. Word would spread—about Chelsea, and about how Tony came within one game of winning this tournament. Still, it felt good to cash another little ticket.

from

Fixer Chao

by Han Ong

THE SKELETON AT the Savoy were applauding A young white guy with an unshaven face and a small potbelly was being, cradled motherlike. In the arms of a pretty black drag queen. The song was something by Patsy Cline. Barney saw me and nodded, and for him it was as close as he would ever get to normal human interaction. I sat at the bar and ordered a beer.

No tequila? Barney asked, surprised.

I resisted the urge to tell him that I'd had my quota of water for the day.

I nursed my drink in silence. The clock with the tinfoil rays said that it was midnight. Any minute now . . .

There was Shem, looking directly at the bar and seeing me. His passive face was like a senator's or a preacher's with important information that he didn't want to surrender so quickly.

We shook hands. He ordered a beer, which Barney brought pronto. Did you read the material? he asked. What do you think? he asked.

I had a feeling that I was not expected to think but instead to make myself blank and pliant, ready to translate whatever information I received into action.

His plan was very simple. He needed me to pretend to be an expert on, what else, Feng Shui. That way, he could take me into a series of homes owned by those people who formed the circle he so detested.

In these people's self-projections, they appeared as colorful characters given distinct outlines by private areas of expertise—admen, screenwriters, Wall Streeters, realtors, magazine editors—but really they were nothing more than blind lemmings with the instinct to follow. And what they all seemed so eager to get behind was this new trend.

They fancied themselves to have artistic sensibilities and/or sympathies—who talked about "inspiration" and "the muse" as things more concrete and vivid than anything from their hidden pasts—and therefore had a natural predisposition to believe in the unseen. And if this unseen was given the weighty cultural imprimatur of two thousand years of Chinese civilization—well, that was as good as gold!

It was a group that knew how to perpetuate itself. What was that bit of Catholic prayer? World without end? For them, it was the very same thing.

More new people kept finding themselves suddenly prosperous and, desiring the inoculation that prosperity can buy, would get referrals from members of the established circle for brand names—interior designers; books to catch up on whose titles could then be conspicuously dropped at parties; restaurants in which to be seen; charities to support—and in this way, would build up the same glass bubble by which a group begins to recognize and protect itself . . . Marianna, Bill Hood, his own disgusting father, the people who stood in for the entire circle who not only laughed at him but, what's worse, had by this time forgotten all about him.

The way he talked reminded me of Preciosa and myself discussing Divina Valencia as she swam to and fro inside her goldfish bowl: everything seen from a giant's distant, haughty perspective.

As he talked, his hands moved the same way that his daughter's did, first going from a position of holding an invisible football, and then dropping it and lengthening the distance between his hands, and then keeping his hands in the same position but adding a single, subtle touch: turning the ends of his fingers crooked, into claws: from "big" to "scary": this time he really was talking about himself.

What exactly would *I* do?

Study the book he gave me, by which he meant the pamphlet. And study some more. Check out titles from the library—there was an ever-growing list on the subject. Learn the terminologies, get comfortable with those foreign, shaken-out-of-a-bag syllables because I would be counted upon, when declaiming and performing in these people's houses, to have a flair that was the decisive complement of authority. Once more, I ran my Agatha Christie vocabulary list through my head: obfuscate, obstinate, obstreperous, ostentatious, oracular. The last word, in particular, began to ring bells.

And he needed me to know exactly what principles to follow, how to rearrange the furniture and suggest color schemes and locate props that would assist these people in their quest for buffers against the harsh world of New York: *peace, harmony, prosperity* settling over their frantic modern lives: words to which the Chinese, by virtue of age and an evanescent sense of spiritual superiority, have become attached as experts and expediters . . . Except . . . He paused tantalizingly . . . Except he needed me to do just one thing wrong. Do one thing that was the exact contradiction of what those manuals said to do. For a banker, for example, he needed me to do the one thing that would ensure that his money schemes would be met with failure. He needed me to familiarize myself with that one thing, and then carry it out, like planting a secret, ticking time bomb.

But, I asked Shem, wouldn't that be contingent on the veracity of this Feng Shui thing? What if it wasn't true at all?

If it's not true, we'll still have scammed them. And it'll still be like a big fuck-you in the middle of where they live. Like a rape, he said. Like sneaking into their homes and doing ugly, hateful things to the things they love. And what's worse, all with their cooperation. And if this Feng Shui is true, so much the better. Suffering and pestilence. I've got the best of both worlds.

And my second question was: Why me?

He looked at me, as if the answer couldn't have been more obvious. I need an Oriental, he said, because this thing, this Feng Shui, is the province of an Oriental. And I've looked. I've looked and haven't found anyone who can go as low as you've gone. You've gone low, you can go low again. He made this sound like a compliment. You and me, he said. You and me are the right team. With your face and my plans . . .

And I sat there, mentally going back years to when I knew this guy, Sam M, a confidence trickster. He conducted his various scams on the streets, in pool halls, bus depots, airports, at the racetrack, anyplace where the flurry of crowds ruled and which helped give his face an erased-over aspect. He put on a show and hustled. And oh boy, what a show that was, aided by his aging priest's look, which, when you encountered it, made you blindly drop all your defenses, and then he'd cinch his hold over you by lubricating Ripley's Believe It or Not hard-luck stories with expertly squeezed tears. But it was strictly small-scale, one sucker at a time, and only for whatever pocket money they happened to have at the moment. A mom-and-pop operation. Had he graduated by now?

What Shem was proposing was bigger. Could we pull it off? The books I loved, after all, depended on apprehension and punishment as part of their ritual satisfaction.

When I came to, Shem was looking at his shot glass as if trying to divine something from the oily smudges of his own fingerprints. There was a mirror behind the bar, a yellow thing with my face on it. Looking at it made me afraid. Oriental, said the invisible caption beneath my face. This caption was crowding out another, which said: Saint. My heart was beating fast. And I realized I was feeling the kind of big fear I'd vowed I would be smart enough never to open the door to next time around. But here I was nevertheless, poised . . . Oh, wait a minute. There was another question I wanted to ask Shem: Who's Suzy Yamada? But when I turned to him, there was only an empty shot glass and neatly arranged bills on top of it. The indentation on his barstool was slowly filling up again. The vivid red doorway bore no trace. And when Barney collected the bills, he found a piece of paper. I think this is for you, he said, handing it to me. On it was a phone number.

THERE WERE SO many sick people here tonight. And they were all given a momentary outline by lights in the ceiling, illustrating some unknown lesson, before being returned once more to the ashen crowd.

A noisy group, buzzing away, and as they buzzed, they were busy examining each other's clothes and jewelry and new tans and fixed-up lips or eyes or noses with the squinched-together expressions of old women inspecting price tags.

Everyone seemed to be connected to me. In my mind they were all gathered in a circle, reaching out an arm toward my rotating body in the center, and it was my job to touch them—a hollow gesture to me but to which they brought all the transporting belief of children as to a fairy tale.

I heard so many words of calm that belied the sick and tortured natures of their speakers. These words were like the sound of insect wings flapping very close to my ears, and gave me a sensation of swimming in a gentle tide, a feeling of being buffeted and laundered, pushed around and molded into a shape by some unknown force to which I had to surrender if I wanted to be changed. And I did. I wanted to be changed just like these people wanted to be changed. I wanted to put on a new shirt and discard the old, sweat-soaked one I had.

I was standing in the vast living room beside some kind of shoulder-height totem carved out of dark wood. Was it African? It looked African, with lips that protruded like a movie star's and eyes that were big and hooded as if in warning. Yes, I was sure it was African. I was beginning to become more knowledgeable about the things I'd begun by regarding with the same laughter as children's at a Sunday matinee.

In the distance I could see a glass door open, and beyond it, more people were gathered on the red-tiled veranda, under skies that shared in the refracted glow of a thousand jiggling lightbulbs strung around four bamboo poles planted at each corner.

Most of the women wore sleeveless shirts and slightly above-the-knee skirts, or slip dresses with barely-there straps, made of light materials like cotton and linen, that upon contact with the breeze were revealed to be things made explicitly for seduction. The clinking of ice in glasses and the scootch-slide of footwear on the wood floors made everything seem inconsequential. There was a heightened feeling that we were truly alive only for this length of time, bracketed by the hours of the party as printed on the invitation cards mailed three weeks ago: 9 p.m. and 3 a.m. And whatever else had happened to us or would happen to us—all these things seemed very far away.

And then among all the sick people there was Shem, who wasn't sick at all. He circulated freely, a gold-colored drink sweating in his hand. I didn't always know where he was in the apartment—which was palatial, and which I realized neither Condé Nast nor *Metropolitan Home* did any justice to—but every once in a while, like a dot pulsating on a tracking screen, there would be Shem's shirt, a shimmering, billowing thing that was neither purple nor gray but instead combined the worst qualities of both, making him stand out like a signal flare even among a field of Mardi Gras tones. He would hold forth for minutes at a time, surrounded by people riveted by his speech, and then he would move on, begin another conversation with a whole new group who would just naturally cluster around his standing figure or he would interject something into a conversation already started, adding expert comments that were either serious or flippant depending on his reading of the crowd. He freshly insinuated himself into a corner by the kitchen doors where a bunch of teeny women were gathered. At the sight of him their eyes lit up. What could he possibly be talking to them about? Certainly not Do you suck cock? Riveted, they were riveted. Look at those hands, flying as he narrated. Those skeletal and wide-spaced fingers that always led people to ask whether he played the piano. He touched them on the shoulders, the elbows, why was he expending such energy on these women? Knowing him, it could only be disdain. Maybe I would be ushered to them later on, introduced by the name of my new religion: Master Chao. Oh, they would think, he's too young to be a master. And this disparity, this chasm between my age and my publicized skills, drawing disbelief at first, would very soon develop a skin of truth around it, as if these listeners were sick and tired of listening to the credible and wanted to cast their lot with the fantastic instead, hoping to be rewarded with whatever the fantastic rewarded its believers.

Riveted listeners, nodding along with his musical speech. As I suppose I had been. Not that I no longer was. Shem still exerted his beautiful control. Intelligence did indeed shine forth in the eyes, and Shem's eyes were—They blazed. Behind them were the fires of a plan in motion. He was back in a circle of people that he saw as tormentors. They had opened their arms once more, courtesy of me.

So many of these people I had helped. They each took me into their homes and revealed the thing that they would never dare speak of in public, the thing that was their big shame, for which their reputations were no more than paperback covers—about to be blown open. They had sons and daughters who were drug addicts. Spouses with drinking problems. They were the children of country bumpkin parents they were embarrassed to present to city friends. They had ailing health for which they held themselves responsible—unwholesome inclinations finally metastasizing into little balls that were blocking their windpipes and arteries and intestines.

Shem pointed out a common denominator in their homes: stacks of glossy magazines underneath coffee tables or beside beds or piled high at the foot of bookshelves. Shem said: They read these things, gulp them down, and cannot avoid seeing themselves as falling far short of their magazine counterparts. They do not have—and will never have—enough possessions, and the ones that they have will never be as shiny, or quiet, always requiring upkeep. And as for their careers—the magazines are always raising the imaginary ceiling of accomplishment. Picture it this way, said Shem: These people on treadmills with speeds which can only go in one direction: plus. Never enough. They covet, said Shem. As I once did.

He had typed up a fake article about me, giving it to me to read. I was impressed. From it I could gather something of the talent he claimed to possess. Its tone was one of casual validation, as if I had been interviewed on a Sunday afternoon, with my feet up on a table, interviewer and subject merely passing the time companionably. It tossed made-up facts carelessly, putting in quotes that sought to establish me as everything I wasn't: offhand, serene, gifted. The picture that emerged of this person, this Master Chao, seemed entirely accidental. You read, not aware that points were being made, or themes being engaged, and in the end you had this sudden sensation of a whole world assembled, a clarity that emerged from sentences that had the look and feel of rubble. This m.o. described Shem's style perfectly: under the radar.

He then had the article designed and then printed up—complete with a photograph—in a copy shop. The entire thing cost him less than five dollars. The article was attributed to a made-up "lifestyle" magazine from Europe. He xeroxed a hundred copies of the article and this was the way I was legitimized, my existence verified, poked into, but only superficially, to give a little "flavor," a little human face to a trend that was on the upswing and didn't seem likely to die for at least the next five years, which, in magazine time, was an eternity. Feng Shui Master Chats with Us, said the subhead beneath the main title, which said: Go East! And there I was, in the lower right-hand corner, above a caption that read. Young Master Chao. I looked like I was smiling, though I wasn't smiling at all. This fact alone made me look more Chinese, more mysterious, gifted with powers that the magazine article didn't even have to elaborate on.

For the photograph, he'd taken me to a furniture emporium in Brooklyn. We'd found an empty showroom for couches and Shem had simply sat me down and started snapping away. This one serious, this one casual, here I'm even smiling, this one looking to my left, then to my right, at some mysterious source of light outside the frame that was nothing more than a dinky floor lamp with a broken glass shade.

In the photograph he eventually used, the plush red velvet of a sofa behind me was cropped in such a way as to suggest that it was so much more: a painting, a flag, the red of a column in a Chinese pavilion. Red for luck, a Chinese preoccupation. And besides, Shem said, it was the one picture where I looked handsomest, the most serious, without any hint of mischief, or of betraying our true purpose—which, in me, came out as a clear shine in the eyes, complemented by a slight arching of my left eyebrow and this look seemed to come out in picture after worrisome picture that Shem took. I was familiar with that look. I had seen it in many photographs taken of me before and had always thought it made me look more handsome, which was why I continued doing it. But now I realized it was only that I confused handsomeness with inane mimicry of pop star poses in magazines, poses calculated to establish a pop star's integrity by aligning him with black traits: surliness, indifference, mischief. Well, Shem and I didn't want any of that. What we wanted was a look that was the opposite of a pop star, or rather a pop star whose aura was white rather than black, sexless and filled with wisdom.

In the picture, my hair was greased with newfangled pomade that was supposed to coat the hair with protective proteins. The amount of money it cost, though it made me wince—forty-two dollars for a six-ounce container—was like a down payment for a future of returns, a thousandfold.

Every picture tells a lie, Devo the stylist for photo shoots, the concealer, the fixer, the rearranger, quipped to me once.

Well, this picture Shem took was the image these people were projecting back onto the blank screen of my face tonight. It was that man these people had shaken hands with, behind whom doors had closed with little ceremonies of embarrassment and supplication. Please come into my humble home, more than a few of them had said, stepping aside for this man. And the truth was, not one of those homes could even be remotely described as humble. Ugly, yes. Intimidating, of course. Palatial, some. Even the ones that adhered strictly to the modish principles of minimalism, given the buffed sensuality of a Japanese or even a Shaker environment—even those homes could not be described as humble: There might only have been one table and one chair in a vast room that could easily house a family of five, but that table was made entirely of marble and the chair, of hand-sewn double-stitched leather. See? My eyes were beginning to wrap around confronted objects better. With the first big money I got—five thousand dollars from Lindsay S, minus Shem's cut—along with a second savings account that I opened in another bank, I bought subscriptions to three magazines: *Metropolitan Home*, Condé

Nast *House & Garden*, and newly, *Elle Décor*. This was my little joke to myself. Even my own slummy apartment was beginning to show the influences of this reading: like a rusted tin can repainted and then pierced with holes and then, with a lighted votive placed inside, made to shine.

Some of my clients and their homes I first encountered in the pages of these magazines. I enlarged on the revelations in the various articles or read between the lines, deciding on likely troubles for the subjects—taken for diagnostic clairvoyance and greeted with breathy But-how-do-you-know's—before offering my occult solutions.

For example, there was a woman whose child's spine had been permanently crushed in a car accident and who stuffed every single seat in her home with thick pillows, referring to them as "posts of much-needed comfort": I told her to get rid of those pillows. I said that I "sensed" a tragedy that had occurred in the past hanging in the air and for which the pillows had been trotted out as "palliatives."

You feel guilt about this accident, and the guilt has been building and concentrating on your back (giving her back pain; hence the pillows), but as soon as you get rid of the pillows, your back will have to learn to straighten instead of curve and, straightening, will have to release the guilt locked inside for a long time.

This woman, hearing me speak, opened her mouth but could say nothing.

Poker in the Strand

by John Molyneux

Of course, it's all different now. For a start, nowadays there are always beggars and rough sleepers in the doorways in that part of The Strand. In those days, in the mid-sixties, I had to go to New York, to the Bowery, to see such things and very shocking it was too. In those days of The Beatles and Mary Quant there was 'something in the air' in swinging London. . . . but this is not an exercise in nostalgia for that mythologised golden age, this is an exercise in nostalgia for a particular place, a particular institution, in the London of that time, which existed at a much lower, more subterranean level of sixties society.

Nor is there now any visible trace of this institution—I checked it out just the other day. The building is still there, of course; they haven't knocked down and rebuilt The Strand but from the street, there's no sign the En Passant ever existed—well, there wouldn't be, would there? But if you had passed that way when I first visited in 1965 and were not *in the know*, you would also have seen nothing.

I first found my way there with a chess-playing friend when I was sixteen by tagging along with (more accurately trailing along after) the chess master, Bob Wade, and some prodigious young chess players after a London chess tournament. I was still at school, just starting to find my way round London by night and had very little idea where I was going, except that it was in a vague way notorious. Anyway, we followed Wade and his disciples to a shop in The Strand, nearly opposite The Savoy and just in between The Adelphi and Vaudeville theatres. The shop sold off property lost on London Transport and had a U-shaped glass front for the display of its wares. The shop entrance set back in the center was, obviously, closed but just before the entrance, on the right hand side, was an unmarked door which, when tried, turned out to be open (permanently as I discovered later). Behind the door was a dingy bare wooden staircase, which led our band to the first floor above the shop. This turned out to be a large, minimally decorated room devoid of people or signs of life, except for several long tables with chairs and benches and, on the tables, a few chess sets. Wade and his group sat at one table, my friend and I at another. They chatted and, as serious chess players do, started to set up positions and analyse them. We, feeling very awkward, half tried to eavesdrop on their conversation and half played our own game. Soon, however, we became aware of sounds, voices, faint but quite animated, coming from above and we saw there was another staircase leading upwards. After about twenty minutes a rather nondescript man came up the stairs from the street, passed through our room without a word and disappeared upstairs to the next floor. Fifteen minutes after that, another nondescript but to us rather tough-looking guy came down the stairs and left, again without a word. No one from the Wade group made any move towards going upstairs so neither did we. After an hour or so they left and we followed with our tails between our legs.

When I came back, now three months older and three months bolder and just turned 17, with my friend from school, Chris Carvell (who went on to become a croupier at The Golden Nugget), we climbed the second set of stairs to the En Passant proper.

The En Passant was a poker club, hiding behind the very tiniest fig leaf of a chess club. Actually, this is not quite true. It was really a poker *game*, not a club. There was nothing one could join, no membership fee or list, no records of any kind, no entrance fee, no reception or receptionist, no doormen, no security—though the people who went there, some of them at least, were more than capable of dealing with any trouble that might present itself and capable, if they chose, of creating more trouble than any doorman or security could handle. There was just a game of poker, occasionally two games—seven or eight men sitting round a table playing cards permanently. Every now and then a player would get up and go to be replaced by someone waiting or there would be a vacant seat till the next punter arrived but the game would go on. In its heyday the poker game at the En Passant ran continuously 24 hours round the clock, one endless game of cards without beginning or end. It was also, to my knowledge, the hardest game in London at that time and by hardest, I mean the one with the highest average level of skill in which it was most difficult to be a regular winner.

In every society at given points in time, there exist unofficial places, hidden from the overwhelming majority, where intriguing social interactions take place. Such were the 'buffet flats' frequented by the likes of Bessie Smith on the black music scene in the US in the twenties, or the extra-legal raves in the 1987 'summer of love' or the squatter organized events in Hackney today. Such was the En Passant. These places are either completely unknown to the mainstream society or else radically different in reality to whatever vague public image they might have developed. The danger is that if they are not recorded, all knowledge of their existence may be lost. It may be true that 'one picture is worth a thousand words' and one may wish that Brassai could have been transported from Paris in the thirties to record the scene at the En Passant but he wasn't, so now the only recourse is to words based on memories.

I have already given some impression of the En Passant's grim physical appearance. Let me add that the second floor, the scene of the action, resembled the first in its barren dinginess. It may have been above street level rather than below it but the En Passant was a dive of the first water. With no décor or decoration worth mentioning, lighting that was adequate but on the dim side and furniture consisting only of the main card table, a couple of spares and a scattering of chairs, this was minimalism resembling that of a Carl Andr—brick sculpture. In addition, there was a kitchen–cum–office, whence tea and not much else was served—no alcohol, occasionally a sandwich. There *must* have been a toilet and washroom—punters spent days and nights there—but I don't remember them. They could not have been very salubrious. Looking back, however, I have no doubt that this very minimalism, this absence of distractions, the 'purist' focus on the main thing, men playing poker, was one of the En Passant's attractions.

Regarding the origins and history of the En Passant, I can say very little. I encountered the place as an established fact in circumstances in which the last thing on my mind was historical research or enquiring about the past and there is no book to look things up in. All I know is the hearsay I picked up on the poker scene, which amounts to this: the En Passant was set up and opened, I don't know when, as a bona fide chess and card club (hence its name taken from the chess move, en passant) by an émigré Russian entrepreneur known as Boris Watson. Boris, whom I played poker with and therefore got to know in the extremely limited sense one did get to know people in the poker world, closely resembled in girth, facial appearance and manner, the actor Sidney Greenstreet, who played the fat man in *The Maltese Falcon*. For Boris, the En Passant was one of three related business ventures, the others being The Mandrake, a drinking club in Meard Street in Soho and The Prompt Corner, a chess café at the corner of Pond Street and South End Green near Hampstead Heath. The Mandrake closed and The Prompt Corner was sold to a Greek Cypriot called Mr Kanou (who appeared to dislike the chess players but nevertheless tolerated them with the result that The Prompt remained an interesting place for some years). The En Passant also failed but in a peculiar way. Boris's problem was that he was a very bad but completely compulsive poker player. Over a period of time he lost so much money in his own game that he had to hand over control of the 'club' to two of the most regular and successful players, who then paid him a modest weekly rent. It was these two, Ted Iles and Colin Kennedy, who ran the game at the En Passant during all my time there. Their method was to work alternate twelve-hour shifts, organizing and running the game, playing in it and cutting the pot—taking sixpence or a shilling for the house out of every pound bet—at the same time. They were an unlikely partnership. Ted, who was clearly the dominant one of the two, was a large, thick set man, supremely solid rather than fat, in, probably, his late thirties or early forties. (I do not know his exact age or that of anyone else featured here and I don't think seventeen year olds are good at estimating the ages of their elders). He was an ex-policeman—rumour had it that he had been kicked out of the cops in disgrace following some involvement with a teenage runaway girl—but he also possessed a powerful intelligence having been a county standard chess and bridge player. Everything about Ted Iles exuded strength, hardness and there was something else, a hint of real malevolence, a touch of evil just below the surface. Colin Kennedy was about ten years younger, a gangly, rather shy, somewhat intellectual gay Irishman. By what route he arrived at the En Passant I do not know but he was something of an oddity in that environment. Although he was cool and competent in his management of the poker game, he came over as weak in comparison to the intimidating Ted. This was certainly Ted's view. "My partner is a wanker", he would say from time to time. Despite this, Colin Kennedy was a formidable poker player.

There are many kinds of poker and they are played with a wide variety of rules and arrangements in different venues, clubs and parts of the world. Classic 'Draw Poker', in which each player is dealt five cards face down and then draws, i.e. exchanges one, two, three or four cards to try to improve his hand, is the form of the game most often featured in films and on TV—usually as a plot device—but in my experience it is hardly ever played, at least in clubs as opposed to private games. The same is true of 'pure' Five Card Stud—one card dealt face down, one face up, followed by three up cards with a round of betting after each—probably because, for all the legends about 'Aces-in-the-Hole' and so on, the vast majority of hands are very low, less than one pair and this is not conducive to exciting play or big pots. Today the dominant form of poker is 'Texas Hold'em' imported from Las Vegas; in the sixties it was generally Five Card Stud stripped deck, that is with cards below the seven removed, which greatly increases the size of the average hand.

At The Strand, however, the main game was Seven Card Stud—two down cards and one up card, followed by three more up cards and a final down card with five rounds of betting in all. In my opinion, Seven Card is the best, most interesting and most demanding form of poker. The five rounds of betting allow for sustained and subtle bluffing and remarkable feats of card reading (working out an opponent's hand) and from time to time, produce a buildup to a real dramatic showdown in which everything depends on the players' correct judgement on whether to call, pass or raise.

All poker is a combination of luck and skill: luck in what cards you are dealt, skill in how you bet them. In the long run, therefore, poker is a game of skill like bridge or chess because in the long run the luck evens out. But the fact that luck plays a big part in the short run and is the main factor determining who wins each hand is what makes poker attractive to the gambler in a way that chess is not. The weak player can always tell himself he has a chance of beating even the strongest professional and, *in the short run,* he does have such a chance. At the same time the weak player can always tell himself, and anyone else, that the reason he lost was because he was unlucky. But the balance of luck and skill is not the same in all kinds of poker. Texas Hold'em with its high antes, heavy betting on the first two cards and its flop of three cards at once is a version that increases the element of luck. Seven Card Stud is a version that maximizes the element of skill. This was especially true of the way the game was played at the En Passant. The ante put in by the dealer and the first bet from the player showing the highest card, were very low, usually only one shilling, occasionally half a crown in a 'big' game. After that, betting was pot limit, i.e. if there was three shillings (or three pounds) in the pot, player A could bet up to three shillings (or three pounds), then player B could call that bet and raise up to nine shillings (or nine pounds). This meant that it was possible to play very tight, sitting and waiting patiently for a very good initial hand, without losing too much in antes (high antes work against this strategy). However, once a pot got going, the size of the bets could escalate rapidly, especially in the later stages. A hand that began with bets of a few shillings could end in bets of thirty, fifty or even hundreds of pounds if there were raises and re-raises. This put a very high premium on precise judgement in certain highly pressured situations.

After Seven Card Stud, the next most popular game at The Strand was Dealer's Choice. In this, the dealer got to choose which version of poker would be played for that round (eight hands if there were seven players). Dealer's Choice was poker for aficionados. In fact, unless you were quite experienced, or very sharp, you would not be able to understand how to play the games at all, never mind how to play them well enough to cope with the sharks at the En Passant. Players chose the most weird and wonderful versions of poker imaginable and often invented new forms on the spot. Characteristic features of these Dealer's Choice games were: proliferating wild cards—not just deuces wild but *leaners* (adjacent cards of the same suit, 9-10 of Hearts, A-2 of Clubs etc) or *jumpers* (next but one cards of same suit, 6-8-10 of Spades etc) or *pairs* (so that Kings up, KK55, equaled four kings); hi-lo games where the pot was divided between the highest and the lowest hand; multiple rounds of betting with complex card exchanges. A typical game, therefore, might be announced by the dealer as follows, "We'll play . . . Seven Card hi-lo, leaners wild, changes on the third, fifth and last cards, dealer sees the changes, simultaneous declaration". Sometimes the cards lost their usual values and were measured by their point count or some strange combination of the two, as in Seven Card Stud, eight point count and the best hand, three exchanges.

In this, only cards up to eight counted for the point count side of the pot while everything counted for the best hand side. In this game what you wanted was something like 88877—very strong for both point count and best hand. What you didn't want was AAAJ10 or KKQQ4—no use for the point count and probably beaten for best hand. One key feature of Dealer's Choice was that players delighted in inventing games with tricky rules that gave an advantage to the dealer; an extreme example of this was 'the Tim Swindle', invented by my friend Tim, the complexities of which I shall not attempt to describe, save to say that if you understood how the Tim Swindle worked, you simply didn't play, no matter how good your cards, unless you were the dealer when you played whatever you had. Despite its giveaway name, there were many occasions on which the Tim Swindle proved an effective way of relieving mugs of their cash.

Other aspects of poker at The Strand also contributed to the game's particular atmosphere. There was the fact that it was illegal, which created an attractive frisson of danger for the middle class elements in the clientele. Legal poker was available in London at this time, at established casinos, such as Crockford's or the Victoria Sporting Club but these games, initially, were organized in a very genteel way with low stakes and restricted betting limits. They had none of the drama and tension of a pot limit game. The illicit status of the En Passant game, however, raised an interesting question. How was it possible for an illegal poker game to operate undisturbed twenty-four hours a day on one of central London's main thoroughfares without even a lock or a doorman on the door? I don't know for certain but I can think of only one plausible explanation: the cops were being paid off, which, given what we know about the Met in the sixties is hardly surprising. Then there was the absence of any croupiers or dealers, the players dealing for themselves and finally, the use of actual cash instead of chips. These features, which if not absolutely unique, were at least pretty unusual, both made for a heightened feeling of gritty realism, like the use of black and white in classic film noir.

In the end, however, it was not the minimalist décor or the kind of poker, or the cash pots or any of these things that made the En Passant what it was. It was the people who went to play there. The majority of these fell into three main categories: a criminal, small gangster element from London's East and West Ends; a middle class intellectual/professional element—lawyers, journalists and the like—and the professional poker players. Each of these groups brought its own particular 'flavour' to

The Strand but it was the interaction between them that was the crucial factor in the game's distinctive atmosphere.

The small gangster types all had Runyonesque nicknames: Johnny the Builder, Chills Tony, Little Art, Jumbo, Scouse Billy, Paddy George, Chrissy Doobie, Brian the Burglar and such like. By and large, these were hard men, some with that keen, hunted look in their eyes that, in my experience, goes with having been in prison. Johnny the Builder was a small wiry man, middle aged going on old, with a harsh rasping voice that testified to chain smoking and could hardly utter a sentence without several expletives. "Fucking cards. I ain't seen a fucking pair since bloody eight o'clock". That sort of thing. Chills Tony, whose nickname certainly had the desired effect on me, was probably in his late twenties. He was lean, muscled and had a fearsome reputation. One day a newcomer to the scene, whose name I forget, got into a dispute with Chills over the table. He was a young man, early twenties, tall and broad shouldered. Either he fancied his chances or just got carried away but he wagged his finger in Tony's face. "Don't do that, son", said one of the older hands sitting next to the youngster. "He'll hit you over the head with an iron bar!" And such was the matter of fact realism of this helpful advice, that the young man realized instantly that he was making a mistake and the matter was sorted. However, the enormous Jumbo, whose soubriquet did not deceive, once told me that in his view, Chills Tony was not the hardest man at The Strand, the honour belonged to Little Art. "If I had to I could just about handle Tony", said Jumbo (I did not really believe this—Jumbo was too nice), "but Little Art . . . no way!" Little Art was, or had been, a stunt man on one of the first Bond films, it was said—and Little Art's strength, Jumbo explained, lay in his exceptional speed.

Interestingly, physical violence was a rarity at the poker table, despite the presence of these potentially violent men. I think the psychological aggression of the game itself worked as a kind of sublimation. In all my poker-playing days I only once saw an actual serious blow struck at or around the table. That was by Vivian, the Irish queer basher, in a dispute over a £5 bet and happened not at The Strand but at The Primrose Club in Belsize Park, an altogether safer place. Vivian 'earned' his living by picking up gay men (no one used this term yet), taking them to The Strand Palace Hotel or somewhere similar, bashing them and robbing them. I was told that he once turned up to play at the En Passant with notes covered in fresh blood. But Vivian was an outsider, a pariah even among the villains. On one occasion I found myself obliged to share a cab with him. He complained bitterly of the coldness of the English. "No one seems to want to be friends", he said. That this might be related to his 'profession' did not seem to occur to him.

Violence away from the table was a different matter. Paddy George, for instance, was disfigured by a large and hideous scar from the corner of his mouth to his ear—clearly the product of some knife or razor attack. George hung out with the terse and hard-bitten Scouse Billy. One day George and Billy disappeared from the scene. The word was that they were on the run. Apparently some doorman had tried to deny them entry to a late-night drinking club. With the aid of a third accomplice, they had captured the doorman, dragged him into the back of a car, cut up his face with a broken bottle and thrown him out of the car at speed. I never saw either of them again, except for one night on Greek Street I saw Scouse crossing the road towards me. "Hi Billy", I said, without thinking. He swept past me without a word and dodged into an entrance.

The most attractive personality among the villains, to me at any rate, was Brian the Burglar. Brian was thirtyish, tall, good looking and generally charming. In a delicious irony, his real surname was Law. His nickname, however, was a simple statement of fact; he was a professional thief, a housebreaker. His method of earning a living was to go to an apartment block in a fairly well heeled area at an appropriate time—say 2pm when people were likely to be out—ring the doorbell and, on receiving no reply, effect an entry by means of a piece of plastic, like a credit card. He would then help himself to whatever cash, jewellery or other portable valuables were lying around and beat a hasty retreat. Brian's career was assisted by the unstated policy of the Metropolitan Police at that time (I don't know if it is still the same today) not to investigate house break-ins, on account of their great frequency. This meant that so long as he did not get caught in the act, he was in the clear, barring any accidents such as getting stopped and searched in a car full of stolen goods. Despite this 'indulgence', Brian, when I met him, had already been inside a couple of times and was therefore looking at a long stretch should he be convicted again.

In his personal dealings I found Brian both affable and genuinely kind. For some reason he took a liking to me and for a time, took me under his wing, which greatly assisted my transition from isolated callow youth to member of the rather louche poker scene. On occasion, after an all-night poker session, we would drive out at dawn to have breakfast at London Airport. I remember it then as deserted, eerie and vaguely exciting—now it has changed beyond recognition. The thing with Brian was that you felt that if you ever really needed help, he would go the distance for you and this I tried to reciprocate.

As poker players, the villains—with the exception of Jumbo who was definitely 'loose' and weak—were generally quite good. They were sharp, intelligent, nobody's fools and usually had plenty of bottle at the table. They were not the best however. I think this was because for them, poker was a leisure, not a work activity. They had other means of earning their living and therefore did not play with the absolute intensity and 'commitment' necessary to be a consistent winner, a real professional.

The middle-class element brought an essential ingredient to the En Passant: its money. Every poker game needs its quota of mugs or losers to supply the lubricant to keep its wheels turning smoothly. If the proportion of pots and tight players in a game gets too high, the game dries up and becomes no good to anyone. This was especially true of a game like The Strand where the House was cutting the pot. By the standards of many clubs and private games these were quite good players but by the standards of The Strand they were a weak link, inferior to both the villains and the pro-gamblers.

Typical of the middle class crowd were men like the young lawyer, Jeff Abrahams, Stewart Reuben (who was part of the chess-poker crossover and who is still around as an organizer of chess events), Charlie Gale and the journalists, Jeremy Hornsby and David Spanier. Charlie Gale lived with and off his parents in Hampstead Garden Suburb. He had been to Oxford but he preferred ducking and diving to the disciplines of a proper job or career. I knew Charlie from the Prompt Corner and it was partly through me that he got involved in poker. Often we would drive to games together in his tiny Fiat car. An interesting case was David Spanier. He was quite a prestigious journalist at The Times, who won some kind of European Journalist of the Year award for his reporting on the Common Market and who played in the 'famous' private game with Al Alvarez and Anthony Holden—famous because they were media people who publicized their own exploits. In later years, Spanier presented himself as a poker 'expert', writing a book, making the odd TV appearance etc. but at The Strand he was a mug. The news that 'David of The Times' was on his way would always raise spirits at the table since it meant that a welcome injection of cash was coming. On one occasion, I fleeced Spanier in a two-handed game of Dealer's Choice with the crude device of repeatedly choosing the Tim Swindle. David, for all his intellectual status, seemed unable to work out the fairly obvious catch. These middle class characters were, of course, drawn by the frisson of danger provided by The Strand's low life clientele but they had to pay for their thrills at the table.

From among this group there was one individual who stood out, at least from my point of view, and who is the only person from those days I'm still in touch with. This was Maurice Sumray. When I first saw Maurice at the En Passant he was a small unshaven man in his mid-forties, scruffily dressed and wearing a floppy old cordouroy hat, which made him look a down and out. "Ask him for a lift home", said Ted Iles one morning, with a psychological insight that was in a way typical of this unpleasant man. "He may look like a tramp but he has on E-type Jag parked downstairs." So I did and he agreed and this proved the start of our friendship.

Maurice was a Jewish artist who had set aside his art to make a pile of money with an engraving business. At this point in time, he was busy dissipating his fortune on wine, women and poker. He had a beautiful house in Muswell Hill with an extraordinary private art collection, including a small original Picasso (!) and other great 20th century originals. His wife, Pat, was also stunningly beautiful—in an artistic bohemian not bimboish or show business way—but there was evident strain and pain in the relationship, maybe because of Maurice's gambling and philandering. Superficially, Maurice could be cocky, cheeky, arrogant, aggressive and humorous by turns. There was always a twinkle in his eye, which could be exceptionally charming to women and men alike and which is still there now that he is eighty. But the real thing about Maurice was that he had been, was, a serious artist, a real painter. He had exhibited at the Whitechapel and Gimpel Fils galleries and been described by Wyndham Lewis as one of 'the best artists in England' and knew Francis Bacon, Lucian Freud and such. He therefore understood all too well the high calling of being a real artist and beneath his bluff, gruff exterior, there was a deep sadness and profound human sympathy with the downtrodden, which showed itself in his work and his half denied left wing politics (he remembered Mosley and the Battle of Cable St in the East End) and his choice of company. Like me, Maurice also played chess at the Prompt Corner and was close friends with Brian the Burglar.

The professional poker players were the kings of the En Passant and, at the same time, its humble servants and its lowly parasites. They were, of course, few in number. Apart from Ted Iles and Colin Kennedy there were only three real pros: Ray 'Doc' Joseph, Paddy Joe and Irish John Turner.

Ray Joseph was a tall, thin young man in his late twenties, with a long face and long bony fingers, which handled the cards with elegant precision. Ray had once been a student at the nearby London School of Economics but had abandoned his studies for poker. He was the extreme example of the 'scientific' player. Someone who new all the odds and stuck strictly to them—the tightest man at the table who would wait hours for a decent hand if necessary. They called him 'the Doc' in honour of Dr. Death, the wrestler who strangled his opponents into submission. (To have someone 'strangled' is poker parlance for having a hand so strong that the other player(s) cannot possible beat it. In stud, this is not uncommon e.g. in Five Card Stud a pair of Aces has the whole table strangled if no pair is showing and there is no possible straight or flush).

Away from the game, Doc was an amiable fellow but he could be tetchy at the table, especially if things were not going well. He was married with children and found playing for a living a strain. "I have to clear two grand a year before I start to live," he would say, referring to his domestic commitments. Certainly Doc was tight but he was also a very skillful subtle player, a good 'reader' of the cards and master of the unexpected raise and deceptive bet or check. I once asked Ray if his reputation for caution didn't make it difficult for him to get paid when he did have a hand. "Yeah," he said, "but there are compensations." "How do you mean?" I asked. "Well, you don't get people trying to bluff Jumbo out of a full house, do you!" The Doc could sit quietly, almost unnoticed, in a game for many hours but at the end of the night he was usually ahead. Sometimes he would go for a drink with other players, especially the pros but usually he would go home to his family in Blackheath.

When I first met them, John Turner and Paddy Joe were mates, two young Irishmen who had come over on the boat together when they were sixteen and graduated from snooker hustlers to poker pros. By the time I left the scene a few years later, their ways had parted as John's star rose and Joe's declined.

Paddy Joe was small, quiet of voice but intense in his feelings and concentration. He lived a life totally devoted to and within the gambling world, moving from poker game to roulette wheel to dice table and always back to poker again. Ray Joseph once said of Joe, "Sometimes he plays like a God and sometimes like a complete mug". His passion for the game enabled him to play very tight for a long time and then go absolutely fearlessly for a really big pot. Then the fearlessness could suddenly turn into reckless self-destructiveness. One night in a big five card stripped deck game, not at The Strand, Joe patiently built his last five pounds into £450. He then put the lot—a small fortune in those days—in a single bet on a pair of Queens against a showing Ten, only to be called and outdrawn with a middle pin straight on the last card. When Joe was doing well he would rent a nice flat, buy himself a good suit and watch—these were the limits of his ambition. When he was broke he would give up the flat for a bedsit, pawn the watch and suit and hustle to get back in the big time. Some pro players, Ted Iles for example and I was like this too, are not really gamblers; they play a game of skill for money and have no interest in betting for its own sake. Joe was a fantastically good poker player but he was also a mad compulsive gambler. This was probably his downfall. Occasionally Joe would interrupt his gambling binges to take in a movie. The last time I saw him he had been entranced by the *Woodstock* film and had started smoking dope.

John Turner was the most fearsome and most feared player on our circuit. He was probably the best poker player in London at the time and certainly the best I saw. Medium to short, stockily built, barrel chested, he was the Diego Maradonna of the poker table with a personality to match. Ted Iles once said of him that John Turner managed to play more cards, drink more booze and sleep with more women than anyone else he knew.

At the table, John Turner was all energy and action. From the moment he sat down he sought and usually achieved a personal domination of the game. His method was to unleash a flurry of small bets and raises combined with a stream of mildly aggressive banter, in such a way as to make himself the center of attention. This simultaneously created the illusion—and it was an illusion—that he was basically a loose player and aroused the envy of almost every other player in the game. Unlike Ted, there was nothing seriously malicious in John Turner but he used his pugnacious personality to provoke other players to engage with him. When you played with John Turner you felt harried, got at and personally challenged so that you put your money in the middle when you shouldn't and whenever that money was substantial, you could be sure that Turner would produce the goods. This was only possible because John was a superb 'reader' of both cards and people. No player I ever saw made fewer mistakes, fewer errors of judgement in betting, calling and passing in critical situations.

If Turner had a weakness, it was his heavy drinking but even this he could turn to his advantage. He would turn up at the table obviously the worse for wear and spread some easy money around. Then he would sober up rapidly and catch people on the rebound who thought he was still drunk. The interesting thing about John was that despite his aggressive, provocative personality and his way of getting under everyone's skin and making them play badly, almost no one bore a grudge against him or actually disliked him. On the contrary, he was generally popular, especially with the villains, who admired his 'bottle.' What happened to him later I've no idea, but I fear that in the long run, the drinking must have taken its toll.

Naturally, not everyone at The Strand fitted into my three main types. There was, for example, Tony Tea—a rather camp youngish man, employed by Ted to make the tea. Whenever Tony could scrape together enough from his doubtless meager wages, he would chance his arm at the table—not very successfully. From time to time Tony would appear with the odd younger lad in tow, who would also do a stint in the kitchen. It was clear from the odd comment he made that Ted Iles had a certain 'interest' in these young gay men but Ted was overtly straight and my guess is that his interest was 'psychological' rather than directly sexual.

Another gay guy on the En Passant scene for a time was Johnny Mew. Johnny was a somewhat rough looking, working class man in his forties, who, I was told, had had a rich sugar daddy. The sugar daddy had died and left Johnny a very considerable sum—maybe £30,000 or something like that. But Johnny was a total poker addict and the world's worst player. While he had money, Ted courted him, reserved him a seat at the table, even allowed him to stay in his flat and drip fed him credit £10 at a time. In this way, Johnny Mew, who *always* lost, contributed £100 or more a night to the En Passant game and the house cut until his inheritance was all gone and Ted discarded him like a used rag.

So far I have spoken only of men. Obviously in the mid sixties, the poker scene as a whole and The Strand especially, was overwhelmingly male but there were a few women players. Two that I remember were

Diane and Edna. Diane, I hardly knew at all but Jumbo claimed to have had an affair with her and Brian the Burglar, from the manner of his greeting of her that I saw on one occasion, may also have had some kind of relationship with her. She was, as far as I can recall, not a bad player. Edna, I came to know very well. She was half Italian, half Irish, swarthy of complexion, plump and in her forties. Edna was sort of half professional. On the one hand, she was a very regular player who was certainly not a mug and who clearly lacked the source of income to sustain a losing poker habit. On the other hand, she clearly was not in the same league as the Doc or John Turner. Edna played sometimes at The Strand and could just about survive there but, generally, she preferred the gentler game at The Primrose, which anyway was nearer to her Kilburn home. Both on and off the table, Edna was kind and friendly to me in a mildly maternal way.

One aspect of The Strand of which I am more aware today than I was at the time, was its 'whiteness.' The poker scene as a whole was very cosmopolitan. A number of the clubs I used, including The Primrose and the Double One, were run by Asians and frequented by many Indian, Pakistani and Chinese players. There was also substantial participation from the Greek community but none of this was true of the En Passant, which remained almost exclusively white (though, as we have seen, very Jewish). Not, I hasten to add, that there was a colour bar. As far as I can recall, no one of any description was barred from The Strand, especially if they had money to lose but it seems it was just not a place black and Asian people felt drawn to.

Finally, I should say something about my own position within this scene. My main distinguishing feature was my youth. At seventeen, just out of school, as I was by some distance the youngest person around and as a result they called me Schoolboy John. By education and background, I was closest to the middle class professional/intellectual element but I was a rebel and tended to despise the respectable bourgeois types (except the bohemian Maurice). Also I had little or no money so I had to play to win like the real pros. A feat I managed in a small way most, if not all, of the time. Luckily for me I was not a gambler—games of chance held no interest for me—or an addict and when the time came for me to move on in my life, I was able to give up poker without difficulty.

Up to this point, I have not offered up what dominates most depictions of poker on the page and the screen, namely the tall poker tale or the description of the dramatic pot. This has been intended as a deliberate corrective to the way poker is usually represented. Mostly poker features in stories as a plot device, a set piece scene focusing on a single hand, leading to a gunfight or a confrontation between hero and villain. Typically, all we see is a huge pot in which the guy required by the storyline to be the winner has four Aces against the predetermined loser's four Kings, or the dramatic climax in which The Man does or does not have the Jack of Diamonds in the hole to make a straight flush. Real poker is not like that. Ninety, no ninety-nine per cent of the time, it is a matter of routine pots in which Two Pair beats a pair of Kings or a Straight outdraws a pair of Aces and winning at poker is basically a question of trying to ensure that when you have the Two Pair against the pair of Kings, you win more money than you lose when the hands are reversed. This is why poker is a boring game unless it is played for stakes that are high enough to hurt if you lose. You've got to really care that you have a pair of Queens and your opponent only has Jacks or Tens and you have to be very pleased that you managed to pass your Aces Up when you read the other guy for Three Fours. Only the money makes you that.

Nevertheless, there were some incidents that stood out and which I can still remember more than thirty years later. One of these involved Maurice Sumray and Ray Joseph. It was Seven Card Stud and on the fourth card, Maurice, holding a pair of Aces (showing A6 with A4 in the hole) bet the pot. The Doc, showing Q10, raised just below the maximum but a strong bet. Maurice, mistakenly, called—unless it was an out and out bluff, which was unlikely, Ray would never raise in that situation unless he could beat the possible Aces. On card five, Maurice hit a four making Aces Up and the Doc drew an irrelevant seven. Maurice checked. The Doc paused, checked his hole cards, pondered some more and eventually said, "I don't believe you've got Aces Up!" He then bet the pot. The remark riled Maurice. "Is he allowed to make comments like that?" he said. "At Crockfords they'd call that 'cheating'". Colin Kennedy, who was in charge, shrugged his shoulders. "This is not Crockfords", he said. "Right, I call", said Maurice, his dander up. On the sixth card neither player improved and Maurice checked again. The Doc bet the pot. As he leant forward to place the money in the middle, Maurice grabbed him by the wrist and looking straight in his eyes, said, "Don't worry, I'm staying to the end, whatever you bet. But if you've got the Three Queens I think you've got, you'll never get a penny of the money."

Doc never wanted trouble at the table, he already regretted his 'clever' remark but her wanted the money, badly. "Calm down, Maurice. Just play your cards," he said, extricating himself. Maurice called the bet, anything but calm. When the final down card was dealt Maurice saw that the Doc only had a few pounds left. "I set you in," he announced rather pompously. Ray Joseph called immediately. "Aces Up", said Maurice, defiantly. The Doc turned over his inevitable Three Queens. In an instant Maurice reached forward, seized the pot, comprising some £80–£100 in five and ten pound notes, tore the notes in half and then again into quarters and threw the whole lot high into the air.

To this day Maurice, with his artist's eye for the visual, recalls the scraps of paper money 'floating down to the table like confetti.'

At that point Maurice simply got up and walked out. Anywhere else he would have been barred, probably for life; at The Strand a phone call to Ted a couple of weeks later and he was back, everything forgotten and forgiven. Apparently he and Ray Joseph had a good laugh about it in later years.

Another particularly spectacular and memorable pot, possibly the biggest ever played there, featured Brian the Burglar, flush with the proceeds of a lucrative job, Colin Kennedy running the game, an unnamed American serviceman on his first visit and Ted Iles, not playing but attending to some business in the office. The American had sat down earlier in the evening and said he would play, call or pass (i.e. cover any bet made at the table without limit). He had played quietly for several hours without being involved in any dramatic action. Brian arrived sometime in the small hours in a rather excited mood. He too announced he would play, call or pass. Normally only one person could be call or pass at one time but by this time, people had sort of forgotten the Yank and nothing was said. (Strictly speaking this was Colin's fault).

After a while the American was dealing with Brian to his left and Colin on his right. It was Seven Card and Brian showed an Ace, Colin a ten and the Yank a deuce. Brian, as high card, opened the compulsory half-crown and received three or four callers, including Colin. The Yank raised the pot, fifteen shillings. Brian just called and the others passed but Colin reraised three pounds more. The Yank called and Brian raised another tenner. Colin and the Yank called.

This was already exceptional betting for the first of five rounds of betting. The next card made no apparent difference to anyone—a five to the

Ace, a seven to the ten and a Jack to the deuce. Brian bet forty pounds, Colin called and the Yank raised another hundred. Brian called and Colin, after a long pause, declared that he was going all in the hundred plus another hundred and twenty. The Yank, who was starting to sweat profusely, checked his money in his wallet and, with a touch of agitation in his voice said, "I call". At this point Brian rather triumphantly announced, "Well I'm raising. How much is there in the pot?" Colin counted the large pile of notes. "With your one twenty, it comes to nearly eight hundred", he said. Brian reached into his inside pocket and fetched out a huge roll of notes. "I raise five hundred", he said.

The American's face fell through the floor. Frantically he checked his wallet. "I can't cover the bet", he mumbled. "Then you must fold", said Colin, with a slight smirk. "You said you were playing call or pass". "No, no. I'll go all in".

"Oh no you won't", said Brian, starting to get angry. "Call or pass is call or pass". There was a general muttering of agreement round the table. Everyone was tense—it was a huge pot by the standards of the game and the time—but everyone was on Brian's side.

The Yank was getting desperate. "I-I'll get the money", he said. "I'll leave the hand here and I'll get the money. Give me an hour".

"Hmm . . .", Colin hesitated.

"Look mate", said Brian, who had made a decision. "I've got three Aces here and you're strangled. I'd swallow it if I were you". He flipped over his hole cards to prove his point.

"I've got over a hundred and fifty in this pot. I want to carry on. I'll get the money", the American protested.

Then a voice came from the back. It was Ted. "I have to tell you that if you get the money, we shall be cutting the deck before the hand continues".

This was decisive. Ted had rumbled that there must be a rigged deck and the Yank knew he was rumbled.

"I-I'm getting the money", he said, and rose from the table. He was running before he reached the door. Everyone knew he wasn't coming back. Colin, who had three tens back-to-back, now suggested the pot should be split. "No way", said Brian with his three Aces.

"What we will do", said Ted, taking control, "is deal out the top cards to see what would have happened, then we'll reshuffle the deck and deal again for real". Colin wasn't happy but he couldn't buck Ted. The next three cards told the whole story. There, on cue, was the fourth deuce for the absent Yank. But when they re-dealt, there was a bitter twist. Colin paired his seven to make a full house but Brian did not improve. And that was how Colin won the biggest pot in the short history of the En Passant. "Oh well! Easy come, easy go", said Brian the Burglar.

When now, from the vantage point of middle age and a new century, I reflect on the En Passant and my experience of it, two things stand out: one personal, one social. Personally, it assisted and in large part effected, my rapid transition from a socially isolated, nerdish, certainly very gauche adolescence into the adult world. In the space of a few months it enabled me to leapfrog over the 'normal' teenage scene of dances, parties, pubs, dates—from which I had largely felt excluded by the peculiarities of my sheltered upbringing. Hindsight has revealed this to be a mixed blessing but at the time I was deeply grateful.

Socially, I think it was symptomatic at a subterranean level of a trend that was evident in the higher reaches of the culture in the sixties, namely the arrival on the stage of a young non-deferential working class which challenged the hitherto uncontested cultural hegemony of the traditional middle and upper classes. In its own tiny way, therefore, the world of the *En Passant was* a part of the cultural wave that gave us *Saturday Night and Sunday Morning, Room at the Top, The Loneliness of the Long Distance Runner* and indeed, The Beatles. And from the clear fact that John Turner was loads smarter than David Spanier and Brian the Burglar an infinitely preferable human being to Ted Iles or Jeremy Hornsby, I learned the invaluable lesson that, contrary to everything I had been taught at school, neither intelligence nor decency were linked to social status or respectability.

Permissions

"The Lottery in Bablyon" from *Collected Fictions* by Jorge Luis Borges, translated by Andrew Hurley. Copyright © 1998 by Maria Kodama; translation Copyright © 1998 by Penguin Putnam, Inc. Used by permission of Viking Penguin, a division of Penguin Putnam, Inc.

Excerpt from *Poker—Bets, Bluffs and Bad Beats* by Al Alvarez. Copyright © 2001 by A. Alvarez. Published by Chronicle Books, San Francisco, LLC. Used with permission.

Excerpt from *The Alchemy of Opposites* by Rodolfo Scarfalloto. Copyright © 1997 by Rodolfo Scarfalloto. Used by permission of the author.

Excerpt from *Con Men and Cutpurses* by Lucy Moore. Copyright © 2000 by Lucy Moore and Allen Lane, The Penguin Press. Reprinted with permission of The Penguin Group (UK).

"A Word About Confidence Men" from *The Big Con* by David Maurer. Copyright © 1999 by David Maurer. Reprinted by permission of Doubleday, a division of Random House, Inc.

"Chance" *Low Life* by Luc Sante. Copyright © 1991 by Luc Sante. Reprinted by permission of Farrar, Straus & Giroux, LLC.

Excerpt from *Oscar Wilde* by Richard Ellman. Copyright © 1987 by The Estate of Richard Ellman. Used by permission of Compass, a division of Random House, Inc.

"There's a One-Eyed Man in the Game" from *Wondrous Times on the Frontier* by Dee Alexander Brown. Copyright © 1992 by Dee Alexander Brown. Used by permission of Sterling Lord Literistic, Inc.

"Four Men and a Poker Game" from *Collected Stories* by Bertolt Brecht. Copyright © 1967 by Suhrkamp Verlag. Translation Copyright © 1983 by Stephan S. Brecht. Published by Arcade Publishing, New York, NY. Reprinted with permission of the Publisher.

"The Snatching of Bookie Bob" from *Guys and Dolls and Other Stories* by Damon Runyon. Used by permission of Penguin Putnam, Inc.

"A Talk With the Yellow Kind" by Saul Bellow. Copyright © 1956 by Saul Bellow. Reprinted with the permission of The Wylie Agency, Inc.

Excerpt from *The Hustler* by Walter Tevis. Copyright © 1959 by The Walter Tevis Literary Trust. Used by permission of the Susan Schulman Literary Agency and The Walter Tevis Literary Trust.

"Birds of a Feather" from *The Big Con* by David Maurer. Copyright © 1999 by David Maurer. Reprinted by permission of Doubleday, a division of Random House, Inc.

Excerpt from *Casino* by Nicholas Pileggi. Copyright © 1995 by Pileggi Literary Properties, Inc. Reprinted with the permission of Simon & Schuster Adult Publishing Group.

"Painter Jailed for Committing Masterpieces" by Robert Anton Wilson. Copyright © 1995 by Robert Anton Wilson. Used by arrangement with New Falcon Publications.

"A Law Degree is Just an Illegal Technicality" from *Catch Me If You Can* by Frank W. Abangale. Copyright © 1980 by Frank Abangale. Used by permission of Grosset & Dunlap, Inc., a division of Penguin Putnam, Inc.

Excerpt from *Fear and Loathing in Las Vegas* by Hunter S. Thompson. Copyright © 1972 by Hunter S. Thompson. Used by permission of Random House, Inc.

"Pool Halls" and "Things I Have Learned Player Poker on the Hill" from *A Whore's Profession* by David Mamet. Copyright © 1994 by David Mamet. Reprinted with permission of Faber & Faber Ltd., London.

Excerpt from *Cut Numbers* by Nick Tosches. Copyright © 1989 by Martin Amis. Used by permission of Vintage Books, a division of Random House, Inc.

Excerpt from *London Fields* by Martin Amis. Copyright © 1989 by Martin Amis. Used by permission of Vintage Books, a division of Random House, Inc.

Excerpt from *Love Is a Racket* by John Ridley. Copyright © 1998 by International Famous Player Radio Picture Corporation. Used by permission of A. Knopf, a division of Random House, Inc.

Excerpt from *Son of a Grifter* by Kent Walker. Copyright © 2001 by Kent Walker and Mark Schone. Reprinted by permission of HarperCollins Publishers, Inc.

"The Chelsea Rip" from *Playing Off the Rail* by David McCumber. Copyright © 1996 by David McCumber. Used by permission of Random House, Inc.

Excerpt from *Fixer Chao* by Han Ong. Copyright © 2001 by Han Ong. Reprinted with permission of Susan Bergholz Literary Services.

About the Editors

Stephen Hyde graduated in film at the University of Westminster, London. He has worked as a researcher and has co-edited the anthologies *Players* and *White Lines* for Thunder's Mouth Press. He lives in Portsmouth, England.

Geno Zanetti is the editor of the acclaimed anthology, *She's a Bad Motorcycle,* which *Jane* magazine described as "super cool" and *Rocky Mountain News* described as "a remarkable collection." He divides his time between Solentsea, England and New York City.

LaVergne, TN USA
28 July 2010
191191LV00003B/36/P